ELEVENTH
EDITION

BECOMING A
MASTER
STUDENT

CONCISE

DAVE ELLIS

ELEVENTH EDITION
Concise

Becoming a Master Student

Doug Toft
Contributing Editor

Dean Mancina
Faculty Advisor

Eldon L. McMurray
Faculty Advisor

Houghton Mifflin Company   Boston   New York

Publisher: Patricia A. Coryell
Executive Editor: Mary Finch
Sponsoring Editor: Shani B. Fisher
Assistant Editor: Andrew Sylvester
Senior Project Editor: Cathy Labresh Brooks
Editorial Assistant: Susan Miscio
Composition Buyer: Chuck Dutton
Art and Design Manager: Jill Haber
Manufacturing Manager: Karen Fawcett
Marketing Manager: Elinor Gregory
Marketing Associate: Evelyn Yang

Cover credit: Cover image © Robert Schoen Photography,
Alistair Berg/Getty Images

College Survival
2075 Foxfield Drive, Suite 100
St. Charles, IL 60174
1-800-528-8323
collegesurvival@hmco.com

Photo and illustration credits appear on page 248.

Printed in the U.S.A.

Library of Congress Control Number: 2005929683

Student Edition
ISBN 13: 978-0-618-59538-9
ISBN 10: 0-618-59538-4
Annotated Instructor's Edition
ISBN 13: 978-0-618-60419-7
ISBN 10: 0-618-60419-7

3 4 5 6 7 8 9 – WC – 09 08 07 06

As part of Houghton Mifflin's ongoing
commitment to the environment, this text
has been printed on recycled paper.

advisory board

brief table of contents

table of contents

Making Transitions

1 First Steps

2 Planning

3 Memory

4 Reading

5 Notes

6

Tests

7

Thinking

8 Communicating

9 Technology

INTRODUCTION
Making Transitions

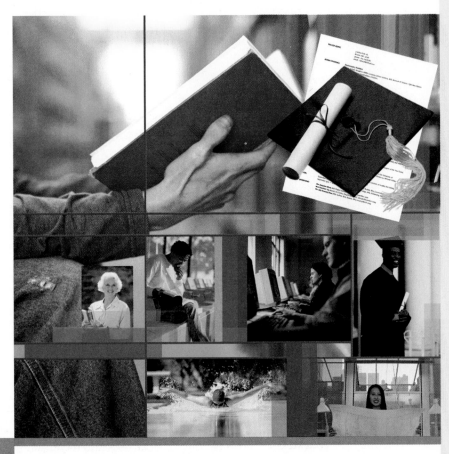

why
the Introduction matters . . .

Acquiring new strategies can help you make a smooth and successful transition to the world of higher education, help you feel more at ease in this new world, and help you succeed.

what
is included . . .

This book is worthless—if you just read it
Get the most out of this book
The Discovery and Intention Journal Entry system
Discovery and Intention Statement guidelines
Making the transition to higher education
Making a healthy transition
Connect to resources
Link to the world of work
Attitudes, values, and visualizations
Ways to change a habit
Motivation
Power Process: "Discover what you want"

how
you can use this Introduction . . .

Discover a way to interact with books that multiplies their value.
Use writing to translate personal discoveries into powerful new behaviors.
Connect with people and organizations that can support your success.

As you read, ask yourself
what if . . .

I could use the ideas in this Introduction to master any transition in my life?

STUDENT VOICES

" *I am now 37 years old and have returned to college. I am very apprehensive about this experience. However, I am not trying to conquer my fear. My fear has become my friend. When I embraced my fear, it was a moment of enlightenment. I thought I would appear foolish, old, and unsuccessful. By recognizing these feelings and taking away their powers over me, they become harmless. They also became the fuel for my drive for success.*"

—RICHARD HERBERT

This book is worthless—if you just read it

The first edition of this book began with the sentence *This book is worthless.* Many students thought this was a trick to get their attention. It wasn't. Others thought it was reverse psychology. It wasn't that, either. Still others thought it meant that the book was worthless if they didn't read it. It's more than that.

This book is worthless *even if you read it*—if reading is all you do. What was true of that first edition is true of this one. Until you take action and use the ideas in it, *Becoming a Master Student* really is worthless.

The purpose of this book is to help you make a successful transition to higher education by setting up a pattern of success that will last the rest of your life. You probably won't take action and use the ideas in this book until you are convinced that you have something to gain. That's the reason for this introduction—to persuade you to use this book actively.

Before you stiffen up and resist this sales pitch, remember that you have already bought the book. Now you can get something for your money by committing yourself to take action—in other words, by committing yourself to becoming a master student. Here's what's in it for you.

Pitch #1: You can save money now and make more later. Start with money. Your college education is one of the most expensive things you will ever buy. Typically, it costs students $30 to $70 an hour to sit in class. Unfortunately, many students think their classes aren't worth even 50 cents an hour.

As a master student, you control the value you get out of your education, and that value can be considerable. The joy of learning aside, college graduates make more money during their lifetimes than their nondegreed peers.[1] The income advantage you gain through higher education could total over half a million dollars. It pays to be a master student.

Pitch #2: You can rediscover the natural learner in you. Joy is important, too. As you become a master student, you will learn to gain knowledge in the most effective way possible by discovering the joyful, natural learner within you.

Children are great natural students. They quickly master complex skills, such as language, and they have fun doing it. For them, learning is a high-energy process involving experimentation, discovery, and sometimes broken dishes. Then comes school. For some students, drill and drudgery replace discovery and dish breaking.

Learning can become a drag. You can use this book to reverse that process and rediscover what you knew as a child—that laughter and learning go hand in hand.

Sometimes learning does take effort, especially in college. As you become a master student, you will learn many ways to get the most out of that effort.

Pitch #3: You can choose from hundreds of techniques. *Becoming a Master Student* is packed with hundreds of practical, nuts-and-bolts techniques. And you can begin using them immediately. For example, during the textbook reconnaissance on page 2, you can practice three powerful learning techniques in one 15-minute exercise. Even if you doze in lectures, drift during tests, or dawdle on term papers, you'll find ideas in this book that you can use to become a more effective student.

Not all of these ideas will work for you. That's why there are so many of them in *Becoming a Master Student.* You can experiment with the techniques. As you discover what works, you will develop a unique style of learning that you can use for the rest of your life.

Pitch #4: You get the best suggestions from thousands of students. The concepts and techniques in this book are here not because learning theorists, educators, and psychologists say they work. They are here because tens of thousands of students from all kinds of backgrounds have tried them and say that they work. These are people who dreaded giving speeches, couldn't read their own notes, and fell behind in their course work. Then they figured out how to solve these problems. Now you can use their ideas.

Pitch #5: You can learn about you. The process of self-discovery is an important theme in *Becoming a Master Student.* Throughout the book you can use Discovery and Intention Statements for everything from organizing your desk to choosing long-term goals. Studying for an organic chemistry quiz is a lot easier with a clean desk and a clear idea of the course's importance to you.

Pitch #6: You can use a proven product. The first ten editions of this book have proved successful for hundreds of thousands of students. In schools where it was widely used, the dropout rate decreased as much as 25 percent, and in some cases, 50 percent. Student feedback has been positive. In particular, students with successful histories have praised the techniques in this book.

Pitch #7: You can learn the secret of student success. If this sales pitch still hasn't persuaded you to use this book actively, maybe it's time to reveal the secret of student success. (Provide your own drum roll here.) The secret is—that there are no secrets. Perhaps the ultimate formula is to give up formulas and keep inventing.

The strategies and tactics that successful students use are well known. You have hundreds of them at your fingertips right now, in this book. Use them. Modify them. Invent new ones. You're the authority on what works for you.

However, what makes any technique work is commitment—and action. Without them, the pages of *Becoming a Master Student* are just 2.1 pounds of expensive mulch. Add your participation to the mulch, and these pages are priceless. ◩

This book is worth $1,000

Houghton Mifflin Student Success is proud to present three students each year with a $1,000 scholarship for tuition reimbursement. Any post-secondary school in the United States and Canada can nominate one student for the scholarship. In order to be considered, students must write an essay that answers the question "How do you define success?"

For more details, go to (masterstudent.college.hmco.com)

TEXTBOOK RECONNAISSANCE

Start becoming a master student this moment by doing a 15-minute "textbook reconnaissance." Here's how.

First, read the table of contents. Do it in three minutes or less. Next, look at every page in the book. Move quickly. Scan headlines. Look at pictures. Notice forms, charts, and diagrams. Don't forget the last few pages in back, which include extra copies of planning forms that you might find useful.

A textbook reconnaissance shows you where a course is going. It gives you the big picture. That's useful because brains work best when going from the general to the specific. Getting the big picture before you start makes it easier to recall and understand details later on.

Your textbook reconnaissance will work even better if, as you scan, you look for ideas you can use. When you find one, write the page number and a short description of it in the space below. If you run out of room, just continue your list on a separate sheet of paper. Or use Post-it Notes to flag the pages that look useful. You could even use notes of different colors to signal priority, such as green for ideas to use right away and yellow for those to apply later. The idea behind this technique is simple: It's easier to learn when you're excited, and it's easier to get excited about a course if you know it's going to be useful, interesting, or fun.

Remember, look at every page, and do it quickly. And here's another useful tip for the master student: Do it now.

Page number   *Description*

_____

_____

_____

_____

_____

_____

_____

_____

_____

_____

_____

_____

Get the most out of this book

1. Rip 'em out. The pages of *Becoming a Master Student* are perforated because some of the information here is too important to leave in the book and some your instructor might want to see. For example, Journal Entry #2 asks you to list some important things you want to get out of your education. To keep yourself focused, you could rip that page out and post it on your bathroom mirror or some other place where you'll see it several times a day.

You can reinsert the page later by sticking it into the spine of the book. A piece of tape will hold it in place.

2. Skip around. You can use this book in several different ways. Read it straight through. Or pick it up, turn to any page, and find an idea you can use. Look for ideas you can use right now. For example, if you are about to choose a major or are considering changing schools, skip directly to the articles on these topics in Chapters 7 and 10, respectively.

3. If it works, use it. If it doesn't, lose it. If there are sections of the book that don't apply to you at all, skip them—unless, of course, they are assigned. Then see if you can gain value from these sections anyway. When you are committed to getting value from this book, even an idea that seems irrelevant or ineffective at first can turn out to be a powerful tool.

4. Put yourself into the book. As you read about techniques in this book, create your own scenarios, starring yourself in the title role. For example, when reading through Exercise #1: "Textbook reconnaissance," picture yourself using this technique on your world history textbook.

5. Listen to your peers. At the beginning of each chapter, you will find Student Voices, quotations from students who used *Becoming a Master Student* to promote their success. As you dig into the following chapters, think about what you would say if you could add your voice to theirs. Look for tools and techniques that can make a huge difference in your life.

6. Own this book. Right now, put your name, address, and related information on the inside cover of this book, and don't stop there. Determine what you want to get out of school and create a record of how you intend to get it by reading the Power Process and completing the Journal Entries in this Introduction. Every time your pen touches a page, you move closer to mastery of learning.

7. Do the exercises. Action makes this book work. To get the most out of an exercise, read the instructions carefully before you begin. To get the most out of this book, do most of the exercises. More important, avoid feeling guilty if you skip some. And by the way, it's never too late to go back and do the ones you skipped.

These exercises invite you to write, touch, feel, move, see, search, ponder, speak, listen, recall, choose, commit, and create. You might even sing and dance. Learning often works best when it involves action.

8. Practice critical thinking. Throughout this book are Practicing Critical Thinking activities. Their purpose is to reinforce contemplation and problem solving. Note that other elements of this text, including the exercises and Journal Entries, also promote critical thinking.

9. Learn about learning styles. Check out the Learning Styles Application in each chapter. These exercises are included to increase your awareness of your preferred learning styles and to help you explore new styles. Each application will guide you through experiencing four specific modes of learning as applied to the content of the chapter. The modes can be accessed by asking four basic questions: *Why? What? How?* and *What if?* You'll find more details in the Learning Style Inventory in Chapter One.

10. Navigate through learning experiences with the Master Student Map. You can orient yourself for maximum learning every time you open this book by asking those same four questions. That's the idea behind the

Master Student Map included on the first page of each chapter. Eventually, you'll be able to use the four-part structure of this map to guide yourself in effectively learning anything.

11. Link to the Web. Throughout this book, you'll notice reminders to visit the Web site for *Becoming a Master Student*:

> masterstudent.college.hmco.com

Check regularly for articles, online exercises, and links to other useful Web sites.

12. Sweat the small stuff. Look for sidebars—short bursts of words and pictures placed between longer articles—throughout this book. These short pieces might offer an insight that transforms your experience of higher education. Remember this related point: Shorter chapters in this book are just as important as longer chapters.

13. Take this book to work. With a little tweaking in some cases, you can apply nearly all of the techniques in this book to your career. For more details, see the Put It to Work articles in each chapter. Use them to make a seamless transition from success in school to success on the job.

14. Get used to a new look and tone. This book looks different from traditional textbooks. *Becoming a Master Student* presents major ideas in magazine-style articles. You will discover lots of lists, blurbs, one-liners, pictures, charts, graphs, illustrations, and even a joke or two.

Even though this book is loaded with special features, you'll find some core elements. For example, the two pages that open each chapter include a "lead" article and an introductory Journal Entry. And at the end of each chapter you'll find a Power Process, Put It to Work article, chapter quiz, Learning Styles Application, and Master Student Profile—all noted in a toolbar at the top of the page.

Note: As a strategy for avoiding sexist language, this book alternates the use of feminine and masculine pronouns. ✖

COMMITMENT

This book is worthless unless you actively participate in its activities and exercises. One powerful way to begin taking action is to make a commitment. Conversely, without commitment, sustained action is unlikely, and the result is again a worthless book. Therefore, in the interest of saving your valuable time and energy, this exercise gives you a chance to declare your level of involvement up front. From the choices below, choose the sentence that best reflects your commitment to using this book. Write the number in the space provided at the end of the list.

1. "Well, I'm reading this book right now, aren't I?"
2. "I will skim the book and read the interesting parts."
3. "I will read the book and think about how some of the techniques might apply to me."
4. "I will read the book, think about it, and do the exercises that look interesting."
5. "I will read the book, do some exercises, and complete some of the Journal Entries."
6. "I will read the book, do some exercises and Journal Entries, and use some of the techniques."
7. "I will read the book, do most of the exercises and Journal Entries, and use some of the techniques."
8. "I will study this book, do most of the exercises and Journal Entries, and use some of the techniques."
9. "I will study this book, do most of the exercises and Journal Entries, and experiment vigorously with most of the suggestions in order to discover what works best for me."
10. "I promise myself to get value from this book, beginning with Exercise #1: 'Textbook reconnaissance,' even if I have to rewrite the sections I don't like and invent new techniques of my own."

Enter your commitment level and today's date here:

Commitment level _____   Date _____

If you selected commitment level 1 or 2, you might consider passing this book on to a friend. If your commitment level is 9 or 10, you are on your way to terrific success in school. If your level is somewhere in between, experiment with the techniques and learning strategies in this book. If you find that they work, consider returning to this exercise and raising your level of commitment.

The Discovery and Intention Journal Entry system

AIRPORT

One way to become a better student is to grit your teeth and try harder. There is another way. You can use the Discovery and Intention Journal Entry system to focus your energy.

The Discovery and Intention Journal Entry system is a little like flying a plane. An airplane is seldom exactly on course. But because of constant observation and course correction, it arrives at the right destination.

You can use a similar system. Most Journal Entries throughout this book are labeled as either Discovery Statements or Intention Statements—and some are Discovery/Intention Statements. Each Journal Entry will contain suggestions for writing.

Discovery Statements are a record of your strengths and weaknesses. Discovery Statements can also declare your goals, describe your attitudes, state your feelings, transcribe your thoughts, and chronicle your behavior.

Sometimes Discovery Statements chronicle an "aha!" moment—a flash of insight or a solution to a longstanding problem. Don't let such moments disappear. Capture them in Discovery Statements.

Intention Statements can be used to alter your course. They are statements of your commitment to do a specific task. An intention arises out of your choice to direct your energy toward a particular goal. While Discovery Statements promote awareness, Intention Statements are blueprints for action.

The Journal Entry process is a cycle. First, you write Discovery Statements about where you are now and where you want to be. Next, you write Intention Statements about the specific steps you will take to get there. Then you follow up with Discovery Statements about

whether you completed those steps and what you learned in the process, followed by more Intention Statements, and so on. Sometimes a statement will be long and detailed. Usually, it will be short—maybe just a line or two. With practice, the cycle will become automatic.

While Discovery Statements promote awareness, Intention Statements are blueprints for action. The two processes reinforce each other.

Don't panic when you fail to complete an intended task. Straying off course is normal. Simply make the necessary corrections. Stay with the cycle. Use Discovery Statements to get a clear view of your world and what you want out of it. Then use Intention Statements to direct your actions. When you notice progress, record it.

The following statement might strike you as improbable, but it is true: It often takes the same amount of energy to get what you want in school as it takes to get what you *don't* want.

Sometimes getting what you don't want takes even more effort. An airplane burns the same amount of fuel flying away from its destination as it does flying toward it. It pays to stay on course. ◩

GOAL

Discovery and Intention Statement guidelines

Discovery Statements

1 Record specifics. Observe your actions and record the facts. If you spent 90 minutes chatting online instead of reading your anatomy text, write about it and include the details, such as when you did it, where you did it, and how it felt. Record your observations quickly, as soon as you make them. Notice how you feel when you function well. Use Discovery Statements to pinpoint exactly where and when you learn most effectively.

2 Use discomfort as a signal. When you approach a daunting task, such as a difficult accounting problem, notice your physical sensations. Feeling uncomfortable, bored, or tired might be a signal that you're about to do valuable work. Stick with it. Tell yourself you can handle the discomfort just a little bit longer. You will be rewarded.

3 Suspend judgment. When you are discovering yourself, be gentle. If you continually judge your behaviors as "bad" or "stupid," sooner or later your mind will quit making discoveries.

4 Tell the truth. The closer you get to the truth, the more powerful your Discovery Statements will be. And if you notice that you are avoiding the truth, don't blame yourself. Just tell the truth about it.

Intention Statements

1 Make intentions positive. Focus on what you want. Instead of writing "I will not fall asleep while studying accounting," write "I intend to stay awake when studying accounting."

Also avoid the word *try*. Trying is not doing. When we hedge our bets with *try*, we can always tell ourselves, "Well, I *tried* to stay awake."

2 Make intentions observable. Rather than writing "I intend to work harder on my history assignments," write "I intend to review my class notes and make summary sheets of my reading." Then, when you review your progress, you can determine more precisely whether you accomplished your intention.

3 Make intentions small and keepable. Break large goals into small, specific tasks to do quickly. If you want to get an A in biology, ask yourself, What can I do today? You might choose to study biology for an extra hour. Make that your intention.

Be careful of intentions that depend on others. If you intend for your study group to complete an assignment by Monday, then your success depends on the other students in the group.

4 Set timelines that include rewards. If you are assigned to write a paper, break the assignment into small tasks and set a precise due date for each one. Remember that you create timelines for your own benefit, not to set yourself up to feel guilty. And you can always change the timeline.

When you meet your goal on time, reward yourself. Rewards that are an integral part of a goal are powerful. For example, your reward for earning a degree might be the career you've always dreamed of. External rewards, such as a movie or an afternoon in the park, are valuable, too. These rewards work best when you're willing to withhold them. If you plan to take a nap on Sunday afternoon whether or not you've finished your English assignment, the nap is not an effective reward.

Another way to reward yourself is to sit quietly after you have finished your task and savor the feeling. One reason why success breeds success is that it feels good. ▨

journal entry 1

Discovery Statement

Welcome to the first Journal Entry in this book. You'll find Journal Entries in every chapter, all with a similar design that allow space for you to write.

In the space below, write a description of a time in your life when you learned or did something well. This experience does not need to be related to school. Describe the details of the situation, including the place, time, and people involved. Describe how you felt about it, how it looked to you, how it sounded. Describe the physical sensations you associate with the event. Also describe your emotions.

I discovered that . . .

_____

_____

_____

You share one thing in common with other students at your vocational school, college, or university: Entering higher education represents a major change in your life. You've joined a new culture with its own set of rules, both spoken and unspoken.

Making the transition to higher education

Whether they've just graduated from high school or have been out of the classroom for decades, students new to higher education immediately face many differences between secondary and post-secondary education. The sooner you understand such differences, the sooner you can deal with them. Some examples include:

- *New academic standards.* Often there are fewer tests in higher education than in high school, and the grading might be tougher. You'll probably find that teachers expect you to study more than you did in high school. At the same time, your instructors might give you less guidance about what or how to study, and less feedback about how you are doing.

- *Differences in teaching styles.* Instructors at colleges, universities, and vocational schools are often steeped in their subject matter. Many did not take courses on how to teach and might not be as interesting as some of your high school teachers. And some professors might seem more focused on research than on teaching.

- *A larger playing field.* The institution you've just joined might seem immense, impersonal, and even frightening. The sheer size of the campus, the variety of courses offered, the large number of departments—all of these can add up to a confusing array of options.

There's an opportunity that comes with all of these changes. Higher education presents you with a new world of choices. You are now responsible for deciding what classes to take, how to structure your time, and with whom to associate. Perhaps more than ever before, you'll find that your education is your own creation. When making decisions that lead to the future of your dreams, keep the following in mind.

Decrease the unknowns. Before classes begin, get a map of the school property and walk through your first day's schedule, perhaps with a classmate or friend. Visit your instructors in their offices and introduce yourself. Anything you can do to get familiar with the new routine will help.

Admit your feelings—whatever they are. School can be an intimidating experience for new students. People of diverse cultures, adult learners, commuters, and people with disabilities can feel excluded. Anyone can feel anxious, isolated, homesick, or worried about doing well academically.

Those emotions are common among new students, and there's nothing wrong with them. Simply admitting the truth about how you feel—to yourself and to someone else—can help you cope. And you can almost always do something constructive, no matter how you feel.

If your feelings about this transition make it hard for you to carry out the activities of daily life—going to class, working, studying, and relating to people—then get professional help. Start with a counselor at the student health service on your campus. The mere act of seeking help can make a difference.

Access resources. A supercharger increases the air supply to an internal combustion engine. The resulting difference in power can be dramatic. You can make just as powerful a difference in your education by using all of the resources available to students. In this case, your "air supply" includes people, campus clubs and organizations, and school and community services.

Of all resources, people are the most important. You can isolate yourself, study hard, and get a good education. When you make the effort to establish relationships with teachers, staff members, fellow students, and employers, you can get a *great* education.

Meet with your academic advisor. One person in particular can help you access resources and make the transition to higher education—your academic advisor. Meet with this person regularly. Advisors generally have a big picture of course requirements, options for declaring majors, and the resources available at your school. Peer advisory programs might also be available.

When you work with an advisor, remember that you're a paying customer and have a right to be satisfied with the service you get. Don't be afraid to change advisors when that seems appropriate.

Learn the language of higher education. Terms such as *grade point average (GPA)*, *prerequisite*, *accreditation*, *matriculation*, *tenure*, and *syllabus* might be new to you. Ease your transition to higher education by checking your school catalog for definitions of these words and others that you don't understand. Also ask your academic advisor for clarification.

Attend class. In higher education, teachers generally don't take attendance. Yet you'll find that attending class is essential to your success. The amount that you pay in tuition and fees makes a powerful argument for going to classes regularly and getting your money's worth. In large part, the material that you're tested on comes from events that take place in class.

"Showing up" for class occurs on two levels. The most visible level is being physically present in the classroom. Even more important is showing up mentally. This includes taking detailed notes, asking questions, and contributing to class discussions.

Don't assume that you already know how to study. You can cope with increased workloads and higher academic expectations by putting all of your study habits on the table and evaluating them. Keep the habits that serve you, drop those that hold you back, and adopt new ones to promote your success. On every page of this book, you'll find helpful suggestions.

Succeed as an adult learner. If you're returning to school after a long break from the classroom, there's no reason to feel out of place. Returning adults and other nontraditional students are already a majority in some schools.

You share a central goal with students of any age: succeeding in school. Consider pooling resources with younger students. Share notes, form study groups, or edit each other's term papers. Introduce yourself to other adult learners.

Rather than returning to study habits from previous school experiences, many adult learners find it more effective to treat their school assignments exactly as they would treat a project at work. They use the same tactics in the library as they do on the job, which often helps them learn more actively.

Take the initiative in meeting new people. Promise yourself to meet one new person each week; then write an Intention Statement describing specific ways to do this. Introduce yourself to classmates. Just before or after class is a good time to do so. Realize that most of the people in this new world of higher education are waiting to be welcomed. You can help them and help yourself at the same time. ✉

Perhaps more than ever before, you'll find that your education is your own creation.

For more strategies on mastering the art of transition, visit the Master Student Web site at

masterstudent.college.hmco.com

Making a healthy transition

Healthy people meet the demands of daily life with energy to spare. Preserving your health is one way to maintain the personal resources needed to succeed in higher education.

Eat for health *and* pleasure

By remembering and acting on three key words, you can eat to maintain energy, manage weight, and prevent disease:

Quantity. To avoid becoming overweight, begin by choosing *how much* you eat. Notice portion sizes. Pass on seconds and desserts, or just indulge occasionally.

Quality. To prevent heart disease and cancer—major sources of premature death in developed countries—the United States Department of Agriculture now recommends a plant-based diet. Build most of your meals from plant foods—whole grains, fruits, and vegetables. You can get complete proteins from low-fat dairy products, lean meats, and soy foods. Enjoy fats and sweets in moderation. Also keep in mind that your body is mostly water, so drink plenty of it.

Enjoyment. Eating can be one of life's greatest pleasures. Take the time to enjoy your food. If you eat slowly and savor each bite, you can be satisfied with smaller portions—a way to reduce calories while increasing your enjoyment.

For students with eating disorders, food becomes a source of suffering rather than joy. These disorders involve overeating or extreme reduction of food intake, as well as irrational concern about body shape or weight. Eating disorders can lead to many complications, some life-threatening. If you're worried that you might have an eating disorder, visit a doctor, campus health service, or local public health clinic. If you see signs of an eating disorder in someone else, express your concern now.

Do exercise you enjoy

Regular exercise can improve your alertness and ability to learn. Exercising is also a way to dissipate the tension that you build up while hunched over a keyboard hammering out a term paper.

Do something you enjoy. Start by walking briskly for at least 15 minutes every day. Increase that time gradually and add a little running. Once you're in reasonable shape, you can stay there by doing aerobic activity on most days of the week. An hour of daily activity is ideal, but do whatever you can. Some activity is better than none.

Manage stress

There are three things you can do as immediate first-aid for stress:

- *Learn to relax.* There are many types of relaxation exercises, ranging from yoga to guided visualization. One of the simplest is to close your eyes, sit in a relaxed yet upright position, and count your breaths. As thoughts and body sensations arise, just notice them and let them go. Over time, and with consistent practice, your mind will gradually clear.

- *Get aerobic exercise.* Vigorous movement is good for your heart, and it's also good for your mood.

- *Get sound sleep.* If you have problems sleeping, avoid taking naps during the daytime. Monitor your caffeine intake, especially in the afternoon and evening.

Get help for alcohol or other drug abuse

According to researchers from the Harvard School of Public Health, at least 40 percent of American college students are regular binge drinkers. The results include nearly 1,400 deaths annually from alcohol-related injuries and accidents. Other costs of binge drinking include assault, rape, vandalism, and suicide.[2]

When people continue to use alcohol or other drugs despite negative consequences, they're abusing chemicals. If they find it impossible to stop using drugs on their own, they may be alcoholics or addicts.

Be willing to admit the truth about your relationship to alcohol and other drugs. If you have any concerns, go to the student health service on your campus and ask about treatment options. There are many—everything from confidential counseling and self-help groups to formal treatment programs. Taking charge of your relationship to alcohol and other drugs can remove one of the greatest obstacles to success in higher education. ⊠

Connect to resources

As a student in higher education, you can access a world of student services and community resources. Any of them can help you succeed in school. Many of them are free.

Name a problem that you're facing right now or that you anticipate facing in the future: Finding money to pay for classes. Deciding which courses to take. Resolving conflicts with a teacher. Getting treatment for a sexually transmitted disease or an eating disorder. Lining up a job after graduation. Chances are good that a school or community resource can help you.

Resources often go unused—even when people pay taxes to fund them. You can demonstrate an alternative. Following are a few examples of resources. Check your school and city Web sites for the specific resources available to you.

Academic advisors can help you with selecting courses, choosing majors, planning your career, and adjusting in general to the culture of higher education.

Arts organizations energize local museums, concert venues, clubs, and stadiums.

Athletic centers often open weight rooms, swimming pools, indoor tracks, basketball courts, and racquet-sport courts to all students.

Childcare is sometimes made available to students at a reasonable cost through the early childhood education department on campus or through community agencies.

Computer labs where students can go 24 hours a day to work on projects and access the Internet are usually free. Instruction on computer use might also be offered.

Churches, synagogues, mosques, and temples have members happy to welcome fellow worshippers who are away from home.

Consumer credit counseling can help, even if you've really blown your budget. And it's usually free. Remember, no matter how bad your financial picture is, you are probably in better shape than most governments.

Counseling centers in the community can assist you with a problem when you can't get help at school. Look for job and career planning services, rehabilitation offices, veterans' outreach programs, church and social service agencies, and mental health clinics.

The **financial aid office** assists students with loans, scholarships, and grants. To find ways to finance your education, visit this office.

Governments (city, county, state, and federal) often have programs for students. Check the government listings in your local telephone directory.

Libraries are a treasure on campus and in any community. Most employ people who are happy to help you locate information.

Job placement offices can help you find part-time employment while you are in school and a job after you graduate.

Legal aid services provide free or inexpensive assistance to low-income people.

Newspapers published on campus and in the local community list events and services that are free or inexpensive.

The **school catalog** lists course descriptions and tuition fees, requirements for graduation, and information on everything from the school's history to its grading practices.

School security agencies can tell you what's safe and what's not. They can also provide information about parking, bicycle regulations, and traffic rules. Some offer safe escorts at night for female students.

Support groups exist for people with almost any problem, from drug addiction to cancer. You can find people with problems who meet every week to share suggestions, information, and concerns. Some examples are groups for single parents, recently widowed people, alcoholics or drug addicts, breast cancer survivors, and parents who have lost a child.

Student health clinics often provide free or inexpensive counseling and other medical treatment.

Student organizations present opportunities for extracurricular activities. Explore student government, fraternities, sororities, service clubs, veterans' organizations, religious groups, sports clubs, and political groups. Find women's centers, multicultural student centers, and organizations for international students, disabled students, and gay and lesbian students.

Student unions are hubs for social activities, special programs, and free entertainment.

Tutoring is usually free and is available through academic departments or counseling centers. ⬛

Link to the world of work

The suggestions in this book can help you succeed both inside and outside the classroom. Apply the techniques you gain from this course to any learning situation you encounter, whether at home, at school, or at work.

Staying current in the job market means continually expanding your knowledge and skills. You might change careers several times during your working life—a possibility that calls for continuous learning. As a master student, you can gain favor with employers by getting up to speed quickly on new jobs and new projects.

Starting now, read this book with a mental filter in place. Ask yourself: How can I use this idea to meet my career goals? How can I apply this technique to my current job or the next job I see for myself? The answers can help you thrive in any job, whether you work full- or part-time. To stimulate your thinking, look for the Put It to Work article located in each chapter. In addition, invent techniques of your own based on what you read and test them at work. There's no limit to the possibilities.

For example, you can use the Discovery and Intention Journal Entry system while you're in the work force. Write Discovery Statements to note your current job skills as well as areas for improvement. Also use Discovery Statements to describe what you want from your career.

Follow up with Intention Statements that detail specifically what you want to be doing one year, five years, and ten years or more from today. Write additional Intention Statements about specific actions you can take right now to meet those career goals.

Below is a textbook reconnaissance that lists articles in this book with workplace applications. These are just a few examples. As you read, look for more.

- The skills you learn as you are *making the transition to higher education* (page 7) can help you make the transition to a new job. For example, you can decrease unknowns by working for a company on a temporary, part-time, or contract basis. These positions can lead to an offer of full-time employment. If that happens, you'll already know a lot about the company.

- The article *Getting the most out of now* (page 59) is packed with ideas you can transfer to the workplace. For example, tackle difficult tasks first in the day, or at any other time when your energy peaks. Also find five-minute tasks that you can complete while waiting for a meeting to start.

- The article *Choosing to remember* (page 74) will come in handy as you learn the policies and procedures for a new job.

- Techniques presented in *Remembering names* (page 79) can help as you meet people during your job search and as you are being introduced to new coworkers.

- Use *Muscle Reading* (page 91) to keep up with journals and books in your field. This set of techniques can also help you scan Web sites for the information you want, keep up with ever-increasing volumes of e-mail, and reduce mountains of interoffice memos to manageable proportions.

- *The note-taking process flows* (page 113) explains different formats for taking notes—mind maps, concept maps, the Cornell format, and more. These are tools you can use to document what happens at work-related meetings.

- Adapt the ideas mentioned in *Cooperative learning—Study with people* (page 139) in order to cooperate more effectively with members of a project team.

- Use the thinking skills presented in *Gaining skill at decision making* (page 170) when it comes time to choose a career, weigh job offers, or make work-related decisions.

- Ideas from *The fine art of conflict management* (page 188) can help you defuse tensions among coworkers.

- The suggestions in *Communicating across cultures* (page 190) can assist you in adapting to the culture of a new job. Each company, large or small, develops its own culture—a set of shared values and basic assumptions. Even if you are self-employed, you can benefit by discovering and adapting to a client's corporate culture.

Attitudes, values, and visualizations

"I have a bad attitude." Some of us say this as if we were talking about having the flu. An attitude can be as strong as the flu, but it isn't something we have to blindly accept.

Attitudes are powerful. They shape behavior. If your attitude is that you're not a successful student, then your behavior will probably match your attitude. If your attitude is that you can learn to succeed in school, then you're more likely to benefit from all the money and time you invest in higher education.

You can change your attitudes by acting on your values and visualizing new results in your life.

Act on your values. Values are the things in life that you want for their own sake. Values guide your choices, including your moment-by-moment choices. Some people are guided by values that they adopt without thinking. These people could be missing the opportunity to live a life that's truly of their own choosing.

Values are pivotal to this book. In fact, *Becoming a Master Student* is based on a particular set of values:

- Focused attention
- Taking responsibility for your life
- Giving and keeping your word
- Risk taking
- Contributing to others

Suggestions throughout this book flow from these values. The Time Monitor/Time Plan exercise, for example, calls for focused attention. And even the simple act of sharing your notes with a student who missed a class is an example of contributing.

Don't read the previous list of values with the idea that it is the "right" one for you. Instead, use these values as a point of departure when creating your own list.

Also translate your values into behavior. Though defining your values is powerful, it doesn't guarantee any results. To achieve your goals, take actions that align with your values.

Visualize it. Visualization is the technique of seeing yourself as being successful right now.

Decide what you want to improve, and write down what it would look like, sound like, and feel like to have that improvement in your life. If you are learning to play the piano, write down briefly what you would see, hear, and feel if you were playing skillfully. If you want to improve your relationships with your children, write down what you would see, hear, and feel if you were communicating with them successfully.

Once you have an image of what it would be like to be successful, practice it in your imagination—successfully. As you play out the scenario, include as many details as you can. Always have your practices be successes. Whenever you toss the basketball, it swishes through the net. Every time you invite someone out on a date, the person says yes. Each test the teacher hands back to you is graded an A. Practice at least once a day.

To support your visualization, experiment with affirmations. An affirmation is a statement describing what you want. Effective affirmations are personal, positive, detailed, and written in the present tense. For example: "I, Malika Jones, am a master student. I take full responsibility for my education. I learn with joy, and I use my experiences in each course to create the life that I want."

Or: "I, Susan Webster, have a wonderful job. I respect and love my colleagues, and they feel the same way about me. I look forward to going to work each day."

Once you have written an affirmation, repeat it. Practice saying it out loud several times a day. This works best if you say it at a regular time, such as just before you go to sleep or just after you wake up.

Values, visualizations, and affirmations are ways to change your attitudes and behaviors. Be clear about what you want from your education and your life—and then support yourself to get it. ⊠

Ways to change a habit

Imagine for a moment that many of our most troublesome problems and even our most basic traits are just habits.

An expanding waistline may just be a habit called overeating.

An outcome that "couldn't" be avoided, such as dropping out of school, may just be a cluster of habits—failing to complete reading assignments and skipping classes.

Procrastination, stress, and money shortages might just be names that we give to collections of habits—scores of simple, small, repeated behaviors that combine to create a huge result.

When you confront an obstacle to getting what you want, consider a new attitude: It's just a habit. And it can be changed.

Choose and commit

It often helps to choose a new habit to replace an old one. Then make a commitment to practice the new habit. Tell key people in your life about your decision to change. Set up a plan for when and how. Answer questions such as these: When will I apply the new habit? Where will I be? Who will be with me? What will I be seeing, hearing, touching, saying, or doing? Exactly how will I think, speak, or act differently?

Take the student who always snacks when he studies. He decides to change this habit by studying at a desk in his bedroom instead of at the kitchen table. And every time he feels the urge to bite into a potato chip, he drinks from a glass of water instead.

Get feedback and support

This is a crucial step and a point at which many plans for change break down. It's easy to practice your new behav-ior with great enthusiasm for a few days. After the initial rush of excitement, however, things can get a little tougher. We begin to find excuses for slipping back into old habits: "One more cigarette won't hurt." "I can get back to my diet tomorrow." "It's been a tough day. I deserve this beer."

One way to get feedback is to bring other people into the picture. Ask others to remind you that you are changing your habit.

Support from others can be as simple as a quick phone call: "Hi. Have you started that outline for your research paper yet?" Or it can be as formal as a support group that meets once weekly to review everyone's goals and action plans.

You are probably the most effective source for your own support and feedback. You know yourself better than anyone else does and can design a system to monitor your behavior. You can create your own charts or diagrams to track your behavior, or you can write about your progress in your journal. Figure out a way to monitor your progress.

Practice, practice, practice—without self-judgment

Psychologists such as B. F. Skinner define learning as a stable change in behavior that comes as a result of practice.[3] This idea is key to changing habits. Act on your intention. If you fail or forget, let go of any self-judgment. Just keep practicing the new habit and allow whatever time it takes to make a change.

Accept the feelings of discomfort that might come with a new habit. Keep practicing the new behavior, even if it feels unnatural. If you fail or forget, don't scold yourself. Just return to practicing the new behavior and allow whatever time it takes to make a change.

Making mistakes as you practice doesn't mean that you've failed. Even when you don't get the results you want from a new behavior, you learn something valuable in the process. Once you understand ways to change one habit, you understand ways to change almost any habit.

Motivation

The terms *self-discipline, willpower,* and *motivation* are often used to describe something missing in ourselves. Time after time we invoke these words to explain another person's success—or our own short-comings: "If I were more motivated, I'd get more in-volved in school." "Of course she got an A. She has self-discipline." "If I had more willpower, I'd lose weight."

An alternative is to stop assuming that motivation is mysterious, determined at birth, or hard to come by. Perhaps what we call *motivation* is something that you already possess—or simply a habit that you can develop with practice. Test this idea yourself with the following suggestions.

Promise it. Motivation can come simply from being clear about your goals and acting on them. Say that you want to start a study group. You can commit yourself to inviting people and setting a time and place to meet. Promise your classmates that you'll do this, and ask them to hold you accountable. Self-discipline, willpower, motivation—none of these mysterious characteristics needs to get in your way. Just make a promise and keep your word.

Befriend your discomfort. Sometimes keeping your word means doing a task you'd rather put off. The mere thought of doing laundry, reading a chapter in a statistics book, or proofreading a term paper can lead to discomfort.

If you feel this kind of discomfort, stay with it. Don't run from it. Don't judge it as good or bad.

Discomfort is just a name we give to thoughts and sensations that rise and pass away. They do not have to stop you from acting on your intentions. Simply notice discomfort, accept it, and then move into action. On the other side of discomfort lies mastery.

Sweeten the task. Sometimes it's just one aspect of a task that holds us back. We can stop procrastinating merely by changing that aspect. If distaste for our physical environment keeps us from studying, we can change that environment. Reading about social psychology might seem like a yawner when we're alone in a dark corner of the house. Moving to a cheery, well-lit library can sweeten the task.

Compare the payoffs to the costs. Behaviors such as cramming for exams have payoffs. For example, skipping a reading assignment can give you time to go to the movies. However, you might be unprepared for class and have twice as much to read the following week.

Maybe there is another way to get the payoff (going to the movies) without paying the cost (skipping the reading assignment). With some thoughtful weekly planning, you might choose to give up a few hours of television and end up with enough time to read the assignment *and* go to the movies.

Comparing the costs and benefits of any behavior can fuel our motivation. We can choose new behaviors because they align with what we want most.

Do it later. At times, it's effective to save a task for later. For example, writing a résumé can wait until you've taken the time to analyze your job skills and map out your career goals. This is not a lack of motivation—it's planning.

Heed the message. Sometimes lack of motivation carries a message that's worth heeding. An example is the student who majors in accounting but seizes every chance to be with children. His chronic reluctance to read accounting textbooks might not be a problem. Instead, it might reveal his desire to major in elementary education. His original career choice might have come from the belief that "real men don't teach kindergarten." In such cases, an apparent lack of motivation signals a deeper wisdom trying to get through. ▨

power process

Discover what you want

Imagine a person who walks up to a counter at the airport to buy a plane ticket for his next vacation. "Just give me a ticket," he says to the reservation agent. "Anywhere will do."

The agent stares back at him in disbelief. "I'm sorry, sir," he replies. "I'll need some more details. Just minor things—such as the name of your destination city and your arrival and departure dates."

"Oh, I'm not fussy," says the would-be vacationer. "I just want to get away. You choose for me."

Compare this with another traveler who walks up to the counter and says, "I'd like a ticket to Ixtapa, Mexico, departing on Saturday, March 23, and returning Sunday, April 7. Please give me a window seat, first class, with vegetarian meals."

Now, ask yourself which traveler is more likely to end up with a vacation that he'll enjoy.

The same principle applies in any area of life. Knowing where we want to go increases the probability that we will arrive at our destination. Discovering what we want makes it more likely that we'll attain it. Once our goals are defined precisely, our brains reorient our thinking and behavior to align with those goals—and we're well on the way there.

Mastery lies in the details

The example about the traveler with no destination seems far-fetched. Before you dismiss it, do an informal experiment: Ask three other students what they want to get out of their education. Be prepared for hemming and hawing, vague generalities, and maybe even a helping of pie-in-the-sky à la mode.

That's amazing, considering the stakes involved. Our hypothetical vacationer is about to invest a couple weeks of his time and hundreds of dollars—all with no destination in mind. Students routinely invest years of their lives and thousands of dollars with an equally hazy idea of their destination in life.

Suppose that you ask someone what she wants from her education and you get this answer: "I plan to get a degree in journalism with double minors in earth science and Portuguese so that I can work as a reporter covering the environment in Brazil." Chances are you've found a master student. The details of a person's vision offer a clue to mastery.

Discover the benefits

Discovering what you want greatly enhances your odds of succeeding in higher education. Many students quit school simply because they are unsure of their goals. With well-defined objectives in mind, you can constantly look for connections between what you want and what you study. The more connections you discover, the more likely you'll stay in school—and the more likely you'll benefit from higher education.

Having a clear idea of your goals makes many decisions easier. Knowing what you want from your education helps you choose the school you'll attend, the courses you'll take, the major you'll declare, and the next career you'll pursue.

Discovering what you want also enhances your study skills. An example is memorizing. A skydiver will not become bored learning how to pack her parachute. Her reward for learning the skill is too important. Likewise, when information helps you get something you want, it becomes easier to remember.

You can have more energy when your daily activities lead to what you want. If you're bogged down in quadratic equations, stand back for a minute. Think about how that math course ties in with your goal of becoming an electrical engineer, how your philosophy course relates to your aim of becoming a minister, or how your English course can help you become a better teacher.

Succeeding in higher education takes effort. When you follow the path of getting what you truly want, you can enjoy yourself even if the path is uphill. You can expend great energy and still feel fresh and eager to learn. When you take on courses that you care about and prepare for a career that you look forward to, you can play full out. You can work even to the point of exhaustion at times, and do it happily.

That's one purpose of discovering what you want. Your vision is not meant to be followed blindly—it's meant to pull you forward.

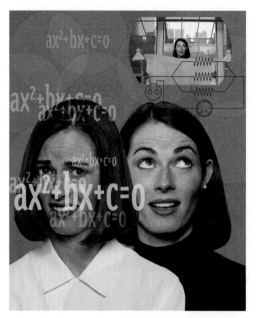

Perhaps you want to restore the integrity of the ozone layer or eliminate racism through international law. Or perhaps you simply want to be more physically fit, more funny, or more loving. Whatever you want, write it down.

Later, if you want, you can let go of some goals. First, though, live with them for a while. Goals that sound outlandish right now might seem more realistic in a few weeks, months, or years. Time often brings a more balanced perspective, along with an expanded sense of possibility.

Put it in writing

For maximum clarity, write down what you want. Goals that reside strictly in your head can remain fuzzy. Writing them down brings them into sharper focus.

As you write about what you want, expand your imagination to many different time frames. Define what you want to be, do, and have next week, next month, and next year. Write about what you want five years from now—and five minutes from now.

Approach this process with a sense of adventure and play. As you write, be willing to put any option on the table. List the most outrageous goals—those that sound too wonderful to ever come true.

You might want to travel to India, start a consulting business, or open a library in every disadvantaged neighborhood. Write those goals down.

You might want to own a ranch in a beautiful valley, become a painter, or visit all of the hot springs in the world. Write those down, too.

With well-defined objectives in mind, you can constantly look for connections between what you want and what you study.

Move from discovery to action

Discovering what you want can be heady fun. And it can quickly become an interesting but irrelevant exercise unless you take action to get what you want. Most discoveries come bundled with hints to *do* something—perhaps to change a habit, contact someone, travel, get educated, or acquire a new skill. Dreams that are not followed with action tend to die on paper. On the other hand, dreams that lead to new behaviors can lead to new results in your life.

To move into action, use this book. It's filled with places to state what you want to accomplish and how you intend to go about it. Every Journal Entry and exercise exists for this purpose. Fill up those pages. Take action and watch your dreams evolve from fuzzy ideals into working principles.

With your dreams and new behaviors in hand, you might find that events fall into place almost magically. Start telling people about what you want, and you'll eventually find some who are willing to help. They might offer an idea or two or suggest a person to call or an organization to contact. They might even offer their time or money. The sooner you discover what you want, the sooner you can create the conditions that transform your life. ⬛

journal entry 2

Discovery Statement

Success is a choice—your choice. To *get* what you want, it helps to *know* what you want. That is the purpose of this Journal Entry, which has two parts.

You can begin choosing success right now by setting a date, time, and place to complete this Journal Entry. Write your choices here; then block out the time on your calendar.

Date: _____

Time: _____

Place: _____

Part 1

Select a time and place when you know you will not be disturbed for at least 20 minutes. (The library is a good place to do this.) Relax for two or three minutes, clearing your mind. Next, complete the following sentences—and then keep writing.

When you run out of things to write, stick with it just a bit longer. Be willing to experience a little discomfort. Keep writing. What you discover might be well worth the extra effort.

What I want from my education is . . .

_____

_____

_____

When I complete my education, I want to be able to . . .

_____

_____

_____

_____

I also want . . .

_____

_____

_____

_____

Part 2

After completing Part 1, take a short break. Reward yourself by doing something that you enjoy. Then come back to this Journal Entry.

Now, review the above list of things that you want from your education. See if you can summarize them in a one-sentence, polished statement. This will become a statement of your purpose for taking part in higher education.

Allow yourself to write many drafts of this mission statement, and review it periodically as you continue your education. With each draft, see if you can capture the essence of what you want from higher education and from your life. State it in a vivid way—a short sentence that you can easily memorize, one that sparks your enthusiasm and makes you want to get up in the morning.

You might find it difficult to express your purpose statement in one sentence. If so, write a paragraph or more. Then look for the sentence that seems most charged with energy for you.

Following are some sample purpose statements:

- My purpose for being in school is to gain skills that I can use to contribute to others.

- My purpose for being in school is to live an abundant life that is filled with happiness, health, love, and wealth.

- My purpose for being in school is to enjoy myself by making lasting friendships and following the lead of my interests.

Write at least one draft of your purpose statement below:

_____

_____

_____

_____

_____

_____

_____

1

First Steps

why

this chapter matters . . .

Visible measures of success—such as top grades and résumés filled with accomplishments—start with invisible assets called attitudes.

what

is included . . .

First Step: Truth is a key to mastery
If you skipped the Introduction . . .
The Discovery Wheel
The Master Student
Claim your multiple intelligences
Learning by seeing, hearing, and moving: The VAK system
Learning styles: Discovering how you learn
Learning Style Inventory
Using your learning style profile to succeed in school
The value of higher education
Power Process: "Ideas are tools"
Master Student Profile: Ruth Handler

how

you can use this chapter . . .

Experience the power of telling the truth about your current skills.
Discover your preferred learning styles and develop new ones.
Consciously choose attitudes that promote your success.

As you read, ask yourself

what if . . .

I could create attitudes that would help me achieve my goals?

STUDENT VOICES

" *At first I was very angry about being left behind and was discouraged because of my learning style. In fact, I spent a lot of energy resenting my lost opportunities. Then I realized that the energy I was spending on resentment could be turned into something positive. I wrote a speech and shared my experiences; I addressed problems that can result from not recognizing learning styles. In the speech, I pointed out ways to identify learning styles and ways to get those styles met. I received a lot of good feedback from the speech, and I think it actually helped other students.*"

—REBECCA GULLEDGE

First Step: Truth is a key to mastery

The First Step technique is simple: Tell the truth about who you are and what you want. End of discussion. Now proceed to Chapter Two.

Well, it's not *quite* that simple.

The First Step is one of the most valuable tools in this book. It magnifies the power of all the other techniques. It is a key to becoming a master student. Unfortunately, a First Step is easier to explain than it is to use. Telling the truth sounds like pie-in-the-sky moralizing, but there is nothing pie-in-the-sky or moralizing about a First Step. It is a practical, down-to-earth way to change our behavior. No technique in this book has been field-tested more often or more successfully—or under tougher circumstances.

Success starts with telling the truth about what *is* working—and what *isn't*—in our lives right now. When we acknowledge our strengths, we gain an accurate picture of what we can accomplish. When we admit that we have a problem, we free up energy to find a solution. Ignoring the truth, on the other hand, can lead to problems that stick around for decades. The principle of telling the truth is applied universally by people who want to turn their lives around. For members of Alcoholics Anonymous, the First Step is acknowledging that they are powerless over alcohol. For people who join Weight Watchers, the First Step is admitting how much they weigh.

It's not easy to tell the truth about ourselves. And for some of us, it's even harder to recognize our strengths. Maybe we don't want to brag. Maybe we're attached to poor self-images. The reasons don't matter. The point is that using the First Step technique in *Becoming a Master Student* means telling the truth about our positive qualities, too.

Many of us approach a frank evaluation of ourselves about as enthusiastically as we'd anticipate an audit by the IRS. There is another way to think about self-evaluations. If we could see them as opportunities to solve problems and take charge of our lives, we might welcome them. Believe it or not, we can begin working with our list of weaknesses by celebrating them.

Consider the most accomplished, "together" people you know. If they were totally candid with you, you'd soon hear about their mistakes and regrets. The more successful people are, the more willing they are to look at their flaws.

It might seem natural to judge our own shortcomings and feel bad about them. Some people believe that such feelings are necessary in order to bring about change. Others think that a healthy dose of shame can turn negatives into positives. There is an alternative. We can discover a way to gain skill without feeling rotten about the past. By taking a First Step, we can change the way things *are* without having to be upset about the way things *have been*. We can learn to see shame or blame as excess baggage and just set it aside. It might also help to remember that weaknesses are often strengths taken to an extreme. The student who carefully revises her writing can make significant improvements in a term paper. If she hands in the paper late, though, her grade might suffer. Any success strategy carried too far can backfire. Whether written or verbal, First Steps are more powerful when

If you skipped the Introduction...

"Tell the truth about who you are and what you want."

they are specific. For example, if you want to improve your note-taking skills, you might write, "I am an awful note taker." It would be more effective to write, "I can't read 80 percent of the notes I took in Introduction to Psychology last week, and I have no idea what was important in that class." Be just as specific about what you plan to achieve. You might declare, "I want to take legible notes that help me predict what questions will be on the final exam."

Complete the exercises in this chapter, and your courage will be rewarded. The Discovery Wheel exercise and the rest of the activities in this book can help you tap resources you never knew you had. They're all First Steps—no kidding. It's just that simple. The truth has power. ◙

Some people think introductions have little to offer and are a waste of time. The Introduction to *Becoming a Master Student* is important. It suggests ways to get your money's worth out of this book—and out of your education.

Here are some of the informative articles that await you:

- This book is worthless—if you just read it
- Get the most out of this book
- The Discovery and Intention Journal Entry system
- Making the transition to higher education
- Making a healthy transition
- Connect to resources
- Link to the world of work
- Attitudes, values, and visualizations
- Ways to change a habit
- Motivation
- Power Process: "Discover what you want"

Please go back and read the Introduction now. ◙

TAKING THE FIRST STEP

The purpose of this exercise is to give you a chance to discover and acknowledge your own strengths, as well as areas for improvement. For many students, this is the most difficult exercise in the book. To make the exercise worthwhile, do it with courage.

Some people suggest that looking at areas for improvement means focusing on personal weaknesses. They view it as a negative approach that runs counter to positive thinking. Well, perhaps. Positive thinking is a great technique. So is telling the truth, especially when we see the whole picture—the negative aspects as well as the positive ones.

If you admit that you can't add or subtract and that's the truth, then you have taken a strong, positive First Step toward learning basic math. On the other hand, if you say that you are a terrible math student and that's not the truth, then you are programming yourself to accept unnecessary failure.

The point is to tell the truth. This exercise is similar to the Discovery Statements that appear in every chapter. The difference is that in this case, for reasons of confidentiality, you won't write down your discoveries in the book.

Be brave. If you approach this exercise with courage, you are likely to disclose some things about yourself that you wouldn't want others to read. You might even write down some truths that could get you into trouble. Do this exercise on separate sheets of paper; then hide or destroy them. Protect your privacy.

To make this exercise work, follow these suggestions:

Be specific. It is not effective to write "I can improve my communication skills." Of course you can. Instead, write down precisely what you can *do* to improve your communication skills, for example, "I can spend more time really listening while the other person is talking, instead of thinking about what I'm going to say next."

Look beyond the classroom. What goes on outside of school often has the greatest impact on your ability to be an effective student.

Be courageous. This exercise is a waste of time if it is done half-heartedly. Be willing to take risks. You might open a door that reveals a part of yourself that you didn't want to admit was there. The power of this technique is that once you know what is there, you can do something about it.

Part 1

Time yourself, and for 10 minutes write as fast as you can, completing each of the following sentences at least 10 times with anything that comes to mind. If you get stuck, don't stop. Just write something—even if it seems crazy.

> I never succeed when I . . .
>
> I'm not very good at . . .
>
> Something I'd like to change about myself is . . .

Part 2

When you have completed the first part of the exercise, review what you have written, crossing off things that don't make any sense. The sentences that remain suggest possible goals for becoming a master student.

Part 3

Here's the tough part. Time yourself, and for 10 minutes write as fast as you can, completing the following sentences with anything that comes to mind. As in Part 1, complete each sentence at least 10 times. Just keep writing, even if it sounds silly.

> I always succeed when I . . .
>
> I am very good at . . .
>
> Something I like about myself is . . .

Part 4

Review what you have written and circle the things that you can fully celebrate. This is a good list to keep for those times when you question your own value and worth.

THE DISCOVERY WHEEL

The Discovery Wheel is another opportunity to tell the truth about the kind of student you are and the kind of student you want to become.

This is not a test. There are no trick questions, and the answers will have meaning only for yourself.

Here are two suggestions to make this exercise more effective. First, think of it as the beginning of an opportunity to change. There is another Discovery Wheel at the end of this book. You will have a chance to measure your progress, so be honest about where you are now. Second, lighten up. A little laughter can make self-evaluations a lot more effective.

Here's how the Discovery Wheel works. By the end of this exercise, you will have filled in a circle similar to the one on this page. The Discovery Wheel circle is a picture of how you see yourself as a student. The closer the shading comes to the outer edge of the circle, the higher the evaluation of a specific skill. In the example to the right, the student has rated her reading skills low and her note-taking skills high.

The terms *high* and *low* are not meant to reflect a negative judgment. The Discovery Wheel is not a permanent picture of who you are. It is a picture of how you view your strengths and weaknesses as a student today. To begin this exercise, read the following statements and award yourself points for each one, using the point system described below. Then add up your point total for each section and shade the Discovery Wheel on page 25 to the appropriate level.

5 points
This statement is always or almost always true of me.

4 points
This statement is often true of me.

3 points
This statement is true of me about half the time.

2 points
This statement is seldom true of me.

1 point
This statement is never or almost never true of me.

1. _____ I enjoy learning.

2. _____ I understand and apply the concept of multiple intelligences.

3. _____ I connect my courses to my purpose for being in school.

4. _____ I make a habit of assessing my personal strengths and areas for improvement.

5. _____ I am satisfied with how I am progressing toward achieving my goals.

6. _____ I use my knowledge of learning styles to support my success in school.

7. _____ I am willing to consider any idea that can help me succeed in school—even if I initially disagree with that idea.

8. _____ I regularly remind myself of the benefits I intend to get from my education.

_____ Total score (1) *Motivation*

Do this exercise online at masterstudent.college.hmco.com

1. _____ I set long-term goals and periodically review them.
2. _____ I set short-term goals to support my long-term goals.
3. _____ I write a plan for each day and each week.
4. _____ I assign priorities to what I choose to do each day.
5. _____ I plan regular recreation time.
6. _____ I adjust my study time to meet the demands of individual courses.
7. _____ I have adequate time each day to accomplish what I plan.
8. _____ I am confident that I will find the resources to finance my education.

_____ Total score (2) *Planning*

1. _____ I am confident of my ability to remember.
2. _____ I can remember people's names.
3. _____ At the end of a lecture, I can summarize what was presented.
4. _____ I apply techniques that enhance my memory skills.
5. _____ I can recall information when I'm under pressure.
6. _____ I remember important information clearly and easily.
7. _____ I can jog my memory when I have difficulty recalling.
8. _____ I can relate new information to what I've already learned.

_____ Total score (3) *Memory*

1. _____ I preview and review reading assignments.
2. _____ When reading, I ask myself questions about the material.
3. _____ I underline or highlight important passages when reading.
4. _____ When I read textbooks, I am alert and awake.
5. _____ I relate what I read to my life.
6. _____ I select a reading strategy to fit the type of material I'm reading.

7. _____ I take effective notes when I read.
8. _____ When I don't understand what I'm reading, I note my questions and find answers.

_____ Total score (4) *Reading*

1. _____ When I am in class, I focus my attention.
2. _____ I take notes in class.
3. _____ I am aware of various methods for taking notes and choose those that work best for me.
4. _____ I distinguish important material and note key phrases in a lecture.
5. _____ I copy down material that the instructor writes on the chalkboard or overhead projector.
6. _____ I can put important concepts into my own words.
7. _____ My notes are valuable for review.
8. _____ I review class notes within 24 hours.

_____ Total score (5) *Notes*

1. _____ I feel confident and calm during an exam.
2. _____ I manage my time during exams and am able to complete them.
3. _____ I am able to predict test questions.
4. _____ I adapt my test-taking strategy to the kind of test I'm taking.
5. _____ I understand what essay questions ask and can answer them completely and accurately.
6. _____ I start reviewing for tests at the beginning of the term.
7. _____ I continue reviewing for tests throughout the term.
8. _____ My sense of personal worth is independent of my test scores.

_____ Total score (6) *Tests*

1. _____ I have flashes of insight and often think of solutions to problems at unusual times.

2. _____ I use brainstorming to generate solutions to a variety of problems.

3. _____ When I get stuck on a creative project, I use specific methods to get unstuck.

4. _____ I see problems and tough decisions as opportunities for learning and personal growth.

5. _____ I am willing to consider different points of view and alternative solutions.

6. _____ I can detect common errors in logic.

7. _____ I construct viewpoints by drawing on information and ideas from many sources.

8. _____ As I share my viewpoints with others, I am open to their feedback.

_____ Total score (7) *Thinking*

1. _____ I am candid with others about who I am, what I feel, and what I want.

2. _____ Other people tell me that I am a good listener.

3. _____ I can communicate my upset and anger without blaming others.

4. _____ I can make friends and create valuable relationships in a new setting.

5. _____ I can effectively resolve conflict.

6. _____ I can persuade others to accept my ideas by writing a research paper or speaking in public.

7. _____ I am aware of my biases and am open to understanding people from other cultures, races, and ethnic groups.

8. _____ I can point out examples of discrimination and sexual harassment and effectively respond to them.

_____ Total score (8) *Communicating*

1. _____ I learn effectively from course materials and activities that are posted online.

2. _____ I can efficiently find information on the Internet.

3. _____ I think critically about information and ideas that I access online.

4. _____ I write clear and concise e-mail messages that generate the results I want.

5. _____ My online communication is fair and respectful to other people.

6. _____ I monitor new technology that can support my success in school.

7. _____ I monitor new technology that can support my success in my career.

8. _____ I effectively use libraries to find the resources and information I want.

_____ Total score (9) *Technology*

1. _____ I see learning as a lifelong process.

2. _____ I relate school to what I plan to do for the rest of my life.

3. _____ I learn by contributing to others.

4. _____ I revise my plans as I learn, change, and grow.

5. _____ I am clear about my purpose in life.

6. _____ I know that I am responsible for my own education.

7. _____ I take responsibility for the quality of my life.

8. _____ I am willing to accept challenges even when I'm not sure how to meet them.

_____ Total score (10) *Purpose*

Filling in your Discovery Wheel

Using the total score from each category, shade in each section of the Discovery Wheel. Use different colors, if you want. For example, you could use green to denote areas you want to work on. When you have finished, complete the Journal Entry on the next page.

journal entry 4

Discovery/Intention Statement

Now that you have completed your Discovery Wheel, spend a few minutes with it. Get a sense of its weight, shape, and balance. Can you imagine running your hands around it? If you could lift it, would it feel light or heavy? How would it sound if it rolled down a hill? Would it roll very far? Would it wobble? Make your observations without judging the wheel as good or bad. Simply be with the picture you have created.

After you have spent a few minutes studying your Discovery Wheel, complete the following sentences in the space below. Don't worry if you can't think of something to write. Just put down whatever comes to mind. Remember, this is not a test.

This wheel is an accurate picture of my ability as a student because . . .

_____

_____

My self-evaluation surprises me because . . .

_____

_____

The two areas in which I am strongest are . . .

_____

_____

The areas in which I want to improve are . . .

_____

_____

I want to concentrate on improving these areas because . . .

_____

_____

Now, select one of your discoveries and describe how you intend to benefit from it. Complete the statement below.

To gain some practical value from this discovery, I will . . .

_____

_____

→ Textbook reconnaissance, take two

The first chapter of a textbook usually includes key material—ideas that the author wants you to have up front. Likewise, this book is packed with articles that could benefit you right now. There just wasn't enough room to put them all in the first chapter.

While skimming the book for Exercise #1: "Textbook reconnaissance," you might have spotted the following articles in later chapters. If not, consider sampling them right now.

The seven-day antiprocrastination plan, page 57

Getting the most out of now, page 58

Choosing to remember, page 74

Muscle Reading, page 91

The note-taking process flows, page 113

Disarm tests, page 135

Gaining skill at decision making, page 170

Communicating across cultures, page 190

Writing and delivering speeches, page 197

Becoming an online learner, page 211

Jumpstart your career plan, page 227

Cruising for jobs on the Internet, page 232

In 1482, **Leonardo da Vinci** wrote a letter to a wealthy baron, applying for work. In excerpted form, he wrote,

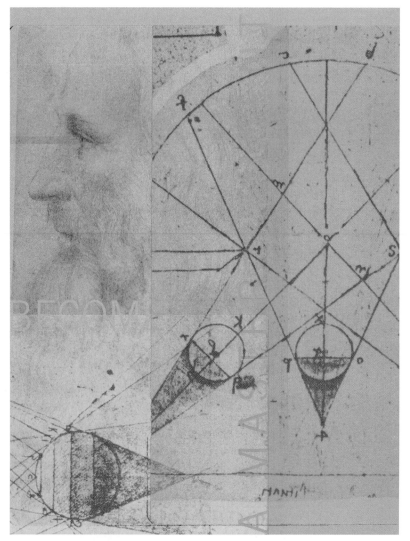

"I can contrive various and endless means of offense and defense.... I have all sorts of extremely light and strong bridges adapted to be most easily carried.... I have methods for destroying every turret or fortress.... I will make covered chariots, safe and unassailable.... In case of need I will make big guns, mortars, and light ordnance of fine and useful forms out of the common type." And then he added, almost as an afterthought, "In times of peace I believe I can give perfect satisfaction and to the equal of any other in architecture ... can carry out sculpture ... and also I can do in painting whatever may be done."

The **Mona Lisa,** for example.

The Master Student

This book is about something that cannot be taught. It's about becoming a master student.

A master is a person who has attained a level of skill that goes beyond technique. For a master, methods and procedures are automatic responses to the needs of the task. Work is effortless; struggle evaporates. The master carpenter is so familiar with her tools, they are part of her. To a master chef, utensils are old friends. Because these masters don't have to think about the details of the process, they bring more of themselves to their work.

Mastery can lead to flashy results—an incredible painting, for example, or a gem of a short story. In basketball, mastery might result in an unbelievable shot at the buzzer. For a musician, it might be the performance of a lifetime, the moment when everything comes together. Often the result of mastery is a sense of profound satisfaction, well-being, and timelessness. Work seems self-propelled. The master is *in* control by being *out* of control. He lets go and allows the creative process to take over. That's why after a spectacular performance, it is often said of an athlete or a performer, "He was playing out of his mind."

Likewise, the master student is one who "learns out of her mind." Of course, that statement makes no sense. Mastery, in fact, doesn't make sense. It cannot be captured with words. It defies analysis. Mastery cannot be taught, only learned and experienced.

Examine the following list of characteristics of master students in light of your own experience. The list is not complete. It merely points in a direction. Look in that direction, and you'll begin to see the endless diversity of master students. These people are old and young, male and female. They exist in every period of history. And they come from every culture, race, and ethnic group.

Also remember to look to yourself. No one can teach us to be master students; we already *are* master students. We are natural learners by design. As students, we can discover that every day.

Following are some traits shared by master students.

Inquisitive. The master student is curious about everything. By posing questions, she can generate interest in the most mundane, humdrum situations. When she is bored during a biology lecture, she thinks to herself, "I always get bored when I listen to this instructor. Why is that? Maybe it's because he reminds me of my boring Uncle Ralph, who always tells those endless fishing stories. He even looks like Uncle Ralph. Amazing! Boredom is certainly interesting." Then she asks herself, "What can I do to get value out of this lecture, even though it seems boring?" And she finds an answer.

Able to focus attention. Watch a 2-year-old at play. Pay attention to his eyes. The wide-eyed look reveals an energy and a capacity for amazement that keep his attention absolutely focused in the here and now. The master student's focused attention has a childlike quality. The world, to a child, is always new. Because the master student can focus attention, to him the world is always new, too.

Willing to change. The unknown does not frighten the master student. In fact, she welcomes it—even the unknown in herself. We all have pictures of who we think we are, and these pictures can be useful. They also can prevent learning and growth. The master student is open to changes in her environment and in herself.

Able to organize and sort. The master student can take a large body of information and sift through it to discover relationships. He can play with information, organizing data by size, color, function, timeliness, and hundreds of other categories.

Competent. Mastery of skills is important to the master student. When she learns mathematical formulas, she studies them until they become second nature. She practices until she knows them cold, then puts in a few extra minutes. She also is able to apply what she learns to new and different situations.

Joyful. More often than not, the master student is seen with a smile on his face—sometimes a smile at nothing in particular other than amazement at the world and his experience of it.

Able to suspend judgment. The master student has opinions and positions, and she is able to let go of them when appropriate. She realizes she is more than her thoughts. She can quiet her internal dialogue and listen to an opposing viewpoint. She doesn't let judgment get in the way of learning. Rather than approaching discussions with a "Prove it to me and then I'll believe it" attitude, she asks herself, What if this is true? and explores possibilities.

Energetic. Notice the student with a spring in his step, the one who is enthusiastic and involved in class. When he reads, he often sits on the very edge of his chair, and he plays with the same intensity. He is a master student.

Well. Health is important to the master student, though not necessarily in the sense of being free of illness. Rather, she values her body and treats it with respect. She tends to her emotional and spiritual health, as well as her physical health.

Self-aware. The master student is willing to evaluate himself and his behavior. He regularly tells the truth about his strengths and those aspects that could be improved.

Responsible. There is a difference between responsibility and blame, and the master student knows it well. She is willing to take responsibility for everything in her life—even for events that most people would blame on others.

For example, if a master student is served cold eggs in the cafeteria, she chooses to take responsibility for getting cold eggs. This is not the same as blaming herself for cold eggs. Rather, she looks for ways to change the situation and get what she wants. She could choose to eat breakfast earlier, or she might tell someone in the kitchen that the eggs are cold and request a change. The cold eggs might continue. Even then, the master student takes responsibility and gives herself the power to choose her response to the situation.

Willing to take risks. The master student often takes on projects with no guarantee of success. He participates in class dialogues at the risk of looking foolish. He tackles difficult subjects in term papers. He welcomes the risk of a challenging course.

Willing to participate. Don't look for the master student on the sidelines. She's in the game. She is a player who can be counted on. She is willing to make a commitment and to follow through on it.

A generalist. The master student is interested in everything around him. He has a broad base of knowledge in many fields and can find value that is applicable to his specialties.

Willing to accept paradox. The word *paradox* comes from two Greek words, *para* (beyond) and *doxen* (opinion). A paradox is something that is beyond opinion or, more accurately, something that might seem contradictory or absurd yet might actually have meaning.

For example, the master student can be committed to managing money and reaching her financial goals. At the same time, she can be totally detached from money, knowing that her real worth is independent of how much money she has. The master student recognizes the limitations of the mind and is at home with paradox. She can accept that ambiguity.

Courageous. The master student admits his fear and fully experiences it. For example, he will approach a tough exam as an opportunity to explore feelings of anxiety and tension related to the pressure to perform. He does not deny fear; he embraces it.

Self-directed. Rewards or punishments provided by others do not motivate the master student. Her motivation to learn comes from within.

Spontaneous. The master student is truly in the here and now. He is able to respond to the moment in fresh, surprising, and unplanned ways.

Relaxed about grades. Grades make the master student neither depressed nor euphoric. She recognizes that sometimes grades are important, and grades are not the only reason she studies. She does not measure her worth as a human being by the grades she receives.

Intuitive. The master student has an inner sense that cannot be explained by logic. He has learned to trust his feelings, and he works to develop this intuitive sense.

Creative. Where others see dull details and trivia, the master student sees opportunities to create. She can gather pieces of knowledge from a wide range of subjects and put them together in new ways. The master student is creative in every aspect of her life.

Willing to be uncomfortable. The master student does not place comfort first. When discomfort is necessary to reach a goal, he is willing to experience it. He can endure personal hardships and can look at unpleasant things with detachment.

Accepting. The master student accepts herself, the people around her, and the challenges that life offers.

Willing to laugh. The master student might laugh at any moment, and his sense of humor includes the ability to laugh at himself.

Going to school is a big investment. The stakes are high. It's OK to be serious about that, but you don't have to go to school on the deferred-fun program. A master student celebrates learning, and one of the best ways to do that is to have a laugh now and then.

Hungry. Human beings begin life with a natural appetite for knowledge. In some people it soon gets dulled. The master student has tapped that hunger, and it gives her a desire to learn for the sake of learning.

Willing to work. Once inspired, the master student is willing to follow through with sweat. He knows that genius and creativity are the result of persistence and work. When in high gear, the master student works with the intensity of a child at play.

Caring. A master student cares about knowledge and has a passion for ideas. She also cares about people and appreciates learning from others. She flourishes in a community that values "win-win" outcomes, cooperation, and love.

The master student in you. The master student is in all of us. By design, human beings are learning machines. We have an innate ability to learn, and all of us have room to grow and improve.

It is important to understand the difference between learning and being taught. Human beings can resist being taught anything. Carl Rogers goes so far as to say that anything that can be taught to a human being is either inconsequential or just plain harmful.[1] What is important in education, Rogers asserts, is *learning*. And everyone has the ability to learn.

Unfortunately, people also learn to hide that ability. As they experience the pain that sometimes accompanies learning, they shut down. If a child experiences embarrassment in front of a group of people, he could learn to avoid similar situations. In doing so, he restricts his possibilities.

Some children "learn" that they are slow learners. If they learn it well enough, their behavior comes to match that label.

As people grow older, they sometimes accumulate a growing list of ideas to defend, a catalog of familiar experiences that discourages them from learning anything new.

Still, the master student within survives. To tap that resource, you don't need to acquire anything. You already have everything you need. Every day you can rediscover the natural learner within you. ✖

PRACTICING CRITICAL THINKING

1

Review the article *The Master Student* in this chapter. Then skim the master student profiles throughout this book. Finally, choose one of the people profiled and describe in the space below how this person embodies qualities of a master student.

_____

_____

_____

_____

_____

_____

_____

_____

_____

_____

_____

_____

*The Practicing Critical Thinking exercises that appear throughout this book incorporate ideas from Peter Facione, Dean of the College of Arts and Sciences, Santa Clara University, and creator of the California Critical Thinking Disposition Inventory. Mr. Facione provided substantial suggestions for these exercises and edited them. He can be contacted through the California Academic Press on the World Wide Web at **http://www.insightassessment.com/about.html**.*

Adapted with permission from Critical Thinking: What It Is and Why It Counts *by Peter Facione (Millbrae, CA: The California Academic Press, 1996).*

 Master Student Profiles

In each chapter of this text there is an example of a person who embodies several qualities of a master student. As you read about these people and others like them, ask yourself: How can I apply this? Look for the timeless qualities in the people you read about. Many of the strategies used by master students from another time or place are tools that you can use today.

The master students in this book were chosen because they demonstrate unusual and effective ways to learn. Re-member that these are just 10 examples of master students (one for each chapter). You can read more about them in the Master Student Hall of Fame at **masterstudent.college.hmco.com**. Also reflect on other master students you've read about or know personally. As you meet new people, look for those who excel at learning. The master student is not a vague or remote ideal. Rather, master students move freely among us.

In fact, there's one living inside your skin.

Claim your multiple intelligences

People often think that being smart means the same thing as having a high IQ, and that having a high IQ automatically leads to success. However, psychologists are finding that IQ scores do not always foretell which students will do well in academic settings—or after they graduate.

Howard Gardner of Harvard University believes that no single measure of intelligence can tell us how smart we are. Instead, Gardner identifies many types of intelligence, as described below.[2] Gardner's theory of several types of intelligence complements the discussion in this chapter on different learning styles—both recognize that there are alternative ways for people to learn and assimilate knowledge. You can use Gardner's concepts to explore additional methods for achieving success in school, work, and relationships. People using **verbal/linguistic intelligence** are adept at language skills and learn best by speaking, writing, reading, and listening. They are likely to enjoy activities such as telling stories and doing crossword puzzles.

Those using **mathematical/logical intelligence** are good with numbers, logic, problem solving, patterns, relationships, and categories. They are generally precise and methodical, and are likely to enjoy science.

When people learn visually and by organizing things spatially, they display **visual/spatial intelligence.** They think in images and pictures, and understand best by seeing the subject. They enjoy charts, graphs, maps, mazes, tables, illustrations, art, models, puzzles, and costumes.

People using **bodily/kinesthetic intelligence** prefer physical activity. They enjoy activities such as building things, woodworking, dancing, skiing, sewing, and crafts. They generally are coordinated and athletic, and would rather participate in games than just watch.

Those using **musical/rhythmic intelligence** enjoy musical expression through songs, rhythms, and musical instruments. They are responsive to various kinds of sounds, remember melodies easily, and might enjoy drumming, humming, and whistling.

People using **intrapersonal intelligence** are exceptionally aware of their own feelings and values. They are generally reserved, self-motivated, and intuitive.

Evidence of **interpersonal intelligence** is seen in outgoing people. They do well with cooperative learning and are sensitive to the feelings, intentions, and motivations of others. They often make good leaders.

Those using **naturalist intelligence** love the outdoors and recognize details in plants, animals, rocks, clouds, and other natural formations. These people excel in observing fine distinctions among similar items.

Each of us has all of these intelligences to some degree. And each of us can learn to enhance them. Experiment with learning in ways that draw on a variety of intelligences—including those that might be less familiar. When we acknowledge all of our intelligences, we can constantly explore new ways of being smart. The following chart summarizes the multiple intelligences discussed in this article and suggests ways to apply them. This is not an exhaustive list or a formal inventory, so take what you find merely as points of departure. You can invent strategies of your own to cultivate different intelligences. ◪

Multiple intelligences

Type of intelligence	Possible characteristics	Possible learning strategies	Possible careers
Verbal/linguistic	You enjoy reading, writing, and listening to and telling stories.	• Highlight, underline, and write other notes in your textbooks. • Recite new ideas in your own words. • Edit your class notes. • Talk to other people about your classes.	Librarian, lawyer, editor, journalist, English teacher
Mathematical/logical	You enjoy puzzles, math, science, and planning.	• Analyze tasks into a sequence of steps. • Look for ways to express ideas in numerical terms.	Accountant, auditor, mathematician, computer programmer, math or science teacher
Visual/spatial	• You draw pictures to give an example or to clarify an explanation. • You understand maps and illustrations more readily than text.	• Take notes in visual form (see Chapter Five). Use different colors to highlight main topics, major points, and key details.	Architect, artist, graphic designer, photographer, interior decorator
Bodily/kinesthetic	You enjoy physical exercise and working with your hands.	• Pace as you recite, read while standing up, and create flash cards. • Create hands-on activities related to key concepts; for example, create a game based on course content.	Physical education teacher, athlete, athletic coach, physical therapist, dancer
Musical/rhythmic	• You often sing in the car or shower. • You tap your foot to the beat of a song. • You play a musical instrument. • You feel most engaged and productive when music is playing.	• During a study break, play music or dance to restore energy. • Write your own songs based on course content.	Musician, music teacher, music therapist, musical instrument sales representative
Intrapersonal	• You enjoy writing in a journal and prefer individual projects more than group projects.	• Study a topic alone before attending a study group. • Keep a journal that relates your course work to events in your daily life.	Minister, priest, rabbi, professor of religion, creator of a home-based or small business
Interpersonal	• You prefer group work more than working alone. • You have plenty of friends and regularly spend time with them.	• Form and conduct study groups. • Volunteer to give a speech or to lead group presentations.	Manager, administrator, salesperson, teacher, counselor, arbitrator, police officer, nurse, public relations specialist, creator of a midsize to large business
Naturalist	• You enjoy being outdoors. • You find that important insights occur during times you spend in natural surroundings.	• During study breaks, take walks outside. • Invite classmates to discuss course work while taking a hike or going on a camping trip.	Recreation supervisor, museum curator, biologist, criminologist, mechanic, construction worker

Learning by seeing, hearing, and moving:

The VAK system

You can approach the topic of learning styles with a simple and powerful system—one that focuses on just three ways of perceiving through your senses:

- Seeing, or *visual* learning
- Hearing, or *auditory* learning
- Movement, or *kinesthetic* learning

To recall this system, remember the letters *VAK*, which stand for **v**isual, **a**uditory, and **k**inesthetic. The theory is that each of us prefers to learn through one of these sense channels. And we can enrich our learning with activities that draw on the other channels.

To reflect on your VAK preferences, answer the following questions. Each question has three possible answers. Circle the answer that best describes how you would respond in the stated situation. This is not a formal inventory—just a way to prompt some self-discovery.

When you have problems spelling a word, you prefer to:
1. *Look it up in the dictionary.*
2. *Say the word out loud several times before you write it down.*
3. *Write out the word with several different spellings and choose one.*

You enjoy courses the most when you get to:
1. *View slides, overhead transparencies, videos, and readings with plenty of charts, tables, and illustrations.*
2. *Ask questions, engage in small-group discussions, and listen to guest speakers.*
3. *Take field trips, participate in lab sessions, or apply the course content while working as a volunteer or intern.*

When giving someone directions on how to drive to a destination, you prefer to:
1. *Pull out a piece of paper and sketch a map.*
2. *Give verbal instructions.*
3. *Say, "I'm driving to a place near there, so just follow me."*

When planning an extended vacation to a new destination, you prefer to:

1. *Read colorful, illustrated brochures or articles about that place.*
2. *Talk directly to someone who's been there.*
3. *Spend a day or two at that destination on a work-related trip before taking a vacation there.*

You've made a commitment to learn to play the guitar. The first thing you do is:
1. *Go to a library or music store and find an instruction book with plenty of diagrams and chord charts.*
2. *Pull out your favorite CDs, listen closely to the guitar solos, and see if you can sing along with them.*
3. *Buy or borrow a guitar, pluck the strings, and ask someone to show you how to play a few chords.*

You've saved up enough money to lease a car. When choosing from among several new models, the most important factor in your decision is:
1. *The car's appearance.*
2. *The information you get by talking to people who own the cars you're considering.*
3. *The overall impression you get by taking each car on a test drive.*

You've just bought a new computer system—monitor, central processing unit, keyboard, CD burner, cable modem, and external speakers. When setting up the system, the first thing you do is:
1. *Skim through the printed instructions that come with the equipment.*
2. *Call up someone with a similar system and ask her for directions.*
3. *Assemble the components as best as you can, see if everything works, and consult the instructions only as a last resort.*

You get a scholarship to study abroad next semester, which starts in just three months. You will travel to a country where French is the most widely spoken language. To learn as much French as you can before you depart, you:
1. *Buy a video-based language course that's recorded on a DVD.*

2. Set up tutoring sessions with a friend who's fluent in French.

3. Sign up for a short immersion course in an environment in which you speak only French, starting with the first class.

Now take a few minutes to reflect on the meaning of your responses. All of the answers numbered "1" are examples of visual learning. The "2's" refer to auditory learning, and the "3's" illustrate kinesthetic learning. Finding a consistent pattern in your answers indicates that you prefer learning through one sense channel more than the others. Or you might find that your preferences are fairly balanced.

Listed below are suggestions for learning through each sense channel. Experiment with these examples and create more techniques of your own. Use them to build on your current preferences and develop new options for learning.

To enhance *visual* learning:

- Preview reading assignments by looking for elements that are highlighted visually—bold headlines, charts, graphs, illustrations, and photographs.

- When taking notes in class, leave plenty of room to add your own charts, diagrams, tables, and other visuals later.

- Whenever an instructor writes information on a blackboard or overhead projector, copy it exactly in your notes.

- Transfer your handwritten notes to your computer. Use word processing software that allows you to format your notes in lists, add headings in different fonts, and create visuals in color.

- Before you begin an exam, quickly sketch a diagram on scratch paper. Use this diagram to summarize the key formulas or facts you want to remember.

- During tests, see if you can visualize pages from your handwritten notes or images from your computer-based notes.

To enhance *auditory* learning:

- Reinforce memory of your notes and readings by talking about them. When studying, stop often to recite key points and examples in your own words.

- After doing several verbal summaries, record your favorite version or write it out.

- Read difficult passages in your textbooks slowly and out loud.

- Join study groups and create short presentations about course topics.

- Visit your instructors during office hours to ask questions.

To enhance *kinesthetic* learning:

- Look for ways to translate course content into three-dimensional models that you can build. While studying biology, for example, create a model of a human cell using different colors of clay.

- Supplement lectures with trips to museums, field observations, lab sessions, tutorials, and other hands-on activities.

- Recite key concepts from your courses while you walk or exercise.

- Intentionally set up situations in which you can learn by trial and error.

- Create a practice test and write out the answers in the room where you will actually take the exam.

Note: This chapter introduces several approaches to learning styles: the Learning Style Inventory, multiple intelligences, and the VAK system. That's a lot of information to absorb. Remember that each approach presents an option, not the final word on learning styles. Above all, look for ideas from any of these methods that you can put to immediate use. When you write Intention Statements, keep these questions in mind: How can I use this idea to *be* more successful in school? What will I *do* differently as a result of reading about learning styles? If I develop new learning styles, what skill will I *have* that I don't have now? ✖

learning styles

what
if
why
how
what

Discovering how you learn

When we learn, two things initially happen. First, we notice new information. We *perceive* and take in what's before us. Second, we make sense of the information. We *process* it in a way that helps us understand what's going on and makes the information our own. *Learning styles* is a term that takes into account differences in how people prefer to perceive and process information.

Knowing your preferred learning style helps you understand why some courses appeal to you while others seem dull or boring. Figuring out when to use your preferences—and when it might be helpful to include another style of learning—can help you create value from any class and function successfully as a student in many different settings.

Perceiving information

The ways that people perceive information typically range from a preference for concrete experience (CE) to a preference for abstract conceptualization (AC):

■ People who favor perceiving by concrete experience like to absorb information through their five senses. They learn by getting directly involved in new experiences. When solving problems, they rely on their intuition as much as their intellect. These people

typically function well in unstructured learning classes that allow them to take the initiative.

■ People who favor perceiving by *abstract conceptualization* take in information best when they can think about it as a subject separate from themselves. They analyze, intellectualize, and create theories. Often these people take a scientific approach to problem solving and excel in traditional classrooms.

Processing information

The ways that people process information typically range from a preference for active experimentation (AE) to a preference for reflective observation (RO):

■ People who favor processing information by *active experimentation* prefer to jump in and start doing things immediately. They do not mind taking risks as they attempt to make sense of things because this helps them learn. They are results-oriented and look for practical ways to apply what they have learned.

■ People who favor processing information by *reflective observation* prefer to stand back, watch what is going on, and think about it. Often they consider several points of view as they attempt to make sense of things and can generate many ideas about how something happens. They value patience, good judgment, and a thorough approach to understanding information.

According to David Kolb, a psychologist who developed the theory of experiential learning, learners have natural preferences for how they perceive and process information.[3] Yet they benefit most fully if they allow themselves to participate in all four points of the continuums described above. Successful learners:

1. involve themselves fully, openly, and without bias in new experiences (CE);

2. observe and reflect on these experiences from many points of view (RO);

3. integrate these observations into logically sound theories (AC) that include predictions about the consequences of new behaviors; and

4. use these theories to make decisions, solve problems, and take effective action (AE). This view of learning is quite flexible. You can start learning at any one of the four points listed above and cycle through the rest. In any case, the power of your learning derives from testing theories in your daily life—and in changing those theories based on the feedback you get from concrete experiences.

You can use Kolb's ideas to increase your skills at learning anything. First, start by understanding your natural preferences. Then balance them with activities that you consciously choose to support your learning.

Taking your Learning Style Inventory

To help you become more aware of what you currently do to support your learning, David Kolb has developed the Learning Style Inventory (LSI), which is included on the next few pages. Completing this inventory will help you discover more about how you learn.

Step 1   Keep in mind that this is not a test. There are no right or wrong answers. Your goal is to develop a profile of your learning. Take the inventory quickly. There's no need to agonize over your responses. Recalling a recent situation in which you learned something new at school,

at work, or in your life might make it easier for you to focus and answer the questions.

Step 2   Remove the sheet of paper following page LSI-2. When you're ready to write on the inventory, press firmly so that your answers will show up on the page underneath the questions.

Step 3   Note that the LSI consists of 12 sentences, each with four different endings. You will read each sentence, then write a "4" next to the ending that best describes the way you currently learn. Then you will continue ranking the other endings with a "3," "2," or "1." This is a forced choice inventory, so you must rank each ending; no items can be left out. *Look at the example provided at the top of page LSI-1 before you begin.*

When you understand the example, you're ready to respond to the 12 sentences of the LSI:

- After you answer item #1, check to be sure that you wrote one "1," one "2," one "3," and one "4."

- Also check to make sure that your markings are showing through onto the scoring page (LSI-3).

- After you have responded to the 12 items, go to page LSI-3, which has instructions for computing your results. ◪

Learning Style Inventory

Fill in the following blanks like this example:

A. When I learn: ___2___ I am happy. ___3___ I am fast. ___4___ I am logical. ___1___ I am careful.

Remember: **4** = Most like you **3** = Second most like you **2** = Third most like you **1** = Least like you

Remove the sheet of paper following this page. Press firmly while writing.

1. When I learn: _____ I like to deal with my feelings. _____ I like to think about ideas. _____ I like to be doing things. _____ I like to watch and listen.

2. I learn best when: _____ I listen and watch carefully. _____ I rely on logical thinking. _____ I trust my hunches and feelings. _____ I work hard to get things done.

3. When I am learning: _____ I tend to reason things out. _____ I am responsible about things. _____ I am quiet and reserved. _____ I have strong feelings and reactions.

4. I learn by: _____ feeling. _____ doing. _____ watching. _____ thinking.

5. When I learn: _____ I am open to new experiences. _____ I look at all sides of issues. _____ I like to analyze things, break them down into their parts. _____ I like to try things out.

6. When I am learning: _____ I am an observing person. _____ I am an active person. _____ I am an intuitive person. _____ I am a logical person.

7. I learn best from: _____ observation. _____ personal relationships. _____ rational theories. _____ a chance to try out and practice.

8. When I learn: _____ I like to see results from my work. _____ I like ideas and theories. _____ I take my time before acting. _____ I feel personally involved in things.

9. I learn best when: _____ I rely on my observations. _____ I rely on my feelings. _____ I can try things out for myself. _____ I rely on my ideas.

10. When I am learning: _____ I am a reserved person. _____ I am an accepting person. _____ I am a responsible person. _____ I am a rational person.

11. When I learn: _____ I get involved. _____ I like to observe. _____ I evaluate things. _____ I like to be active.

12. I learn best when: _____ I analyze ideas. _____ I am receptive and open-minded. _____ I am careful. _____ I am practical.

Interpreting your Learning Style Graph

Four modes of learning

When we're learning well, we tend to search out the answers to four key questions: *Why? What? How?* and *What if?* Each of these questions represents a different *mode of learning.* The modes of learning are patterns of behavior—unique combinations of concrete experience, reflective observation, abstract conceptualization, and active experimentation. When you are in a learning situation, you might find that you continually ask yourself one of these key questions more than the others. Or you might routinely ask several of these questions. Read the descriptions below to get a better idea of how you approach learning.

Mode 1: Why? Some of us question why we are learning things. We seek a purpose for information and a personal connection with the content. We want to know a rationale for what we're learning—why the course content matters and how it challenges or fits in with what we already know.

Mode 2: What? Some of us crave information. When learning something, we want to know critical facts. We seek a theory or model to explain what's happening and follow up to see what experts have to say on the topic. We break a subject down into its key components or steps and master each one.

Mode 3: How? Some of us hunger for an opportunity to try out what we're studying. We ask ourselves: Does this idea make sense? Will it work, and, if so, *how* does it work? How can I make use of this information? We want to apply and test theories and models. We excel at taking the parts or key steps of a subject and assembling them into a meaningful sequence.

Mode 4: What if? Some of us get excited about going beyond classroom assignments. We aim to adapt what we're learning to another course or to a situation at work or at home. By applying our knowledge, we want to make a difference in some area that we care about. We ask ourselves: What if we tried…? or What if we combined…?

Your preferred learning mode

When you examine your completed Learning Style Graph on page LSI-5, you will notice that your learning style profile (the "kite" that you drew) might be located primarily in one part of the graph. This will give you an idea of your preferred mode of learning, that is, the kind of behaviors that feel most comfortable and familiar to you when you are learning something. Using the descriptions below and the sample graphs, identify your preferred learning mode.

Mode 1: Why? If the majority of your learning style profile is in the upper right-hand corner of the Learning Style Graph, you probably prefer Mode 1 learning. You like to consider a situation from many different points of view and determine why it is important to learn a new idea or technique.

Mode 2: What? If your learning style profile is mostly in the lower right-hand corner of the Learning Style Graph, you probably prefer Mode 2 learning. You are interested in knowing what ideas or techniques are important. You enjoy learning lots of facts and then arranging these facts in a logical and concise manner.

Mode 3: How? If most of your learning style profile is in the lower left-hand corner of the Learning Style Graph, you probably prefer Mode 3 learning. You get involved with new knowledge by testing it out. You investigate how ideas and techniques work, and you put into practice what you learn.

Mode 4: What if? If most of your learning style profile is in the upper left-hand corner of the Learning Style Graph, you probably prefer Mode 4 learning. You like to take what you have practiced and find other uses for it. You seek ways to apply this newly gained skill or information at your workplace or in your personal relationships.

Combinations. Some learning style profiles combine all four modes. The profile to the right reflects a learner who is focused primarily on gathering information—lots of information! People with this profile tend to ask for additional facts from an instructor, or they want to know where they can go to discover more about a subject.

The profile to the right applies to learners who focus more on understanding what they learn and less on gathering lots of information. People with this profile prefer smaller chunks of data with plenty of time to process it. Long lectures can be difficult for these learners.

The profile to the right indicates a learner whose preferences are fairly well balanced. People with this profile can be highly adaptable and tend to excel no matter what the instructor does in the classroom. These people enjoy learning in general and do well in school. ⬒

Remove this sheet before completing the Learning Style Inventory.

This page is inserted to ensure that the other writing you do in this book doesn't show through on page LSI-3.

Remove this sheet before completing the Learning Style Inventory.

This page is inserted to ensure that the other writing you do in this book doesn't show through on page LSI-3.

Scoring your Inventory

Now that you have taken the Learning Style Inventory, it's time to fill out the Learning Style Graph (page LSI-5) and interpret your results. To do this, please follow the next five steps.

1 First, add up all of the numbers you gave to the items marked with brown **F** letters. Then write down that total to the right in the blank next to "**Brown F**." Next, add up all of the numbers for "**Teal W**," "**Purple T**," and "**Orange D**," and also write down those totals in the blanks to the right.

2 Add the four totals to arrive at a GRAND TOTAL and write down that figure in the blank to the right. (*Note:* The grand total should equal 120. If you have a different amount, go back and re-add the colored letters; it was probably just an addition error.) Now remove this page and continue with Step 3 on page LSI-5.

Brown F total	_____
Teal W total	_____
Purple T total	_____
Orange D total	_____
GRAND TOTAL	_____

F	T	D	W
W	T	F	D
T	D	W	F
F	D	W	T
F	W	T	D
W	D	F	T
W	F	T	D
D	T	W	F
W	F	D	T
W	F	D	T
F	W	T	D
T	F	W	D

Remove this page after you have completed Steps 1 and 2 on page LSI-3. Then continue with Step 3 on page LSI-5.

Once you have completed Step 3, discard this page so that you can more easily compare your completed Learning Style Graph with the examples on page LSI-2.

Learning Style Graph

3 Remove the piece of paper that follows this page and then transfer your totals from Step 2 on page LSI-3 to the lines on the Learning Style Graph below. On the brown (F) line, find the number that corresponds to your "**Brown F**" total from page LSI-3. Then write an X on this number. Do the same for your "**Teal W**," "**Purple T**," and "**Orange D**" totals.

4 Now, pressing firmly, draw four straight lines to connect the four X's and shade in the area to form a "kite." This is your learning style profile. Each X that you placed on these lines indicates your preference for a different aspect of learning:

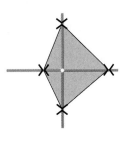

Concrete experience ("Feeling"). The number where you put your X on this line indicates your preference for learning things that have personal meaning. The higher your score on this line, the more you like to learn things that you feel are important and relevant to yourself.

Reflective observation ("Watching"). Your number on this line indicates how important it is for you to reflect on the things you are learning. If your score is high on this line, you probably find it important to watch others as they learn about an assignment and then report on it to the class. You probably like to plan things out and take the time to make sure that you fully understand a topic.

Abstract conceptualization ("Thinking"). Your number on this line indicates your preference for learning ideas, facts, and figures. If your score is high on this line, you probably like to absorb many concepts and gather lots of information on a new topic.

Active experimentation ("Doing"). Your number on this line indicates your preference for applying ideas, using trial and error, and practicing what you learn. If your score is high on this line, you probably enjoy hands-on activities that allow you to test out ideas to see what works.

5 Read page LSI-2 to understand further your preferences for learning.

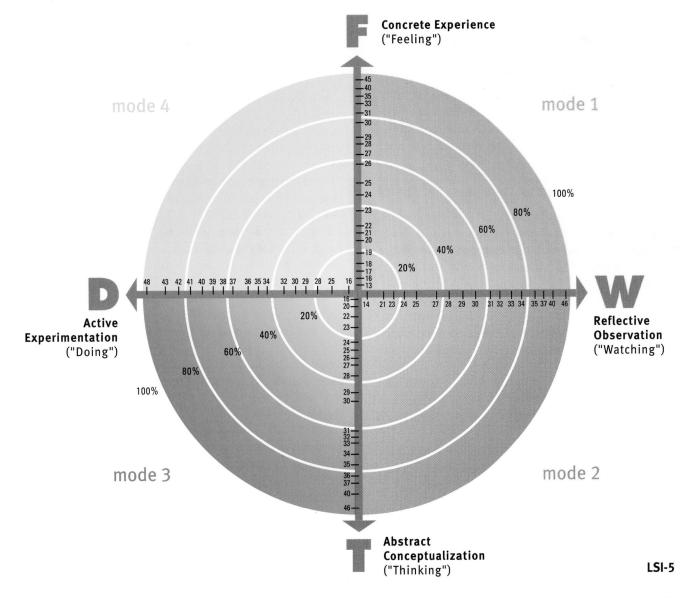

Cycle of learning

These examples show how the learning cycle works. You're interested in something (Mode 1), so you gather information about it (Mode 2). You try out what you're learning (Mode 3), then you integrate it into your day-to-day life (Mode 4). You go through this cycle many times as one learning experience generates another.

Example 1 Learning about a historical issue

You're required to take an elective in history, and you decide to take a course on the history of immigration in the United States. Your great-grandparents came to this country as immigrants, and immigration is still taking place today. You conclude that this topic is interesting—in part, because of your family background (Mode 1: *Why?*).

Soon you're in class, and you learn that from the early years of the country's history, many Americans have had misconceptions and fears about immigration that persist to the present day (Mode 2: *What?*).

You find yourself re-evaluating your own beliefs and assumptions. You wonder whether new immigrants in your city are experiencing some of the same stereotyping that was commonplace in earlier times. You decide to become more active in a community organization that deals firsthand with the impact of immigration policies (Mode 3: *How?*).

You also start to consider what it would be like to become an attorney and devote your career to creating a system that treats all immigrants with fairness and respect. You realize that you want to make a positive difference in the lives of people who are coming to live in the United States today (Mode 4: *What if?*).

Example 2 Learning to use a personal digital assistant (PDA)

Learning begins with developing an interest in this technology. Maybe you want to manage your to-do lists and appointments in a way that is more efficient than writing notes to yourself on random bits of paper. Maybe you never want to buy another pocket calendar. Or maybe you want to store your planning information digitally and exchange files with your personal computer. You conclude that this technology could help you finally get organized and feel on top of your schedule (Mode 1: *Why?*). Next, you learn as much as you can about the different PDAs on the market. You visit Web sites, go to a computer store, and ask for a demonstration. You also talk to friends who swear by PDAs—and those who swear never to use them—and weigh their advice and differing opinions (Mode 2: *What?*).

After you gather this information, you decide to buy your own PDA. You take the handwritten information from your pocket calendar and to-do lists and enter it all into your new PDA. This takes several hours, including the time spent learning to write with a stylus (Mode 3: *How?*).

Once you've conquered the mechanics of using a PDA, you begin to use it on a daily basis—and encounter some unexpected hassles. For one thing, writing with the stylus requires you to form individual letters in a special way. Also, your friends who stick with paper-based planning can simply open up their pocket calendars and quickly pencil in appointments. Meanwhile, you have to turn on your PDA and wait for it to boot up before you can use it. Instead of feeling more organized, you end up feeling behind. You wonder what it would be like to switch back to paper-based planning. After your experiences with a PDA, you decide to do just that. This time, however, you introduce a change in your behavior. Instead of recording your to-do items on any scrap of paper that is lying around, you put a pen and some 3x5 index cards in your pocket and carry them with you at all times. Whenever you want to make a note to yourself, you simply pull out a card and jot down your thoughts. Cards are easy to store and sort. This new system, while it seems so simple and so "low-tech," finally helps you achieve that sense of organization you've been craving (Mode 4: *What if?*).

Example 3 Thinking about the effects of television

Your sociology instructor asks you to write a 2,000-word paper about the impact of television on our society. As part of the assignment, you're asked to envision a society without television. This interests you since you've often wondered what it would be like to give up television (Mode 1: *Why?*).

One of your first steps in writing this paper is to ask what purposes television serves. You conclude that, based on the varieties of programming, several purposes are involved: entertainment, news and information, documentaries, sports, and, of course, advertising. To research the paper, you also read two books on the history of American television (Mode 2: *What?*).

Still wondering how your own life would change if you were to give up television, you choose to do so on a trial basis—for two weeks—and observe the effects. This change in your behavior frees up several hours each week, which you use for reading newspapers and magazines. You find that you don't miss television news and that reading leaves you better informed about the world (Mode 3: *How?*).

As a result of your personal experiment with television, you wonder what it would be like to give up television news permanently. You choose to do this for at least six more months. You also volunteer for a local literacy campaign that encourages people to go television-free for one month each year and devote the time they save to reading (Mode 4: *What if?*).

Remove this sheet before completing the Learning Style Graph.

This page is inserted to ensure that the other writing you do in this book doesn't show through on page LSI-7.

Remove this sheet before completing the Learning Style Graph.

This page is inserted to ensure that the other writing you do in this book doesn't show through on page LSI-7.

Name _____ Date _____/_____/_____

Note: After completing your Learning Style Inventory (page LSI-1) and filling in the Learning Style Graph (page LSI-5), be sure to read the sections titled "Interpreting Your Learning Style Graph" (page LSI-2) and "Cycle of Learning" (page LSI-6). Then complete the following Journal Entry.

journal entry 5

Discovery/Intention Statement

To make this concept of the learning cycle more useful, start applying it right away. You can begin with the content of this book. For example, as you read the Master Student Profiles, ask questions based on each mode of learning: *Why* is this person considered a master student? *What* attitudes or behaviors helped to create her mastery? *How* can I develop those qualities? *What if* I could use her example to create significant new results in my own life? (Or, *What if* I ignore the lessons to be learned from this Master Student Profile and experience significant costs as a result?) Also see the Master Student Map at the beginning of each chapter for sample answers to *Why? What? How?* and *What if?* questions.

Regarding my preferences for learning, I discovered that . . .

_____

_____

Given my preferences for learning, I intend to . . .

_____

_____

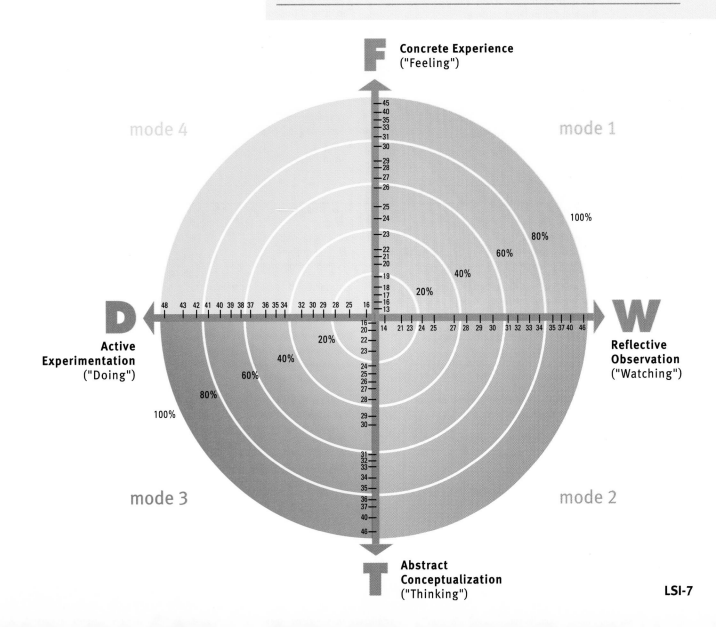

Balancing your preferences

The chart below identifies some of the natural talents as well as challenges for people who have a strong preference for any one mode of learning. For example, if most of your "kite" is in Mode 2 of the Learning Style Graph, then look at the lower right-hand corner of the following chart to see if this is an accurate description of yourself.

After reviewing the description of your preferred learning mode, read all of the sections that start with the words "People with other preferred modes." These sections explain what actions you can take to become a more balanced learner.

Concrete Experience

mode 4

Strengths:
Getting things done
Leadership
Risk taking

Too much of this mode can lead to:
Trivial improvements
Meaningless activity

Too little of this mode can lead to:
Work not completed on time
Impractical plans
Lack of motivation to achieve goals

People with other preferred modes can develop Mode 4 by:
• Making a commitment to objectives
• Seeking new opportunities
• Influencing and leading others
• Being personally involved
• Dealing with people

mode 1

Strengths:
Imaginative ability
Understanding people
Recognizing problems
Brainstorming

Too much of this mode can lead to:
Feeling paralyzed by alternatives
Inability to make decisions

Too little of this mode can lead to:
Lack of ideas
Not recognizing problems and opportunities

People with other preferred modes can develop Mode 1 by:
• Being aware of other people's feelings
• Being sensitive to values
• Listening with an open mind
• Gathering information
• Imagining the implications of ambiguous situations

Active Experimentation

Reflective Observation

Strengths:
Problem solving
Decision making
Deductive reasoning
Defining problems

Too much of this mode can lead to:
Solving the wrong problem
Hasty decision making

Too little of this mode can lead to:
Lack of focus
Reluctance to consider alternatives
Scattered thoughts

People with other preferred modes can develop Mode 3 by:
• Creating new ways of thinking and doing
• Experimenting with fresh ideas
• Choosing the best solution
• Setting goals
• Making decisions

mode 3

Strengths:
Planning
Creating models
Defining problems
Developing theories

Too much of this mode can lead to:
Vague ideals ("castles in the air")
Lack of practical application

Too little of this mode can lead to:
Inability to learn from mistakes
No sound basis for work
No systematic approach

People with other preferred modes can develop Mode 2 by:
• Organizing information
• Building conceptual models
• Testing theories and ideas
• Designing experiments
• Analyzing quantitative data

mode 2

Abstract Conceptualization

Using your learning style profile
to succeed in school

what if   why

how   what

To get the most value from knowing your learning style profile, look for ways to apply this knowledge in school and at work. Remember that in this exercise the term *preferred learning mode* refers to the way you've typically approached learning in the past. It does not describe the way you have to learn in the future. No matter what aspects of learning you've tended to prefer, you can develop the ability to use all four modes. Doing so offers many potential benefits. For example, you can excel in different types of courses, seize more opportunities for learning outside the classroom, and expand your options for declaring a major and choosing a career. In addition, you can more fully understand people who learn differently than you, decreasing the potential for conflict while increasing the effectiveness of your working relationships. Exploring all of the learning modes provides more opportunities for you to achieve your goals. Consider the suggestions that follow.

Tolerate discomfort. Discomfort is a natural part of the learning process. As you participate in modes of learning that do not energize you, allow yourself to notice your struggle with a task or your lack of interest in completing it. Realize that you are balancing your learning preferences. Resist the temptation to skip a mode of learning or move too quickly through it. By tolerating discomfort and using all of the modes, you increase your chances for success.

Match activities to your learning style profile. You might want to examine your learning style profile when choosing your major and planning your career. You could focus on courses or jobs that suit your preferred modes of learning. Consulting with people who have different learning preferences can also be beneficial when you approach course work or other learning situations.

Ask for what you want. You might find that the way an instructor teaches is not the way you prefer to learn and that teachers don't always promote all four modes of learning. Once you know your learning preferences, you can take a more active role in ensuring that your learning needs are met.

- *If you have a strong preference for Mode 1,* you are likely to spend time observing others and planning out your course of action. You probably also enjoy working with other students. To assist yourself in school, ask questions that help you understand why it is important for you to learn about a specific topic. You might also want to form a study group.

- *If you have a strong preference for Mode 2,* you are skilled in understanding theories and concepts. When in learning situations, you are likely to enjoy lectures and individual class assignments. Chances are that you also enjoy solitary time and are not fond of working in groups. To assist yourself in school, ask questions that help you gather enough information to understand what you are learning. You might also increase your effectiveness by choosing not to concentrate equally on all of the material in a chapter, focusing primarily on specific parts of the text.

- *If you have a strong preference for Mode 3,* you probably excel at working with your hands and at laboratory stations. When in a learning situation, you are interested in knowing how things work. In addition, you probably enjoy working alone or with a small group. To assist yourself in school, ask questions that help you understand how something works and how you can experiment with these new ideas. Also allow time to practice and apply what you learn. You can conduct experiments, create presentations, tabulate findings, or even write a rap song that summarizes key concepts. Such activities provide an opportunity to internalize your learning through hands-on practice.

- *If you have a strong preference for Mode 4,* you are skilled at teaching others what you have learned and helping them see the importance of these concepts. Whether in a learning situation or in everyday life, you like to apply facts and theories. You probably enjoy carrying out plans and having new and challenging experiences. You also prefer working with others and are likely to have a large social circle. To assist yourself in school, ask questions that help you determine where else in your life you can apply what you have just learned. Also seek opportunities to demonstrate your understanding. You could coach a classmate about what you have learned, present findings from your research, explain how your project works, or perform a rap song that someone else might have written.

Associate with students who have different learning style profiles. If your instructor asks your class to form groups to complete an assignment, avoid joining a group in which everyone shares your preferred modes of learning. Get together with people who both complement and challenge you. This is one way you can develop skills in all four learning modes and become a more well-rounded student.

Resolve conflicts in learning styles. When they experience difficulty in school, some students say: "The classroom is not conducive to the way that I learn" or "The instructor doesn't teach to my learning style." Such statements can prevent you from taking responsibility for your own education. To stay in charge of your learning, replace them with statements such as "I will create value from this course" and "Working with this instructor will help me discover new ways to learn."

Use this book with the modes of learning in mind. The four modes of learning are part of a natural cycle.

Master students learn in all four ways. If you strongly prefer one mode, then experiment with the others. Becoming a Master Student can help. This book is designed to move you through all four modes of learning.

- At the beginning of each chapter, you are asked to complete a Journal Entry designed to stimulate your thinking and connect the chapter content to your current life experience—to help you see why learning this material is beneficial (a Mode 1 activity).

- Next, you read articles that are filled with ideas, information, and suggestions that can help you succeed in school (a Mode 2 activity).

- You are also asked to practice new skills with exercises provided throughout each chapter (a Mode 3 activity).

- Finally, at the end of each chapter, Discovery and Intention Statements and Learning Styles Applications help you tie all of this information together and suggest ways that you can use it in your future (a Mode 4 activity).

This article and the previous one were written following the same four-mode learning cycle. The previous article, "Learning styles: Discovering how you learn," first reviewed the value of knowing about learning styles (Mode 1). Then facts and theories about learning styles were discussed (Mode 2). Next, you took action and did the Learning Style Inventory (Mode 3). Finally, this article invites you to apply your newfound knowledge of learning styles in your daily life (Mode 4). ⊠

➤ The magic of metacognition

It's pronounced "metta-cog-ni-shun." "Meta" means *beyond* or *above*, "cognition" refers to everything that goes on inside your brain—thinking, perceiving, and learning. Metacognition is thinking about thinking, learning about learning. It's your ability to stand "above" your mental processes—to observe them and to take conscious control of them.

Metacognition is one of the main benefits of higher education. Mastering this skill allows you to learn anything you want, any time.

Students who master metacognition can do things such as:

- state the ways that they'll benefit from learning a subject;

- describe their preferred learning styles and develop new ones;

- make accurate statements about their current abilities;

- monitor their behavior and change their habits;

- choose and apply various strategies for reading, writing, speaking, listening, managing time, and related tasks; and

- modify strategies so that they work in several contexts.

With metacognition, you can view any course as one step along the path to learning what you want to learn—in the way that you prefer to learn it. The magic of metacognition is that you become your own best teacher.

When you're waist-deep in reading assignments, writing papers, and studying for tests, you might well ask yourself: Is all this effort going to pay off someday?

The value of higher education

That's a fair question. And it addresses a core issue—the value of getting an education beyond high school. Be reassured. The potential benefits of higher education are enormous.

Gain a broad vision

As workers in different fields become more specialized, they run the risk of forgetting how to talk to each other.

Higher education can change that. People with a liberal arts background are aware of the various kinds of problems tackled in psychology and theology, philosophy and physics, literature and mathematics. They understand how people in all of these fields arrive at conclusions and how these fields relate to each other.

Master the liberal arts

The liberal arts promote mastery of the basic processes of communication: reading, writing, speaking, and listening. In addition, courses in mathematics and science help us understand the world in quantitative terms. The abilities to communicate and calculate are essential to almost every profession. Excellence at these skills has long been considered an essential characteristic of an educated person.

The word *liberal* comes from the Latin verb *libero*, which means "to free." Liberal arts are those that promote critical thinking. Studying them can free us from irrational ideas, half-truths, racism, and prejudice.

Discover your values

We do not spend all of our waking hours at our jobs. That leaves us with a decision that affects the quality of our lives: how to spend leisure time. By cultivating our interest in the arts and community affairs, the liberal arts provide us with many options for activities outside of work. These studies add a dimension to life that goes beyond having a job and paying the bills.

Discover new interests

Taking a broad range of courses has the potential to change your direction in life. A student previously committed to a career in science might try out a drawing class and eventually switch to a degree in studio arts. Or a person who swears that she has no aptitude for technical subjects might change her major to computer science after taking an introductory computer course.

To make effective choices about your long-term goals, base those choices on a variety of academic and personal experiences.

Hang out with the great

Today we enjoy a huge legacy from our ancestors. The creative minds of our species have given us great works of art and systems of thought that defy the imagination. These creations are inexhaustible. We can return to them time after time and gain new insights. These are the works we can justifiably deem great. Hanging out with them transforms us. Getting to know them exercises our minds, just as running exercises our bodies.

The world's finest scientists and artists have joined voices in a conversation that spans centuries and crosses cultures. This is a conversation about the nature of truth and beauty, knowledge and compassion, good and evil—ideas that form the basis of human society. Our greatest thinkers have left behind tangible records of these ideas. You'll find them in libraries, concert halls, museums, and scientific laboratories across the world. Through higher education, you gain an opportunity to add your own voice.

Learn skills that apply across careers

Jobs that involve responsibility, prestige, and higher incomes depend on self-management skills. These include knowing ways to manage time, resolve conflicts, set goals, learn new skills, and control stress. Higher education is a place to learn and practice such skills. ☒

power process

Ideas are tools

There are many ideas in this book. When you first encounter them, don't believe any of them. Instead, think of them as tools.

For example, you use a hammer for a purpose—to drive a nail. When you use a new hammer, you might notice its shape, its weight, and its balance. You don't try to figure out whether the hammer is "right." You just use it. If it works, you use it again. If it doesn't work, you get a different hammer.

This is not the attitude most people adopt when they encounter new ideas. The first thing most people do with new ideas is to measure them against old ones. If a new idea conflicts with an old one, the new one is likely to be rejected.

People have plenty of room in their lives for different kinds of hammers, but they tend to limit their capacity for different kinds of ideas. A new idea, at some level, is a threat to their very being—unlike a new hammer, which is simply a new hammer.

Most of us have a built-in desire to be right. Our ideas, we often think, represent ourselves. And when we identify with our ideas, they assume new importance in our lives. We put them on our mantels. We hang them on our walls. We wear them on our T-shirts and display them on our bumpers. We join associations of people who share our most beloved ideas. We make up rituals about them, compose songs about them, and write stories about them. We declare ourselves dedicated to these ideas.

Some ideas are worth dying for. But please note: This book does not contain any of those ideas. The ideas on these pages are strictly "hammers."

Imagine someone defending a hammer. Picture this person holding up a hammer and declaring, "I hold this hammer to be self-evident. Give me this hammer or give me death. Those other hammers are flawed. There are only two kinds of people in this world: people who believe in this hammer and people who don't."

That ridiculous picture makes a point. This book is not a manifesto. It's a toolbox, and tools are meant to be used. This viewpoint is much like one advocated by psychologist and philosopher William James. His approach to philosophy, which he called "pragmatism," emphasized the usefulness of ideas as a criterion of truth.[4] James liked to talk about the "cash value" of an idea—whether it leads to new actions and new results.

If you read about a tool in this book that doesn't sound "right" or one that sounds a little goofy, remember that the ideas here are for using, not necessarily for believing. Suspend your judgment. Test the idea for yourself.

If it works, use it. If it doesn't, don't.

Ask: What if it's true?

When presented with a new idea, some of us take pride in being critical thinkers. We look for problems. We probe for weaknesses. We continue to doubt the idea until there's clear proof. Our main question seems to be "What's wrong with this idea?"

This approach can be useful when it is vital to expose flaws in ideas or reasoning. On the other hand, when we constantly look for what's wrong with new ideas, we might not recognize their value. A different and potentially more powerful approach is to ask yourself: What if that idea is true? This opens up all sorts of new possibilities and variations. Rather than looking for what's wrong, we can look for what's potentially valuable. Faced with a new idea, we can stay in the inquiry, look deeper, and go further.

Keep looking for answers

The light bulb, the airplane, the computer chip, the notion of the unconscious—these and many other tools became possible when their inventors practiced the art of continually looking for additional answers.

Another way to expand your toolbox is to keep on looking for answers. Much of your education will be about finding answers to questions. Every subject you study—from algebra to history to philosophy—poses a unique set of questions. Some of the most interesting questions are those that admit many answers: How can we create a just society? How can we transmit our values to the next generation? What are the purposes of higher education? How can we prevent an environmental crisis?

Other questions are more personal: What career shall I choose? Shall I get married? Where shall I live and how shall I spend my leisure time? What shall I have, do, and be during my time on earth?

Perhaps you already have answers to these questions. Answers are wonderful, especially when they relate to our most persistent and deeply felt questions. Answers can

also get in the way. Once we're convinced that we have the "right" answer, it's easy to stop looking for more answers. We then stop learning. Our range of possible actions becomes limited.

Instead of latching on to one answer, we can look for more. Instead of being content with the first or easiest options that come to mind, we can keep searching. Even when we're convinced that we've finally handled a problem, we can brainstorm until we find five more solutions.

When we keep looking for answers, we uncover fresh possibilities for thinking, feeling, and behaving. Like children learning to walk, we experience the joy of discovery.

A caution

A word of caution: Any tool—whether it's a hammer, a computer program, or a study technique—is designed to do a specific job. A master mechanic carries a variety of tools because no single tool works for all jobs. If you throw a tool away because it doesn't work in one situation, you won't be able to pull it out later when it's just what you need. So if an idea doesn't work for you and you are satisfied that you gave it a fair chance, don't throw it away. File it away instead. The idea might come in handy sooner than you think.

And remember, this book is not about figuring out the "right" way. Even the "ideas are tools" approach is not "right."

It's a hammer . . . (or maybe a saw). ⊠

This book is not a manifesto. It's a toolbox, and tools are meant to be used.

put it to work

At work, you can benefit by remembering the concept of learning styles. In the workplace, people act in a variety of ways that express their preferences for perceiving information, processing ideas, and acting on what they learn.

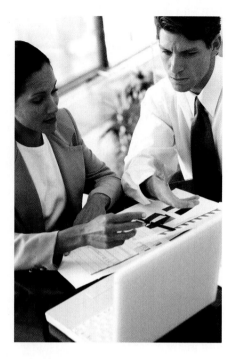

The worker who's continually moving might prefer concrete experience over memos and meetings. She likes to learn by doing. The person who's usually on the phone might prefer to learn by listening and talking. She likes to reflect on her experiences and forge relationships.

You might have a supervisor who enjoys working with concepts as much as working with people. She might prefer to decide on a long-range goal and a detailed plan before taking action.

Discover learning styles in your workplace. You can learn a lot about your coworkers' learning styles simply by observing them during the workday. Just look for clues.

One clue is how they *approach a learning task*. Some people process new information or ideas by sitting quietly and reading or writing. When learning to use a piece of equipment, such as a new computer, they'll read the instruction manual first. Those who use a trial-and-error approach will skip the manual, unpack all the boxes, and start setting up equipment. Other coworkers might ask a more experienced colleague to guide them in person, step by step.

Another clue is *word choice*. Some people like to process information visually. You might hear them say, "I'll look into that" or "Give me the big picture first." Those who like to solve problems verbally might say, "Let's talk though this problem" or "I hear you!" In contrast, some of your coworkers express themselves using body sensations ("This product feels great") or action ("Let's run with this idea and see what happens").

In addition, notice *process preferences*—patterns in the way that your coworkers meet goals. When attending meetings, for example, some might stick closely to the agenda and keep an eye on the clock. Others might prefer to "go with the flow," even if it means working an extra hour or scrapping the agenda.

Once you've discovered such differences among your coworkers, look for ways to accommodate their learning styles.

Gear presentations to different learning styles. When you want coworkers to agree to a new procedure or promote a new product, you'll probably make a speech or give a presentation. To persuade more people, gear your presentation to several learning styles.

For example, some people want to see the overall picture first. You can start by saying, "This product has four major features." Then explain the benefits of each feature in order.

Also allow time for verbally oriented people to ask questions and make comments. For those who prefer a hands-on approach, offer a chance to try out the new product for themselves—to literally "get the feel of it."

Finish with a handout that includes plenty of illustrations, charts, and step-by-step instructions. Visual learners and people who like to think abstractly will appreciate it.

Gear projects to different learning styles. When working on project teams, look for ways to combine complementary skills. If you're adept at planning, find someone who excels at active experimentation. Also seek people who can reflect on and interpret the team members' experiences. Pooling different learning styles allows you to draw on everyone's strengths.

Remember that a person's learning style is both stable and dynamic. People gravitate toward the kinds of tasks they've succeeded at in the past. They can also broaden their learning styles by taking on new tasks to reinforce different aspects of learning. For example, ask people who enjoy taking immediate action to step back more often and reflect on the overall purpose of a project. ▓

quiz

Name _____ Date _____/_____/_____

1. Explain three ways that you can use knowledge of your learning styles to succeed in school.

2. Define the term *mastery* as it is used in this chapter.

3. The First Step technique refers only to telling the truth about your areas for improvement. True or False? Explain your answer.

4. Examples of effective First Steps include:
   (a) I am an awful public speaker.
   (b) After I speak in front of a class, people say that they had a hard time hearing me.
   (c) I want to create more effective notes to use when I speak in public.
   (d) All of the above.

5. The four modes of learning are associated with certain questions. List the appropriate question for each mode.

6. Give three examples of the benefits of getting an education beyond high school.

7. Briefly describe how being aware of your own multiple intelligences can help you thrive in higher education.

8. According to the Power Process: "Ideas are tools," if you want the ideas in this book to work, you must believe in them. True or False? Explain your answer.

9. Students who are skilled in metacognition can do which of the following:
   (a) Choose and apply various strategies for reading, writing, speaking, listening, managing time, and related tasks.
   (b) Modify strategies so that they work in several contexts.
   (c) Monitor their behavior and change habits.
   (d) State the ways that they'll benefit from learning a subject.
   (e) All of the above.

10. List two strategies that you can use to enhance kinesthetic learning.

learning styles application

Even though you have preferred ways to learn new ideas or skills, you can benefit from using several learning styles. The questions below will "cycle" you through four styles, or modes, of learning as explained in the article "Learning styles: Discovering how you learn" in this chapter. Each question will help you explore a different mode. You can answer the questions in any order.

Remember that you do not have to start with *Why?* of Mode 1. Any of the four questions can serve as your point of entry into the cycle of learning.

Look for a similar Learning Styles Application at the end of every chapter in this book. Also notice that the first page of each chapter includes a preview based on the four questions that represent the four modes of learning: *Why? What? How?* and *What if?*

what if *Review this chapter and the Introduction, looking for ideas that could help you make the transition from being in school to working in your next career. List two or three suggestions, stating each one in a short sentence.*

why *Think about why the subject of transitions matters to you. Describe a major transition that you have experienced in the past. Examples might include changing schools, moving to a new city, starting a job, or going to college. In a sentence or two, describe what you did to cope with this change in your life.*

how *In a short paragraph, explain how you can use one suggestion from this book to master a future transition that you will experience in education. Examples include declaring a major, changing majors, or transferring to a new school.*

what *Review this chapter and the Introduction, looking for ideas that could help you make a major transition in your life. List two or three suggestions, stating each one in a short sentence.*

master student

profile

RUTH HANDLER

(1916–2002) As a cofounder of Mattel, she invented the Barbie doll in 1959. After being diagnosed with breast cancer and undergoing a mastectomy, she designed a prosthetic breast that was later patented as Nearly Me.

When Ruth Handler first proposed the idea of a grown-up doll to the toy designers at Mattel—the company she and her husband ran—the designers thought she was crazy. Little girls want to pretend to be mommies, she was told.

No, said Handler. Little girls want to pretend to be bigger girls. And she knew this because she spent a lot of time observing one little girl in particular—her daughter, Barbara, nicknamed "Barbie."

All her life, Ruth has considered the word "no" just another challenge.

When Ruth graduated from East Denver High School and announced her intention to attend college, her family didn't give her a lot of encouragement. Marrying her high-school sweetheart—a broke-but-talented artist named Elliot Handler—was more traditional than going to college. But she ended up at the University of Denver. And she married Elliot anyway. When she took two semesters of business education at the University of California at Los Angeles, she was the only married woman in her class. And she became the first woman to complete the program.

Ruth fell in love with Southern California and was hired as a stenographer at Paramount Studios in Hollywood. The year was 1937. Ruth worked at Paramount until 1941, when she became pregnant with Barbara, and stayed home until after the birth of her son, Ken, in 1944. Staying home made Ruth restless; she wanted to help [her husband] Elliot run his giftware and costume jewelry business. "You make something; I'll sell it," she told him.

In 1944, while the United States was embroiled in World War II, Elliot designed a new style of picture frame made out of the then-revolutionary new plastics. His partner, Harold "Matt" Matson, built samples and Ruth took the frames to a chain of photography studios and got a large order. The three celebrated, calling their new business "Mattel" after MATT and ELliot.

Soon after, plastic was needed for the war effort and became unavailable for civilian use. Fortunately, Elliot came up with the idea of making frames out of scrap wood. Ruth took the samples back to the photography studio and got an even bigger order. Mattel could continue operating. The leftover wood from the picture frames led to a thriving business making doll house furniture.

Worldwide, Mattel sold millions of Ruth Handler's Barbie dolls, boosting the company's sales to $18 million. Within ten years, customers had bought $500 million worth of Barbie products.

Over the years, Ruth moved up from cofounder of the company to executive vice president to president to cochairman of the board of directors. These titles were practically unheard of for women in the 1960s.

Handler remembers one episode that occurred despite her executive status. A brokerage house was holding a meeting with the investment community at a private club, and Handler was to be the keynote speaker. When she arrived at the club, the program planners ushered her into the club through the alley and kitchen. Later, she discovered that she was sneaked into the building because the club didn't allow women.

From Ethlie Ann Vare and Greg Placek, *Women Inventors and Their Discoveries.* Copyright ©1993. Reprinted by permission of The Oliver Press.

For more biographical information on Ruth Handler, visit the Master Student Hall of Fame at the *Becoming a Master Student* Web site at

masterstudent.college.hmco.com

2

Planning

" *Making lists has been one of my favorite tools to stay on track and prioritize. Not much gives me more pleasure than to cross off duties one by one and to see the number of items left to do shrink to nothing—or to what can be put off until another time.*"

—LAURIE MURRAY

why

this chapter matters . . .

Your ability to manage time and money is a major predictor of your success in school.

what

is included . . .

You've got the time
Setting and achieving goals
The ABC daily to-do list
The seven-day antiprocrastination plan
Getting the most out of now
Financial planning: Meeting your money goals
Power Process: "Be here now"
Master Student Profile: Ron Brown

how

you can use this chapter . . .

Know exactly what you want to accomplish today, this month, this year—and beyond.
Eliminate stress due to poor planning and procrastination.
Gain freedom from money worries.

As you read, ask yourself

what if . . .

I could have more than enough time and money to accomplish whatever I choose?

You've got the time

The words *planning* and *time management* can call forth images of restriction and control. You might visualize a prune-faced Scrooge hunched over your shoulder, stopwatch in hand, telling you what to do every minute. Bad news.

Good news: You do have enough time for the things you want to do. All it takes is learning to plan.

Planning is about time, and time is an equal opportunity resource. All of us, regardless of gender, race, creed, or national origin, have exactly the same number of hours in a week. No matter how newsworthy we are, no matter how rich or poor, we get 168 hours to spend each week—no more, no less.

Time is also an unusual commodity. It cannot be saved. You can't stockpile time like wood for the stove or food for the winter. It can't be seen, felt, touched, tasted, or smelled. You can't sense time directly. Even scientists and philosophers find it hard to describe. Because time is so elusive, it is easy to ignore. That doesn't bother time at all. Time is perfectly content to remain hidden until you are nearly out of it. And when you are out of it, you are out of it.

Time is a nonrenewable resource. If you're out of wood, you can chop some more. If you're out of money, you can earn a little extra. If you're out of love, there is still hope. If you're out of health, it can often be restored. But when you're out of time, that's it. When this minute is gone, it's gone. Time seems to pass at varying speeds. Sometimes it crawls and sometimes it's faster than a speeding bullet. On Friday afternoons, classroom clocks can creep. After you've worked a 10-hour day, reading the last few pages of an economics assignment can turn minutes into hours. A year in school can stretch out to an eternity. At the other end of the spectrum, time flies. There are moments when you are so absorbed in what you're doing that hours disappear like magic.

Approach time as if you are in control. Sometimes it seems that your friends control your time, that your boss controls your time, that your teachers or your parents or your kids or somebody else controls your time. Maybe that is not true. When you say you don't have enough time, you might really be saying that you are not spending the time you *do* have in the way that you want.

This chapter used to be called *Time*. The new title—*Planning*—puts this material in a bigger context. Planning involves determining what you want to achieve and how you intend to go about it. You can state your wants as written goals. Then use your time-management skills to schedule activities that will help you meet those goals.

As you plan, be willing to include all areas of your life. In addition to setting academic goals, write down goals relating to your career, family life, social life, or anything else that matters to you. Since money is a concern for many students, this chapter includes specific suggestions for financial planning.

Planning gives you a chance to spend your most valuable resource in the way you choose. Start by observing how you use time. The next exercise gives you this opportunity. ⬧

journal entry 6

Discovery/Intention Statement

Think back to a time during the past year when you rushed to finish a project or when you did not find time for an activity that was important to you. List one thing you might have done to create this outcome.

I discovered that I . . .

_____

_____

_____

Take a few minutes to skim this chapter. Find three to five articles that might help you avoid such outcomes in the future and list them below.

Title	Page number

If you don't have time to read these articles in depth right now, schedule a time to do so.

I intend to . . .

_____

_____

_____

_____

THE TIME MONITOR/TIME PLAN PROCESS

The purpose of this exercise is to transform time into a knowable and predictable resource. You can do this by repeating a two-phase cycle of monitoring and planning.

This exercise takes place over two weeks. During the first week, you can monitor your activities to get a detailed picture of how you spend your time. Then you can plan the second week thoughtfully. Monitor your time during the second week, compare it to your plan, and discover what changes you want to make in the following week's plan.

Monitor your time in 15-minute intervals, 24 hours a day, for seven days. Record how much time you spend sleeping, eating, studying, attending lectures, traveling to and from class, working, watching television, listening to music, taking care of the kids, running errands—everything.

If this sounds crazy, hang on for a minute. This exercise is not about keeping track of the rest of your life in 15-minute intervals. It is an opportunity to become conscious of how you spend your time, your life. Use the Time Monitor/Time Plan process only for as long as it is helpful to do so.

When you know how your time is spent, you can find ways to adjust and manage it so that you spend your life doing the things that are most important to you. Monitoring your time is a critical first step toward putting you in control of your life.

Some students choose to keep track of their time on 3x5 cards, calendars, campus planners, or software designed for this purpose. You might even develop your own form for monitoring your time.

1. Get to know the Time Monitor/Time Plan. Look at the Time Monitor/Time Plan on page 49. Note that each day has two columns, one labeled "monitor" and the other labeled "plan." During the first week, use only the "monitor" column. After that, use both columns simultaneously to continue the monitor-plan process.

To become familiar with the form, look at the example on page 49. When you begin an activity, write it down next to the time you begin and put a line just above that spot. Round off to the nearest 15 minutes. If, for example, you begin eating at 8:06, enter your starting time as 8:00. Over time, it will probably even out. In any case, you will be close enough to realize the benefits of this exercise. (Note that you can use the blank spaces in the "monitor"

Do this exercise online at

masterstudent.college.hmco.com

and "plan" columns to cover most of the day.)

On Monday, the student in this example got up at 6:45 a.m., showered, and got dressed. He finished this activity and began breakfast at 7:15. He put this new activity in at the time he began and drew a line just above it. He ate from 7:15 to 7:45. It took him 15 minutes to walk to class (7:45 to 8:00), and he attended classes from 8:00 to 11:00.

Keep your Time Monitor/Time Plan with you every minute you are awake for one week. Take a few moments every two or three hours to record what you've done. Or enter a note each time you change activities.

Here's an eye opener for many students. If you think you already have a good idea of how you manage time, predict how many hours you will spend in a week on each category of activity listed in the form on page 50. (Four categories are already provided; you can add more at any time.) Do this before your first week of monitoring. Write your predictions in the margin to the left of each category. After monitoring your time for one week, see how accurate your predictions were.

2. Remember to use your Time Monitor/Time Plan. It might be easy to forget to fill out your Time Monitor/Time Plan. One way to remember is to create a visual reminder for yourself. You can use this technique for any activity you want to remember.

Relax for a moment, close your eyes, and imagine that you see your Time Monitor/Time Plan. Imagine that it has arms and legs and is as big as a person. Picture the form sitting at your desk at home, in your car, in one of your classrooms, or in your favorite chair. Visualize it sitting wherever you're likely to sit. When you sit down, the Time Monitor/Time Plan will get squashed.

You can make this image more effective by adding sound effects. The Time Monitor/Time Plan might scream, "Get off me!" Or since time can be related to money, you might associate the Time Monitor/Time Plan with the sound of an old-fashioned cash register. Imagine that every time you sit down, a cash register rings.

3. Evaluate the Time Monitor/Time Plan. After you've monitored your time for one week, group your activities together by categories. The form on page 54 lists the categories "sleep," "class," "study," and "meals." Think of other categories you could add. "Grooming" might include showering, putting on makeup, brushing teeth, and getting dressed. "Travel" can include walking, driving, taking the bus, and

MONDAY 9 / 12

Monitor	Time	Plan
Get up		
Shower		
	7:00	7:00
Breakfast	7:15	
	7:30	
Walk to	7:45	
class	8:00	8:00
	8:15	
Econ 1	8:30	
	8:45	
	9:00	9:00
	9:15	
	9:30	
	9:45	
Bio 1	10:00	10:00
	10:15	
	10:30	
	10:45	
	11:00	11:00
Study	11:15	
	11:30	
	11:45	
	12:00	12:00
Lunch	12:15	
	12:30	
	12:45	
	1:00	1:00
Eng. Lit	1:15	
	1:30	
	1:45	
	2:00	2:00
Coffeehouse	2:15	
	2:30	
	2:45	
	3:00	3:00
	3:15	
	3:30	
	3:45	
	4:00	4:00
Study	4:15	
	4:30	
	4:45	
	5:00	5:00
Dinner	5:15	
	5:30	
	5:45	
	6:00	6:00
	6:15	
Babysit	6:30	
	6:45	
	7:00	7:00

TUESDAY 9 / 13

Monitor	Time	Plan
Sleep		
	7:00	7:00
	7:15	
	7:30	
Shower	7:45	
Dress	8:00	8:00
Eat	8:15	
	8:30	
	8:45	
Art	9:00	9:00
Apprec.	9:15	
Project	9:30	
	9:45	
	10:00	10:00
	10:15	
	10:30	
	10:45	
Data	11:00	11:00
process	11:15	
	11:30	
	11:45	
	12:00	12:00
	12:15	
	12:30	
	12:45	
	1:00	1:00
Lunch	1:15	
	1:30	
	1:45	
Work	2:00	2:00
on book	2:15	
report	2:30	
	2:45	
Art	3:00	3:00
Apprec.	3:15	
	3:30	
	3:45	
	4:00	4:00
	4:15	
	4:30	
	4:45	
Dinner	5:00	5:00
	5:15	
	5:30	
	5:45	
Letter to	6:00	6:00
Uncle Jim	6:15	
	6:30	
	6:45	
	7:00	7:00

riding your bike. Other categories might be "exercise," "entertainment," "work," "television," "domestic," and "children."

Write in the categories that work for you, and then add up how much time you spent in each of your categories. Put the totals in the "monitored" column on page 50. Make sure that the grand total of all categories is 168 hours.

Now take a minute and let these numbers sink in. Compare your totals to your predictions and notice your reactions. You might be surprised. You might feel disappointed or even angry about where your time goes. Use those feelings as motivation to plan your time differently. Go to the "planned" column and decide how much time you want to spend on various daily activities. As you do so, allow yourself to have fun. Approach planning in the spirit of adventure. Think of yourself as an artist who's creating a new life.

In several months you might want to take another detailed look at how you spend your life. You can expand the two-phase cycle of monitoring and planning to include a third phase: evaluating. Combine this with planning your time, following the suggestions in this chapter. You can use a continuous cycle: monitor, evaluate, plan; monitor, evaluate, plan. When you make it a habit, this cycle can help you get the full benefits of time management for the rest of your life. Then time management becomes more than a technique. It's transformed into a habit, a constant awareness of how you spend your lifetime.

Planning is a broad word that refers to all aspects of creating a vision for your future. Goal setting, time management, budgeting—all are tools that allow you to maximize your freedom and live a full life. Few architects propose a building project without a blueprint. Few entrepreneurs get venture capital without a sound business plan. And few film producers begin shooting a movie without a script. In each case, the rationale is to avoid actions that waste time, money, effort, and talent. In this light, it's amazing that so many people lack a plan for something as important as their own lives.

Planning and motivation are mutually reinforcing. When your goals connect to your deepest desires, you discover new reserves of energy. Moving into action becomes almost effortless. When you clearly define a goal, your mind and body start to operate more consistently in ways to achieve your dreams. As you meet goals and cross them off your list, you experience the satisfaction of success.

WEEK OF ___ / ___ / ___ /		
Category	Monitored	Planned
Sleep		
Class		
Study		
Meals		

MONDAY ___ / ___ / ___ /

Monitor	Plan
7:00	7:00
7:15	
7:30	
7:45	
8:00	8:00
8:15	
8:30	
8:45	
9:00	9:00
9:15	
9:30	
9:45	
10:00	10:00
10:15	
10:30	
10:45	
11:00	11:00
11:15	
11:30	
11:45	
12:00	12:00
12:15	
12:30	
12:45	
1:00	1:00
1:15	
1:30	
1:45	
2:00	2:00
2:15	
2:30	
2:45	
3:00	3:00
3:15	
3:30	
3:45	
4:00	4:00
4:15	
4:30	
4:45	
5:00	5:00
5:15	
5:30	
5:45	
6:00	6:00
6:15	
6:30	
6:45	
7:00	7:00
7:15	
7:30	
7:45	
8:00	8:00
8:15	
8:30	
8:45	
9:00	9:00
9:15	
9:30	
9:45	
10:00	10:00
10:15	
10:30	
10:45	
11:00	11:00
11:15	
11:30	
11:45	
12:00	12:00

TUESDAY ___ / ___ / ___ /

Monitor	Plan
7:00	7:00
7:15	
7:30	
7:45	
8:00	8:00
8:15	
8:30	
8:45	
9:00	9:00
9:15	
9:30	
9:45	
10:00	10:00
10:15	
10:30	
10:45	
11:00	11:00
11:15	
11:30	
11:45	
12:00	12:00
12:15	
12:30	
12:45	
1:00	1:00
1:15	
1:30	
1:45	
2:00	2:00
2:15	
2:30	
2:45	
3:00	3:00
3:15	
3:30	
3:45	
4:00	4:00
4:15	
4:30	
4:45	
5:00	5:00
5:15	
5:30	
5:45	
6:00	6:00
6:15	
6:30	
6:45	
7:00	7:00
7:15	
7:30	
7:45	
8:00	8:00
8:15	
8:30	
8:45	
9:00	9:00
9:15	
9:30	
9:45	
10:00	10:00
10:15	
10:30	
10:45	
11:00	11:00
11:15	
11:30	
11:45	
12:00	12:00

WEDNESDAY ___ / ___ / ___ /

Monitor	Plan
7:00	7:00
7:15	
7:30	
7:45	
8:00	8:00
8:15	
8:30	
8:45	
9:00	9:00
9:15	
9:30	
9:45	
10:00	10:00
10:15	
10:30	
10:45	
11:00	11:00
11:15	
11:30	
11:45	
12:00	12:00
12:15	
12:30	
12:45	
1:00	1:00
1:15	
1:30	
1:45	
2:00	2:00
2:15	
2:30	
2:45	
3:00	3:00
3:15	
3:30	
3:45	
4:00	4:00
4:15	
4:30	
4:45	
5:00	5:00
5:15	
5:30	
5:45	
6:00	6:00
6:15	
6:30	
6:45	
7:00	7:00
7:15	
7:30	
7:45	
8:00	8:00
8:15	
8:30	
8:45	
9:00	9:00
9:15	
9:30	
9:45	
10:00	10:00
10:15	
10:30	
10:45	
11:00	11:00
11:15	
11:30	
11:45	
12:00	12:00

THURSDAY ___ / ___ / ___ /		FRIDAY ___ / ___ / ___ /		SATURDAY ___ / ___ / ___ /	
Monitor	Plan	Monitor	Plan	Monitor	Plan
7:00	7:00	7:00	7:00		
7:15		7:15			
7:30		7:30			
7:45		7:45			
8:00	8:00	8:00	8:00		
8:15		8:15			
8:30		8:30			
8:45		8:45			
9:00	9:00	9:00	9:00		
9:15		9:15			
9:30		9:30			
9:45		9:45			
10:00	10:00	10:00	10:00		
10:15		10:15			
10:30		10:30			
10:45		10:45			
11:00	11:00	11:00	11:00		
11:15		11:15			
11:30		11:30			
11:45		11:45			
12:00	12:00	12:00	12:00		
12:15		12:15			
12:30		12:30			
12:45		12:45			
1:00	1:00	1:00	1:00		
1:15		1:15			
1:30		1:30			
1:45		1:45			
2:00	2:00	2:00	2:00		
2:15		2:15			
2:30		2:30			
2:45		2:45			
3:00	3:00	3:00	3:00		
3:15		3:15			
3:30		3:30			
3:45		3:45		SUNDAY ___ / ___ / ___ /	
4:00	4:00	4:00	4:00	Monitor	Plan
4:15		4:15			
4:30		4:30			
4:45		4:45			
5:00	5:00	5:00	5:00		
5:15		5:15			
5:30		5:30			
5:45		5:45			
6:00	6:00	6:00	6:00		
6:15		6:15			
6:30		6:30			
6:45		6:45			
7:00	7:00	7:00	7:00		
7:15		7:15			
7:30		7:30			
7:45		7:45			
8:00	8:00	8:00	8:00		
8:15		8:15			
8:30		8:30			
8:45		8:45			
9:00	9:00	9:00	9:00		
9:15		9:15			
9:30		9:30			
9:45		9:45			
10:00	10:00	10:00	10:00		
10:15		10:15			
10:30		10:30			
10:45		10:45			
11:00	11:00	11:00	11:00		
11:15		11:15			
11:30		11:30			
11:45		11:45			
12:00	12:00	12:00	12:00		

Discovery Statement

After one week of monitoring my time, I discovered that . . .

_____

_____

I want to spend more time on . . .

_____

_____

I want to spend less time on . . .

_____

_____

_____

I was surprised that I spent so much time on . . .

_____

_____

_____

I was surprised that I spent so little time on . . .

_____

_____

_____

I had strong feelings about my use of time when (describe the feeling and the situation) . . .

_____

_____

_____

Setting and achieving goals

Many of us have vague, idealized notions of what we want out of life. These notions float among the clouds in our heads. They are wonderful, fuzzy, safe thoughts such as "I want to be a good person," "I want to be financially secure," or "I want to be happy."

Such outcomes are great possible goals. Left in a generalized form, however, these goals can leave us confused about ways to actually achieve them.

If you really want to meet a goal, translate it into specific, concrete behaviors. Find out what that goal looks like. Listen to what it sounds like. Pick it up and feel how heavy that goal is. Inspect the switches, valves, joints, cogs, and fastenings of the goal. Make your goal as real as a chain saw.

There is nothing vague or fuzzy about chain saws. You can see them, feel them, and hear them. They have a clear function. Goals can be every bit as real and useful.

Writing down your goals exponentially increases your chances of meeting them. Writing exposes undefined terms, unrealistic time frames, and other symptoms of fuzzy thinking. If you've been completing Intention Statements as explained in the Introduction to this book, then you've already had experience writing goals. Goals and Intention Statements both address changes you want to make in your behavior, your values, your circumstances—or all of these. To keep track of your goals, write each one on a separate 3x5 card or key them all into a word processing file on your computer.

There are many useful methods for setting goals. Following is one of them. This method is based on writing specific goals in several time frames and areas of your life. Experiment with it and modify it as you see fit. You're also encouraged to reflect regularly on your goals. The key words to remember are *specific, time, areas,* and *reflect.* Combine the first letter of each word and you get the acronym *STAR.* Use this acronym to remember the suggestions that follow.

Write specific goals. In writing, state your goals as observable actions or measurable results. Think in detail about how things will be different once your goals are attained. List the changes in what you'd see, feel, touch, taste, hear, be, do, or have.

Suppose that one of your goals is to become a better student by studying harder. You're headed in a powerful direction; now go for the specifics. Translate that goal into a concrete action, such as "I will study two hours for every hour I'm in class." Specific goals make clear what actions are needed or what results are expected. Consider these examples:

Vague goal	Specific goal
Get a good education.	Graduate with B.S. degree in engineering, with honors, by 2009.
Enhance my spiritual life.	Meditate for 15 minutes daily.
Improve my appearance.	Lose six pounds during the next six months.

When stated specifically, a goal might look different to you. If you examine it closely, a goal you once thought you wanted might not be something you want after all. Or you might discover that you want to choose a new path to achieve a goal that you are sure you want.

Write goals in several time frames. To get a comprehensive vision of your future, write down:

- *Long-term goals.* Long-term goals represent major targets in your life. These goals can take five to 20 years to achieve. In some cases, they will take a lifetime. They can include goals in education, careers, personal relationships, travel, financial security—whatever is important to you. Consider the answers to the following questions as you create your long-term goals: What do you want to accomplish in your life? Do you want your life to make a statement? If so, what is that statement?

- *Mid-term goals.* Mid-term goals are objectives you can accomplish in one to five years. They include goals such as completing a course of education, paying off a car loan, or achieving a specific career level. These goals usually support your long-term goals.

- *Short-term goals.* Short-term goals are the ones you can accomplish in a year or less. These goals are specific achievements, such as completing a particular course or group of courses, hiking down the Appalachian Trail, or organizing a family reunion.

A financial goal would probably include an exact dollar amount. Whatever your short-term goals are, they will require action now or in the near future.

Write goals in several areas of life. People who set goals in only one area of life—such as their career—can find that their personal growth becomes one-sided. They could experience success at work while neglecting their health or relationships with family members and friends.

To avoid this outcome, set goals in a variety of categories. Consider what you want to experience in your:

- education
- career
- financial life
- family life
- social life
- spiritual life
- level of health

Add goals in other areas as they occur to you.

Reflect on your goals. Each week, take a few minutes to think about your goals. You can perform the following "spot checks":

- *Check in with your feelings.* Think about how the process of setting your goals felt. Consider the satisfaction you'll gain in attaining your objectives. If you don't feel a significant emotional connection with a written goal, consider letting it go or filing it away to review later.

- *Check for alignment.* Look for connections between your goals. Do your short-term goals align with your mid-term goals? Will your mid-term goals help you achieve your long-term goals? Look for a "fit" between all of your goals and your purpose for taking part in higher education, as well as your overall purpose in life.

- *Check for obstacles.* All kinds of things can come between you and your goals, such as constraints on time and money. Anticipate obstacles and start looking now for workable solutions.

- *Check for immediate steps.* Here's a way to link goal setting to time management. Decide on a list of small, achievable steps you can take right away to accomplish each of your short-term goals. Write these small steps down on a daily to-do list. If you want to accomplish some of them by a certain date, enter them in a calendar that you consult daily. Then, over the coming weeks, review your to-do list and calendar. Take note of your progress and celebrate your successes. ☒

GET REAL WITH YOUR GOALS

One way to make goals effective is to examine them up close. That's what this exercise is about. Using a process of brainstorming and evaluation, you can break a long-term goal into smaller segments until you have taken it completely apart. When you analyze a goal to this level of detail, you're well on the way to meeting it.

For this exercise, you will use a pen, extra paper, and a watch with a second hand. (A digital watch with a built-in stopwatch is even better.) Timing is an important part of the brainstorming process, so follow the stated time limits. This entire exercise takes about an hour.

Part one: Long-term goals

Brainstorm. Begin with an eight-minute brainstorm. For eight minutes write down everything you think you want in your life. Write as fast as you can and write whatever comes into your head. Leave no thought out. Don't worry about accuracy. The object of a brainstorm is to generate as many ideas as possible. Use a separate sheet of paper for this part of the exercise.

Evaluate. After you have finished brainstorming, spend the next six minutes looking over your list. Analyze what you wrote. Read the list out loud. If something is missing, add it. Look for common themes or relationships between goals. Then select three long-term goals that are important to you—goals that will take many years to achieve. Write these goals below in the space provided.

_____

_____

_____

Before you continue, take a minute to reflect on the process you've used so far. What criteria did you use to select your top three goals? For example, list some of the core values (such as love, wealth, or happiness) underlying these goals.

Part two: Mid-term goals

Brainstorm. Read out loud the three long-term goals you selected in Part One. Choose one of them. Then brainstorm a list of goals you might achieve in the next one to five years that would lead to the accomplishment of that

Do this exercise online at

(masterstudent.college.hmco.com)

one long-term goal. These are mid-term goals. Spend eight minutes on this brainstorm. Remember, neatness doesn't count. Go for quantity.

Evaluate. Analyze your brainstorm of mid-term goals. Then select three that you determine to be important in meeting the long-term goal you picked. Allow yourself six minutes for this part of the exercise. Write your selections below in the space provided.

_____

_____

_____

Again, pause for reflection before going on to the next part of this exercise. Why do you see these three goals as more important than the other mid-term goals you generated? Write about your reasons for selecting these three goals.

Part three: Short-term goals

Brainstorm. Review your list of mid-term goals and select one. In another eight-minute brainstorm, generate a list of short-term goals—those you can accomplish in a year or less that will lead to the attainment of that mid-term goal. Write down everything that comes to mind. Do not evaluate or judge these ideas yet. For now, the more ideas you write down, the better.

Evaluate. Analyze your list of short-term goals. The most effective brainstorms are conducted by suspending judgment, so you might find some bizarre ideas on your list. That's fine. Now is the time to cross them out. Next, evaluate your remaining short-term goals and select three that you are willing and able to accomplish. Allow yourself six minutes for this part of the exercise; then write your selections below in the space provided.

_____

_____

_____

The more you practice, the more effective you can be at choosing goals that have meaning for you. You can repeat this exercise, employing the other long-term goals you generated or creating new ones. By using this brainstorm and evaluation process, you can make goals come to life in the here and now.

While the Time Monitor/Time Plan gives you a general picture of the week, a daily to-do list itemizes specific tasks you want to complete within the next 24 hours.

The ABC daily to-do list

It's easy to forget an important task on a busy day. When that task is written down on a to-do list, you don't have to rely on your memory.

Step 1 **Brainstorm tasks.** To get started, list all of the tasks you want to get done tomorrow. Write them on a sheet of paper or a planning calendar, or in a special notebook. You can also use 3x5 cards, writing one task on each card.

Step 2 **Estimate time.** For each task you wrote down in step 1, estimate how long it will take you to complete it. This can be tricky. For now, give it your best guess. Your estimates will improve with practice.

Add up the time needed to complete all your to-do items. Also add up the number of unscheduled hours in your day. Then compare the two totals. The power of this step is that you can spot overload in advance. If you have eight hours' worth of to-do items but only four unscheduled hours, that's a potential problem. To solve it, proceed to step 3.

Step 3 **Rate each task by priority.** One way to stay focused on important tasks comes from the book *How to Get Control of Your Time and Your Life* by Alan Lakein: Simply label each task A, B, or C.[1]

The A's on your list are those things that are the most critical. These are assignments that are coming due or jobs that need to be done immediately. Also included are activities that lead directly to your short-term goals.

The B's on your list are important, but less so than the A's. They can be postponed, if necessary, for another day.

The C's do not require immediate attention. These are often small, easy tasks with no set timeline. These, too, can be postponed.

Once you've labeled the items on your to-do list, schedule time for all of the A's. The B's and C's can be done randomly during the day when you are not yet ready to start the next A.

Step 4 **Cross off tasks.** Keep your to-do list with you at all times, crossing off activities when you finish them. Crossing off tasks can be fun—a visible reward for your diligence.

You might experience an ailment common to students: C fever. This is the uncontrollable urge to drop that A task and begin crossing C's off your to-do list. If your history paper is due tomorrow, you might feel compelled to vacuum the rug, call your third cousin in Tulsa, and make a trip to the store for shoelaces.

Don't panic or berate yourself when you realize that in the last six hours, you have completed 11 C's and not a single A. Calmly return to the A's.

Step 5 **Evaluate.** At the end of the day, look for A priorities you didn't complete. Look for items that repeatedly turn up as B's or C's on your list and never seem to get done. Consider changing these to A's or dropping them altogether. Similarly, you might consider changing an A that didn't get done to a B or C priority. When you're done evaluating, start on tomorrow's to-do list.

In any case, make starting your own to-do list an A priority. ⊠

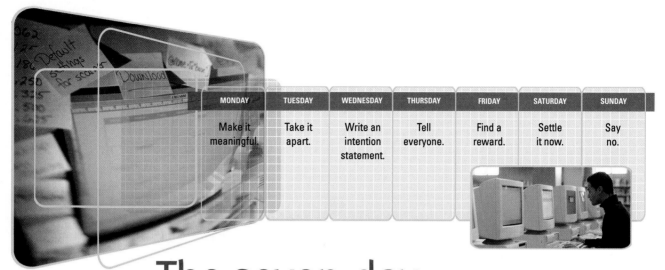

MONDAY	TUESDAY	WEDNESDAY	THURSDAY	FRIDAY	SATURDAY	SUNDAY
Make it meaningful.	Take it apart.	Write an intention statement.	Tell everyone.	Find a reward.	Settle it now.	Say no.

The seven-day
antiprocrastination plan

Listed here are seven strategies you can use to reduce or eliminate many sources of procrastination. The suggestions are tied to the days of the week to help you remember them. Use this list to remind yourself that each day of your life presents an opportunity to stop the cycle of procrastination.

Monday: Make it meaningful. What is important about the task you've been putting off? List all the benefits of completing it. Look at it in relation to your short-, mid-, or long-term goals. Be specific about the rewards for getting it done, including how you will feel when the task is completed. To remember this strategy, keep in mind that it starts with the letter *M*, like the word *Monday*.

Tuesday: Take it apart. Break big jobs into a series of small ones you can do in 15 minutes or less. If a long reading assignment intimidates you, divide it into two-page or three-page sections. Make a list of the sections and cross them off as you complete them so you can see your progress. Even the biggest projects can be broken down into a series of small tasks. This strategy starts with the letter *T*, so mentally tie it to *Tuesday*.

Wednesday: Write an Intention Statement. For example, if you can't get started on a term paper, you might write, "I intend to write a list of at least 10 possible topics by 9 p.m. I will reward myself with an hour of guilt-free recreational reading." Write your intention on a 3x5 card and carry it with you, or post it in your study area where you can see it often. In your memory, file the first word in this strategy—*write*—with *Wednesday*.

Thursday: Tell everyone. Publicly announce your intention to get a task done. Tell a friend that you intend to learn 10 irregular French verbs by Saturday. Tell your spouse, roommate, parents, and children. Include anyone who will ask whether you've completed the assignment or who will suggest ways to get it done. Make the world your support group. Associate *tell* with *Thursday*.

Friday: Find a reward. Construct rewards to yourself carefully. Be willing to withhold them if you do not complete the task. Don't pick a movie as a reward for studying biology if you plan to go to the movie anyway. And when you legitimately reap your reward, notice how it feels. Remember that *Friday* is a fine day to *find* a reward. (Of course, you can find a reward on any day of the week. Rhyming *Friday* with *fine day* is just a memory trick.)

Saturday: Settle it now. Do it now. The minute you notice yourself procrastinating, plunge into the task. Imagine yourself at a cold mountain lake, poised to dive. Gradual immersion would be slow torture. It's often less painful to leap. Then be sure to savor the feeling of having the task behind you. Link *settle* with *Saturday*.

Sunday: Say no. When you keep pushing a task into a low-priority category, re-examine your purpose for doing it at all. If you realize that you really don't intend to do something, quit telling yourself that you will. That's procrastinating. Just say no. Then you're not procrastinating. You don't have to carry around the baggage of an undone task. *Sunday*—the last day of this seven-day plan—is a great day to finally let go and just *say* no. ✖

Getting the most out of now

The following time-management techniques are about:

- When to study
- Where to study
- Ways to handle the rest of the world
- Things to ask yourself if you get stuck

When to study

Study two hours for every hour in class. In higher education, it's standard advice to allow two hours of study time for every hour spent in class. Students making the transition from high school to college are often unaware that more is expected of them. However, this guideline is just that—a guideline, not an absolute rule. Consider what's best for you.

Study difficult subjects first. If your chemistry problems put you to sleep, get to them first, while you are fresh. We tend to give top priority to what we enjoy studying, yet the courses we find most difficult often require the most creative energy. Save your favorite subjects for later.

Use your times of peak energy. Study your most difficult subjects during the times when your energy peaks. Many people can concentrate more effectively during daylight hours. The early morning hours can be espe-

cially productive, even for those who hate to get up with the sun. Observe the peaks and valleys in your energy flow during the day and adjust study times accordingly. Perhaps you will experience surges in memory power during the late afternoon or evening.

Use waiting time. Five minutes waiting for a subway, 20 minutes waiting for the dentist, 10 minutes in between classes—waiting time adds up fast. Have short study tasks ready to do during these periods. For example, you can carry 3x5 cards with facts, formulas, or definitions and pull them out anywhere.

Where to study

Use a regular study area. Your body and your mind know where you are. Using the same place to study, day after day, helps train your responses. When you arrive at that particular place, you can focus your attention more quickly.

Study where you'll be alert. In bed, your body gets a signal. For most students, that signal is more likely to be "Time to sleep!" than "Time to study!" Just as you train your body to be alert at your desk, you also train it to slow down near your bed. For that reason, don't study where you sleep.

Use a library. Libraries are designed for learning. The lighting is perfect. The noise level is low. A wealth of ma-

→ **Remember cultural differences**

There are as many different styles for managing time as there are people. These styles vary across cultures.

In the United States and England, for example, business meetings typically start on time. That's also true in Scandinavian countries such as Norway and Sweden. However, travelers to Panama might find that meetings start about a half-hour late. And people who complain about late meetings while doing business in Mexico might be considered rude.

Cultural differences can get even more pronounced. In her book *Freedom and Culture*, anthropologist Dorothy Lee writes about a group of people in the Trobriand Islands east of New Guinea.[2] Their language has no verb tenses—

no distinction among past, present, and future. The Trobrianders celebrate each event as an end in itself, not as a means to achieve some future goal. In this culture, the whole concept of time management would have little meaning.

When you study or work with people of different races and ethnic backgrounds, look for differences in their approach to time. A behavior that you might view as rude or careless—such as showing up late for appointments—could simply result from seeing the world in a different way.

Find additional articles about cultural differences online at (mastersstudent.college.hmco.com)

terial is available. Entering a library is a signal to focus the mind and get to work. Many students can get more done in a shorter time frame at the library than anywhere else. Experiment for yourself.

Ways to handle the rest of the world

Agree with living mates about study time. This includes roommates, spouses, and children. Make the rules clear, and be sure to follow them yourself. Explicit agreements—even written contracts—work well. One student always wears a colorful hat when he wants to study. When his wife and children see the hat, they respect his wish to be left alone.

Get off the phone. The telephone is the ultimate interrupter. People who wouldn't think of distracting you might call at the worst times because they can't see that you are studying. You don't have to be a telephone victim. If a simple "I can't talk; I'm studying" doesn't work, use dead silence. It's a conversation killer.

Learn to say no. This is a timesaver and a valuable life skill for everyone. Some people feel it is rude to refuse a request. But saying no can be done effectively and courteously. Others want you to succeed as a student. When you tell them that you can't do what they ask because you are busy educating yourself, most people will understand.

Call ahead. Before you go shopping, call the store to see if it carries the items you're looking for. If you're driving, call for directions to your destination. A few

seconds on the phone can save hours in wasted trips and wrong turns.

Avoid noise distractions. To promote concentration, avoid studying in front of the television and turn off the radio.

If you live in a residence hall, ask if study rooms are available. Or go somewhere else where it's quiet, such as the library. Some students have even found refuge in quiet cafés, self-service laundries, and places of worship.

Notice how others misuse your time. Ask yourself if there are certain friends or relatives who consistently interrupt your study time. If avoiding the interrupter is impractical, send a clear message. Sometimes others don't realize that they are breaking your concentration. You can give them a gentle yet firm reminder.

Things to ask yourself if you get stuck

Ask: Am I balancing short-term and long-term planning? Consider planning a whole week—or even two weeks—at a time. If you have an especially busy period coming up, you'll spot it in advance. You can also spread to-do items out over a longer period instead of trying to get them all done in one day.

As you get comfortable with this technique, see if you can extend your planning even further out in time. Get a planner with an overview of each month, academic term, or calendar year. Enter key events such as due dates for major assignments in all your courses. Also mark significant events in your life outside school. Examples are birthdays, anniversaries, medical and dental checkups, car maintenance schedules, and due dates for major bills.

The art of planning is balancing a short-term view of your activity with a long-range vision for your life. Set goals for today, this week, this month, this term, this year, and beyond. Then you can be more confident that you're advancing in the direction of your dreams.

Ask: Is this a piano? Carpenters who construct rough frames for buildings have a saying they use when they bend a nail or accidentally hack a chunk out of a two-by-four: "Well, this ain't no piano." It means that perfection is not necessary. Ask yourself if what you are doing needs to be perfect. If you can complete a job 95 percent perfectly in two hours and 100 percent perfectly in four hours, ask yourself whether the additional 5 percent improvement is worth doubling the amount of time you spend.

Ask: Would I pay myself for what I'm doing right now? If you were employed as a student, would you be earning your wages? Ask yourself this question when you notice that you've taken your third snack break in 30 minutes.

Ask: Can I do just one more thing? Ask yourself this question at the end of a long day. Almost always you will have enough energy to do just one more short task. The overall increase in your productivity might surprise you.

Ask: Am I making time for things that are important but not urgent? Examples include exercising regularly, reading, praying or meditating, spending quality time alone or with family members and friends, traveling, and cooking nutritious meals. Each of these can contribute directly to a long-term goal or life mission. Yet when schedules get tight, we often forgo these things, waiting for that elusive day when we'll "finally have more time."

Ask: Can I delegate this? Instead of doing all the housework or cooking by yourself, for example, you can assign some of the tasks to family members or roommates. Rather than making a trip to the library to look up a simple fact, you can call and ask a librarian to research it for you. Instead of driving across town to deliver a package, you can hire a delivery service to do so. All of these tactics can free up extra hours for studying.

Ask: Am I allowing flexibility in my schedule? Recognize that unexpected things will happen. Leave some holes in your schedule; build in blocks of unplanned time. Use these hours for emergencies, spontaneous activities, errands, catching up, seizing new opportunities—or simply having fun.

Ask: How did I just waste time? Notice when time passes and you haven't accomplished what you had planned to do. Take a minute to review your actions and note the specific ways you wasted time. We tend to operate by habit, wasting time in the same ways over and over again. When you are aware of things you do that drain your time, you are more likely to catch yourself in the act next time.

Ask: Could I find the time if I really wanted to? The next time you're tempted to say, "I just don't have time," pause for a minute. Question the truth of this statement. Could you find four more hours this week for studying? Suppose that someone offered to pay you $10,000 to find those four hours. Suppose, too, that you will get paid only if you don't lose sleep, call in sick for work, or sacrifice anything important to you. Could you find the time if vast sums of money were involved?

Remember that when it comes to school, vast sums of money *are* involved.

Ask: Am I willing to promise it? If you want to find time for a task, promise yourself—and others—that you'll get it done.

Promises can work magic. When our word is on the line, it's possible to discover reserves of time and energy we didn't know existed. Promises can push us to exceed our expectations. ◨

CREATE A LIFELINE

On a large sheet of paper, draw a horizontal line. This line will represent your lifetime. Now add key events in your life to this line in chronological order. Examples are birth, first day at school, graduation from high school, and enrollment in higher education.

Now extend the lifeline into the future. Write down key events you would like to see occur in one year, five years, and 10 or more years from now. Choose events that align with your core values. Work quickly in the spirit of a brainstorm, bearing in mind that this is not a final plan.

Afterward, take a few minutes to review your lifeline. Select one key event for the future and list any actions you

could take in the next month to bring yourself closer to that goal. Do the same with the other key events on your lifeline. You now have the rudiments of a comprehensive plan for your life.

Finally, extend your lifeline another 50 years beyond the year when you would reach age 100. Describe in detail what changes in the world you'd like to see as a result of the goals you attained in your lifetime.

Do this exercise online at

masterstudent.college.hmco.com

PRACTICING CRITICAL THINKING
2

In the space below, create an alternative to the statement you just wrote about. Write a sentence that puts you back in charge of your time and no longer offers an excuse for procrastination. For example: "Even if I don't complete a task perfectly, I can give it my best shot and learn from my mistakes."

Some thoughts fuel procrastination and keep you from experiencing the rewards in life that you deserve. Psychologists Jane Burka and Lenora Yuen list these examples:[3]

I must be perfect.
Everything I do should go easily and without effort.
It's safer to do nothing than to take a risk and fail.
If it's not done right, it's not worth doing at all.
If I do well this time, I must always do well.
If I succeed, someone will get hurt.

Choose one of these statements—or think of a similar one—and write a sentence or two about how it could promote procrastination.

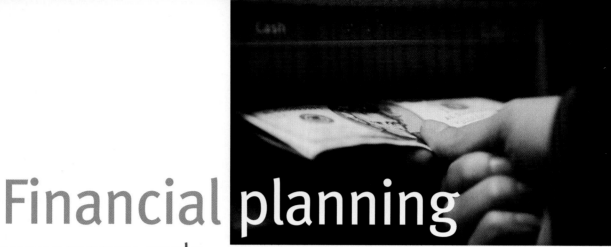

Financial planning

Meeting your money goals

Some people shy away from financial planning. They think that money is a complicated subject. Yet most money problems result from simply spending more than is available.

The solution also is simple: *Don't spend more than you have.* If you are spending more money than you have, increase your income, decrease your spending, or do both. This idea has never won a Nobel Prize in economics, but you won't go broke applying it.

Increase money in. There are several ways to increase your income while you go to school. One of the most obvious ways is to get a job. You could also apply for scholarships and grants. You might borrow money, inherit it, or receive it as a gift. You could sell property, collect income from investments, or use your savings. Other options—such as lotteries and gambling casinos—pose obvious risks. Stick to making money the old-fashioned way: Earn it.

If you work while you go to school, you can earn more than money. Working helps you gain experience, establish references, and expand your contacts in the community. Doing well at a work-study position or an internship while you're in school can also help you land a good job after you graduate.

Decrease money out. For many of us, making more money is the most appealing way to fix a broken budget. When our income increases, however, most of us still continue to spend more than we make. You can avoid this dilemma by managing your expenses no matter how much money you make.

When you look for places to cut expenses, start with the items that cost the most. Your choices about which school to attend, what car to buy, and where to live can save you tens of thousands of dollars. For example, keep your housing costs reasonable. Sometimes a place a little farther from your school or a smaller house will be much less expensive.

Decreasing the money you spend on small purchases can also help you balance your budget. A three-dollar cappuccino is tasty, but the amount that some people spend on such treats over the course of a year could give anyone the jitters.

In addition, shop around for the best prices and avoid buying things on impulse. Whenever possible, use public transportation rather than a car. Look for free entertainment, including on-campus theater, concerts, films, and dances.

Also tame the credit card tiger. Keep track of how much you spend using credit cards each month. Then save an equal amount in cash. That way, you can pay off the card balances each month and avoid interest charges. Following this suggestion alone might transform your financial life.

Monitor money out. These are just a few examples of ways to decrease spending. Invent more of your own, and reinforce them all with awareness. Know exactly how much you earn and spend.

Each month, review your checkbook, receipts, and other financial records. Sort your expenditures into major categories such as school expenses, housing, personal debt, groceries, eating out, and entertainment. At the end of the month, total up how much you spend in each category. You might be surprised. Once you discover the truth, it might be easier to decrease unnecessary spending.

Remember that education is worth it—and you can pay for it. A college degree is one of the safest and most worthwhile investments you can make. Money invested in land, gold, oil, or stocks can be lost, but your education will last a lifetime.

In the long run, education pays off in increased income, job promotions, career satisfaction, and more creative use of your leisure time.

Most students can afford higher education. This includes using grants, scholarships, loans, and work-study placement. If you demonstrate financial need, you can usually get financial aid. In general, financial need equals the cost of your schooling minus the amount that you can reasonably be expected to pay. Receiving financial assistance has little to do with "being poor." Your prospects for aid depend greatly on the costs of the school you attend.

Create a master plan—a long-term budget listing how much you need to complete your education and where you plan to get the money. Having a plan for paying for your entire education makes completing your degree work a more realistic possibility.

Create money for the future. Saving is one of the most effective ways to reach your money goals. Aim to save at least 10 percent of your monthly take-home pay.

First, build a cushion for financial emergencies—savings equal to six months of your living expenses. Then save for major, long-term expenses.

Put your money into insured savings accounts, money market funds, savings bonds, or certificates of deposit. These are low-risk options that you can immediately turn into cash. Even a small amount of money set aside each month at compound interest can grow rapidly.

Remember that investing in stocks and bonds is risky. Invest only money that you can afford to lose. Consider something safe, such as Treasury securities (bills, notes, and bonds backed by the federal government), no-load mutual funds, or blue chip stocks.

Avoid taking a friend's advice on how to invest your hard-earned money. Be wary, too, of advice from someone who has something to sell, such as a stockbroker or a realtor. See your banker or an independent certified financial planner instead. ⌧

EDUCATION BY THE HOUR

Determine exactly what it costs you to go to school. Fill in the blanks below using totals for a semester, quarter, or whatever term system your school uses.

Note: Include only the costs that relate directly to going to school. For example, under "Transportation," list only the amount that you pay for gas to drive back and forth to school—not the total amount you spend on gas for a semester.

Tuition	$_____
Books	$_____
Fees	$_____
Transportation	$_____
Clothing	$_____
Food	$_____
Housing	$_____
Entertainment	$_____
Other (such as insurance, medical, childcare)	$_____
Subtotal	$_____
Salary you could earn per term if you weren't in school	$_____
Total (A)	$_____

Now figure out how many classes you attend in one term. This is the number of your scheduled class periods per week multiplied by the number of weeks in your school term. Put that figure below:

Total (B) _____

Divide the **Total (B)** into the **Total (A)** and put that amount here:

$_____

This is what it costs you to go to one class one time.

On a separate sheet of paper, describe your responses to discovering this figure. Also list anything you will do differently as a result of knowing the hourly cost of your education.

power process

Be here now

Being right here, right now is such a simple idea. It seems obvious. Where else can you be but where you are? When else can you be there but when you are there?

The answer is that you can be somewhere else at any time—in your head. It's common for our thoughts to distract us from where we've chosen to be. When we let this happen, we lose the benefits of focusing our attention on what's important to us in the present moment.

To "be here now" means to do what you're doing when you're doing it and to be where you are when you're there. Students consistently report that focusing attention on the here and now is one of the most powerful tools in this book.

Leaving the here and now

We all have a voice in our head that hardly ever shuts up. If you don't believe it, conduct this experiment: Close your eyes for 10 seconds and pay attention to what is going on in your head. Please do this right now.

Notice something? Perhaps your voice was saying, "Forget it. I'm in a hurry." Another might have said, "I wonder when 10 seconds is up." Another could have been saying, "What little voice? I don't hear any little voice." That's the voice.

This voice can take you anywhere at any time—especially when you are studying. When the voice takes you away, you might appear to be studying, but your brain is at the beach.

All of us have experienced this voice, as well as the absence of it. When our inner voices are silent, time no longer seems to exist. We forget worries, aches, pains, reasons, excuses, and justifications. We fully experience the here and now. Life is magic. There are many benefits of such a state of consciousness. It is easier to discover the world around us when we are not chattering away to ourselves about how we think it ought to be, has been, or

will be. Letting go of inner voices and pictures—being totally in the moment—is a powerful tool. Do not expect to be rid of daydreams entirely. That is neither possible nor desirable. Inner voices serve a purpose. They enable us to analyze, predict, classify, and understand events out there in the "real" world.

Your stream of consciousness serves a purpose. When you are working on a term paper, your inner voices might suggest ideas. When you are listening to your sociology instructor, your inner voices can alert you to possible test questions. When you're about to jump out of an airplane, they could remind you to take a parachute. The trick is to consciously choose when to be with your inner voices and when to let them go.

Returning to the here and now

A powerful step toward returning to the here and now is to notice when we leave it. Our mind has a mind of its own, and it seems to fight back when we try to control it too much. If you doubt this, for the next 10 seconds do not, under any circumstances, think of a pink elephant. Please begin not thinking about one now.

Persistent image, isn't it? Most ideas are this insistent when we try to deny them or force them out of our consciousness.

For example, during class you might notice yourself thinking about a test you took the previous day, or a party planned for the weekend, or the DVD player you'd like to have.

Instead of trying to force a stray thought out of your head—a futile enterprise—simply notice it. Accept it. Tell yourself, "There's that thought again." Then gently return your attention to the task at hand. That thought, or another, will come back. Your mind will drift. Simply notice again where your thoughts take you and gently bring yourself back to the here and now.

Another way to return to the here and now is to notice your physical sensations. Notice the way the room looks or smells. Notice the temperature and how the chair feels. Once you've regained control of your attention by becoming aware of your physical surroundings, you can more easily take the next step and bring your full attention back to your present task.

We can often immediately improve our effectiveness—and our enjoyment—by fully entering into each of our activities, doing one thing at a time.

For example, take something as simple as peeling and eating an orange. Carefully notice the color, shape, and texture of the orange. Hold it close to your nose and savor the pungent, sweet smell. Then slowly peel the orange and see if you can hear every subtle sound that results. Next take one piece of the orange and place it in your mouth. Notice the feel of the fruit on your tongue. Chew the piece slowly, letting the delicious juice bathe your taste buds. Take note of each individual sensation of pleasure that ripples through your body as you sample this delicious treat.

"Be here now" can turn the act of eating an orange into a rich experience. Imagine what can happen when you bring this quality of attention to almost everything that you do.

Choose when to be here now

Remember that no suggestion is absolute—including the suggestion to do one thing at a time with full, focused attention. Sometimes choosing to do two or more things at once is useful, even necessary. For example, you might study while doing laundry. You might ask your children to quiz you with flash cards while you fix dinner.

The key to this Power Process is to *choose*. When you choose, you overcome distractions and stay in charge of your attention.

Experiment with noticing your inner voices. Let go of the ones that prevent you from focusing on learning. Practice the process. Be here now, moment by moment.

To "be here now" means to do what you're doing when you're doing it and to be where you are when you're there.

The here and now in your future

You also can use this Power Process to keep yourself pointed toward your goals. In fact, one of the best ways to get what you want in the future is to realize that you do not have a future. The only time you have is right now.

The problem with this idea is that some students might think: "No future, huh? Terrific! Party time!" Being in the here and now, however, is not the same as living for today and forgetting about tomorrow.

Nor is the "be here now" idea a call to abandon goals. Goals are merely tools we create to direct our actions right now. They are useful only in the present. Goals, like our ideas of the past and future, are creations of our minds. The only time they are real is in the here and now.

The power of this idea lies in a simple but frequently overlooked fact: The only time to do anything is now. You can think about doing something next Wednesday. You can write about doing something next Wednesday. You can daydream, discuss, ruminate, speculate, and fantasize about what you will do next Wednesday.

But you can't do anything on Wednesday until it is Wednesday.

Sometimes students think of goals as things that exist in the misty future. And it's easy to postpone action on things in the misty future, especially when everyone else is going to a not-so-misty party.

However, the word *goal* comes from the Anglo-Saxon *gaelan,* which means "to hinder or impede," as in the case of a boundary. That's what a goal does. It restricts, in a positive way, our activity in the here and now. It channels our energy into actions that are more likely to get us what we really want. That's what goals are for. And they are useful only when they are directing action in the here and now.

The idea behind this Power Process is simple. When you plan for the future, plan for the future. When you listen to a lecture, listen to a lecture. When you read this book, read this book. And when you choose to daydream, daydream. Do what you're doing when you're doing it.

Be where you are when you're there. Be here now . . . and now . . . and now. ◪

put it to work

Being skilled at managing time and money will serve you in any career you choose. Following are ways that you can transfer techniques from this chapter to the workplace.

Monitor work time. Use the Time Monitor/Time Plan process to analyze the way you currently use your time at work. With this awareness, you can minimize downtime and boost your productivity. Look for low-value activities to eliminate. Also note your peak periods of energy during the workday and schedule your most challenging tasks for these times.

Use a long-term planner to manage major projects at work. Besides scheduling a due date for the final product, set interim due dates—what you'll produce at key points leading up to that final date. For example, you're planning to launch a new in-house training program in one year. Set individual due dates for finishing each major component of the program, such as manuals, Web sites, and videotapes.

Avoid the perils of multi-tasking. Our effectiveness often decreases when we try to do several things at once, such as talking on a cell phone while driving. When you get busy at work, you might feel tempted to multi-task. Yet studies indicate that multi-tasking reduces metabolic activity in the brain, lowers ability to complete tasks efficiently, and increases the number of errors made in following a procedure.[4] Turn to the Power Process: "Be here now" to find a solution. Plan your workday as a succession of tasks, then do each task with full attention. Use the ABC priority system to weed out tasks of lower importance. This can give you more time to focus on the A's.

Overcome procrastination. This problem is as widespread in the workplace as it is on any campus. Apply the suggestions from "The seven-day antiprocrastination plan" to work tasks as well as academic tasks.

Calculate the cost of attending meetings. Meetings are a way of life for countless people in the workplace. In fact, if you're in a management or supervisory position, meetings can take up most of your workday. See if you can modify the "Education by the hour" exercise to calculate what it costs you to attend a one-hour business meeting. With this data in hand, write an Intention Statement about how you plan to get the most value out of the meetings you will attend in the future.

Use a lifeline to chart your career path. Your career plan can extend decades into the future. Below are some possible lifeline entries for a person focusing on a career in education.

May 2009	Graduate with a teaching degree
August 2010	Begin teaching high school physics
September 2017	Begin saving 5 percent of income to fund a personal sabbatical
September 2021	Return to school for a graduate degree in school administration
September 2023	Begin career as a high school principal
September 2027	Take a one-year sabbatical to live and work part-time in New Zealand
September 2028	Return to job as a high school principal
January 2031	Begin a home-based consulting business advising teachers and principals about ways to avoid job burnout

Do long-term planning for your organization. The strategies for long-term planning in this chapter can help you set goals for your company that extend well into the future. For example, create a lifeline for your organization, listing specific outcomes to achieve during each of the next five years.

Name _____ Date _____/_____/_____

quiz

1. Time is referred to in this chapter as an "equal opportunity resource." List a reason for describing time in this way.

2. Describe the difference between a mid-term goal and a short-term goal.

3. Suppose that after you choose where to focus your attention, your mind wanders. The Power Process: "Be here now" suggests that one of the most effective ways to bring your focus back to the here and now is to:
   (a) Slap your cheek and shout, "Attention" as loudly as you can.
   (b) Notice that your thoughts have wandered and gently bring them back.
   (c) Sleep.
   (d) Concentrate as hard as you can to force distracting thoughts out of your head.
   (e) Ignore physical sensations.

4. What are at least five suggestions for getting the most out of now?

5. In time-management terms, what is meant by "This ain't no piano"?

6. Define "C fever" as it applies to the ABC priority method.

7. Making promises can be an effective strategy for managing time. True or False? Explain your answer.

8. Describe at least three strategies for overcoming procrastination.

9. According to this chapter, most money problems have a simple source. What is it?

10. List three ways to decrease expenses.

learning styles application

The questions below will "cycle" you through four styles, or modes, of learning as explained in the article "Learning styles: Discovering how you learn" in Chapter One. Each question will help you explore a different mode. You can answer the questions in any order.

what if *After implementing a method of improving your planning skills from this chapter, consider how well this new method has worked for you. Which actions do you intend to continue on a regular basis? Are there any new actions you intend to take?*

why *Suppose that you could use the techniques in this chapter to free up four additional hours each week to do whatever you please. Describe the things you would do with this extra time and why these activities matter to you.*

how *Choose one technique from this chapter and create a plan for how you will implement this strategy in your life. Then put this experiment into action.*

what *Choose three techniques from this chapter that you could use to free up four additional hours in the next week. Summarize those techniques in a single phrase or sentence and list them here.*

master student

profile

RON BROWN

(1941–1996) first African American secretary of commerce and first African American chairman of the Democratic National Committee. Died in a plane crash in Bosnia while on a diplomatic mission.

Ron Brown was born in Washington, D.C., to William and Gloria Brown, both graduates of Howard University. The family moved to New York City when he was relatively young. His father managed the legendary Hotel Theresa in Harlem. Here, Ron encountered the social, artistic, political, and powerful elite of the African American community. He encountered people who ran the race of life brilliantly, daring to be first in what they did. They were people like Jackie Robinson, the first African American to play professional baseball; W. E. B. Du Bois, one of the first African Americans to receive a Ph.D. from Harvard; Duke Ellington, one of the first African Americans to own and lead an internationally acclaimed big band; Ralph Ellison, one of the first widely successful African American writers; Adam Clayton Powell, the first African American congressman from Harlem. . . . Often as he peered out of the twelfth floor window of the Hotel Theresa, and observed the hustle and bustle of 125th St. below, he realized how easy it was to get lost in the superficial crowd of everyday life. He realized that the view from the top was a little better than the view from the bottom and that the Hotel Theresa with its legendary reputation and world famous clientele was simply his personal tutoring ground, training him to see above and beyond the crowded streets of New York City.

From the many heated discussions that Ron was involved in at the Hotel Theresa, Ron developed an agile mind and a disciplined tongue. He became almost invincible in his ability to present sound and convincing arguments. In this black cultural Mecca, he studied how creative, artistic, and powerful African American people behaved. He learned early that hard work, commitment, and perseverance characterized people of position and power. He learned the importance of appearance, preparation, and personal influence in the race called life as he listened intensely to guests' lively stories and daring escapades of world travel.

With this strong sense of self and the willingness to seek different academic and cultural experiences, he got himself accepted by Middlebury College in rural Vermont. This was significant, in that Middlebury was the first college known to have graduated an African American (Alexander L. Twight, in 1823). At Middlebury, far from the blacktop boulevards and the high-rise tenements of Harlem, Ron really began to excel. He was the first black initiated into the Middlebury chapter of the national, all-white fraternity Sigma Phi Epsilon, which eventually lost its national charter because of his induction. . . .

Paramount in Ronald Harmon Brown's strategies for success was knowing how to solicit trust from himself. He learned early to accept himself for who he was and what he could or couldn't do. Knowing his own strengths and weaknesses, he never shortchanged himself. He learned self-reliance by preparing for every area of his life. He was confident in his ability to lead, orchestrate, mediate, and guide. He knew the importance of building lasting relationships. . . .

Ron Brown's life shouts to each of us, "Be your own best cheerleader. Root for a winner. Be that winner yourself." ◼

Osborne Robinson, Jr., *African American Master Student Profiles.* Copyright © 1998 by Houghton Mifflin Company. Reprinted with permission.

For more biographical information about Ron Brown, visit the Master Student Hall of Fame on the *Becoming a Master Student* Web site at

masterstudent.college.hmco.com

3

Memory

"*The one technique of* Becoming a Master Student *that has helped me the most is definitely going over and repeating the material within 24 hours. After reading about it, I decided to try it and it truly made a difference when it came time to take a test.*"

—MACHEALA JACQUEZ

why
this chapter matters . . .

Learning memory techniques can boost your skills at test taking, reading, note taking, and many other academic tasks.

what
is included . . .

Take your memory out of the closet
The memory jungle
Choosing to remember
Remembering names
Mnemonic devices
Power Process: "Love your problems (and experience your barriers)"
Master Student Profile: Cesar Chavez

how
you can use this chapter . . .

Focus your attention.
Make conscious choices about what to remember.
Recall facts and ideas with more ease.

As you read, ask yourself
what if . . .

I could use my memory to its full potential?

Take your memory out of the closet

Once upon a time, people talked about human memory as if it were a closet. You stored individual memories there like old shirts and stray socks. Remembering something was a matter of rummaging through all that stuff. If you were lucky, you found what you wanted.

This view of memory creates some problems. For one thing, closets can get crowded. Things too easily disappear. Even with the biggest closet, you eventually run out of space. If you want to pack some new memories in there—well, too bad. There's no room. Brain researchers have shattered this image to bits. Memory is not a closet. It's not a place or a thing. Instead, memory is a *process*.

On a conscious level, memories appear as distinct and unconnected mental events: words, sensations, images. They can include details from the distant past—the smell of cookies baking in your grandmother's kitchen or the feel of sunlight warming your face through the window of your first-grade classroom. On a biological level, each of those memories involves millions of nerve cells, or neurons, firing chemical messages to each other. If you could observe these exchanges in real time, you'd see regions of cells all over the brain glowing with electrical charges at speeds that would put a computer to shame.

When a series of cells connects several times in a similar pattern, the result is a memory. Psychologist Donald Hebb uses the aphorism "Neurons which fire together, wire together" to describe this principle.[1] This means that memories are not really "stored." Instead, remembering is a process in which you *encode* information as links between active neurons that fire together and *decode*, or reactivate, neurons that wired together in the past. Memory is the probability that certain patterns of brain activity will occur again in the future. In effect, you re-create a memory each time you recall it.

Whenever you learn something new, your brain changes physically by growing more connections between neurons. The more you learn, the greater the number of connections. For all practical purposes, there's no limit to how many memories your brain can encode.

There's a lot you can do to wire those neural networks into place. That's where the memory techniques described in this chapter come into play. Step out of your crowded mental closet into a world of infinite possibilities.

journal entry 8

Discovery/Intention Statement

Write a sentence or two describing the way you feel when you want to remember something but have trouble doing so. Think of a specific incident in which you experienced this problem, such as trying to remember someone's name or a fact you needed during a test.

I discovered that I . . .

_____

_____

_____

Now spend five minutes skimming this chapter and find three to five memory strategies you think could be helpful. List the strategies below and note the page numbers where they are explained. Then write an Intention Statement scheduling a time to study them in more detail.

Strategy   *Page number*

_____

_____

_____

_____

I intend to . . .

_____

_____

_____

_____

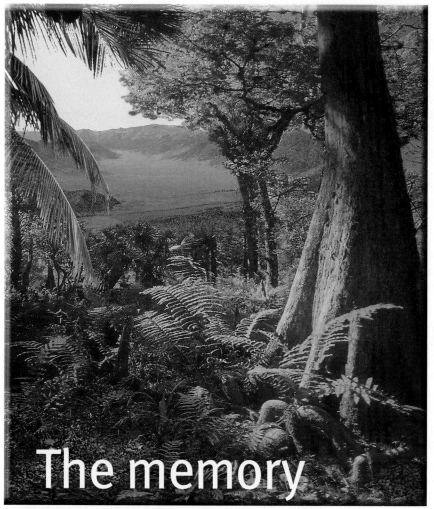

The memory jungle

Think of your memory as a vast, overgrown jungle. This memory jungle is thick with wild plants, exotic shrubs, twisted trees, and creeping vines. It spreads over thousands of square miles— dense, tangled, forbidding.

The more often you recall information, and the more often you put the same information into your memory, the easier it is to find.

Imagine that the jungle is encompassed on all sides by towering mountains. There is only one entrance to the jungle, a small meadow that is reached by a narrow pass through the mountains.

In the jungle there are animals, millions of them. The animals represent all of the information in your memory. Imagine that every thought, mental picture, or perception you ever had is represented by an animal in this jungle. Every single event ever perceived by any of your five senses—sight, touch, hearing, smell, or taste—has also passed through the meadow and entered the jungle. Some of the thought animals, such as the color of your seventh-grade teacher's favorite sweater, are well hidden. Other thoughts, such as your cell phone number or the position of the reverse gear in your car, are easier to find.

There are two rules of the memory jungle. Each thought animal must pass through the meadow at the entrance to the jungle. And once an animal enters the jungle, it never leaves.

The meadow represents short-term memory. You use this kind of memory when you look up a telephone number and hold it in your memory long enough to make a call. Short-term memory appears to have a limited capacity (the meadow is small) and disappears fast (animals pass through the meadow quickly).

The jungle itself represents long-term memory. This is the kind of memory that allows you to recall information from day to day, week to week, and year to year. Remember that thought animals never leave the long-term memory jungle. The following visualizations can help you recall useful concepts about memory.

Visualization #1: A well-worn path

Imagine what happens as a thought, in this case we'll call it an elephant, bounds across short-term memory and into the jungle. The elephant leaves a trail of broken twigs and footprints that you can follow. Brain research suggests that thoughts can wear paths in the memory.[2] These paths are called *neural traces*. The more well-worn the neural trace, the easier it is to retrieve (find) the thought. In other words, the more often the elephant retraces the path, the clearer the path becomes. The more often you recall information, and the more often you put the same information into your memory, the easier it is to find. When you buy a new car, for example, the first few times you try to find reverse, you have to think for a moment. After you have found reverse gear every day for a week, the path is worn into your memory. After a year, the path is so well-worn that when you dream about driving your car backward, you even dream the correct motion for putting the gear in reverse.

Visualization #2: A herd of thoughts

The second picture you can use to your advantage is the picture of many animals gathering at a clearing—like thoughts gathering at a central location in the memory. It is easier to retrieve thoughts that are grouped together, just as it is easier to find a herd of animals than it is to find a single elephant.

Pieces of information are easier to recall if you can associate them with similar information. For example,

you can more readily remember a particular player's batting average if you can associate it with other baseball statistics.

Visualization #3: Turning your back

Imagine releasing the elephant into the jungle, turning your back, and counting to 10. When you turn around, the elephant is gone. This is exactly what happens to most of the information you receive.

Generally, we can recall only 50 percent of the material we have just read. Within 24 hours, most of us can recall only about 20 percent. This means that 80 percent of the material has not been encoded and is wandering around, lost in the memory jungle.

The remedy is simple: Review quickly. Do not take your eyes off the thought animal as it crosses the short-

term memory meadow, and review it soon after it enters the long-term memory jungle. Wear a path in your memory immediately.

Visualization #4: You are directing the animal traffic

The fourth picture is one with you in it. You are standing at the entrance to the short-term memory meadow, directing herds of thought animals as they file through the pass,

across the meadow, and into your long-term memory. You are taking an active role in the learning process. You are paying attention. You are doing more than sitting on a rock and watching the animals file past into your brain. You have become part of the process, and in doing so, you have taken control of your memory. ⬚

Experience these visualizations online at ⬤ masterstudent.college.hmco.com

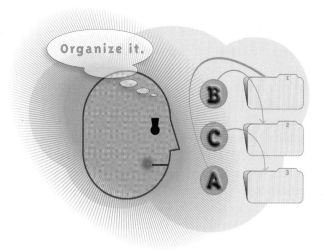

Organize it.

B
C
A

Choosing to remember

Experiment with these techniques to develop a flexible, custom-made memory system that fits your style of learning.

The techniques are divided into four categories. Each category represents a general principle for improving memory: organize it, use your body, use your brain, and recall it.

Organize it

Be selective. To a large degree, the art of memory is the art of selecting what to remember in the first place.

As you dig into your textbooks and notes, make choices about what is most important to learn. Imagine that you are going to create a test on the material and consider the questions you would ask.

Make it meaningful. One way to create meaning from your reading and notes is to learn from the general to the specific. Before you begin your next reading assignment, skim it to locate the main idea. If you're ever lost, step back and look at the big picture. The details might then make more sense.

Create associations. To remember more, associate new facts and ideas with something you already know.

Think about your favorite courses, for example. They probably relate to subjects that you already know something about.

Even when you're tackling a new subject, you can build a mental store of basic background information—the raw material for creating associations. Preview reading assignments, and complete those readings before you attend lectures. Before taking upper-level courses, master the prerequisites.

Use your body

Learn it once, actively. According to an old saying, we remember what we *do* far more than what we see or hear. This statement might not be scientifically accurate, but the underlying principle is sound.

To remember an idea, go beyond thinking about it. *Do* something with it.

You can use simple, direct methods to infuse your learning with action. When you sit at your desk, sit up straight. Sit on the edge of your chair, as if you were about to spring out of it and sprint across the room.

Also experiment with standing up when you study. It's harder to fall asleep in this position. Some people insist that their brains work better when they stand.

Pace back and forth and gesture as you recite material out loud. Use your hands. Get your whole body involved in studying.

Relax. When you're relaxed, you absorb new information quickly and recall it with greater ease.

Relaxing might seem to contradict the idea of active learning, but it doesn't. Being relaxed is not the same as being drowsy, zoned out, or asleep. You can be active, alert, *and* relaxed.

Create pictures. Draw diagrams. Make cartoons. Use these images to connect facts and illustrate relationships. Associations within and among abstract concepts can be "seen" and recalled more easily when they are visualized. Use your imagination.

For example, Boyle's law states that at a constant temperature, the volume of a confined ideal gas varies inversely with its pressure. Simply put, cutting the volume in half doubles the pressure. To remember this concept, you might picture someone "doubled over" using a bicycle pump. As she increases the pressure in the pump by decreasing the volume in the pump cylinder, she seems to be getting angrier. By the time she has doubled the pressure (and halved the volume) she is boiling ("Boyle-ing") mad.

Recite and repeat. When you repeat something out loud, you anchor the concept in two different senses. First, you get the physical sensation in your throat, tongue, and lips when voicing the concept. Second, you hear it. The combined result is synergistic, just as it is when you create pictures. That is, the effect of using two different senses is greater than the sum of their individual effects.

Write it down. This technique is obvious, yet easy to forget. Writing a note to yourself is a physical action that helps you remember an idea—even if you never look at the note again.

Writing engages a different kind of memory than speaking. Writing prompts us to be more logical, coherent, and complete. Written reviews reveal gaps in knowledge that oral reviews miss, just as oral reviews reveal gaps that written reviews miss.

Another advantage of written reviews is that they more closely match the way you're asked to remember materials in school. During your academic career, you'll probably take far more written exams than oral exams. Writing can be an effective way to prepare for such tests.

Use your brain

Engage your emotions. One powerful way to enhance your memory is to make friends with your amygdala. This is an area of your brain that lights up with extra neural activity each time you feel a strong emotion. When a topic excites love, laughter, or fear, the amygdala sends a flurry of chemical messages that say, in effect: *This information is important and useful. Don't forget it.*

You can use this strategy even when a subject seems boring at first. If you're not naturally interested in a topic, then create interest. Find a study partner in the class—if possible, someone you know and like—or form a study group. Also consider getting to know the instructor personally. When a course creates a bridge to human relationships, you engage the content in a more emotional way.

Overlearn. One way to fight mental fuzziness is to learn more than you need to know about a subject simply to pass a test. You can pick a subject apart, examine it, add to it, and go over it until it becomes second nature.

This technique is especially effective for problem solving. Do the

•Amygdala

The amygdala, highlighted in this illustration, is an area of your brain that sends neural messages associated with strong emotions. When you link new material to something that you feel strongly about, you activate this part of your brain. In turn, you're more likely to remember that material.

assigned problems, and then do more problems. The potential rewards are speed, accuracy, and greater confidence at exam time.

Be aware of attitudes. If you think a subject is boring, remind yourself that everything is related to everything else. Look for connections that relate to your own interests.

For example, consider a person who is fanatical about cars. She can rebuild a motor in a weekend and has a good time doing so. From this apparently specialized interest, she can explore a wide realm of knowledge. She can relate the workings of an engine to principles of physics, math, and chemistry. Computerized parts in newer cars can lead her to the study of data processing. She can research how the automobile industry has changed our cities and helped create suburbs, a topic that includes urban planning, sociology, business, economics, psychology, and history.

Being aware of your attitudes is not the same as fighting them or struggling to give them up. Acknowledge them. Notice them. Simple awareness can deflate an attitude that is blocking your memory.

Keep your brain fit for life. Your brain is an organ that needs regular care and exercise. Higher education promotes brain fitness. In addition, adopt habits to keep your brain lean and fit for the rest of your life.

One is to seek out new experiences. If you sit at a desk most of the workday, take a dance class. If you seldom travel, start reading maps of new locations and plan a cross-country trip. Seek out new museums, theaters, concerts, and other cultural events. Even after you graduate, consider taking classes for fun. Your brain thrives on novelty. Build it into your life.

Also take care of your health. Exercising regularly, staying tobacco-free, and getting plenty of sleep can reduce your risk of cancer, heart disease, stroke, and other conditions that interfere with memory. Eating well also helps. A diet rich in fruits and vegetables boosts your supply of antioxidants—natural chemicals that nourish your brain. Drink alcohol moderately, if at all.

Recall it

Remember something else. When you are stuck and can't remember something that you're sure you know, remember something else that is related to it.

If you can't remember your great-aunt's name, remember your great-uncle's name. During an economics exam, if you can't remember anything about the aggregate demand curve, recall what you do know about the aggregate supply curve.

Notice when you do remember. To develop your memory, notice when you recall information easily and ask yourself what memory techniques you're using naturally. Also notice when it's difficult to recall information. Get the facts and then adjust your learning techniques. And remember to congratulate yourself when you remember.

Use it before you lose it. To remember something, access it a lot. Read it, write it, speak it, listen to it, apply it—find some way to make contact with the material regularly.

Another way to make contact with the material is to teach it. Teaching demands mastery. When you explain the function of the pancreas to a fellow student, you discover quickly whether you really understand it yourself.

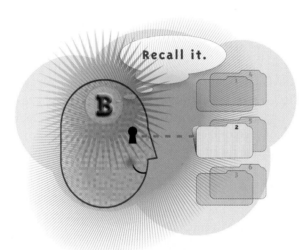

Recall it.

Adopt the attitude that you never forget. You might not believe that an idea or a thought never leaves your memory. That's OK.

Test the concept. Instead of saying, "I don't remember," say, "It will come to me." The latter statement implies that the information you want is encoded in your brain and that you can retrieve it—just not right now.

People sometimes use the flip side of this technique. "I never remember anything," they say over and over again. Perhaps that kind of negative talk is self-fulfilling.

Instead, use affirmations that support you in developing your memory: "I recall information easily and accurately." "At any time I choose, I will be able to recall key facts and ideas." "My memory serves me well."

Or even "I choose to remember." ✖

➔ Set a trap for your memory

When you want to remind yourself to do something, link this activity to another event you know will take place. The key is to "trap" your memory by picking events that are certain to occur.

Say that you're walking to class and suddenly remember that your accounting assignment is due tomorrow. Switch your watch to the opposite wrist. Now you're "trapped." Every time you glance at your wrist and remember that you have switched your watch, it becomes a reminder that you were supposed to remember something else. (You can do the same with a ring.)

If you empty your pockets every night, put an unusual item in your pocket in the morning to remind yourself to do something before you go to bed. For example, to remember to call your younger sister on her birthday, pick an object from the playpen—a teething toy, perhaps—and

put it in your pocket. When you empty your pocket that evening and find the teething toy, you're more likely to make the call.

Everyday rituals that are seldom neglected, such as feeding a pet, listening to the weather report, and unlacing shoes, provide opportunities for setting traps. For example, tie a triple knot in your shoelace as a reminder to set the alarm for your early morning study group meeting. You can even use imaginary traps. To remember to write a check for the phone bill, picture your phone hanging on the front door. In your mind, create the feeling of reaching for the doorknob and grabbing the phone instead. When you get home and reach to open the front door, the image is apt to return to you.

Link two activities together, and make the association unusual.

USE Q-CARDS TO REINFORCE MEMORY

One memory strategy you might find useful involves a special kind of flash card. It's called a *Question Card*, or *Q-Card* for short.

To create a standard flash card, you write a question on one side of a 3x5 card and its answer on the other side. Q-Cards have a question on *both* sides. Here's the trick: The question on each side of the card contains the answer to the question on the other side.

The questions you write on Q-Cards can draw on both lower- and higher-order thinking skills. Writing these questions forces you to encode material in different ways. You activate more areas of your brain and burn the concepts even deeper into your memory.

For example, say that you want to remember the subject of the 18th Amendment to the United States Constitution, the one that prohibited the sale of alcohol. On one side of a 3x5 card, write *What amendment prohibited the sale of alcohol?* Turn the card over and write *What did the 18th Amendment do?*

To get the most from Q-Cards:

- Add a picture to each side of the card. This helps you learn concepts faster and develop a more visual learning style.

- Read the questions and recite the answers out loud. Two keys to memory are repetition and novelty, so use a different voice whenever you read and recite. Whisper the first time you go through your cards; then shout or sing the next time. Doing this develops an auditory learning style.

- Carry Q-Cards with you and pull them out during waiting times. To develop a kinesthetic learning style, handle your cards often.

- Create a Q-Card for each new and important concept within 24 hours after attending a class or completing an assignment. This is your *active stack* of cards. Keep answering the questions on these cards until you learn each new concept.

- Review all of the cards from the term for a certain subject on one day each week. For example, on Monday, review all cards from biology; on Tuesday, review all cards from history. These cards make up your *review stacks*.

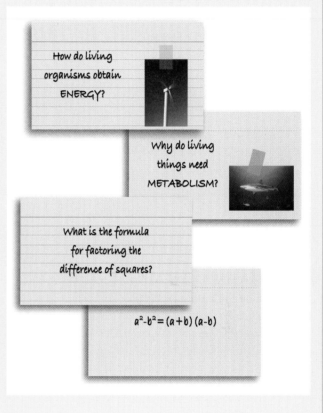

Notable failures

You might feel discouraged about your failure to remember information at critical moments, such as during a test. Before you despair over your test scores or grade point average, remember that history is filled with examples of people who struggled academically and then went on to achieve great things. These notable failures, some of whom are listed below, are emblazoned in our collective memory, while their detractors are long forgotten.

Einstein was four years old before he could speak and seven before he could read. **Isaac Newton** did poorly in grade school. **Beethoven**'s music teacher once said of him, "As a composer he is hopeless."

When **Thomas Edison** was a boy, his teachers told him he was too stupid to learn anything. **F. W. Woolworth** got a job in a dry goods store when he was 21, but his employers would not let him wait on customers because he "didn't have enough sense."

A newspaper editor fired **Walt Disney**, claiming that he had "no good ideas." **Caruso**'s music teacher told him,

"You can't sing. You have no voice at all." The director of the Imperial Opera in Vienna told **Madame Schumann-Heink** that she would never be a singer and advised her to buy a sewing machine. **Leo Tolstoy** flunked out of college. **Wernher von Braun** flunked ninth-grade algebra. Admiral **Richard E. Byrd** had been retired from the navy as "unfit for service" until he flew over both Poles.

Louis Pasteur was rated as "mediocre" in chemistry when he attended the Royal College. **Abraham Lincoln** entered the Black Hawk War as a captain and came out as a private. **Louisa May Alcott** was told by an editor that she could never write anything that would have popular appeal. **Fred Waring** was once rejected for high school chorus. **Winston Churchill** failed the sixth grade.

"Humbling Cases for Career Counselors," by Dr. Milton E. Larson, from *Phi Delta Kappan,* February 1973 issue, Volume LVI, no. 6, p. 374. © 1973. Reprinted by permission.

exercise 10

REMEMBERING YOUR CAR KEYS— OR ANYTHING ELSE

Pick something you frequently forget. Some people chronically lose their car keys or forget to write down checks in their check register. Others let anniversaries and birthdays slip by.

Pick an item or a task you're prone to forget. Then design a strategy for remembering it. Use any of the techniques from this chapter, research others, or make up your own from scratch. Describe your technique and the results in the space below.

_____

_____

_____

_____

In this exercise, as in most of the exercises in this book, a failure is also a success. Don't be concerned with whether your technique will work. Design it, and then find out. If it doesn't work for you this time, use another method.

journal entry 9

Discovery Statement

Take a minute to reflect on the memory techniques in this chapter. You probably use some of them already without being aware of it. In the space below, list at least three techniques you have used in the past and describe how you used them.

_____

_____

_____

_____

_____

_____

_____

_____

_____

_____

_____

Remembering names

One powerful way to immediately practice memory techniques is to use them to remember names.

Recite and repeat in conversation. When you hear a person's name, repeat it. Immediately say it to yourself several times without moving your lips. You could also repeat the name out loud in a way that does not sound forced or artificial: "I'm pleased to meet you, Maria."

Ask the other person to recite and repeat. You can let other people help you remember their names. After you've been introduced to someone, ask that person to spell the name and pronounce it correctly for you. Most people will be flattered by the effort you're making to learn their names.

Visualize. After the conversation, construct a brief visual image of the person. For a memorable image, make it unusual. Imagine the name painted in hot pink fluorescent letters on the person's forehead.

Admit you don't know. Admitting that you can't remember someone's name can actually put people at ease. Most of them will sympathize if you say, "I'm working to remember names better. Yours is right on the tip of my tongue. What is it again?" (By the way, that's exactly what psychologists call that feeling—the "tip of the tongue" phenomenon.)

Introduce yourself again. Most of the time we assume introductions are one-shot affairs. If we miss a name the first time around, our hopes for remembering it are dashed. Instead of giving up, reintroduce yourself: "Hello, again. We met earlier. I'm Jesse, and please tell me your name again."

Use associations. Link each person you meet with one characteristic that you find interesting or unusual. For example, you could make a mental note: "Vicki Cheng—long, black hair" or "James Washington—horn-rimmed glasses." To reinforce your associations, write them on 3x5 cards as soon as you can.

Limit the number of new names you learn at one time. Occasionally, we find ourselves in situations where we're introduced to many people at the same time: "Dad, these are all the people in my Boy Scout troop." "Let's take a tour so you can meet all 32 people in this department."

When meeting a group of people, concentrate on remembering just two or three names. Free yourself from feeling obligated to remember everyone. Few of the people in mass introductions expect you to remember their names. Another way to avoid memory overload is to limit yourself to learning just first names. Last names can come later.

Ask for photos. In some cases, you might be able to get photos of all the people you meet. For example, a small business where you apply for a job might have a brochure with pictures of all the employees. Ask for individual or group photos and write in the names if they're not included. You can use these photos as "flash cards" as you drill yourself on names.

Go early. Consider going early to conventions, parties, and classes. Sometimes just a few people show up on time at these occasions. That means fewer names for you to remember. And as more people arrive, you can overhear them being introduced to others—an automatic review for you.

Make it a game. In situations where many people are new to one another, consider pairing up with another person and staging a contest. Challenge each other to remember as many new names as possible. Then choose an "award"—such as a movie ticket or free meal—for the person who wins.

Intend to remember. The simple act of focusing your attention at key moments can do wonders for your memory. Test this idea for yourself. The next time you're introduced to someone, direct 100 percent of your attention to hearing that person's name. Do this consistently and see what happens to your ability to remember names.

The intention to remember can be more powerful than any single memory technique. ⊠

It's pronounced *ne-mon´-ik.* The word refers to tricks that can increase your ability to recall everything from grocery lists to speeches.

Mnemonic devices

Some entertainers use mnemonic devices to perform "impossible" feats of memory, such as recalling the names of everyone in a large audience after hearing them just once. Waiters use mnemonics to take orders from several tables without the aid of pad and pencil. Using mnemonic devices, speakers can go for hours without looking at their notes. The possibilities for students are endless.

There is a catch. Mnemonic devices have three serious limitations.

First, they don't always help you understand or digest material. Instead of encouraging critical thinking skills, mnemonics rely only on rote memorization.

Second, the mnemonic device itself is sometimes complicated to learn and time-consuming to develop. It

might take more energy to create such a device than to memorize something by using a more traditional memory technique, such as repetition.

Third, mnemonic devices can be forgotten. Recalling a mnemonic device might be as hard as recalling the material itself.

In spite of their limitations, mnemonic devices can be powerful. There are five general categories: new words, creative sentences, rhymes and songs, the loci system, and the peg system.

New words

Acronyms are words created from the initial letters of a series of words. Examples include NASA (**N**ational

Aeronautics and Space Administration), radar (**ra**dio **d**etecting **a**nd **r**anging), scuba (**s**elf-**c**ontained **u**nderwater **b**reathing **a**pparatus), and laser (**l**ight **a**mplification by **s**timulated **e**mission of **r**adiation). You can make up your own acronyms to recall series of facts. A common mnemonic acronym is Roy G. Biv, which has helped thousands of students remember the colors of the visible spectrum (**r**ed, **o**range, **y**ellow, **g**reen, **b**lue, **i**ndigo, and **v**iolet). IPMAT helps biology students remember the stages of cell division (**i**nterphase, **p**rophase, **m**etaphase, **a**naphase, and **t**elophase).

Creative sentences

Acrostics are sentences that help you remember a series of letters that stand for something. For example, the first letters of the words in the sentence "Every good boy does fine" (E, G, B, D, and F) are the music notes of the lines of the treble clef staff.

Rhymes and songs

Madison Avenue advertising executives spend billions of dollars a year on commercials designed to burn their messages into your memory. Coca-Cola's song, "It's the Real Thing," practically stands for Coca-Cola, despite the fact that the soda contains artificial ingredients.

Rhymes have been used for centuries to teach children basic facts: "In fourteen hundred and ninety-two, Columbus sailed the ocean blue" or "Thirty days hath September."

The loci system

The word *loci* is the plural of *locus*, a synonym for *place* or *location*. Use this system to create visual associations with familiar locations. Unusual associations are the easiest to remember.

Example 1

The loci system is an old one. Ancient Greek orators used it to remember long speeches. For example, if an orator's position was that road taxes must be raised to pay for school equipment, his loci visualizations might have looked like the following.

First, as he walks in the door of his house, he imagines a large *porpoise* jumping through a hoop. This reminds him to begin by telling the audience the *purpose* of his speech.

Next, he visualizes his living room floor covered with paving stones, forming a road leading into the kitchen. In the kitchen, he pictures dozens of schoolchildren sitting on the floor because they have no desks.

Now it's the day of the big speech. The Greek politician is nervous. He is perspiring, and his toga sticks to his body. He stands up to give his speech, and his mind goes blank. Then he starts thinking to himself:

I am so nervous that I can hardly remember my name. But no problem—I can remember the rooms in my house. Let's see, I'm walking in the front door and—wow! I see the porpoise. That reminds me to talk about the purpose of my speech. And then there's that road leading to the kitchen. Say, what are all those kids doing there on the floor? Oh, yeah, now I remember—they have no desks! We need to raise taxes on roads to pay for their desks and the other stuff they need in classrooms.

Example 2

The loci system can also be based on parts of your body. When studying biology, for instance, use the loci system to memorize the order of structures of living things.

Start with your toes, the lowest points of your body. Associate them with the lowest structure of living things—*atoms*.

The top of your head is the highest point on your body. So associate it with the highest order of living things—*biosystems*, or groups of species.

Then associate the intermediate structures with points on your body between your head and toes.

exercise 11

BE A POET

Construct your own mnemonic device for remembering some of the memory techniques in this chapter. Make up a poem, jingle, acronym, or acrostic, or use another mnemonic system. Describe your mnemonic device in the space below.

_____

_____

_____

_____

_____

_____

Link *molecules* to your feet.
Link *cells* to your ankles.
Link *tissues* with your knees.
Link *organs* with your waist.
Link *organ systems* with your chest.
Link *organisms* with your neck.

The peg system

This technique employs key words that are paired with numbers. Each word forms a "peg" on which you can "hang" mental associations. To use this system effectively, learn the following peg words and their associated numbers well:

bun goes with 1	*sticks* goes with 6
shoe goes with 2	*heaven* goes with 7
tree goes with 3	*gate* goes with 8
door goes with 4	*wine* goes with 9
hive goes with 5	*hen* goes with 10

Believe it or not, you can use the peg system to remember the Bill of Rights (the first ten amendments to the United States Constitution). For example, amendment number *four* is about protection from unlawful search and seizure. Imagine people knocking at your *door* who are demanding to search your home. This amendment means that you do not have to open your door unless those people have a proper search warrant. ⊠

PRACTICING CRITICAL THINKING 3

Take five minutes to remember a time when you enjoyed learning something. In the space below, describe that experience in a sentence or two. Then make a brief list of the things you found enjoyable about that experience.

_____

_____

Within the next 24 hours, compare your list with those of other classmates. Look for similarities and differences in the descriptions of your learning experiences.

Based on your comparison, form a tentative explanation about what makes learning enjoyable for people. Summarize your explanation here:

_____

_____

_____

_____

_____

MOVE FROM PROBLEMS TO SOLUTIONS

Students who enter higher education immediately face the decision about whether to *stay* in higher education. You can promote your chances of thriving in school by anticipating possible barriers to your success and putting solutions in place now.

Many students find it easy to complain about school and dwell on problems. This exercise gives you an opportunity to change that habit and respond creatively to any problem you're currently experiencing.

The key is to dwell more on solutions than on problems. Do that by inventing as many solutions as possible for any given problem. Shifting the emphasis of your conversation from problems to solutions raises your sense of possibility and unleashes the master learner within you.

In the space below, describe at least three problems that could interfere with your success as a student. The problems can be related to courses, teachers, personal relationships, finances, or anything else that might get in the way of your success.

My problem is that . . .

_____

_____

_____

_____

_____

My problem is that . . .

_____

_____

_____

_____

_____

My problem is that . . .

_____

_____

_____

_____

Next, brainstorm at least five possible solutions to each of those problems. Ten is even better. You might find it hard to come up with that many ideas. That's OK. Stick with it. Stay in the inquiry, give yourself time, and ask other people for ideas.

I could solve my problem by . . .

_____

_____

_____

_____

_____

_____

I could solve my problem by . . .

_____

_____

_____

_____

_____

_____

I could solve my problem by . . .

_____

_____

_____

_____

_____

_____

power process

Love your problems
(and experience your barriers)

We all have problems and barriers that block our progress or prevent us from moving into new areas. Often, the way we respond to our problems puts boundaries on our experiences. We place limitations on what we allow ourselves to be, do, and have.

Our problems might include fear of speaking in front of a group, anxiety about math problems, or reluctance to sound ridiculous when learning a foreign language. We might have a barrier about looking silly when trying something new. Some of us even have anxiety about being successful.

Problems often work like barriers. When we bump up against one of our problems, we usually turn away and start walking along a different path. And all of a sudden—bump!—we've struck another barrier. And we turn away again. As we continue to bump into problems and turn away from them, our lives stay inside the same old boundaries. Inside these boundaries, we are unlikely to have new adventures. We are unlikely to improve or to make much progress.

The word *problem* is a wonderful word coming from the ancient Greek word *proballein,* which means "to throw forward." In other words, problems are there to provide an opportunity for us to gain new skills. If we respond to problems by loving them instead of resisting them, we can expand the boundaries in which we live our lives. When approached with acceptance, and even love, problems can "throw" us forward.

Three ways to handle a barrier

It's natural to have barriers, but sometimes they limit our experience so much that we get bored, angry, or frustrated with life. When this happens, consider the following three ways of dealing with a barrier. One way is to pretend it doesn't exist. Avoid it; deny it; lie about it. It's like turning your head the other way, putting on a fake grin, and saying, "See, there's really no problem at all. Everything is fine. Oh, that problem. That's not a problem—it's not really there."

In addition to making us look foolish, this approach leaves the barrier intact, and we keep bumping into it. We deny the barrier and might not even be aware that we're bumping into it. For example, a student who has a barrier about math might subconsciously avoid enriching experiences that include math.

A second approach is to fight the barrier, to struggle against it. This usually makes the barrier grow. It increases the barrier's magnitude. A person who is obsessed with weight might constantly worry about being fat. She might struggle with it every day, trying diet after diet. And the more she struggles, the bigger the problem gets.

The third alternative is to love the barrier. Accept it. Totally experience it. Tell the truth about it. Describe it in detail. When you do this, the barrier loses its power. You can literally love it to death.

The word *love* might sound like an overstatement. In this Power Process, the word means to accept your problems, to allow and permit them. When we fight a problem, it grows bigger. The more we struggle against it, the stronger it seems to become. When we accept the fact that we have a problem, we are more likely to find effective ways to deal with it.

Suppose one of your barriers is being afraid of speaking in front of a group. You can use any of these three approaches.

First, you can get up in front of the group and pretend that you're not afraid. You can fake a smile, not admitting to yourself or the group that you have any concerns about speaking—even though your legs have turned to rubber bands and your mind to jelly. The problem is that everyone in the room, including you, will know you're scared when your hands start shaking, your voice cracks, and you forget what you were going to say.

The second way to approach this barrier is to fight it. You can tell yourself, "I'm not going to be scared," and then try to keep your knees from knocking. Generally, this doesn't work. In fact, your knee-knocking might get worse.

The third approach is to go to the front of the room, look out into the audience, and say to yourself, "I am scared. I notice that my knees are shaking and my mouth feels dry, and I'm having a rush of thoughts about what might happen if I say the wrong thing. Yup, I'm scared, and that's OK. As a matter of fact, it's just part of me, so I accept it and I'm not going to try to fight it. I'm going to give this speech even though I'm scared." You might not actually eliminate the fear; however, your barrier about the fear—which is what inhibits you—might disappear. And you might discover that if you examine the fear, love it, accept it, and totally experience it, the fear itself also disappears.

Applying this process

Applying this process is easier if you remember three ideas. First, loving a problem is not necessarily the same as enjoying it. Love in this sense means total and unconditional acceptance.

This can work even with problems as thorny as physical pain. When we totally experience pain, it often diminishes and sometimes it disappears. This strategy can work with emotions and even with physical pain. Make it your aim to love the pain, that is, to fully accept the pain and know all the details about it. Most pain has a wavelike quality. It rises, reaches a peak of intensity, and then subsides for a while. See if you can watch the waves as they come and go.

Second, unconditional acceptance is not the same as unconditional surrender. Accepting a problem does not mean escaping from it or giving up on finding a solution. Rather, this process involves freeing ourselves from the

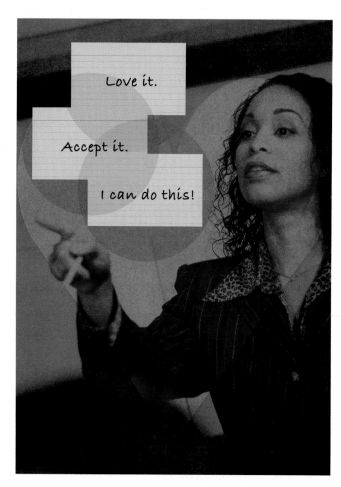

When we accept the fact that we have a problem, we are more likely to find effective ways to deal with it.

grip of the problem by diving *into* the problem head first and getting to know it in detail.

Third, love and laughter are allies. It's hard to resist a problem while you are laughing at it. Sure, that incident when you noticed the spinach in your teeth only *after* you got home from a first date was a bummer. But with the passage of time, you can admit that it was kind of funny. You don't have to wait weeks to gain that perspective. As long as you're going to laugh anyway, why wait? The sooner you can see the humor in your problems, the sooner you can face them.

When people first hear about loving their problems, they sometimes think it means being resigned to problems. Actually, loving a problem does not need to stop us from solving it. In fact, fully accepting and admitting the problem usually helps us take effective action—which can free us of the problem once and for all.

put it to work

Meeting your professional goals might call for continual training to update your skills—perhaps even an advanced degree. The memory techniques in this chapter can serve you at every stage of your career. Following are examples of ways to transfer those techniques to the workplace.

Focus on solving problems.
When applying for jobs, review the Power Process: "Love your problems." Present yourself as someone who can spot an organization's areas for improvement and take appropriate action. During the hiring process, transform yourself from a faceless job applicant to a potent problem solver. For example, you might say, "I've found it difficult to order products from your Web site. Five people have told me the same thing. I have a list of ideas that could solve this problem." Then explain one item from your list. You'll get an employer's attention.

If some of your solutions fail, return to the "Notable failures" article in this chapter to renew your inspiration. Many of the people featured in this article experienced career-related snafus.

Organize your workspace to promote memory. When personal computers first became standard fixtures in office cubicles, some futurists predicted the imminent arrival of the "paperless office." It didn't happen. Data might be stored digitally, but workers in the twenty-first century still handle reams of paper—letters, memos, manuals, meeting minutes, training materials, newsletters, magazines, technical journals, and books. That's all in addition to e-mail, Web pages, and other Internet-based documents.

Faced with such an information glut, you might find it challenging to remember where you *put* a particular document, let alone remember what's *in* it. Memory techniques from this chapter can help:

- **Be selective.** Instead of letting paper-based and digital documents pile up and telling yourself you'll

get to them later, make quick decisions about which documents to keep. You might know right away that you'll never refer to some of them again. Be bold and trash them immediately. If only one article out of a magazine interests you, tear it out and toss the rest. Out of the millions of words and images that filter into your life at work, extract the gems and commit those to memory. A recycling bin that's full of paper is one sign of a healthy brain at work.

- **Create a meaningful organization for your files.** Take the documents you decide to keep and consider your options for filing them. You can group them alphabetically by subject, chronologically by date, or on a continuum from high to low priority. Documents that call for immediate action can go in a file that you check daily. Put lower-priority items in other files to review weekly, monthly, or quarterly. You don't have to memorize everything that's in these documents—even the most urgent ones. Just know where to find them on a moment's notice.

- **Create a personal system of cues and reminders.** In 1999, the winner of the U.S. National Memory Championship was a 27-year-old woman, Tatiana Cooley. To gain her title, she memorized lists of hundreds of randomly organized numbers and words. Yet Cooley confessed to a CNN reporter that she is absent-minded at work and plasters her office with handwritten Post-it Notes to aid her memory.[3] The same approach can work for you. This is a highly kinesthetic memory system.

Name _____ Date _____/_____/_____

1. According to the text, remembering is most accurately described as a process rather than a thing. True or False? Explain your answer.

2. The memory jungle is a visualization that can help you recall which of the following points about memory?
   (a) New information is first encoded as short-term memories.
   (b) Short-term memories decay quickly.
   (c) Short-term memory has a limited capacity.
   (d) The more often you recall information, the easier it is to recall again.
   (e) All of the above.

3. Describe a visualization that can help you remember Boyle's law.

4. Define *acronym* and give an example.

5. Memorization on a deep level can take place if you:
   (a) Repeat the idea.
   (b) Repeat the idea.
   (c) Repeat the idea.
   (d) All of the above.

6. Mnemonic devices are tricks that can increase your ability to:
   (a) Manage your time.
   (b) Understand or digest material.
   (c) Recall information that you already understand.

7. List three limitations of mnemonics.

8. There are five general categories of mnemonic devices given in the text. Briefly describe two of them.

9. Briefly describe the difference between loving a problem and being resigned to a problem.

10. List the four categories of memory techniques presented in the article "Choosing to remember."

learning styles application

The questions below will "cycle" you through four styles, or modes, of learning as explained in the article "Learning Styles: Discovering how you learn" in Chapter One. Each question will help you explore a different mode. You can answer the questions in any order.

what if
Describe how you intend to use a technique from this chapter in a situation outside school where memory skills are important.

why
List some important situations in which you could be more effective by improving your memory skills.

how
Describe how you intend to use a technique from this chapter in a class where memory skills are important.

what
List the three most useful memory techniques you learned from this chapter.

master student

profile

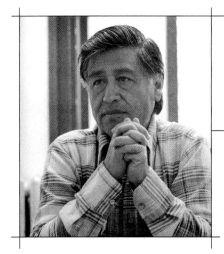

CESAR CHAVEZ

(1927–1993) leader of the United Farm Workers (UFW), organized strikes, boycotts, and fasts to improve conditions for migrant workers.

A *few men and women have* engraved their names in the annals of change through nonviolence, but none have experienced the grinding childhood poverty that Chavez did after the Depression-struck family farm on the Gila River was foreclosed in 1937. Chavez was 10. His parents and the five children took to the picking fields as migrant workers.

Chavez's faith sustained him, but it is likely that it was both knowing and witnessing poverty and the sheer drudgery and helplessness of the migrant life that drove him.

He never lost the outreach that he had learned from his mother, who, despite the family's poverty, told her children to invite any hungry people in the area home to share what rice, beans and tortillas the family had.

He left school to work. He attended 65 elementary schools but never graduated from high school . . . .

It was in the fields, in the 1950s, that Chavez met his wife, Helen. The couple and their eight children gave much to "La Huelga," the strike call that became the UFW trademark, from their eventual permanent home near Bakersfield. Chavez did not own

the home . . . but paid rent out of his $900 a month as a union official.

Yet, in the fields in the 1930s, something happened that changed Chavez's life. He was 12 when a Congress of Industrial Organizations union began organizing dried-fruit industry workers, including his father and uncle. The young boy learned about strikes, pickets and organizing.

For two years during World War II, Chavez served in the U.S. Navy; then it was back to the fields and organizing. There were other movements gaining strength in the United States during those years, including community organizing.

From 1952 to 1962, Chavez was active outside the fields, in voter registration drives and in challenging police and immigration abuse of Mexicans and Mexican Americans.

At first, in the 1960s, only one movement had a noticeable symbol: the peace movement. By the time the decade ended, the United Farm Workers, originally established as the National Farm Workers Association, gave history a second flag: the black Aztec eagle on a red background.

In eight years, a migrant worker son of migrants helped change a nation's perception through non-violent resistance. It took courage, imagination, and the ability to withstand physical and other abuse.

The facts are well-known now. During the 1968 grape boycott, farmers and growers fought him, but

Chavez stood firm. Shoppers hesitated, then pushed their carts past grape counters without buying. The growers were forced to negotiate.

The UFW as a Mexican American civil rights movement in time might outweigh the achievements of the UFW as a labor movement, for Chavez also represented something equally powerful to urban Mexican Americans and immigrants—a nonviolent leader who had achieved great change from the most humble beginnings.

Yet, through the UFW, Chavez and his colleagues brought Americans face-to-face with the true costs, the human costs, of the food on their tables and brought Mexican Americans into the political arena and helped keep them there. . . .

Word of Chavez's death spread to the union halls decorated with the Virgin of Guadalupe and UFW flag, to the fields, to the small towns and larger cities. And stories about the short, compact man with the ready smile, the iron determination, the genuine humility and the deep faith were being told amid the tears.

Reprinted by permission of the *National Catholic Reporter*, Kansas City, MO 64111.

For more biographical information about Cesar Chavez, visit the Master Student Hall of Fame on the *Becoming a Master Student* Web site at

masterstudent.college.hmco.com

4

Reading

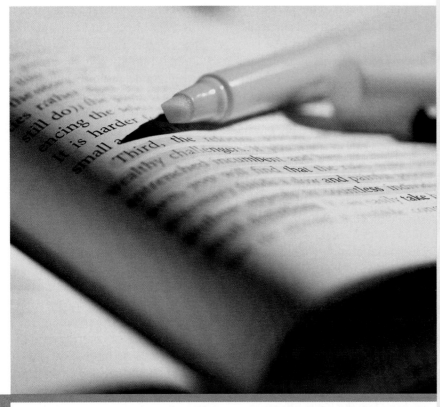

why
this chapter matters ...

Higher education requires extensive reading that results in comprehension of facts, figures, and concepts.

what
is included ...

Muscle Reading
How Muscle Reading works
Phase one: Before you read
Phase two: While you read
Phase three: After you read
When reading is tough
Read with a dictionary in your lap
Reading fast
Reading with children underfoot
Power Process: "Notice your pictures and let them go"
Master Student Profile: Helen Keller

how
you can use this chapter ...

Analyze what effective readers do and experiment with new techniques.
Increase your vocabulary and adjust your reading speed for different types of material.
Comprehend difficult texts with more ease.

As you read, ask yourself
what if ...

I could finish my reading with time to spare and easily recall the key points?

STUDENT VOICES

" *I am 47 years old, have three kids, and just went back to college after being out of school for 28 years. Your book has helped alleviate so many of my 'going back to school' fears. I was skeptical about the reading chapter. I had tried everything to remember what I read . . . ; then I tried the [Muscle Reading] rules. I am now a believer. It really works.*"

—SUE BRUMFIELD

Muscle Reading

Picture yourself sitting at a desk, a book in your hands. Your eyes are open, and it looks as if you're reading. Suddenly your head jerks up. You blink. You realize your eyes have been scanning the page for 10 minutes, and you can't remember a single thing you have read.

Or picture this: You've had a hard day. You were up at 6 a.m. to get the kids ready for school. A coworker called in sick, and you missed your lunch trying to do his job as well as your own. You picked up the kids, then had to shop for dinner. Dinner was late, of course, and the kids were grumpy.

Finally, you get to your books at 8 p.m. You begin a reading assignment on something called "the equity method of accounting for common stock investments." "I am preparing for the future," you tell yourself as you plod through two paragraphs and begin the third. Suddenly, everything in the room looks different. Your head is resting on your elbow, which is resting on the equity method of accounting. The clock reads 11:00 p.m. Say good-bye to three hours.

Sometimes the only difference between a sleeping pill and a textbook is that the textbook doesn't have a warning on the label about operating heavy machinery.

Muscle Reading is a technique you can use to avoid mental minivacations and reduce the number of unscheduled naps during study time, even after a hard day. More than that, Muscle Reading is a way to decrease effort and struggle by increasing energy and skill. Once you learn this technique, you can actually spend less time on your reading and get more out of it.

This is not to say that Muscle Reading will make your education a breeze. Muscle Reading might even look like more work at first. Effective textbook reading is an active, energy-consuming, sit-on-the-edge-of-your-seat business. That's why this strategy is called Muscle Reading. ▧

journal entry 10

Discovery/Intention Statement

Recall a time when you encountered problems with reading, such as words you didn't understand or paragraphs you paused to reread more than once. Sum up the experience and how you felt about it by completing the following statement.

I discovered that I . . .

_____

_____

_____

_____

Now list three to five specific reading skills you want to gain from this chapter.

I intend to . . .

_____

_____

_____

_____

_____

_____

_____

_____

_____

_____

_____

_____

_____

How Muscle Reading works

Muscle Reading is a three-phase technique you can use to extract the ideas and information you want.

Phase one includes steps to take *before* you read.
Phase two includes steps to take *while* you read.
Phase three includes steps to take *after* you read.
Each phase has three steps.

Phase one: Before you read
Step 1: Preview
Step 2: Outline
Step 3: Question

Phase two: While you read
Step 4: Read
Step 5: Underline
Step 6: Answer

Phase three: After you read
Step 7: Recite
Step 8: Review
Step 9: Review again

A nine-step reading strategy might seem cumbersome and unnecessary for a two-page reading assignment. It is. Use the steps appropriately. Choose which ones to apply as you read.

To assist your recall of Muscle Reading strategies, memorize three short sentences:

Pry Out Questions.
Root Up Answers.
Recite, Review, and Review again.

These three sentences correspond to the three phases of the Muscle Reading technique. Each sentence is an acrostic. The first letter of each word stands for one of the nine steps listed above.

Take a moment to invent images for each of those sentences.

For *phase one*, visualize or feel yourself prying out questions from a text. These are questions you want answered based on a brief survey of the assignment. Make a mental picture of yourself scanning the material, spotting a question, and reaching into the text to pry it out. Hear yourself saying, "I've got it. Here's my question." Then for *phase two*, get your muscles involved. Feel the tips of your fingers digging into the text as you root up the answers to your questions.

Finally, you enter *phase three*. Hear your voice reciting what you have learned. Listen to yourself making a speech or singing a song about the material as you review it.

To jog your memory, write the first letters of the Muscle Reading acrostic in a margin or at the top of your notes. Then check off the steps you intend to follow. Or write the Muscle Reading steps on 3x5 cards and then use them for bookmarks.

Muscle Reading could take a little time to learn. At first you might feel it's slowing you down. That's natural when you're gaining a new skill. Mastery comes with time and practice.

PHASE ONE
Before you read

Step 1 Preview.

Before you start reading, preview the entire assignment. You don't have to memorize what you preview to get value from this step. Previewing sets the stage for incoming information by warming up a space in your mental storage area.

If you are starting a new book, look over the table of contents and flip through the text page by page. If you're going to read one chapter, flip through the pages of that chapter. Even if your assignment is merely a few pages in a book, you can benefit from a brief preview of the table of contents.

Keep the preview short. If the entire reading assignment will take less than an hour, your preview might take five minutes. Previewing is also a way to get yourself started when an assignment looks too big to handle. It is an easy way to step into the material.

Keep an eye out for summary statements. If the assignment is long or complex, read the summary first. Many textbooks have summaries in the introduction or at the end of each chapter.

Read all chapter headings and subheadings. Like the headlines in a newspaper, these are usually printed in large, bold type. Often headings are brief summaries in themselves.

When previewing, seek out familiar concepts, facts, or ideas. These items can help increase comprehension by linking new information to previously learned material. Look for ideas that spark your imagination or curiosity. Inspect drawings, diagrams, charts, tables, graphs, and photographs. Imagine what kinds of questions will show up on a test. Previewing helps to clarify your purpose for reading. Ask yourself what you will do with this material and how it can relate to your long-term goals. Are you reading just to get the main points? Key supporting details? Additional details? All of the above? Your answers will guide what you do with each step that follows.

Step 2 Outline.

With complex material, take time to understand the structure of what you are about to read. Outlining actively organizes your thoughts about the assignment and can help make complex information easier to understand.

If your textbook provides chapter outlines, spend some time studying them. When an outline is not provided, sketch a brief one in the margin of your book or at the beginning of your notes on a separate sheet of paper. Later, as you read and take notes, you can add to your outline.

Headings in the text can serve as major and minor entries in your outline. For example, the heading for this article is "Phase one: Before you read," and the subheadings list the three steps in this phase. When you outline, feel free to rewrite headings so that they are more meaningful to you.

The amount of time you spend on this step will vary. For some assignments, a 10-second mental outline is all you might need. For other assignments (fiction and poetry, for example), you can skip this step altogether.

Step 3 Question.

Before you begin a careful reading, determine what you want from an assignment. Then write down a list of questions, including any that resulted from your preview of the materials.

Another useful technique is to turn chapter headings and subheadings into questions. For example, if a heading is "Transference and suggestion," you can ask yourself, "What are *transference* and *suggestion*? How does *transference* relate to *suggestion*?" Make up a quiz as if you were teaching this subject to your classmates. If there are no headings, look for key sentences and turn these into questions. These sentences usually show up at the beginnings or ends of paragraphs and sections.

Have fun with this technique. Make the questions playful or creative. You don't need to answer every question that you ask. The purpose of making up questions is to get your brain involved in the assignment. Take your unanswered questions to class, where they can be springboards for class discussion.

Demand your money's worth from your textbook. If you do not understand a concept, write specific questions about it. The more detailed your questions, the more powerful this technique becomes.

PHASE TWO
While you read

Step 4   **Read.** At last! You have previewed the assignment, organized it in your mind, and formulated questions. Now you are ready to begin reading.

Before you dive into the first paragraph, take a few moments to reflect on what you already know about this subject. Do this even if you think you know nothing. This technique prepares your brain to accept the information that follows.

As you read, be conscious of where you are and what you are doing. Use the Power Process: "Be here now" in Chapter Two. When you notice your attention wandering, gently bring it back to the present moment.

One way to stay focused is to avoid marathon reading sessions. Schedule breaks and set a reasonable goal for the entire session. Then reward yourself with an enjoyable activity for five or 10 minutes every hour or two.

For difficult reading, set more limited goals. Read for a half-hour and then take a break. Most students find that shorter periods of reading distributed throughout the day and week can be more effective than long sessions. You can use the following four techniques to stay focused as you read.

First, visualize the material. Form mental pictures of the concepts as they are presented. If you read that a voucher system can help control cash disbursements, picture a voucher handing out dollar bills. Using visual imagery in this way can help deepen your understanding of the text while allowing information to be transferred into your long-term memory.

Second, read the material out loud, especially if it is complicated. Some of us remember better and understand more quickly when we hear an idea.

Third, get a "feel" for the subject. For example, let's say you are reading about a microorganism, a paramecium, in your biology text. Imagine what it would feel like to run your finger around the long, cigar-shaped body of the organism. Imagine feeling the large fold of its gullet on one side and the tickle of the hairy little cilia as they wiggle in your hand.

Fourth, remember that a goal of your reading is to answer the questions you listed during phase one. After you've identified the key questions, predict how the author will answer them. Then read to find out if your predictions were accurate.

A final note: It's easy to fool yourself about reading. Just having an open book in your hand and moving your eyes across a page doesn't mean you are reading effectively. Reading textbooks takes energy, even if you do it sitting down. There's a saying about corporation presidents—that they usually wear out the front of their chairs first. Approach your reading assignment like a company president. Sit up. Keep your spine straight. Use the edge of your chair. And avoid reading in bed—except for fun.

READ

?

Step 5   **Underline.** Deface your books. Use them up. Have fun writing in them. Indulge yourself as you never could with your grade-school books.

The purpose of making marks in a text is to call out important concepts or information that you will need to review later. Underlining can save lots of time when you are studying for tests.

Underlining offers a secondary benefit. When you read with a pen or pencil in your hand, you involve your kinesthetic senses of touch and motion. Being physical with your books can help build strong neural pathways in your memory.

Avoid underlining too soon. Wait until you complete a chapter or section to make sure you know the key points. Then mark up the text. Sometimes, underlining after you read each paragraph works best.

Underline sparingly, usually less than 10 percent of the text. If you mark up too much on a page, you defeat the purpose—to flag the most important material for review.

In addition to underlining, you can mark up a text in the following ways:

- Place an asterisk (*) or an exclamation point (!) in the margin next to an especially important sentence or term.

- Circle key terms and words to look up later in a dictionary.

➡ Five smart ways to highlight a text

Underlining a text with a pen can make underlined sections—the important parts—harder to read. As an alternative, many students use colored highlighters to flag key words and sentences.

Highlighting can be a powerful tool. It also presents a danger—the ever-present temptation to highlight too much text. Excessive highlighting leads to wasted time during reviews and can also spoil the appearance of your books. Get the most out of all that money you pay for books. Highlight in an efficient way that leaves texts readable for years to come.

Read carefully first. Read an entire chapter or section at least once before you begin highlighting. Don't be in a hurry to mark up your book. Get to know the text first. Make two or three passes through difficult sections before you highlight.

Make choices up front about what to highlight. Perhaps you can accomplish your purposes by highlighting only certain chapters or sections of a text. When you highlight, remember to look for passages that directly answer the questions you posed during step 3 of Muscle Reading. Within these passages, highlight individual words, phrases, or sentences rather than whole paragraphs. The important thing is to choose an overall strategy before you put highlighter to paper.

Recite first. You might want to apply step 7 of Muscle Reading before you highlight. Talking about what you read—to yourself or with other people—can help you grasp the essence of a text. Recite first; then go back and highlight. You'll probably highlight more selectively.

Underline, then highlight. Underline key passages lightly in pencil. Then close your text and come back to them later. Assess your underlining. Perhaps you can highlight less than you underlined and still capture the key points.

Use highlighting to monitor your comprehension. Critical thinking plays a role in underlining and highlighting. When highlighting, you're making moment-by-moment decisions about what you want to remember from a text. You're also making inferences about what material might be included on a test.

Take your critical thinking a step further by using highlighting to check your comprehension. Stop reading periodically and look back over the sentences you've highlighted. See if you are making accurate distinctions between main points and supporting material. Highlighting too much—more than 10 percent of the text—can be a sign that you're not making this distinction and that you don't fully understand what you're reading. See the article "When reading is tough" later in this chapter for suggestions that can help.

- Write short definitions of key terms in the margin.

- Write a "Q" in the margin to highlight possible test questions, passages you don't understand, and questions to ask in class.

- Write personal comments in the margin—points of agreement or disagreement with the author.

- Write mini-indexes in the margin, that is, the numbers of other pages in the book where the same topic is discussed.

- Write summaries by listing the main points or key events covered in a chapter.

- Rewrite chapter titles, headings, and subheadings so that they're more meaningful to you.

- Draw diagrams, pictures, tables, or maps that translate text into visual terms.

- Number each step in a list or series of related points.

Step 6 Answer.

As you read, seek out the answers to your questions and write them down. Fill in your outline. Jot down new questions and note when you don't find the answers you are looking for. Use these notes to ask questions in class, or see your instructor personally.

When you read, create an image of yourself as a person in search of the answers. You are a detective, watching for every clue, sitting erect in your straight-back chair, demanding that your textbook give you what you want—the answers.

PHASE THREE

After you read

Step 7 Recite.

Talk to yourself about what you've read. Or talk to someone else. When you're finished with a reading assignment, make a speech about it. A classic study suggests that you can profitably devote up to 80 percent of your study time to active reciting.[1] When you recite, you practice an important aspect of metacognition—synthesis, or combining individual ideas and facts into a meaningful whole.

One way to get yourself to recite is to look at each underlined point. Note what you marked; then put the book down and start talking out loud. Explain as much as you can about that particular point.

To make this technique more effective, do it in front of a mirror. It might seem silly, but the benefits can be enormous. Reap them at exam time.

Classmates are even better than mirrors. Form a group and practice teaching each other what you have read. One of the best ways to learn anything is to teach it to someone else.

In addition, talk about your reading whenever you can. Tell friends and family members what you're learning from your textbooks.

Talking about your reading reinforces a valuable skill—the ability to summarize. To practice this skill, pick one chapter (or one section of one chapter) from any of your textbooks. State the main topic covered in this chapter. Then state the main points that the author makes about this topic.

For example, the main topic up to this point in this chapter is Muscle Reading. The main point about this topic is that Muscle Reading includes three phases—steps to take before you read, while you read, and after you read. For a more detailed summary, you could name each of the nine steps.

Note: This "topic-point" method does not work so well when you want to summarize short stories, novels, plays, and other works of fiction. Instead, focus on action. In most stories, the main character confronts a major problem and takes a series of actions to solve it.

Describe that problem and talk about the character's key actions—the turning points in the story.

Step 8 Review.

Plan to do your first complete review within 24 hours of reading the material. Sound the trumpets! This point is critical: A review within 24 hours moves information from your short-term memory to your long-term memory.

Review within one day. If you read it on Wednesday, review it on Thursday. During this review, look over your notes and clear up anything you don't understand. Recite some of the main points again.

This review can be short. You might spend as little as 15 minutes reviewing a difficult two-hour reading assignment. Investing that time now can save you hours later when studying for exams.

Step 9 Review again.

The final step in Muscle Reading is the weekly or monthly review. This step can be very short—perhaps only four or five minutes per assignment. Simply go over your notes. Read the highlighted parts of your text. Recite one or two of the more complicated points.

REVIEW

BUT

ONCE AGAIN

→ **Muscle Reading—a leaner approach**

Keep in mind that Muscle Reading is an overall approach, not a rigid, step-by-step procedure. Here's a shorter variation that students have found helpful. Practice it with any chapter in this book:

- *Preview and question.* Flip through the pages, looking at anything that catches your eye—headings, subheadings, illustrations, photographs. Turn the title of each article into a question. For example, "How Muscle Reading works" can become "How does Muscle Reading work?" List your questions on a separate sheet of paper, or write each question on a 3x5 card.

- *Read to answer your questions.* Read each article; then go back over the text and underline or highlight answers to the appropriate questions on your list.

- *Recite and review.* When you're done with the chapter, close the book. Recite by reading each question—and answering it—out loud. Review the chapter by looking up the answers to your questions. (It's easy—they're already highlighted.) Review again by quizzing yourself one more time with your list of questions.

The purpose of these reviews is to keep the neural pathways to the information open and to make them more distinct. That way, the information can be easier to recall. You can accomplish these short reviews anytime, anywhere, if you are prepared.

Conduct a five-minute review while you are waiting for a bus, for your socks to dry, or for the water to boil. Three-by-five cards are a handy review tool. Write ideas, formulas, concepts, and facts on cards and carry them with you.

These short review periods can be effortless and fun.

Sometimes longer review periods are appropriate. For example, if you found an assignment difficult, consider rereading it. Start over, as if you had never seen the material before. Sometimes a second reading will provide you with surprising insights.

Decades ago, psychologists identified the primacy-recency effect, which suggests that we most easily remember the first and last items in any presentation.[2] Previewing and reviewing your reading can put this theory to work for you. ◪

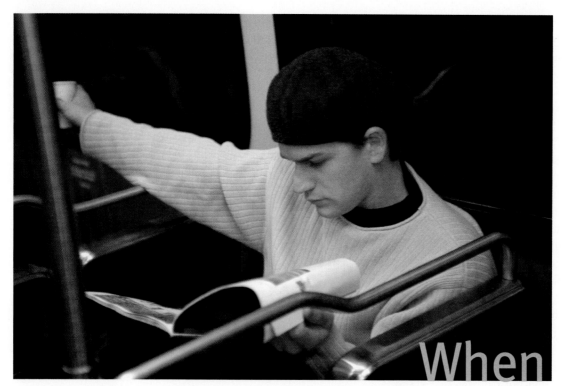

When
reading is tough

Sometimes ordinary reading methods are not enough. Many students get bogged down in a murky reading assignment. If you are ever up to your neck in textbook alligators, you can use the following techniques to drain the swamp.

Read it again. Difficult material—such as the technical writing in science texts—is often easier the second time around. If you read an assignment and are completely lost, do not despair. Admit your confusion. Sleep on it. When you return to the assignment, regard it with fresh eyes.

Look for essential words. If you are stuck on a paragraph, mentally cross out all of the adjectives and adverbs and read the sentence without them. Find the important words. These will usually be verbs and nouns.

Hold a minireview. Pause briefly to summarize—either verbally or in writing—what you've read so far. Stop at the end of a paragraph and recite, in your own words, what you have just read. Jot down some notes or create a short outline or summary.

Read it out loud. Make noise. Read a passage out loud several times, each time using a different inflection and emphasizing a different part of the sentence. Be creative. Imagine that you are the author talking.

Talk to your instructor. Admit when you are stuck and make an appointment with your instructor. Most teachers welcome the opportunity to work individually with students. Be specific about your confusion. Point out the paragraph that you found toughest to understand.

Stand up. Changing positions periodically can combat fatigue. Experiment with standing as you read, especially if you get stuck on a tough passage and decide to read it out loud.

Skip around. Jump immediately to the end of the article or chapter. You might have lost the big picture, and sometimes simply seeing the conclusion or summary is all you need to put the details in context. Retrace the steps in a chain of ideas and look for examples. Absorb facts and ideas in whatever order works for you—which may be different from the author's presentation.

Find a tutor. Many schools provide free tutoring services. If tutoring services are not provided by your school, other students who have completed the course can assist you.

Use another text. Find a similar text in the library. Sometimes a concept is easier to understand if it is expressed another way. Children's books, especially children's encyclopedias, can provide useful overviews of baffling subjects.

Pretend you understand; then explain it. We often understand more than we think we do. Pretend that the material is clear as a bell and explain it to another person, or even yourself. Write down your explanation. You might be amazed by what you know.

Ask: "What's going on here?" When you feel stuck, stop reading for a moment and diagnose what's happening. At these stop points, mark your place in the margin of the page with a penciled "S" for "Stuck." A pattern to your marks over several pages might indicate a question you want to answer before going further. Or you might discover a reading habit you'd like to change.

Stop reading. When none of the above suggestions work, do not despair. Admit your confusion and then take a break. Catch a movie, go for a walk, study another subject, or sleep on it. The concepts you've already absorbed might come together at a subconscious level as you move on to other activities. Allow some time for that process. When you return to the reading material, see it with fresh eyes. ⧖

journal entry 11

Discovery Statement

Now that you've read about Muscle Reading, review your assessment of your reading skills in the Discovery Wheel on page 25. Do you still think your evaluation was accurate? What new insights do you have about the way you read? Are you a more effective reader than you thought you were? Less effective? Record your observations below.

_____

_____

_____

_____

_____

_____

_____

_____

_____

_____

_____

_____

_____

_____

_____

_____

_____

_____

_____

_____

_____

_____

_____

_____

_____

Read with a dictionary in your lap

A large vocabulary makes reading more enjoyable and increases the range of materials you can explore. In addition, building your vocabulary gives you more options for self-expression when speaking or writing. When you can choose from a larger pool of words, you increase the precision and power of your thinking.

Strengthen your vocabulary by taking delight in words. Look up unfamiliar words. Pay special attention to words that arouse your curiosity.

Students regularly use two kinds of dictionaries: the desk dictionary and the unabridged dictionary. A desk dictionary is an easy-to-handle abridged dictionary that you normally use several times in the course of a day. Keep this book within easy reach (maybe in your lap) so you can look up unfamiliar words while reading. You can find a large, unabridged dictionary in a library or bookstore. It provides more complete information about words and definitions not included in your desk dictionary, as well as synonyms, usage notes, and word histories. Both kinds of dictionaries are available on CDs for personal computers.

Construct a word stack. When you come across an unfamiliar word, write it down on a 3x5 card. Below the word, copy the sentence in which it was used. You can look up each word immediately, or you can accumulate a stack of these cards and look up the words later. Write the definition of each word on the back of the 3x5 card,

adding the diacritical marks that tell you how to pronounce it.

To expand your vocabulary and learn the history behind the words, take your stack of cards to an unabridged dictionary. As you find related words in the dictionary, add them to your stack. These cards become a portable study aid that you can review in your spare moments.

Learn—even when your dictionary is across town. When you are listening to a lecture and hear an unusual word or when you are reading on the bus and encounter a word you don't know, you can still build your word stack. Pull out a 3x5 card and write down the word and its sentence. Later, you can look up the definition and write it on the back of the card.

Divide words into parts. Another suggestion is to divide an unfamiliar word into syllables and look for familiar parts. This works well if you make it a point to learn common prefixes (beginning syllables) and suffixes (ending syllables). For example, the suffix *-tude* usually refers to a condition or state of being. Knowing this makes it easier to conclude that *habitude* refers to a usual way of doing something and that *similitude* means being similar or having a quality of resemblance. See an unabridged dictionary for more examples of word parts.

Infer the meaning of words from their context. You can often deduce the meaning of an unfamiliar word simply by paying attention to its context—the surrounding words, phrases, sentences, paragraphs, or images. Later you can confirm your deduction by consulting a dictionary.

Practice looking for context clues such as:

- *Definitions.* A key word might be defined right in the text. Look for phrases such as *defined as* or *in other words.* These often introduce definitions.

- *Examples.* Authors often provide examples to clarify a word meaning. If the word is not explicitly defined, then study the examples. They're often preceded by the phrases *for example, for instance,* or *such as.*

- *Lists.* When a word is listed in a series, pay attention to the other items in the series. They might define the unfamiliar word through association.

- *Comparisons.* You might find a new word surrounded by synonyms—words with a similar meaning. Look for synonyms after words such as *like* and *as.*

- *Contrasts.* A writer might juxtapose a word with its antonym—a word or phrase with the opposite meaning. Look for phrases such as *on the contrary* and *on the other hand.* ⬛

One way to read faster is to read faster. This might sound like double talk, but it is a serious suggestion. The fact is you can probably read faster—without any loss in comprehension—simply by making a conscious effort to do so. Your comprehension might even improve.

The Universal Law of Reading

First corollary:
To read effectively, always sit in a canoe and wear a face mask, snorkel, and flippers.

Second corollary:
Don't believe everything you read.

Reading fast

xperiment with the "just do it" method right now. Read the rest of this article as fast as you can. After you finish, come back and reread the same paragraphs at your usual rate. Note how much you remember from your first sprint through the text. You might be surprised to find out how well you comprehend material even at dramatically increased speeds. Build on that success by experimenting with the following guidelines.

Get your body ready. Gear up for reading faster. Get off the couch. Sit up straight at a desk or table, on the edge of your chair, with your feet flat on the floor. If you're feeling adventurous, read standing up.

Set a time limit. When you read, use a clock or a digital watch with a built-in stopwatch to time yourself. You are not aiming to set speed records, so be realistic. For example, set a goal to read two or three sections of a chapter in an hour, using all of the Muscle Reading steps. If that works, set a goal of 50 minutes for reading the same number of sections. Test your limits. The idea is to give yourself a gentle push, increasing your reading speed without sacrificing comprehension.

The idea is to give yourself a gentle push, increasing your reading speed without sacrificing comprehension.

Relax. It's not only possible to read fast when you're relaxed, it's easier. Relaxation promotes concentration. And remember, relaxation is not the same as sleep. You can be relaxed *and* alert at the same time.

Move your eyes faster. When we read, our eyes leap across the page in short bursts called *saccades* (pronounced *saˇ- käds´*). A saccade is also a sharp jerk on the reins of a horse—a violent pull to stop the animal quickly. Our eyes stop like that, too, in pauses called *fixations*.

Although we experience the illusion of continuously scanning each line, our eyes actually take in groups of words, usually about three at a time. For more than 90 percent of reading time, our eyes are at a dead stop, in those fixations.

One way to decrease saccades is to follow your finger as you read. The faster your finger moves, the faster your eyes move. You can also use a pen, pencil, or 3x5 card as a guide.

Your eyes can move faster if they take in more words with each burst—for example, six instead of three. To practice taking in more words between fixations, find a newspaper with narrow columns. Then read down one column at a time and fixate only once per line.

In addition to using the above techniques, simply make a conscious effort to fixate less. You might feel a little uncomfortable at first. That's normal. Just practice often, for short periods of time.

Notice and release ineffective habits. Our eyes make regressions, that is, they back up and reread words. You can reduce regressions by paying attention to them. Use the handy 3x5 card to cover words and lines that you have just read. You can then note how often you stop and move the card back to reread the text. Don't be discouraged if you stop often at first. Being aware of it helps you regress less frequently.

Also notice vocalizing. You are more likely to read faster if you don't read out loud or move your lips. You can also increase your speed if you don't subvocalize—that is, if you don't mentally "hear" the words as you read them. To stop doing it, just be aware of it.

Another habit to release is reading letter by letter. When we first learn to read, we do it one letter at a time. By now you have memorized many words by their shape, so you don't have to focus on the letters at all. Read this example: "Rasrhcers at Cbmrigae Uivnretisy funod taht eprxert raeedrs dno't eevn look at the lteters." You get the point. Skilled readers recognize many words and phrases in this way, taking them in at a single glance.

When you first attempt to release these habits, choose simpler reading material. That way, you can pay closer attention to your reading technique. Gradually work your way up to more complex material.

If you're pressed for time, skim. When you're in a hurry, experiment by skimming the assignment instead of reading the whole thing. Read the headings, subheadings, lists, charts, graphs, and summary paragraphs. Summaries are especially important. They are usually found at the beginning or end of a chapter or section.

Stay flexible. Remember that speed isn't everything. Skillful readers vary their reading rate according to their purpose and the nature of the material. An advanced text in analytic geometry usually calls for a different reading rate than the Sunday comics.

You also can use different reading rates on the same material. For example, you might first sprint through an assignment for the key words and ideas, then return to the difficult parts for a slower and more thorough reading.

Explore more resources. You can find many books about speed-reading. Ask a librarian to help you find a few. Using them can be a lot of fun. For more possibilities, including courses and workshops, go to your favorite search engine on the Internet and key in the word *speed-reading*.

In your research, you might discover people who offer to take you beyond speed-reading. According to some teachers, you can learn to flip through a book and "mentally photograph" each page—hundreds or even thousands of words at once. To prepare for this feat, you first do relaxation exercises to release tension while remaining alert. In this state, you can theoretically process vast quantities of information at a level other than your conscious mind.

You might find these ideas controversial. Approach them in the spirit of the Power Process: "Ideas are tools." Also remember that you can use more conventional reading techniques at any time.

One word of caution: Courses and workshops range from free to expensive. Before you lay out any money, check the instructor's credentials and talk to people who've taken the course. Also find out whether the instructor offers free "sampler sessions" and whether you can cancel at some point in the course for a full refund.

Finally, remember the first rule of reading fast: Just do it!

exercise 13

RELAX

Eye strain can be the result of continuous stress. Take a break from your reading and use this exercise to release tension.

1. Sit on a chair or lie down and take a few moments to breathe deeply.

2. Close your eyes, place your palms over your eyes, and visualize a perfect field of black.

3. Continue to be aware of the blackness for two or three minutes while you breathe deeply.

4. Now remove your hands from your eyes and open your eyes slowly.

5. Relax for a minute more; then continue reading.

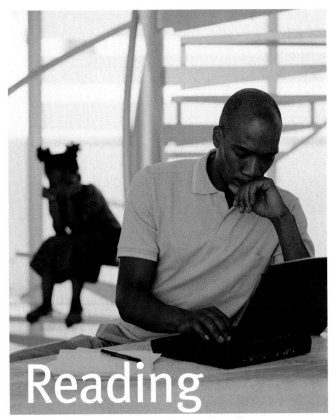

Reading with children underfoot

It is possible to combine effective study time and quality time with children. The following suggestions come mostly from students who are also parents. The specific strategies you use will depend on your schedule and the ages of your children.

Attend to your children first. When you first come home from school, keep your books out of sight. Spend 10 minutes with your children before you settle in to study. Give them hugs and ask about their day. Then explain that you have some work to do. Your children might reward you with 30 minutes of quiet time. A short time of full, focused attention from a parent can be more satisfying than longer periods of partial attention.

Of course, this suggestion won't work with the youngest children. If your children are infants or toddlers, schedule sessions of concentrated study for when they are asleep.

Use "pockets" of time. See if you can arrange study time at school before you come home. If you arrive at school 15 minutes earlier and stay 15 minutes later, you can squeeze in an extra half-hour of study time that day. Also look for opportunities to study in between classes.

Before you shuttle children to soccer games or dance classes, throw a book in the car. While your children are warming up for the game or changing clothes, steal another 15 minutes to read.

Plan special activities for your child. Find a regular playmate for your child. Some children can pair off with close friends and safely retreat to their rooms for hours of private play. You can check on them occasionally and still get lots of reading done.

Another option is to take your children to a public playground. While they swing, slide, and dig in the sand, you can dig into your textbooks. Lots of physical activity will tire out your children in constructive ways. If they go to bed a little early, that's extra time for you to read.

After you set up appropriate activities for your children, don't attend to them every second, even if you're nearby as they play. Obviously, you want to break up fights, stop unsafe activity, and handle emergencies. Short of such incidents, you're free to read.

Use television responsibly. Another option is to use television as a babysitter—when you can control the programming. Rent a videotape for your child to watch as you study. If you're concerned about your child becoming a "couch potato," select educational programs that keep his mind active and engaged.

See if your child can use headphones while watching television. That way, the house stays quiet while you study.

Allow for interruptions. It's possible that you'll be interrupted even if you set up special activities for your child in advance. If so, schedule the kind of studying that can be interrupted. For instance, you could write out or review flash cards with key terms and definitions. Save the tasks that require sustained attention for other times.

Plan study breaks with children. Another option is to spend 10 minutes with your children for every 50 minutes that you study. View this not as an interruption but as a study break.

Or schedule time to be with your children when you've finished studying. Let your children in on the plan: "I'll be done reading at 7:30. That gives us a whole hour to play before you go to bed."

Many children love visible reminders that "their time" is approaching. An oven timer works well for this purpose. Set it for 15 minutes of quiet time. Follow that with five minutes of show-and-tell, storybooks, or another activity with your child. Then set the timer for another 15 minutes of studying, another break, and so on.

Develop a routine. Many young children love routines. They often feel more comfortable and secure when they know what to expect. You can use this to your benefit. One option is to develop a regular time for studying and let your child know this schedule: "I have to do my homework between 4 p.m. and 5 p.m. every day." Then enforce it.

Bargain with children. Reward them for respecting your schedule. In return for quiet time, give your child an extra allowance or a special treat. Children might enjoy gaining "credits" for this purpose. Each time they give you an hour of quiet time for studying, make an entry on a chart, put a star on their bulletin board, or give them a "coupon." After they've accumulated a certain number of entries, stars, or coupons, they can cash them in for a big reward—a movie or a trip to the zoo.

A short time of full, focused attention from a parent can be more satisfying than longer periods of partial attention.

Ask other adults for help. This suggestion for studying with children is a message repeated throughout the book: Enlist other people to help support your success.

Getting help can be as simple as asking your spouse, partner, neighbor, or a fellow student to take care of the children while you study. Offer to trade childcare with a neighbor: You will take his kids and yours for two hours on Thursday night if he'll take them for two hours on Saturday morning. Some parents start blockwide baby-sitting co-ops based on the same idea.

Find community activities and services. Ask if your school provides a day care service. In some cases, these services are available to students at a reduced cost. Community agencies such as the YMCA might offer similar programs.

You can also find special events that appeal to children. Storytelling hours at the library are one example. While your child is being entertained or supervised, you can stay close by. Use the time in this quiet setting to read a chapter or review class notes.

Make it a game. Reading a chemistry textbook with a 3-year-old in the same room is not as preposterous as it sounds. The secret is to involve your child. For instance, use this time to recite. Make funny faces as you say the properties of the transition elements in the periodic table. Talk in a weird voice as you repeat Faraday's laws. Draw pictures and make up an exciting story about the process of titration.

Read out loud to your children, or use them as an audience for a speech. If you invent rhymes, poems, or songs to help you remember formulas or dates, teach them to your children. Be playful. Kids are attracted to energy and enthusiasm.

Whenever possible, involve family members in tasks related to reading. Older children can help you with research tasks—finding books at the library, looking up news articles, even helping with typing.

When you can't read everything, just read something. One objection to reading with children nearby is "I just can't concentrate. There's no way I can get it all done while children are around."

That's OK. Even if you can't absorb an entire chapter while the kids are running past your desk, you can skim the chapter. Or you could just read the introduction and summary. When you can't get it *all* done, just get *something* done.

Caution: If you always read this way, your education might be compromised. Supplement this strategy with others so that you can get all of your reading done. ▨

Discover more ways to study with children underfoot at   masterstudent.college.hmco.com

PRACTICING CRITICAL THINKING

4

Read an editorial in a newspaper or magazine. Analyze this editorial by taking notes in the three-column format below. Use the first column for listing major points, the second for supporting points, and the third for key facts or statistics that support the major or minor points. For example:

Major point

The "female condom" has not yet been proved effective as a method of birth control.

Supporting point

Few studies exist on this method.

Key fact

One of the few studies showed a 26 percent failure rate for the female condom.

Major point	Supporting point	Key fact

Ask another student to do this exercise with you. Then compare and discuss your notes. See if you identified the same main points.

power process

Notice your pictures and let them go

One of the brain's primary jobs is to manufacture images. We use mental pictures to make predictions about the world, and we base much of our behavior on those predictions.

When a cook adds chopped onions, mushrooms, and garlic to a spaghetti sauce, he has a picture of how the sauce will taste and measures each ingredient according to that picture. When an artist is creating a painting or sculpture, he has a mental picture of the finished piece. Novelists often have mental images of the characters that they're about to bring to life. Many parents have a picture about what they want their children to become.

These kinds of pictures and many more have a profound influence on us. Our pictures direct our thinking, our conversations, and our actions—all of which help create our immediate circumstances. That's amazing, considering that we often operate with little, if any, conscious knowledge of our pictures.

Just about any time we feel a need, we conjure up a picture of what will satisfy that need. A baby feels hunger pangs and starts to cry. Within seconds, his mother appears and he is satisfied. The baby stores a mental picture of his mother feeding him. He connects that picture with stopping the hunger pangs. Voilà! Now he knows how to solve the hunger problem. The picture goes on file.

According to psychologist William Glasser, our minds function like a huge photo album.[3] Its pages include pictures of all the ways we've satisfied needs in the past. Whenever we feel dissatisfied, we mentally search the album for a picture of how to make the dissatisfaction go away. With that picture firmly in mind, we act in ways to make the world outside our heads match the pictures inside.

Remember that pictures are not strictly visual images. They can involve any of the senses. When you buy a CD, you have a picture of how it will sound. When you buy a sweater, you have a picture of how it will feel.

A problem with pictures

The pictures we make in our heads are survival mechanisms. Without them, we couldn't get from one end of town to the other. We couldn't feed or clothe ourselves. Without a picture of a socket, we couldn't screw in a light bulb.

Pictures can also get in our way. Take the case of a student who plans to attend a school he hasn't visited. He chose this school for its strong curriculum and good academic standing, but his brain didn't stop there. In his mind, the campus has historic buildings with ivy-covered walls and tree-lined avenues. The professors, he imagines, will be as articulate as Bill Moyers and as entertaining as Oprah Winfrey. His roommate will be his best friend. The cafeteria will be a cozy nook serving delicate quiche and fragrant teas. He will gather there with fellow students for hours of stimulating, intellectual conversation. The library will have every book, while the computer lab will boast the newest technology.

The school turns out to be four gray buildings downtown, next to the bus station. The first class he attends is taught by an overweight, balding professor, who is wearing a purple-and-orange bird of paradise tie and has a bad case of the sniffles. The cafeteria is a nondescript hall with machine-dispensed food, and the student's apartment is barely large enough to accommodate his roommate's tuba. This hypothetical student gets depressed. He begins to think about dropping out of school.

The problem with pictures is that they can prevent us from seeing what is really there. That happened to the student in this story. His pictures prevented him from noticing that his school is in the heart of a culturally vital city—close to theaters, museums, government offices, clubs, and all kinds of stores. The professor with the weird tie is not only an expert in his field, but is also a superior teacher. The school cafeteria is skimpy because it can't compete with the variety of inexpensive restaurants in the area. There might even be hope for a tuba-playing roommate.

Anger and disappointment are often the results of our pictures. We set up expectations of events before they occur, which can lead to disappointment. Sometimes we don't even realize that we have these expectations. The next time you discover you are angry, disappointed, or frustrated, look to see which of your pictures aren't being fulfilled.

Take charge of your pictures

Having pictures is unavoidable. Letting these pictures control our lives *is* avoidable. Some techniques for dealing with pictures are so simple and effortless, they might seem silly.

One way to deal with pictures is to be aware of them. Open up your mental photo album and notice how the pictures there influence your thoughts, feelings, and actions. Just becoming aware of your pictures—and how they affect you—can help you take a huge step toward dealing with them effectively.

Our pictures direct our thinking, our conversations, and our actions—all of which help create our immediate circumstances.

When you notice that pictures are getting in your way, then, in the most gentle manner possible, let your pictures go. Let them drift away like wisps of smoke picked up by a gentle wind.

Pictures are persistent. They come back over and over. Notice them again and let them go again. At first, a picture might return repeatedly and insistently. Pictures are like independent beings. They want to live. If you can see the picture as a thought independent from you, you will likely find it easier to let it go.

You are more than your pictures. Many images and words will pop into your head in the course of a lifetime. You do not have to identify with these pictures. You can let pictures go without giving up yourself.

If your pictures are interfering with your education, visualize them scurrying around inside your head. See yourself tying them to a brightly colored helium balloon and letting them go. Let them float away again and again.

Sometimes we can let go of old pictures and replace them with new ones. We stored all of those pictures in the first place. We can replace them. Our student's new picture of a great education can include the skimpy cafeteria, the professor with the weird tie, and the roommate with the tuba.

We can take charge of the images that float through our minds. We don't have to be ruled by an album of outdated pictures. We can stay aware of our pictures and keep looking for new ones. And when *those* new pictures no longer serve us, we can also let them go. ◪

put it to work

In the year 2000, researchers from the University of California, Berkeley, estimated that the world produces between one and two exabytes of information each year.[4] To put this figure in perspective, consider that one exabyte equals 250 megabytes for each individual on earth. (The complete works of Shakespeare would take up only five megabytes of space on your computer's hard drive.)

Much of your personal 250 megabytes might come in the form of work-related reading: technical manuals, sales manuals, policies and procedures, memos, e-mail, Web pages, newsletters, invoices, application forms, meeting minutes, brochures, annual reports, job descriptions, and more.

The techniques of Muscle Reading will help you plow through all that material and extract what you want to know. Also keep the following suggestions in mind.

Read with a purpose. At work, you're probably reading in order to produce an outcome. Determine your purpose in reading each document and extract only what you need to effect that outcome.

Print out online documents to read later. Research indicates that people can read faster on paper than on the computer screen.[5] Be kind to your eyes. Print out long attachments and e-mails and read them afterwards.

Make several passes through reading material. You don't have to "get it all" the first time you read a document. Make your first pass a quick preview. Then go for a second pass, reading the first sentence of each paragraph or the first and last paragraphs in each section. If you want more detail, then make a third pass, reading the material paragraph by paragraph, sentence by sentence.

Read only the relevant sections of documents. Don't feel obligated to read every document completely. Many business documents include executive summaries. Look for them. Everything you want to know might be there, all in a page or two.

Schedule regular reading time at work. Read during times of the day when your energy peaks.

Discuss what you read with coworkers. Make time for one-on-one, face-to-face conversations. Talking about what you read is a powerful way to transform data into insight.

Create "read anytime" files. Many of the papers and online documents that cross your desk will probably consist of basic background material—items that are important to read but not urgent. Place these documents in a folder and save them for a Friday afternoon or a plane trip. ⊠

Name _____ Date _____/_____/_____

1. Name the acrostic that can help you remember the steps of Muscle Reading.

2. You must complete all nine steps of Muscle Reading to get the most out of any reading assignment. True or False? Explain your answer.

3. Describe at least three strategies you can use to preview a reading assignment.

4. What is one benefit of outlining a reading assignment?

5. Define the terms *prefix* and *suffix*, and explain how they can assist you in learning the meanings of new words.

6. To get the most benefit from marking a book, underline at least 25 percent of the text. True or False? Explain your answer.

7. Explain at least three techniques you can use when reading is tough.

8. According to the Power Process in this chapter, mental pictures are strictly visual images. True or False? Explain your answer.

9. Define the "topic-point" method of summarizing.

10. List at least three techniques for increasing your reading speed.

learning styles application

The questions below will "cycle" you through four styles, or modes, of learning as explained in the article "Learning styles: Discover how you learn" in Chapter One. Each question will help you explore a different mode. You can answer the questions in any order.

what if *Consider how you might adapt or modify Muscle Reading to make it more useful. List any steps that you would add, subtract, or change.*

why *List current reading assignments that you could use to practice Muscle Reading.*

how *Briefly describe how you will approach reading assignments differently after studying this chapter.*

what *List the three most useful suggestions for reading that you gained from this chapter.*

master student profile

HELEN KELLER

(1880–1968) Author and lecturer. Illness left her blind, deaf, and mute at the age of 19 months.

The morning after my teacher came she led me into her room and gave me a doll. The little blind children at the Perkins Institution had sent it and Laura Bridgman had dressed it; but I did not know this until afterward. When I had played with it a little while, Miss Sullivan slowly spelled into my hand the word "d-o-l-l." I was at once interested in this finger play and tried to imitate it. When I finally succeeded in making the letters correctly I was flushed with childish pleasure and pride. Running downstairs to my mother I held up my hand and made the letters for doll. I did not know that I was spelling a word or even that words existed; I was simply making my fingers go in monkey-like imitation. In the days that followed I learned to spell in this uncomprehending way a great many words, among them *pin*, *hat*, *cup*, and a few verbs like *sit*, *stand*, and *walk*. But my teacher had been with me several weeks before I understood that everything has a name.

One day, while I was playing with my new doll, Miss Sullivan put my big rag doll into my lap also, spelled "d-o-l-l" and tried to make me understand that "d-o-l-l" applied to both. Earlier in the day we had had a tussle over the words "m-u-g" and "w-a-t-e-r." Miss Sullivan had tried to impress it upon me that "m-u-g" is mug and that "w-a-t-e-r" is water, but I persisted in confounding the two. In despair she had dropped the subject for the time, only to renew it at the first opportunity. I became impatient at her repeated attempts and, seizing the new doll, I dashed it upon the floor. I was keenly delighted when I felt the fragments of the broken doll at my feet. Neither sorrow nor regret followed my passionate outburst. I had not loved the doll. In the still, dark world in which I lived there was no strong sentiment or tenderness. I felt my teacher sweep the fragments to one side of the hearth, and I had a sense of satisfaction that the cause of my discomfort was removed. She brought me my hat, and I knew I was going out into the warm sunshine. This thought, if a wordless sensation may be called a thought, made me hop and skip with pleasure.

We walked down the path to the well house, attracted by the fragrance of honeysuckle with which it was covered. Someone was drawing water and my teacher placed my hand under the spout. As the cool stream gushed over one hand she spelled into the other the word *water*, first slowly, then rapidly. I stood still, my whole attention fixed upon the motions of her fingers. Suddenly I felt a misty consciousness as of something forgotten—a thrill of returning to thought; and somehow the mystery of language was revealed to me. I knew then that "w-a-t-e-r" meant the wonderful cool something that was flowing over my hand. That living word awakened my soul, it gave it light, hope, joy, set it free! There were barriers still, it is true, but barriers that could in time be swept away.

I left the well house eager to learn. Everything had a name, and each name gave birth to a new thought. As we returned to the house, every object which I touched seemed to quiver with life. That was because I saw everything with the strange, new sight that had come to me. ❖

From Helen Keller, *The Story of My Life* (New York: Doubleday, Page & Company, 1905), 22–24.

For more biographical information on Helen Keller, visit the Master Student Hall of Fame on the *Becoming a Master Student* Web site at

masterstudent.college.hmco.com

5

Notes

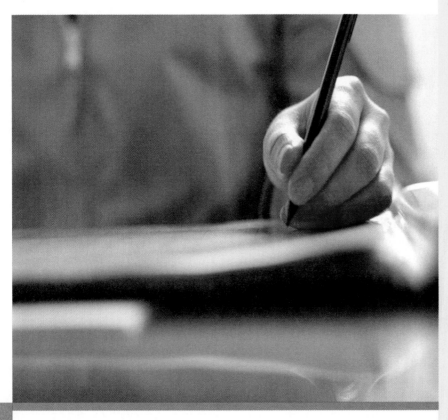

why
this chapter matters . . .

Note taking helps you remember information and influences how well you do on tests

what
is included . . .

The note-taking process flows
Observe
Record
Review
Create your instructor
When your instructor talks fast
Taking notes while reading
Power Process: "I create it all"
Master Student Profile: Craig Kielburger

how
you can use this chapter . . .

Experiment with several formats for note taking.
Create a note-taking format that works especially well for you.
Take effective notes in special situations—while reading, when instructors talk fast, and to chronicle your life.

As you read, ask yourself
what if . . .

I could take notes that remain informative and useful for weeks, months, or even years to come?

STUDENT VOICES

"I had a meeting with my English instructor to look over a paper I had written, and I didn't have the paper with me. He had a look in his eyes that said to me that I was just another average, irresponsible student. Or maybe what I saw in his eyes were my own feelings. Ever since that day, my whole attitude has changed. Since then I have always wanted to be better than average. The biggest step to be better than average is to be responsible."

—RICHARD GREEN, JR.

The note-taking process flows

One way to understand note taking is to realize that taking notes is just one part of the process. Effective note taking consists of three parts: observing, recording, and reviewing. First, you observe an "event"—a statement by an instructor, a lab experiment, a slide show of an artist's works, or a chapter of required reading. Then you record your observations of that event, that is, you "take notes." Finally, you review what you have recorded.

Each part of the process is essential, and each depends on the others. Your observations determine what you record. What you record determines what you review. And the quality of your review can determine how effective your next observations will be. For example, if you review your notes on the Sino-Japanese War of 1894, the next day's lecture on the Boxer Rebellion of 1900 will make more sense.

Legible and speedy handwriting is also useful in taking notes. A knowledge of outlining is handy, too. A nifty pen, a new notebook, and a laptop computer are all great note-taking devices. And they're all worthless—unless you participate as an energetic observer *in* class and regularly review your notes *after* class. If you take those two steps, you can turn even the most disorganized chicken scratches into a powerful tool. Sometimes note taking looks like a passive affair, especially in large lecture classes. One person at the front of the room does most of the talking. Everyone else is seated and silent, taking notes. The lecturer seems to be doing all of the work.

Don't be deceived. Observe more closely, and you'll see some students taking notes in a way that radiates energy. They're awake and alert, poised on the edge of their seats. They're writing, a physical activity that expresses mental engagement. These students listen for levels of ideas and information, make choices about what to record, and compile materials to review. In higher education, you might spend hundreds of hours taking notes. Making them more effective is a direct investment in your success. Think of your notes as a textbook that *you* create—one that's more current and more in tune with your learning preferences than any textbook you could buy. ▨

journal entry 12

Discovery/Intention Statement

Think about the possible benefits of improving your skills at note taking. Recall a recent incident in which you had difficulty taking notes. Perhaps you were listening to an instructor who talked fast, or you got confused and stopped taking notes altogether. Describe the incident in the space below.

_____

_____

_____

_____

_____

Now preview this chapter to find at least five strategies that you can use right away to help you take better notes. Sum up each of those strategies in a few words and note page numbers where you can find out more about each suggestion.

Strategy   *Page number*

_____

_____

_____

_____

_____

Reflect on your intention to experiment actively with this chapter. Describe a specific situation in which you might apply the strategies you listed above. If possible, choose a situation that will occur within the next 24 hours.

I intend to . . .

_____

_____

_____

_____

OBSERVE

The note-taking process flows

Sherlock Holmes, a fictional master detective and student of the obvious, could track down a villain by observing the fold of his scarf and the mud on his shoes. In real life, a doctor can save a life by observing a mole—one a patient has always had—that undergoes a rapid change.

An accountant can save a client thousands of dollars by observing the details of a spreadsheet. A student can save hours of studying by observing that she gets twice as much done at a particular time of day.

Keen observers see facts and relationships. They know ways to focus their attention on the details, then tap their creative energy to discover patterns. Experiment with the following techniques to sharpen your classroom observation skills.

Set the stage

Complete outside assignments. Instructors usually assume that students complete assignments, and they construct their lectures accordingly. The more familiar you are with a subject, the more easily you can absorb important information during class lectures.

Bring the right materials. Make sure you have a pen, pencil, notebook, and any other materials you will need. Bring your textbook to class, especially if the lectures relate closely to the text.

Sit front and center. The closer you sit to the lecturer, the easier it is to hear, and the harder it is to fall asleep. The closer you sit to the front, the fewer interesting, or distracting, classmates are situated between you and the instructor. Material on the board is easier to read from up front. Also, the instructor can see you more easily when you have a question.

Sitting close to the front is a way to commit yourself to getting what you want out of school. One reason students gravitate to the back of the classroom is that they think the instructor is less likely to call on them. Sitting in back can signal a lack of commitment. When you sit up front, you are declaring your willingness to take a risk and participate.

Conduct a short preclass review. Arrive early; then put your brain in gear by reviewing your notes from the previous class. Scan your reading assignment. Look at the sections you have underlined. Review assigned problems and exercises. Note questions you intend to ask.

"Be here now" in class

Accept your wandering mind. The techniques in the Power Process: "Be here now" can be especially useful when your head soars into the clouds. Don't fight daydreaming. When you notice your mind wandering during class, look at this as an opportunity to refocus your attention. If thermodynamics is losing out to beach parties, let go of the beach.

You also can use writing in a direct way to clear your mind of distracting thoughts. Pause for a few seconds and write those thoughts down. Once your distractions are out of your mind and safely stored on paper, you can gently return your attention to taking notes.

Be with the instructor. In your mind, put yourself right up front with the instructor. Imagine that you and the instructor are the only ones in the room and that the lecture is a personal conversation between the two of you. Pay attention to the instructor's body language and facial expressions. Look the instructor in the eye.

Notice your environment. When you become aware of yourself daydreaming, bring yourself back to class by paying attention to the temperature in the room, the feel of your chair, or the quality of light coming through the window. Run your hand along the surface of your desk. Listen to the chalk on the blackboard or the sound of the teacher's voice. Be in that environment. Once your attention is back in the room, you can focus on what's happening in class.

Postpone debate. When you hear something you disagree with, note your disagreement and let it go. Don't allow your internal dialogue to drown out subsequent material. If your disagreement is persistent and strong, make note of this and then move on. Internal debate can prevent you from absorbing new information. It is OK to absorb information you don't agree with. Just absorb it with the mental tag "My instructor says . . . , and I don't agree with this."

Let go of judgments about lecture styles. Don't let your attitude about an instructor's lecture style, habits, or appearance get in the way of your education. You can decrease the power of your judgments if you pay attention to them and let them go.

You can even let go of judgments about rambling, unorganized lectures. Take the initiative and organize the material yourself. While taking notes, separate the key points from the examples and supporting evidence. Note the places where you got confused and make a list of questions to ask.

Participate in class activities. Ask questions. Volunteer for demonstrations. Join in class discussions. Be willing to take a risk or look foolish, if that's what it takes for you to learn. Chances are good the question you think is "dumb" is also on the minds of several of your classmates.

Relate the class to your goals. If you have trouble staying awake in a particular class, write at the top of your notes how that class relates to a specific goal. Identify the reward or payoff for reaching that goal.

Think critically about what you hear. This might seem contrary to "Postpone debate." It's not. Choose not to think critically about the instructor's ideas during the lecture. Do it later as you review and edit your notes. This is a time to list questions or write down your agreements and disagreements.

Watch for clues

Be alert to repetition. When an instructor repeats a phrase or an idea, make a note of it. Repetition is a signal that the instructor thinks the information is important.

Listen for introductory, concluding, and transition words and phrases. These include phrases such as "the following three factors," "in conclusion," "the most important consideration," "in addition to," and "on the other hand." These phrases and others signal relationships, definitions, new subjects, conclusions, cause and effect, and examples. They reveal the structure of the ideas. Use these phrases to organize your notes.

Watch the board or overhead projector. If an instructor takes the time to write something down, consider the material to be important. Copy all diagrams and drawings, equations, names, places, dates, statistics, and definitions.

Watch the instructor's eyes. If an instructor glances at her notes and then makes a point, it is probably a signal that the information is especially important. Anything she reads from her notes is a potential test question.

Highlight the obvious clues. Instructors will often tell students point-blank that certain information is likely to appear on an exam. Make stars or other special marks in your notes next to this information. Instructors are not trying to hide what's important.

Notice the instructor's interest level. If the instructor is excited about a topic, it is more likely to appear on an exam. Pay attention when she seems more animated than usual. ✖

→ What to do when you miss a class

For most courses, you'll benefit by attending every class session. If you miss a class, try to catch up as quickly as possible.

Clarify policies on missed classes. On the first day of classes, find out about your instructors' policies on absences. See if you can make up assignments, quizzes, and tests. Also inquire about doing extra-credit assignments.

Contact a classmate. Early in the semester, identify a student in each class who seems responsible and

dependable. Exchange e-mail addresses and phone numbers. If you know you won't be in class, contact this student ahead of time. When you notice that your classmate is absent, pick up extra copies of handouts, make assignments lists, and offer copies of your notes.

Contact your instructor. If you miss a class, e-mail, phone, or fax your instructor, or put a note in her mailbox. Ask if she has another section of the same course that you could attend so you won't miss the lecture information. Also ask about getting handouts you might need before the next class meeting.

RECORD

The note-taking process flows

The format and structure of your notes are more important than how fast you write or how elegant your handwriting is. The following techniques can improve the effectiveness of your notes.

General techniques for note taking

Use key words. An easy way to sort the extraneous material from the important points is to take notes using key words. Key words or phrases contain the essence of communication. They include technical terms, names, numbers, equations, and words of degree: *most, least, faster,* etc. Key words evoke images and associations with other words and ideas. They trigger your memory. That makes them powerful review tools.

One key word can initiate the recall of a whole cluster of ideas. A few key words can form a chain from which you can reconstruct an entire lecture.

To see how key words work, take yourself to an imaginary classroom. You are now in the middle of an anatomy lecture. Picture what the room looks like, what it feels like, how it smells. You hear the instructor say:

OK, what happens when we look directly over our heads and see a piano falling out of the sky? How do we take that signal and translate it into the action of getting out of the way? The first thing that happens is that a stimulus is generated in the neurons—receptor neurons—of the eye. Light reflected from the piano reaches our eyes. In other words, we see the piano. The receptor neurons in the eye transmit that sensory signal, the sight of the piano, to the body's nervous system. That's all they can do, pass on information. So we've got a sensory signal coming into the nervous

system. But the neurons that initiate movement in our legs are effector neurons. The information from the sensory neurons must be transmitted to effector neurons, or we will get squashed by the piano. There must be some kind of interconnection between receptor and effector neurons. What happens between the two? What is the connection?

Key words you might note in this example include *stimulus, generated, receptor neurons, transmit, sensory signals, nervous system, effector neurons,* and *connection*. You could reduce the instructor's 163 words to these 12 key words. With a few transitional words, your notes might look like this:

> Stimulus (piano) generated in receptor neurons (eye).
> Sensory signals transmitted by nervous system to effector neurons (legs).
> What connects receptor to effector?

Note the last key word of the lecture above—*connection*. This word is part of the instructor's question and leads to the next point in the lecture. Be on the lookout for questions like this. They can help you organize your notes and are often clues for test questions.

Use pictures and diagrams. Make relationships visual. Copy all diagrams from the board and invent your own.

A drawing of a piano falling on someone who is looking up, for example, might be used to demonstrate the relationship of receptor neurons to effector neurons. Label the eyes "receptor" and the feet "effector." This picture implies that the sight of the piano must be translated into a motor response. By connecting the explanation of the process with the unusual picture of the piano falling, you can link the elements of the process together.

Write notes in paragraphs. When it is difficult to follow the organization of a lecture or to put information into outline form, create a series of informal paragraphs. These paragraphs will contain few complete sentences. Reserve complete sentences for precise definitions, direct quotations, and important points that the instructor emphasizes by repetition or other signals—such as the statement "This is an important point." For other material, apply the suggestions in this article for using key words.

Copy material from the board. Record all formulas, diagrams, and problems that the teacher writes down. Copy dates, numbers, names, places, and other facts. If it's on the board, put it in your notes. You can even use your own signal or code to flag that material. If it appears on the board, it can appear on a test.

Use a three-ring binder. Three-ring binders have several advantages over other kinds of notebooks. First, pages can be removed and spread out when you review. This way, you can get the whole picture of a lecture. Second, the three-ring binder format allows you to insert handouts right into your notes. Third, you can insert your own out-of-class notes in the correct order. Fourth, you can easily make additions, corrections, and revisions.

Use only one side of a piece of paper. When you use one side of a page, you can review and organize all your notes by spreading them out side by side. Most students find the benefit well worth the cost of the paper. Perhaps you're concerned about the environmental impact of consuming more paper. If so, you can use the blank side of old notes and use recycled paper.

Use 3x5 cards. As an alternative to using notebook paper, use 3x5 cards to take lecture notes. Copy each new concept onto a separate 3x5 card. Later, you can organize these cards in an outline form and use them as pocket flash cards.

Keep your own thoughts separate. For the most part, avoid making editorial comments in your lecture notes. The danger is that when you return to your notes, you might mistake your own idea for that of the instructor. If you want to make a comment—either a question to ask later or a strong disagreement—clearly label it as your own. Pick a symbol or code and use it in every class.

Use an "I'm lost" signal. No matter how attentive and alert you are, you might get lost and confused in a lecture. If it is inappropriate to ask a question, record in your notes that you were lost. Invent your own signal— for example, a circled question mark. When you write down your code for "I'm lost," leave space for the explanation or clarification that you will get later. The space will also be a signal that you missed something. Later, you can speak to your instructor or ask to see a fellow student's notes. As long as you are honest with yourself when you don't understand, you can stay on top of the course.

Label, number, and date all notes. Develop the habit of labeling and dating your notes at the beginning of each class. Number the page, too. Sometimes the sequence of material in a lecture is important. Write your name and phone number in each notebook in case you lose it. Class notes become more and more valuable as a term or semester progresses.

Use standard abbreviations. Be consistent with your abbreviations. If you make up your own abbreviations or symbols, write a key explaining them in your notes. Avoid vague abbreviations. When you use an abbreviation such as *comm.* for *committee*, you run the risk of not being able to remember whether you meant *committee, commission, common, commit, community, communicate,* or *communist.*

One way to abbreviate is to leave out vowels. For example, *talk* becomes *tlk, said* becomes *sd, American* becomes *Amrcn.*

Leave blank space. Notes tightly crammed into every corner of the page are hard to read and difficult to use for review. Give your eyes a break by leaving plenty of space.

Later, when you review, you can use the blank spaces in your notes to clarify points, write questions, or add other material. Instructors often return to material covered earlier in the lecture.

Take notes in different colors. You can use colors as highly visible organizers. For example, you can signal important points with red. Or use one color of ink for notes about the text and another color for lecture notes. Notes that are visually pleasing can be easier to review.

Use graphic signals. The following ideas can be used with any note-taking format.

- Use brackets, parentheses, circles, and squares to group information that belongs together.

- Use stars, arrows, and underlining to indicate important points. Flag the most important points with double stars, double arrows, or double underlines.

- Use arrows and connecting lines to link related groups and to replace words such as *leads to, becomes,* and *produces.*

- Use equal signs and greater- and less-than signs to indicate compared quantities.

- Use question marks for their obvious purpose. Double question marks can signal tough questions or especially confusing points.

To avoid creating confusion with graphic symbols, use them carefully and consistently. Write a "dictionary" of your symbols in the front of your notebooks, such as the one shown below.

Use recorders effectively. There are persuasive arguments for not using a tape recorder or digital recorder. Here are the main ones.

When you tape a lecture, there is a strong temptation to daydream. After all, you can always listen to the lecture again later on. Unfortunately, if you let the recorder do all of the work, you are skipping a valuable part of the learning process. Actively participating in class can turn a lecture into a valuable study session.

There are more potential problems. Listening to recorded lectures can take a lot of time—more time than reviewing written notes. Recorders can't answer the questions you didn't ask in class. Also, recording devices malfunction. In fact, the unscientific Hypothesis of Recording Glitches states that the tendency of recorders to malfunction is directly proportional to the importance of the material. With those warnings in mind, some students use a recorder effectively. For example, you can use recordings as backups to written notes. (Check with your instructor first. Some prefer not to be recorded.) Turn the recorder on; then take notes as if it weren't there. Recordings can be especially useful if an instructor speaks fast.

You could also record yourself after class, reading your written notes. Teaching the class to yourself is a powerful review tool. Instead of taping all of your notes, for example, you might record only the key facts or concepts.

The Cornell format

A note-taking system that has worked for students around the world is the *Cornell format*.[1] Originally developed by Walter Pauk at Cornell University during the 1950s, this approach continues to be taught across the United States and in other countries as well.

The cornerstone of this system is what Pauk calls the *cue column*—a wide margin on the left-hand side of the paper. The cue column is the key to the Cornell format's many benefits. Here's how to use the Cornell format.

Format your paper. On each sheet of your note paper, draw a vertical line, top to bottom, about two inches from the left edge of the paper. This line creates the cue column—the space to the left of the line.

Take notes, leaving the cue column blank. As you read an assignment or listen to a lecture, take notes on the right-hand side of the paper. Fill up this column with sentences, paragraphs, outlines, charts, or drawings. Do not write in the cue column. You'll use this space later as you do the next steps.

Condense your notes in the cue column. Think of the notes you took on the right-hand side of the paper as a set of answers. In the cue column, list potential test questions that correspond to your notes. Write one question for each major term or point.

As an alternative to questions, you can list key words from your notes. Yet another option is to pretend that your notes are a series of articles on different topics. In the cue column, write a newspaper-style headline for each "article." In any case, be brief. If you cram the cue column full of words, you defeat its purpose—to reduce the number and length of your notes.

Write a summary. Pauk recommends that you reduce your notes even more by writing a brief summary at the bottom of each page. This step offers you another way to engage actively with the material. It can also make your notes easier to review for tests.

Cue column	Notes
What are some key changes in U.S. health over the last 50 years?	Over the past 50 years in the U.S.: — The number of smokers decreased. — Infant mortality dropped to a record low. — Life expectancy hit a record high–about 77 years.
Who announced these changes?	Source: Health, United States 2002, Centers for Disease Control. Health and Human Services Secretary Tommy Thompson announced this report.

Summary
Changes in American health over the last 50 years include fewer smokers, lower infant mortality, and record life expectancy.

Use the cue column to recite. Cover the right-hand side of your notes with a blank sheet of paper. Leave only the cue column showing. Then look at each item you wrote in the cue column and talk about it. If you wrote questions, answer each question. If you wrote key words, define each word and talk about why it's important. If you wrote headlines in the cue column, explain what each one means and offer supporting details. After reciting, uncover your notes and look for any important points you missed. Repeat this cycle of reciting and checking until you've mastered the material.

Mind mapping

This system, developed by Tony Buzan,[2] can be used in conjunction with the Cornell format. In some circumstances, you might want to use mind maps exclusively.

To understand mind maps, first review the features of traditional note taking. Outlines (explained in the next section) divide major topics into minor topics, which, in turn, are subdivided further. They organize information in a sequential, linear way.

This kind of organization doesn't reflect certain aspects of brain function, a point that has been made in discussions about "left brain" and "right brain" activities. People often use the term *right brain* when referring to creative, pattern-making, visual, intuitive brain activity. They use the term *left brain* when talking about orderly, logical, step-by-step characteristics of thought. Writing teacher Gabrielle Rico uses another metaphor. She refers to the left-brain mode as our "sign mind" (concerned with words) and the right-brain mode as our "design mind" (concerned with visuals).[3]

A mind map uses both kinds of brain functions. Mind maps can contain lists and sequences and show relationships. They can also provide a picture of a subject. Mind maps are visual patterns that can serve as a framework for recalling information. They work on both verbal and nonverbal levels.

One benefit of mind maps is that they quickly, vividly, and accurately show the relationships among ideas. Also, mind mapping helps you think from general to specific. By choosing a main topic, you focus first on the big picture, then zero in on subordinate details. And by using only key words, you can condense a large subject into a small area on a mind map. You can review more quickly by looking at the key words on a mind map than

by reading notes word for word.

Give yourself plenty of room. Use blank paper that measures at least 11 by 17 inches. If that's not available, turn regular notebook paper on its side so that you can take notes in a horizontal (instead of vertical) format. Another option is to find software that allows you to draw flow charts or diagrams. Then you can generate mind maps on a computer.

Determine the main concept of the lecture. Write that concept in the center of the paper and circle it, underline it, or highlight it with color. You can also write the concept in large letters. Record concepts related to the main concept on lines that radiate outward from the center. An alternative is to circle these concepts.

Use key words only. Whenever possible, reduce each concept to a single word per line or circle in your mind map. Though this might seem awkward at first, it prompts you to summarize and to condense ideas to their essence. That means fewer words for you to write now and fewer to review when it's time to prepare for tests. (Using shorthand symbols and abbreviations can help.) Key words are usually nouns and verbs that communicate the bulk of the speaker's ideas. Choose words that are rich in associations and that can help you re-create the lecture.

Jazz it up. Use color to organize your mind map. If there are three main subjects covered in the lecture, you can record each subject in a different color. Add symbols and other images as well.

Create links. One mind map doesn't have to include all of the ideas in a book or an article. Instead, you can link mind maps. For example, draw a mind map that sums up the five key points in a chapter, and then make a separate, more detailed mind map for each of those key points. Within each mind map, include references to the other mind maps. This helps explain and reinforce the relationships among many ideas. Some students pin several mind maps next to each other on a bulletin board

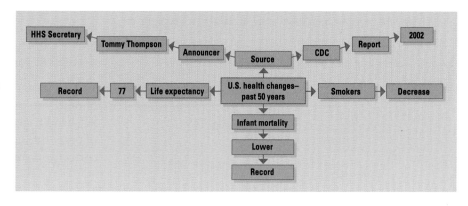

or tape them to a wall. This allows for a dramatic—and effective—look at the big picture.

Outlining

An outline shows the relationship between major points and supporting ideas. One benefit of taking notes in the outline format is that doing so can totally occupy your attention. You are recording ideas and also organizing them. This can be an advantage if the material has been presented in a disorganized way. Perhaps you've had negative experiences with outlining in the past. Teachers might have required you to use complex, rigid outlining formats based exclusively on Roman numerals or on some unfamiliar system. By playing with variations, you can discover the power of outlining to reveal relationships between ideas. Technically, each word, phrase, or sentence that appears in an outline is called a *heading*. These are arranged in different levels:

- In the first or "top" level of headings, note the major topics that are presented in a lecture or reading assignment.

- In the second level of headings, record the key points that relate to each topic in the first-level headings.

- In the third level of headings, record specific facts and details that support or explain each of your second-level headings. Each additional level of subordinate heading supports the ideas in the previous level of heading.

Roman numerals offer one way to illustrate the difference between levels of headings. See the following example.

First-level heading

I. Health and Human Services Secretary Tommy G. Thompson reports that Americans' health changed over the past 50 years.

Second-level heading

   A. Thompson: "When you take the long view, you see clearly how far we've come in combating diseases, making workplaces safer, and avoiding risks such as smoking."
   B. Thompson referred to *Health, United States, 2002*, a report from the Centers for Disease Control and Prevention (CDC).

II. By 2000, infant mortality dropped to a record low and life expectancy hit a record high.
   A. Death rates among children up to age 24 were cut in half.
   B. Americans enjoyed the longest life expectancy in U.S. history.

III. Among working-age adults, fewer are dying from unintentional injuries, heart disease, stroke, and AIDS.

Third-level heading

   A. After 1995, deaths from AIDS dropped.
     1. Powerful new drugs contributed to this result.
     2. Other drugs are now in development.
   B. A decline in smoking contributed to the decline in heart disease.
     1. More than 40 percent of adults were smokers in 1965.
     2. In 2000, just 23 percent smoked.

You can also use other heading styles, as illustrated at right.

Combining formats

Feel free to use different note-taking systems for different subjects and to combine formats. Do what works for you.

For example, combine mind maps along with the Cornell format. You can modify the Cornell format by dividing your note paper in half, reserving one half for mind maps and the other for linear information such as lists, graphs, and outlines as well as equations, long explanations, and word-for-word definitions. You can incorporate a mind map into your paragraph-style notes whenever you feel one is appropriate. Mind maps are also useful for summarizing notes taken in the Cornell format.

John Sperry, a teacher at Utah Valley State College, developed a note-taking system that can include all of the formats discussed in this article:

- Fill up a three-ring binder with fresh paper. Open your notebook so that you see two blank pages—one on the left and one on the right. Plan to take notes across this entire two-page spread.

- During class or while reading, write your notes only on the left-hand page. Place a large dash next to each main topic or point. If your instructor skips a step or switches topics unexpectedly, just keep writing.

- Later, use the right-hand page to review and elaborate on the notes that you took earlier. This page is for anything you want. For example, add visuals such as mind maps. Write review questions, headlines, possible test questions, summaries, outlines, mnemonics, or analogies that link new concepts to your current knowledge.

- To keep ideas in sequence, place appropriate numbers on top of the dashes in your notes on the left-hand page. Even if concepts are presented out of order during class, they'll still be numbered correctly in your notes. ✖

Distinguish levels with indentations only:

First-level heading
   Second-level heading
      Third-level heading
         Fourth-level heading

Distinguish levels with bullets and dashes:

FIRST–LEVEL HEADING
   • Second-level heading
     – Third-level heading

Distinguish headings by size:

FIRST–LEVEL HEADING
Second-level heading
Third-level heading

The note-taking process flows

Think of reviewing as an integral part of note taking rather than as an added task.

Review within 24 hours. This might be the most powerful note-taking technique you can use. It can save you hours of review time later in the term.

If you review your class notes soon enough, you can move that information from short-term to long-term memory. And you can often do it in 10 minutes or less.

The sooner you review your notes, the better, especially if the class was difficult. In fact, you can start reviewing during class. When your instructor pauses to set up the overhead projector or erase the board, scan your notes. Or get to your next class as quickly as you can. Then use the minutes before the lecture begins to review the notes you just took in the previous class. If you do not get to your notes immediately after class, you can still benefit by reviewing later in the day. A review right before you go to sleep can also be valuable.

Think of the day's unreviewed notes as leaky faucets, constantly dripping, losing precious information until you shut them off with a quick review.

Edit notes. During your first review, fix words that are illegible. Write out abbreviated words that might be unclear to you later. Make sure you can read everything. If you can't read something or don't understand something you *can* read, mark it, and make a note to ask your instructor or another student. Check to see that your notes are labeled with the date and class and that the pages are numbered. You can edit with a different colored pen or pencil if you want to distinguish between what you wrote in class and what you filled in later.

Fill in key words in the left-hand column. This task is important if you are to get the full benefit of using the Cornell format. Using the key word principles described earlier in this chapter, go through your notes and write key words, phrases, or questions in the left-hand column. These will speed up the review process later.

Next use the left-hand column as a cue to recite. With a blank sheet of paper, cover your notes, leaving only the left-hand margin showing. Take key words or questions in order and recite as much as you can about them. Then uncover your notes and look for any important points you missed.

Conduct short weekly review periods. Once a week, review all of your notes again. The review sessions don't need to take a lot of time. Even a 20-minute weekly review period is valuable. Some students find that a weekend review, say, on Sunday afternoon, helps them stay in continuous touch with the material. Scheduling regular review sessions on your calendar helps develop the habit.

Consider typing up your notes. Some students type up their handwritten notes using a computer. Typed notes are easier to read, and they take up less space. Also, the process of typing them forces you to review the material.

Another alternative is to bypass handwriting altogether and take notes in class on a laptop computer. However, computer errors can wipe out your notes, leaving you with no handwritten backup.

Experiment with typing notes and see what works for you. For example, you might type up only key portions of notes, such as summaries or outlines.

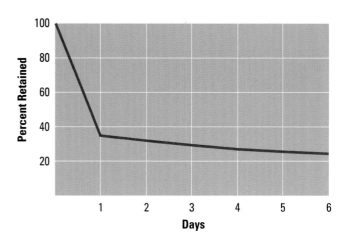

To study the process of memory and forgetting, Hermann Ebbinghaus devised a method for testing memory. The results, shown here in what has come to be known as the Ebbinghaus forgetting curve, demonstrate that forgetting occurs most rapidly shortly after learning and then gradually declines over time.

Create mind map summaries. Mind mapping is an excellent way to make summary sheets. After drawing your map, look at your original notes and fill in anything you missed. This system is fun to use. It's quick, and it gives your brain a hook on which to fasten the material.

journal entry 13

Discovery Statement

Think about the way you have conducted reviews of your notes in the past. Respond to the following statements by checking "Always," "Often," "Sometimes," "Seldom," or "Never" after each.

I review my notes immediately after class.
___Always ___Often ___Sometimes
___Seldom ___Never

I conduct weekly reviews of my notes.
___Always ___Often ___Sometimes
___Seldom ___Never

I make summary sheets of my notes.
___Always ___Often ___Sometimes
___Seldom ___Never

I edit my notes within 24 hours.
___Always ___Often ___Sometimes
___Seldom ___Never

Before class, I conduct a brief review of the notes I took in the previous class.
___Always ___Often ___Sometimes
___Seldom ___Never

exercise 14

TELEVISION NOTE TAKING

You can use evening news broadcasts to practice listening for key words, writing quickly, focusing your attention, and reviewing. As with other skills, the more you practice note taking, the better you become.

The next time you watch the news, use pen and paper to jot down key words and information. During the commercials, review and revise your notes. At the end of the broadcast, spend five minutes reviewing all of your notes. Create a mind map of a few news stories; then sum up the news of the day for a friend.

This exercise will help you develop an ear for key words. Since you can't ask questions or request that the speaker slow down, you train yourself to stay totally in the moment. If you get behind, relax, leave a space, and return your attention to the broadcast.

Don't be discouraged if you miss a lot the first time around. Do this exercise several times and observe how your mind works.

If you find it too difficult to take notes during a fast-paced television news show, check your local broadcast schedule for a news documentary. These are often slower paced. Another option is to tape a program and then take notes. You can stop the tape at any point to review your notes.

You can also ask a classmate to do the same exercise, and then compare notes the next day.

Create your instructor

There are as many definitions of a "poor" instructor as there are students. For some students, "poor" means "boring," "rude," or "insensitive." Or maybe it's an instructor who never remembers what day it is, blows her nose every five minutes, and wears a cologne that could kill a hamster at 30 paces.

Faced with such facts, you have some choices. One is to label the instructor a "dud," "dweeb," "geek," or "airhead," and let it go at that. When you choose this solution, you get to endure class, complain to other students, and wait for a miracle. This choice puts you at the mercy of circumstance. It gives your instructor responsibility for the quality of your education, not to mention responsibility for giving you value for your money.

There is another option. You do not have to give away your power. Instead, you can take responsibility for your education. Use any of the following techniques to change the way you experience your instructors. In effect, you can "create your instructor."

Research the instructor. There are formal and informal sources of information you can turn to before you register for class. One is the school catalog. Alumni magazines or newsletters or the school newspaper might run articles on teachers. In some schools, students circulate informal evaluations of instructors. Also talk to students who have taken courses from the instructor.

Or introduce yourself to the instructor. Set up a visit during office hours and ask about the course. This can help you get the flavor of the class, as well as clues to the instructor's teaching style.

Show interest in class. Students give teachers moment-by-moment feedback in class. That feedback comes through posture, eye contact, responses to questions, and participation in class discussions. If you find a class boring, re-create the instructor through a massive display of interest. Arrive early to class, ask lots of questions, answer questions, and make eye contact. Your enthusiasm might enliven your instructor. If not, you are still creating a more enjoyable class for yourself.

Choose your attitude. Maybe your instructor reminds you of someone you don't like—your annoying Aunt Edna, a rude store clerk, or the fifth-grade teacher who kept you after school. Your attitudes are in your own head and beyond the instructor's control.

An instructor's beliefs about politics, religion, or feminism are not related to teaching ability. Likewise, using a formal or informal lecture style does not indicate knowledge of subject matter. Being aware of such things can help you let go of negative judgments.

Remember classroom etiquette. Certain classroom behaviors promote negative relationships with instructors. Examples are perpetually arriving late or leaving early, wearing headphones, yawning, eating, text messaging, answering a cell phone, arguing about a grade, and showing up with a hangover.

Remembering a few basics of classroom etiquette can help you create the kind of instructor you want. For example, address instructors by their first name only with their permission. Focus your attention in class and avoid behaviors that distract your classmates. Treat instructors respectfully, and you're far more likely to get the same treatment in return.

Classroom etiquette extends to the way that you use any piece of technology. For instance, a cell phone that rings in class offends teachers and irritates almost everyone else in the room. Turn off your cell phone and check voice mail messages after class.

Get to know the instructor better. You might be missing the strong points of an instructor you don't like. Meet with your instructor during office hours. Ask questions that weren't answered in class. Teachers who seem boring in class can be fascinating in person. Send follow-up notes via e-mail. Prepare to notice your pictures and let them go.

Open up to diversity. Sometimes students can create their instructors by letting go of pictures about different races and ethnic groups. According to one picture, a Hispanic person cannot teach English literature. According to other pictures, a white teacher cannot have anything valid to say about African music, a teacher in a wheelchair cannot command the attention of 100 people in a lecture hall, and a male instructor cannot speak credibly about feminism. All of those pictures can clash with reality. Releasing them can open up new opportunities for understanding and appreciation.

Separate liking from learning. You don't have to like an instructor to learn from the person.

One strategy is to focus on content instead of form. Form is the way something is organized or presented. If you are irritated at the sound of an instructor's voice, you're focusing on the form of her presentation. When you put aside your concern about her voice and turn your attention to the points she's making, you're focusing on content.

Remember this strategy if your personal opinions about an instructor's clothes, hairstyle, political views, or mannerisms get in the way of your learning. Notice your reactions without judgment. Then gently return your attention to the class content.

Form your own opinion about each instructor. You might hear conflicting reports about teachers from other students. The same instructor could be described as a riveting speaker or as someone completely lacking in charisma. Decide for yourself.

Seek alternatives. You might feel more comfortable with another teacher's style or method of organizing course materials. Consider changing teachers, asking another teacher for help outside class, or attending an additional section taught by a different instructor. You can also learn from other students, courses, tutors, study groups, books, DVDs, and tapes. You can be a master student, even when you have teachers you don't like. Your education is your own creation.

Avoid excuses. Instructors know them all. Most teachers can see a snow job coming before the first flake hits the ground. Accept responsibility for your own mistakes, and avoid thinking that you can fool the teacher. When you treat instructors honestly, you are more likely to be treated as a responsible adult in return.

Submit professional work. Prepare papers and projects as if you were submitting them to an employer. Imagine that a promotion and raise will be determined by your work. Instructors often grade hundreds of papers during a term. Your neat, orderly, well-organized paper can lift a teacher's spirits after a long night of deciphering gibberish.

Accept criticism. Learn from your teachers' comments about your work. It is a teacher's job to give feedback. Don't take it personally.

Use conference time effectively. Instructors are usually happy to answer questions about class content. To get the most out of conference time, be prepared to ask those questions. Bring your notes, text, and any other materials you might need. During this session you can also address more difficult subjects, such as grades, attendance policies, lecture styles, term papers, or personality conflicts.

Instead of trying to solve a serious problem in the few minutes before or after class, set up a separate meeting. The instructor might feel uncomfortable discussing the problem in front of the other students. The communication techniques suggested in this chapter can help make your conference time more effective.

Use course evaluations. In many classes you'll have an opportunity to evaluate the instructor. When you're asked to do so, respond honestly. Write about the aspects of the class that did not work well for you. Offer specific ideas for improvement. Also note what *did* work well.

Take further steps, if appropriate. Sometimes severe conflict develops between students and instructors. Feedback from students might not be enough to reach a resolution. In such cases, you might decide to file a complaint or ask for help from a third party, such as an administrator.

If you do, be prepared to document your case in writing. When talking about the instructor, offer details. Describe specific actions that created problems for the class. Stick to the facts—events that other class members can verify. Your school might have a set of established grievance procedures to use in these cases. Before you act, understand what the policies are. You are a consumer of education. You have a right and a responsibility to complain if you think you have been treated unfairly.

When your instructor *talks fast*

Take more time to prepare for class. Familiarity with a subject increases your ability to pick up on key points. If an instructor lectures quickly or is difficult to understand, conduct a thorough preview of the material to be covered.

Be willing to make choices. When an instructor talks fast, focus your attention on key points. Instead of trying to write everything down, choose what you think is important. Occasionally, you will make a wrong choice and neglect an important point. Worse things could happen. Stay with the lecture, write down key words, and revise your notes immediately after class.

Exchange photocopies of notes with classmates. Your fellow students might write down something you missed. At the same time, your notes might help them. Exchanging photocopies can fill in the gaps.

Leave large empty spaces in your notes. Leave plenty of room for filling in information you missed. Use a symbol that signals you've missed something so that you can remember to come back to it.

See the instructor after class. Take your class notes with you and show the instructor what you missed.

Use a tape recorder. Taping a lecture gives you a chance to hear it again whenever you choose. Some recorders allow you to vary the speed of the tape. With this feature, you can perform magic and actually slow down the instructor's speech.

Before class, take notes on your reading assignment. You can take detailed notes on the text before class. Leave plenty of blank space. Take these notes with you to class and simply add your lecture notes to them.

Go to the lecture again. Many classes are taught in multiple sections. That gives you the chance to hear a lecture at least twice—once in your regular class and again in another section of the class.

Learn shorthand. Some note-taking systems, known as shorthand, are specifically designed for getting ideas down fast. Books and courses are available to help you learn these systems. You can also devise your own shorthand method by inventing one- or two-letter symbols for common words and phrases.

Ask questions—even if you're totally lost. Many instructors allow a question session. This is the time to ask about the points you missed.

There might be times when you feel so lost that you can't even formulate a question. That's OK. One option is to report this fact to the instructor. She can often guide you to a clear question. Another option is to ask a related question. This might lead you to the question you really wanted to ask.

Ask the instructor to slow down. This is the most obvious solution. If asking the instructor to slow down doesn't work, ask her to repeat what you missed. ⬕

Taking notes while reading

Taking notes while reading requires the same skills that apply to class notes: observing, recording, and reviewing. Just remember that there are two kinds of notes that apply to reading: review notes and research notes.

Review notes. These will look like the notes you take in class. Sometimes you will want more extensive notes than writing in the margin of your text allows. You can't underline or make notes in library books, so these sources will require separate notes, too.

Mind map summaries of textbook materials are particularly useful for review. You can also use outlining or take notes in paragraph form. Single out a particularly difficult section of a text and make separate notes. Or make mind map summaries of overlapping lecture and textbook materials. Use the left-hand column for key words and questions, just as you do in your class notes.

When you read scientific or other technical materials, copy important formulas or equations and write down data that might appear on an exam. Re-create important diagrams and draw your own visual representations of concepts.

Research notes. Writing papers and speeches is a special challenge, and the way you take notes can help you face that challenge.

Use the mighty 3x5 card. There are two kinds of research cards: source cards and information cards. Source cards identify where you found the information contained in your paper or speech. For example, a source card for a book will show the author, title, date and place of publication, and publisher. Source cards are also written for magazine articles, interviews, dissertations, tapes, or any other research materials.

When you write source cards, give each source a code—the initials of the author, a number, or a combination of numbers and letters. A key advantage of using source cards is that you are creating your bibliography as you do the research. When you are done, simply alphabetize the cards by author and—voilà!— instant bibliography.

Write the actual research notes on information cards. At the top of each information card, write the code for the source from which you got the information. Also include the page numbers your notes are based on.

Most important, write only one piece of information on each information card. You can then sort the cards and use them to construct an outline of your paper or speech.

Another option is to take notes using a computer. This offers the same advantage as 3x5 cards—ease of rearranging text and pictures—while enabling you to print out copies to exchange with other students.

Online material. You can print out anything that appears on a computer screen. This includes online course materials, articles, books, manuscripts, e-mail messages, chat room sessions, and more.

One potential problem: Students might skip taking notes on this material altogether. ("I can just print out everything!") These students miss the chance to internalize a new idea by restating it in their own words—a principal benefit of note taking. Result: Material passes from computer to printer without ever intersecting a student's brain.

To prevent this problem, find ways to engage actively with online materials. Take review notes in Cornell, mind map, concept map, or outline format. Write Discovery and Intention Statements to capture key insights from the materials and to state ways you intend to apply them. Also talk about what you're learning. Recite key points out loud and discuss what you read online with other students.

Of course, it's fine to print out online material. If you do, treat your printouts like a textbook and apply the steps of Muscle Reading explained in Chapter Four.

Thinking about notes. Whenever you take notes, use your own words as much as possible. When you do so, you are thinking about what you are reading. If you do quote your source word for word, put that material within quotation marks.

Close the book after reading an assignment and quickly jot down a summary of the material. This writing can be loose, without any structure or format. The important thing is to do it right away, while the material is still fresh in your mind. Restating concepts in this way helps you remember them.

Special cases. The style of your notes can vary according to the nature of the material. If you are assigned a short story or poem, read the entire work once without taking any notes. On your first reading, simply enjoy the piece. When you finish, write down your immediate impressions. Then go over the piece and make brief notes on characters, images, symbols, settings, plot, point of view, or other aspects of the work.

Normally, you would ask yourself questions *before* you read an assignment. When you read fiction or poetry, however, ask yourself questions *after* you have read the piece. Then reread it (or skim it, if it's long) to get answers. Your notes can reflect this question-and-answer process. ⬙

Get to the bones of your book with concept maps

Concept mapping, pioneered by Joseph Novak and D. Bob Gowin, is a tool to make the main ideas in a book leap off the page.[4] In creating a concept map, you reduce an author's message to its essence—its bare bones. Concept maps can also be used to display the organization underlying lectures, discussions, and other reading materials.

To develop the technique of concept mapping, Novak and Gowin drew on ideas from David Ausubel, an educational psychologist.[5] Ausubel stated that human knowledge consists of a series of propositions. A proposition states a relationship between two or more concepts. A subject that you study in school might include dozens or even hundreds of concepts and propositions. However, learning the subject relies on a simple, underlying process: You take one new concept at a time and link it to a concept that you already understand, creating a new proposition.

Concept maps take this process out of your head and put in on paper in a visual format. You list concepts and arrange them in a meaningful order. Then you explicitly state the relationships between concepts, forming meaningful propositions.

Concept maps also promote critical thinking. Creating a concept map can alert you to gaps in your understanding—missing concepts or concepts with illogical links.

To create a concept map, use the following four steps:

1. List the key concepts in the text. Aim to express each concept in three words or less. Most concept words are nouns, including terms and proper names. At this point, you can list the concepts in any order. For ease in ranking the concepts later, write each one on a single 3x5 card.

2. Rank the concepts so that they flow from general to specific. On a large sheet of paper, write the main concept at the top of the

page. Place the most specific concepts near the bottom. Arrange the rest of the concepts in appropriate positions throughout the middle of the page. Circle each concept.

3. Draw lines that connect the concepts. On these connecting lines, add words that describe the relationship between the concepts. Again, limit yourself to the fewest words needed to make an accurate link—three words or less. Linking words are often verbs, verb phrases, or prepositions.

4. Finally, review your map. Look for any concepts that are repeated in several places on the map. You can avoid these repetitions by adding more links between concepts. Also look for accurate linking words and missing concepts.

As you gain facility with concept maps, you might wish to create them on a computer. Use any software with drawing capabilities. For example, the software program Inspiration, a visual thinking and learning tool, is specifically designed to create concept maps.

Sample concept maps based on selected articles in this book are available online at

masterstudent.college.hmco.com

PRACTICING CRITICAL THINKING

5

Use a concept map as a tool to interpret and evaluate a piece of writing. First, list the key concepts from a chapter (or section of a chapter) in a textbook you're reading. Then connect these concepts with linking words, using the format described in the article "Get to the bones of your book with concept maps." Create your concept map on a separate sheet of paper. Then take a few minutes to assess the author's presentation as reflected in your concept map. Pay special attention to the links between concepts. Are they accurate? Do they reveal false assumptions or lack of evidence? Write your evaluation of your concept map on a separate sheet of paper.

power process

I create it all

This is a powerful tool in times of trouble. In a crisis, "I create it all" can lead the way to solutions. "I create it all" means treating experiences, events, and circumstances in your life as if you created them.

When your dog tracks fresh tar on the white carpet, when your political science teacher is a crushing bore, when your spouse dents the car, when your test on Latin American literature focuses on an author you've never read—it's time for a Power Process. Tell yourself, "I created it all."

"Baloney!" you shout. "I didn't let the dog in, that teacher really is a bore, I wasn't even in the car, and nobody told me to read Gabriel García Márquez. I didn't create these disasters."

Good points. Obviously, "I create it all" is one of the most unusual and bizarre suggestions in this book. It certainly is not an idea that is easily believed. In fact, believing it can get you into trouble. "I create it all" is strictly a practical idea. Use it when it works. Don't when it doesn't.

Keeping that caution in mind, consider how powerful this Power Process can be. It is really about the difference between two distinct positions in life: being a victim or being self-responsible. A victim of circumstances is controlled by outside forces. We've all felt like victims at one time or another. When tar-footed dogs tromped on the white carpets of our lives, we felt helpless. In contrast, we can take responsibility. *Responsibility* is the important word. It does not mean "blame." Far from it. Responsibility is "response-ability"—the ability to choose a response.

Practicing resignation

By not taking responsibility, we are acknowledging that the power to determine what happens in our lives is beyond our grasp. When we feel as if we don't have control over our lives, we feel resigned. The opposite of practicing "I create it all" is practicing resignation.

There is a phenomenon called *learned resignation*. An interesting experiment with dogs demonstrates how learned resignation works. A dog is put in a caged pen with a metal floor that can be electrified. When the cage door is left open and the dog is given a mild shock, she runs out of the cage to escape the discomfort. Then the dog is put back into the cage, the door is shut and locked, and a mild shock is given again. The dog runs around, looking for an escape. When she doesn't find one, she just lies down, sits, or stands there, and quits trying to find a way out. She has no control over her circumstances and is learning to be resigned.

Now, here comes the interesting part. After the dog has consistently stopped trying to escape the shock, the door is opened and the dog is led in and out several times. Then the dog is left in the cage, the door is left open, and the shock is administered once again. Amazingly, the dog doesn't even try to escape, even though the open door is right there in front of her. Instead, the dog continues to endure the shock. She has learned to be resigned.

A variety of this phenomenon can occur in human beings as well. When we consistently give control of our lives over to other people and to circumstances, we run the risk of learning to give up. We might develop the habit of being resigned, even though there is abundant opportunity all around us.

Applying this process

Many students approach grades from the position of being victims. When the student who sees the world this way gets an F, she reacts something like this:

"Oh, no!" (Slaps forehead)

"Rats!" (Slaps forehead again) (Students who get lots of F's often have flat foreheads.)

"Another F! That teacher couldn't teach her way out of a wet paper bag. She can't teach English for anything.

And that textbook—what a bore! How could I read it with a houseful of kids making noise all the time? And then friends came over and wanted to party, and . . . ."

The problem with this viewpoint is that in looking for excuses, the student is robbing herself of the power to get any grade other than an F. She's giving all of her power to a bad teacher, a boring textbook, noisy children, and friends.

There is another way, called *taking responsibility*. You can recognize that you choose your grades by choosing your actions. Then you are the source, rather than the result, of the grades you get. The student who got an F could react like this:

"Another F! Oh, shoot! Well, hmmm . . . . How did I choose this F? What did I do to create it?"

Now, that's power. By asking "How did I contribute to this outcome?" you give yourself a measure of control. You are no longer the victim. This student might continue by saying, "Well, let's see. I didn't review my notes after class. That might have done it." Or "I studied in the same room with my children while they watched TV. Then I went out with my friends the night before the test. Well, that probably helped me fulfill some of the requirements for getting an F."

The point is this: When the F is the result of your kids, your friends, the book, or the teacher, you probably can't do anything about it. However, if you *chose* the F, you can choose a different grade next time. You are in charge.

Choosing our thoughts

There are times when we don't create it all. We do not create earthquakes, floods, avalanches, or monsoons. Yet if we look closely, we discover that we *do* create a larger part of our circumstances than most of us are willing to admit.

For example, we can choose our thoughts. And thoughts can control our perceptions by screening information from our senses. We can never be aware of every single thing in our environment. If we could, we'd go crazy from sensory overload. Instead, our brains filter out most sensory inputs. This filtering colors the way we think about the world.

Choosing our behaviors

Moment by moment we make choices about what we will do and where we will go. The results of these choices

are where we are in life. A whole school of psychology called *control theory* is based on this idea, and psychiatrist William Glasser has written extensively about it.[6]

All of those choices help create our current circumstances—even those circumstances that are not "our fault." After a car accident, we tell ourselves, "It just happened. That car came out of nowhere and hit me." We forget that driving five miles per hour slower and paying closer attention might have allowed us to miss the driver who was "to blame."

Some cautions

The presence of blame is a warning that this Power Process is being misused. "I create it all" is not about blaming yourself or others.

Feeling guilty is another warning signal. Guilt actually involves the same dynamic as blame. If you are feeling guilty, you have just shifted the blame from another person to yourself.

Another caution is that this Power Process is not a religion. Saying that you "create it all" does not mean that you have divine powers. It is simply a way to expand the choices you already have. This Power Process is easy to deny. Tell your friends about it, and they're likely to say, "What about world hunger? I didn't cause that. What about people who get cancer? Did they create that?"

These are good arguments—and they miss the point. Victims of rape, abuse, incest, and other forms of violence can still use "I create it all" to choose their response to the people and events that violated them.

Some people approach world hunger, imprisonment, and even cancer with this attitude: "Pretend for a moment that I am responsible for this. What will I do about it?" These people see problems in a new way, and they discover choices that other people miss.

"I create it all" is not always about disaster. It also works when life is going great. We often give credit to others for our good fortune when it's actually time to pat ourselves on the back. By choosing our behavior and thoughts, we can create A's, interesting classes, enjoyable relationships, material wealth, and ways to contribute to a better world.

Whenever tar-footed dogs are getting in the way of your education, remember this Power Process. When you use it, you instantly open up a world of choices. You give yourself power. 🎓

put it to work

You can adapt any of the suggestions in this chapter for use in the workplace. For example:

■ Before meetings, complete background reading on the topics to be discussed. You'll be better prepared to take notes.

■ During meetings, experiment with taking notes in several formats: Cornell, mind mapping, outlining, concept mapping, or some combination.

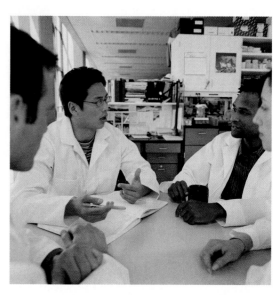

■ After meetings, review the notes you took. Edit or rewrite your notes for clarity. If you took handwritten notes, you might want to key the important points into a computer file.

■ No matter what format you choose for note taking, include key items of information about any meeting: the time and place, the people present, a list of agreements reached, and any items that require follow-up action.

■ During a presentation or training session, let go of any judgments about the presenter's speaking style or appearance. Focus on the content of this person's message and look for ideas to remember and use. Capture those ideas fully and accurately in your notes.

■ When taking notes during fast-paced meetings and conference calls, use suggestions from the article "When your instructor talks fast." Immediately after the call or meeting, review and edit your notes. Flag items that require follow-up action.

■ Remember that the ideas in "Create your instructor" can also help you "create your boss." If you find yourself in conflict with a manager or supervisor, look for ways to take charge of the situation. For example, handle your end of the conflict by doing your job impeccably. Submit your most professional work. Participate actively in meetings. Look for something that you can learn from this conflict—a skill that can help you resolve workplace conflicts in the future.

■ In a personal journal, write about ways to be more effective at work. State a work-related problem and brainstorm to come up with possible solutions. List career goals and write Intention Statements about how you plan to achieve them.

■ Apply the Power Process: "I create it all" to people and situations at work. If you feel tempted to blame a problem on a coworker, look for any ways that you might have contributed to the problem. Consider what you will think, say, and do differently to create a better work environment. ◪

Name _____ Date _____/_____/_____

1. What are the three major steps of effective note taking as explained in this chapter? Summarize each step in one sentence.

2. Techniques you can use to "set the stage" for note taking do *not* include:
   (a) Complete outside assignments.
   (b) Bring the right materials.
   (c) Set aside questions in order to concentrate.
   (d) Conduct a short preclass review.
   (e) Be with the instructor.

3. What is an advantage of sitting in the front and center of the classroom?

4. By the way they behave, instructors sometimes give clues that the material they are presenting is important. Describe at least three of these behaviors.

5. An effective method to postpone debate during a lecture is to ignore your own opinions and passively record the instructor's words. True or False? Explain your answer.

6. When using the Cornell system of note taking:
   (a) Write the main point on a line or in a box, circle, or any other shape.
   (b) Use only Roman numerals in an outline form.
   (c) Copy each new concept on a separate 3x5 card.
   (d) Remember never to combine it with mind mapping.
   (e) Draw a vertical line about two inches from the left edge of the paper.

7. Explain how key words can be used when taking notes. Then select and write down at least five key words from this chapter.

8. Reviewing within 24 hours assists short-term memory only. Long-term memory requires reviews over a longer period of time. True or False? Explain your answer.

9. Compare and contrast source cards and information cards. How are they alike? How are they different?

10. Briefly explain one of the cautions given regarding the use of the Power Process: "I create it all."

learning styles application

The questions below will "cycle" you through four styles, or modes, of learning as explained in the article "Learning styles: Discovering how you learn" in Chapter One. Each question will help you explore a different mode. You can answer the questions in any order.

what if *Create an original format for taking notes. Think about how you could modify or combine the note-taking systems discussed in this chapter. Describe your format here.*

why *Describe a situation in school or at work in which you could benefit by taking more effective notes.*

how *Of the note-taking techniques in this chapter that you like and intend to apply, choose one and describe when and where you will use it.*

what *Think back to the major note-taking systems discussed in this chapter: the Cornell format, mind mapping, outlining, concept mapping, or some combination. Choose one system that you intend to apply and briefly summarize its key features.*

master student

profile

CRAIG KIELBURGER

(1984–   ) In 1995, at age 12, Craig Kielburger founded Free the Children International, an organization of children helping children who are the victims of poverty and exploitation. He has also served as an ambassador to the Children's Embassy in Sarajevo and was named a Global Leader of Tomorrow at the 1998 World Economic Forum.

I *picked up the* **Toronto Star** *and* put it on the table. But I didn't make it past the front page. Staring back at me was the headline, "BATTLED CHILD LABOUR, BOY, 12, MURDERED." It was a jolt. Twelve, the same age as I was. My eyes fixed on the picture of a boy in a bright-red vest. He had a broad smile, his arm raised straight in the air, a fist clenched....

Riding the bus to school later that morning, I could think of nothing but the article I had read on the front page. What kind of parents would sell their children into slavery at four years of age? And who would ever chain a child to a carpet loom?

Throughout the day I was consumed by Iqbal's story. In my Grade Seven class we had studied the American Civil War, and Abraham Lincoln, and how some of the slaves in the United States had escaped into Canada. But that was history from centuries ago. Surely slavery had been abolished throughout the world by now. If it wasn't, why had I never heard about it?

The school library was no help. After a thorough search I still hadn't found a scrap of information. After school, I decided to make the trek to the public library.

The librarian knew me from my previous visits. Luckily, she had read the same article that morning and was just as intrigued. Together, we searched out more information on child labour. We found a few newspaper and magazine articles, and made copies.

By the time I returned home, images of child labour had imbedded themselves in my mind: children younger than me forced to make carpets for endless hours in dimly lit rooms; others toiling in underground pits, struggling to get coal to the surface; others maimed or killed by explosions raging through fireworks factories. I was angry at the world for letting these things happen to children. Why was nothing being done to stop such cruelty?...

At lunchtime that day, some of us got together and talked about what we could do. I was amazed at how enthusiastic they all were. I told them about the youth fair on Friday.

"Do you think we could put together a display?" I asked. "We haven't got much time."

"Sure. Let's do it."

"We can all meet at my house," I said.

That night, twelve of us got together. It was a very tight deadline, with just two days to prepare. We found an old science fair board, and we covered it with coloured paper, pasting on all the information I had found on child labour in the library, then drawing pictures to illustrate it.

We had determined that our first objective should be to inform people of the plight of child labourers. Armed with such knowledge, they might be willing to help. We decided to draw up a petition to present to the government, and called on the expertise of a couple of human rights groups to refine the wording for us.

But we were still without a name for our group. For more than an hour we struggled to come up with something suitable. We flipped through the newspaper clippings for inspiration. One of them reported on a demonstration in Delhi, India, where 250 children had marched through the streets with placards, chanting, "We want an education," "We want freedom," "Free the children!"

"That's it!" someone shouted. "Free the Children." ⬡

From *Free the Children* by Craig Kielburger with Kevin Major. Copyright © 1998 by Craig Kielburger. Reprinted by permission of HarperCollins Publishers, Inc.

For more biographical information on Craig Kielburger, visit the Master Student Hall of Fame on the *Becoming a Master Student* Web site at

masterstudent.college.hmco.com

6

Tests

why
this chapter matters . . .

Adopting a few simple techniques can make a major difference in how you feel about tests—and how you perform on them.

what
is included . . .

Disarm tests
What to do before the test
Ways to predict test questions
Cooperative learning: Studying with people
What to do during the test
Integrity in test taking: The costs of cheating
The test isn't over until . . .
Let go of test anxiety
Taking math and science tests
Celebrate mistakes
Power Process: "Detach"
Master Student Profile: Barbara Jordan

how
you can use this chapter . . .

Predict test questions and use your study time more effectively.
Harness the power of cooperative learning by studying with other people.
See mistakes as ways to gain useful feedback and improve performance.

As you read, ask yourself
what if . . .

I could let go of anxiety about tests— or anything else?

STUDENT VOICES

"*Perhaps the most frightening nightmare I have is taking a test. Although I know that receiving a grade is a measure of how well I did and not a measure of my intelligence, the fear persists. In this dream, though, my favorite tool, the checklist, came to my hand. The items I had to review were popping to attention like little soldiers as I marked them off. I could daydream the day of the test and gently let my anxiety disappear in a gentle puff of wind. I could savor the reward I had promised myself no matter [what] the consequences of the test.*"

—CHARLES R. McINTYRE

Disarm tests

On the surface, tests don't look dangerous, yet sometimes we treat them as if they were land mines. Suppose a stranger walks up to you on the street and asks, "Does a finite abelian P-group have a basis?" Will you break out in a cold sweat? Will your muscles tense up? Will your breathing become shallow?

Probably not. Even if you have never heard of a finite abelian P-group, you are likely to remain coolly detached. However, if you find the same question on a test and if you have never heard of a finite abelian P-group, your hands might get clammy.

Grades (A to F) are what we use to give power to tests. And there are lots of misconceptions about what grades are. Grades are not a measure of intelligence or creativity. They are not an indication of our ability to contribute to society. Grades are simply a measure of how well we do on tests. Some people think that a test score measures what a student has accomplished in a course. This is false. A test score is a measure of what a student scored on a test. If you are anxious about a test and blank out, the grade cannot measure what you've learned. The reverse is also true: If you are good at taking tests and a lucky guesser, the score won't be an accurate reflection of what you know.

Grades are not a measure of self-worth. Yet we tend to give test scores the power to determine how we feel about ourselves. Common thoughts include "If I fail a test, I am a failure" or "If I do badly on a test, I am a bad person." The truth is that if you do badly on a test, you are a person who did badly on a test. That's all.

Carrying around misconceptions about tests and grades can put undue pressure on your performance. It's like balancing on a railroad track. Many people can walk along the rail and stay balanced for long periods. Yet the task seems entirely different if the rail is placed between two buildings, 52 stories up.

It is easier to do well on exams if you don't put too much pressure on yourself. Don't give the test some magical power over your own worth as a human being. Academic tests are not a matter of life and death. Scoring low on important tests—entrance tests for college or medical school, bar exams, CPA exams—usually means only a delay.

Whether the chance of doing poorly is real or exaggerated, worrying about it can become paralyzing. The way to deal with tests is to keep them in perspective. Keep the railroad track on the ground.

journal entry 14

Discovery/Intention Statement

Mentally re-create a time when you had difficulty taking a test. Do anything that helps you re-experience this event. You could draw a picture of yourself in this situation, list some of the questions you had difficulty answering, or tell how you felt after finding out your score on the test. Briefly describe that experience in the space below.

I discovered that I . . .

_____

_____

_____

Now wipe your mental slate clean and declare your intention to replace it with a new scenario. Describe how you want your experience of test taking to change. For example, you might write: "I intend to walk into every test I take feeling well rested and thoroughly prepared."

I intend to . . .

_____

_____

_____

Preview this chapter, looking for at least five strategies that can help you accomplish your goal. List those strategies below and note the page numbers where you can find out more about them.

Strategy   *Page number*

_____

_____

_____

_____

_____

_____

What to do before the test

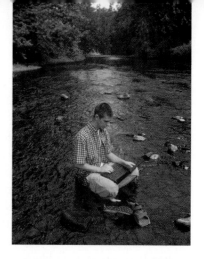

One way to save hours of wasted study time is to look on each test as a performance. From this point of view, preparing for a test means rehearsing. Study for a test in the way that a musician rehearses for a concert or an actor prepares for opening night—by simulating the physical and psychological conditions you'll encounter when you actually enter the exam room.

Rehearsing means doing the kind of tasks that you'll perform during a test—answering questions, solving problems, composing essays. Start this process with regular reviews of course content. Test preparation comes down to answering questions about your self-awareness (What do I know?), task awareness (What do I have to learn?), and strategy awareness (How can I close the gap between what I know and what I don't know?). Answering these questions means managing your review time, creating review tools, and planning your test-taking strategy.

Manage review time

A key to successful test preparation is managing review time. The biggest benefit of early review is that facts have time to roam around in your head. A lot of learning takes place when you are not consciously studying. Your brain has time to create relationships that can show up when you need them—like during a test. Use short daily review sessions to prepare the way for major review sessions. Reviewing with a group often generates new insights and questions.

Daily reviews. Daily reviews include the short pre- and post-class reviews of lecture notes. Research indicates that this is an effective tool for moving ideas from short-term to long-term memory (see Chapter Three: Memory). Also conduct brief daily reviews when you read. Before reading a new assignment, scan your notes and the sections you underlined in the previous assignment. Use the time you spend waiting for the bus or doing the laundry to conduct short reviews. Concentrate daily reviews on two kinds of material: material you have just learned, either in class or in your reading, and material that involves simple memorization (equations, formulas, dates, definitions).

Conduct short daily reviews several times throughout the day. To make sure you do, include them on your daily to-do list. Write down reminders, such as "5 min. review of biology" or "10 min. review of economics," and give yourself the satisfaction of crossing them off your list.

Begin to review on the first day of class. Most instructors outline the whole course at that time. You can start reviewing within seconds after learning. During a lull in class, go over the notes you just took. Then immediately after class, review your notes again.

Weekly reviews. Weekly reviews are longer—about an hour per subject. They are also more structured than short daily reviews. When a subject is complex, the brain requires time to dig into the material. Avoid skipping from subject to subject too quickly. Review each subject at least once a week. Weekly sessions include reviews of assigned reading and lecture notes. Look over any mind map summaries or flash cards you have created. You can also practice working on sample problems.

Major reviews. Major reviews are usually conducted the week before finals or other critical exams. They help integrate concepts and deepen understanding of the material presented throughout the term. These are longer review periods—two to five hours at a stretch, punctuated by sufficient breaks. Remember that the effectiveness of your review begins to drop after an hour or so unless you give yourself a short rest.

After a certain point, short breaks every hour might not be enough to refresh you. That's when it's time to quit. Learn your limits by being conscious of the quality of your concentration. During long sessions, study the most difficult subjects when you are the most alert: at the beginning of the session.

Your commitment to review is your most powerful ally. Create a system of rewards for time spent reviewing. Use the Intention Statements in this chapter or invent your own to draw detailed plans for review time.

Scheduling reviews. If you have a monthly or weekly planner, use it to schedule specific review periods. Plan on at least two major review sessions, lasting two to five hours each, for every course. If you think you'll need extra time for review, consider rearranging tasks or changing their priority in order to free up more study time. Start reviewing key topics at least five days before you'll be tested on them. This allows plenty of time to find the answers to questions and close any gaps in your understanding.

Staying positive. As you review, start every session with affirmations such as "I study with energy and efficiency" or "I am smart and prepared to do well on this test." Keep these statements simple and to the point. This powerful technique can help you stay positive.

Create review tools

Study checklists. Study checklists are used the way a pilot uses a preflight checklist. Pilots go through a standard routine before they take off. They physically mark off each item: test flaps, check magnetos, check fuel tanks, adjust instruments, check rudder. They use a written list to be absolutely certain they don't miss anything. Once they are in the air, it's too late, and the consequences of failing to check the fuel tanks could be drastic. Taking an exam is like flying a plane. Once the test begins, it's too late to memorize that one equation you forgot to include in your review.

Make a list for each subject. List reading assignments by chapters or page numbers. List dates of lecture notes. Write down various types of problems you will need to solve. Write down other skills you must master. Include major ideas, definitions, theories, formulas, and equations. For math and science tests, choose some problems and do them over again as a way to review for the test.

A study checklist is not a review sheet; it is a to-do list. Checklists contain the briefest possible description of each item to study.

Mind map summary sheets. There are several ways to make a mind map as you study for tests. Start by creating a map totally from memory. You might be surprised by how much you already know. Mind maps release floods of information from the brain because the mind works by association. Each idea is linked to many other ideas. You think of one and other associations come to mind.

Let the associations flow. If one seems to go someplace else, simply start another branch on your map. After you have gone as far as you can using recall alone, go over your notes and text and fill in the rest of the map.

Another way to create a mind map summary is to go through your notes and pick out key words. Then, without looking at your notes, create a mind map of everything you can recall about each key word. Finally, go back to your notes and fill in material you left out. You can also start a mind map with underlined sections from your text.

Flash cards. Three-by-five flash cards are like portable test questions. Take them with you everywhere and use them anytime. On one side of the cards, write the questions. On the other, write the answers. It's that simple.

Use flash cards for formulas, definitions, theories, key

words from your notes, axioms, dates, foreign language phrases, hypotheses, and sample problems. Create flash cards regularly as the term progresses. Buy an inexpensive card file to keep your flash cards arranged by subject.

Always carry a pack of flash cards with you, and review them whenever you have a minute to spare.

Monitoring your reviews. Each day that you prepare for a test, assess what you have learned and what you still need to learn. See how many items you've covered from your study checklist. Look at the tables of contents in your textbooks and write an X next to the sections that you've summarized. Using a monitoring system can help you gauge the thoroughness of your reviews and alert you to areas that still need attention.

Plan a test-taking strategy

Knowing what is going to be on a test doesn't require highly sophisticated technology or code breaking. With some practice, you can learn to predict the types of questions and their level of difficulty.

Do a dry run. Write up your own questions and take this "test" several times before the actual exam. Say that the exam will include mainly true/false or short-answer questions. Brainstorm a list of such questions—a mock test—and do a dry run. You might type up this "test" so that it looks like the real thing. Meet with your teacher to go over your mock test. Ask whether your questions focus on appropriate topics and represent the kind of items you can expect to see on the actual test.

Ask the instructor what to expect. One great source of information about the test is your instructor. Ask him what to expect. What topics will be emphasized? What kinds of questions will be included? How can you best allocate your review time? The instructor might decline to give you any of this information. More often, instructors will answer some or all of your questions about the test.

Get copies of old exams. Copies of previous exams for the class might be available from the instructor, the instructor's department, the library, or the counseling office. Old tests can help you plan a review strategy. One caution: If you rely on old tests exclusively, you might gloss over material the instructor has added since the last test. Check your school's policy about making past tests available to students. Some might not allow it. ▨

Ways to predict test questions

Predicting test questions can do more than get you a better grade. It can also keep you focused on the purpose of a course and help you design your learning strategies. Making predictions can be fun, too—especially when they turn out to be accurate.

Ask about the nature of the test. Tests are written from a plan, based on what a teacher considers important. This is not a random or mysterious process. See if you can discover the plan.

Eliminate as much guesswork about tests as possible. Ask your instructor to describe upcoming tests. Do this early in the term so you can be alert for possible test questions throughout the course. Many instructors are happy to answer such questions directly.

Some possible questions to ask are:

- What course material will the test cover—readings, lectures, lab sessions, or a combination?

- Will the test be cumulative, or will it cover just the most recent material you've studied?

- Will the test focus on facts and details or major themes and relationships?

- Will the test call on you to solve problems or apply concepts?

- What types of questions will be on the test—true/false, multiple choice, short-answer, essay?

- Will you have choices about which questions to answer?

- Will your teacher write and score the test—or will a teaching assistant perform those tasks?

Note: In order to study appropriately for essay tests, find out how much detail the instructor wants in your answers. Ask how much time you'll be allowed for the test and how long the essay answers should be (number of pages, blue books, or word limit). Having that information before you begin studying will help you gauge the depth to which you must know the material.

Put yourself in your instructor's shoes. If you were teaching the course, what information would you want students to take away? What kinds of questions would you put on an exam? Make up practice test questions and then answer them. You can also brainstorm test questions with other students—a great activity for study groups.

Look for possible test questions in your notes. Have a separate section in your notebook labeled "Test questions." Add several questions to this section after every lecture and assignment. You can also create your own code or graphic signal—such as a *T!* in a circle—to flag possible test questions in your notes.

See the article "Words to watch for in essay questions" in this chapter. Use it as a guide to turn the key words in your notes into questions.

Look for clues to possible questions during class. During lectures you can predict test questions by observing what an instructor says and how he says it. Instructors often give clues. For example, they might repeat important points several times, write them on the board, or return to them in subsequent classes.

Certain gestures can indicate critical points. For example, your instructor might pause, look at notes, or read passages word for word.

Notice whether your teacher has any strong points of view on certain issues. Questions on those issues are likely to appear on a test. Also pay attention to questions the instructor poses to students, and note questions that other students ask.

When material from reading assignments is covered extensively in class, it is likely to be on a test. For science courses and other courses involving problem solving, work on sample problems using different variables.

Save all quizzes, papers, lab sheets, and graded materials of any kind. Quiz questions have a way of reappearing, in slightly altered form, on final exams. If copies of previous exams and other graded materials are available, use them to predict test questions.

Remember the obvious. Be on the lookout for these words: *This material will be on the test.*

Apply your predictions. To get the most value from your predictions, use them to guide your review sessions.[1] ◪

For suggestions on ways to predict a variety of test questions, go to

masterstudent.college.hmco.com

Cooperative learning
Studying with people

Education often seems like a never-ending competition. We compete for entrance to school, for scholarships and grades while we're in school, and for jobs when we leave school. In that climate, it's easy to overlook the power of cooperation.

If you skip a solo study session, no one else will know. If you declare your intention to study with others who are depending on you, your intention gains strength. In addition to drawing strength from the group, you can help others when they are in need of support.

To multiply the benefits of working with study groups, seek out people of other cultures, races, and ethnic groups. You can get a whole new perspective on the world, along with some valued new friends. And you can experience what it's like to be part of a diverse team—an important asset in today's job market.

Form a study group. Look for dedicated students. Find people you are comfortable with and who share some of your academic goals. Look for students who pay attention, ask questions, and take notes during class, and invite them to join your group.

Studying with friends is fine, but if your common interests are beer and jokes, beware of getting together for schoolwork.

To get the benefit of other perspectives, choose people with similar educational goals who have different backgrounds and methods of learning.

Limit groups to four people. Larger ones can be unwieldy. Begin with a planning session. Ask two or three people to get together for a snack and talk about group goals, meeting times, and other logistics. You don't have to make an immediate commitment.

Test the group first by planning a one-time session. If that session works, plan another. After a few successful sessions, you can schedule regular meetings.

Conduct your study group. There are many ways to conduct a study group. Begin with the following suggestions and see what works.

Set an agenda for each meeting. Select activities from this article, or create other activities to do as a group. Set approximate time limits for each agenda item and determine a quitting time. Finally, end each meeting with assignments for all members.

Test each other by asking questions. Group members can agree to bring five to ten sample test questions to each meeting. Then you can all take a test made up from these questions.

Compare notes. Make sure that you recorded the important information. Ask others to help explain material in your notes that is confusing to you. Do the same for them.

Keep the group on task. If the discussion wanders off-topic, remind members of the time limits and agenda for the meeting.

Ask each member to contribute. Recognize signs that group members are not contributing in equal ways. As a group, brainstorm ways to get unprepared members involved. Reel in a dominating member by reminding him of the importance that everyone's voice be heard.

Work in groups of two at a computer to review a course. One person can operate the keyboard while the other person dictates summaries of lectures and assigned readings. Together, both group members can check facts by consulting textbooks, lecture notes, and class handouts.

Create wall-sized mind maps or concept maps to summarize a textbook or series of lectures.

Pair off to do "book reports." One person can summarize a reading assignment. The other person can act as an interviewer on a talk show, posing questions and asking for further clarification.

Ask members of your group to prepare and deliver full-length lectures on different topics of a course. Volunteer to lecture on the topic that you know least about, and come prepared to answer questions from other group members. ⊠

What to do during the test

Prepare yourself for the test by arriving early. That often leaves time to do a relaxation exercise. While you're waiting for the test to begin and talking with classmates, avoid the question "How much did you study for the test?" This question might fuel anxious thoughts that you didn't study enough.

As you begin

Ask the teacher or test administrator if you can use scratch paper during the test. If you use a separate sheet of paper without permission, you might appear to be cheating. If you get permission, use this paper to jot down memory aids, formulas, equations, facts, or other material you know you'll need and might forget. An alternative is to make quick notes in the margins of the test sheet.

Pay attention to verbal directions given as a test is distributed. Then scan the whole test immediately. Evaluate the importance of each section. Notice how many points each part of the test is worth and estimate how much time you'll need for each section, using its point value as your guide. For example, don't budget 20 percent of your time for a section that is worth only 10 percent of the points.

Read the directions slowly. Then reread them. It can be agonizing to discover that you lost points on a test merely because you failed to follow the directions. When the directions are confusing, ask to have them clarified.

Now you are ready to begin the test. If necessary, allow yourself a minute or two of "panic" time. Notice any tension you feel, and apply one of the techniques explained in the article "Let go of test anxiety" later in this chapter.

Answer the easiest, shortest questions first. This gives you the experience of success. It also stimulates associations and prepares you for more difficult questions. Pace yourself and watch the time. If you can't think of an answer, move on. Follow your time plan.

If you are unable to determine the answer to a test question, keep an eye out throughout the text for context clues that may remind you of the correct answer or provide you with evidence to eliminate wrong answers.

Multiple choice questions

- *Answer each question in your head first.* Do this before you look at the possible answers. If you come up with an answer that you're confident is right, look for that answer in the list of choices.

- *Read all possible answers before selecting one.* Sometimes two answers will be similar, but only one will be correct.

- *Test each possible answer.* Remember that multiple choice questions consist of two parts: the stem (an incomplete statement at the beginning) and a list of possible answers. Each answer, when combined with the stem, makes a complete statement that is either true or false. When you combine the stem with each possible answer, you are turning each multiple choice question into a small series of true/false questions. Choose the answer that makes a true statement.

- *Eliminate incorrect answers.* Cross off the answers that are clearly not correct. The answer you cannot eliminate is probably the best choice.

True/false questions

- *Read the entire question.* Separate the statement into its grammatical parts—individual clauses and phrases—and then test each one. If any part is false, the entire statement is false.

- *Look for qualifiers.* These include words such as *all, most, sometimes,* or *rarely.* Absolute qualifiers such as *always* or *never* generally indicate a false statement.

- *Find the devil in the details.* Double-check each number, fact, and date in a true/false statement. Look for numbers that have been transposed or facts that have been slightly altered. These are signals of a false statement.

- *Watch for negatives.* Look for words such as *not* and *cannot.* Read the sentence without these words and see if you come up with a true or false statement. Then reinsert the negative words and see if the statement makes more sense. Watch especially for sentences with two negative words. As in math operations, two negatives cancel each other out: *We cannot say that Chekov never succeeded at short story writing* means the same as *Chekov succeeded at short story writing*.

Computer-graded tests

- Make sure that the answer you mark corresponds to the question you are answering.

- Check the test booklet against the answer sheet whenever you switch sections and whenever you come to the top of a column.

- Watch for stray marks; they can look like answers.

- If you change an answer, be sure to erase the wrong answer completely, removing all pencil marking completely.

Open-book tests

- Carefully organize your notes, readings, and any other materials you plan to consult when writing answers.

- Write down any formulas you will need on a separate sheet of paper.

- Bookmark the table of contents and index in each of your textbooks. Place Post-it Notes and Index Flags or paper clips on other important pages of books (pages with tables, for instance).

- Create an informal table of contents or index for the notes you took in class.

- Predict which material will be covered on the test and highlight relevant sections in your readings and notes.

Short-answer/fill-in-the-blank tests

- Concentrate on key words and facts. Be brief.

- Overlearning material can really pay off. When you know a subject backward and forward, you can answer this type of question almost as fast as you can write.

Matching tests

- Begin by reading through each column, starting with the one with fewer items. Check the number of items in each column to see if they're equal. If they're not, look for an item in one column that you can match with two or more items in the other column.

- Look for any items with similar wording and make special note of the differences between these items.

- Match words that are similar grammatically. For example, match verbs with verbs and nouns with nouns.

- When matching individual words with phrases, first read a phrase. Then look for the word that logically completes the phrase.

- Cross out items in each column when you are through with them.

Essay questions

Managing your time is crucial to answering essay questions. Note how many questions you have to answer and monitor your progress during the test period. Writing shorter answers and completing all of the questions on an essay test will probably yield a better score than leaving some questions blank.

Find out what an essay question is asking—precisely. If a question asks you to *compare* the ideas of Sigmund Freud and Karl Marx, no matter how eloquently you *explain* them, you are on a one-way trip to No Credit City.

Before you write, make a quick outline. An outline can help speed up the writing of your detailed answer, you're less likely to leave out important facts, and if you don't have time to finish your answer, your outline could win you some points. To use test time efficiently, keep your outline brief. Focus on key words to use in your answer.

Introduce your answer by getting to the point. General statements such as "There are many interesting facets to this difficult question" can cause acute irritation for teachers grading dozens of tests.

One way to get to the point is to begin your answer with part of the question. Suppose the question is "Discuss how increasing the city police budget might or might not contribute to a decrease in street crime." Your first sentence might be "An increase in police expenditures will not have a significant effect on street crime for the following reasons." Your position is clear. You are on your way to an answer.

When you expand your answer with supporting ideas and facts, start out with the most solid points. Be brief and avoid filler sentences.

Write legibly. Grading essay questions is in large part a subjective process. Sloppy, difficult-to-read handwriting might actually lower your grade.

Write on one side of the paper only. If you write on both sides of the paper, writing will show through and obscure the writing on the other side. If necessary, use the blank side to add points you missed. Leave a generous left-hand margin and plenty of space between your answers, in case you want to add to them later.

Finally, if you have time, review your answers for grammar and spelling errors, clarity, and legibility. ⊠

→ Words to watch for in essay questions

The following words are commonly found in essay test questions. If you want to do well on essay tests, study this page thoroughly. Know these words backward and forward. To heighten your awareness of them, underline the words when you see them in a test question.

Analyze: Break into separate parts and discuss, examine, or interpret each part. Then give your opinion.

Compare: Examine two or more items. Identify similarities and differences.

Contrast: Show differences. Set in opposition.

Criticize: Make judgments. Evaluate comparative worth. Criticism often involves analysis.

Define: Explain the exact meaning—usually, a meaning specific to the course or subject. Definitions are usually short.

Describe: Give a detailed account. Make a picture with words. List characteristics, qualities, and parts.

Discuss: Consider and debate or argue the pros and cons of an issue. Write about any conflict. Compare and contrast.

Explain: Make an idea clear. Show logically how a concept is developed. Give the reasons for an event.

Prove: Support with facts (especially facts presented in class or in the text).

Relate: Show the connections between ideas or events. Provide a larger context for seeing the big picture.

State: Explain precisely.

Summarize: Give a brief, condensed account. Include conclusions. Avoid unnecessary details.

Trace: Show the order of events or the progress of a subject or event.

If any of these terms are still unclear to you, consult your unabridged dictionary. A thorough knowledge of these words helps you answer essay questions in a way that best demonstrates your understanding of the course content.

Review these key words and other helpful vocabulary terms by using the online flash cards at

(masterstudent.college.hmco.com)

Integrity in test taking
The costs of cheating

Cheating on tests can be a tempting choice. One benefit is that we might get a good grade without having to study.

Instead of studying, we could spend more time watching TV, partying, sleeping, or doing anything that seems like more fun. Another benefit is that we could avoid the risk of doing poorly on a test—which could happen even if we *do* study.

But before you rush out to make cheating a habit, remember that it also carries costs. Here are some to consider.

We learn less. While we might think that some courses offer little or no value, it is more likely that we can create value from any course. If we look deeply enough, we can discover some idea or acquire some skill to prepare us for future courses or a career after graduation.

We lose money. Getting an education costs a lot of money. Cheating sabotages our purchase. We pay full tuition without getting full value for it.

Fear of getting caught promotes stress. When we're fully aware of our emotions about cheating, we might discover intense stress. Even if we're not fully aware of our emotions, we're likely to feel some level of discomfort about getting caught.

Violating our values promotes stress. Even if we don't get caught cheating, we can feel stress about violating our own ethical standards. Stress can compromise our physical health and overall quality of life.

Cheating on tests can make it easier to violate our integrity again. Human beings become comfortable with behaviors that they repeat. Cheating is no exception.

Think about the first time you drove a car. You might have felt excited—even a little frightened. Now driving is probably second nature, and you don't give it much thought. Repeated experience with driving creates familiarity, which lessens the intense feelings you had during your first time at the wheel.

We can experience the same process with almost any behavior. Cheating once will make it easier to cheat again. And if we become comfortable with compromising our integrity in one area of life, we might find it easier to compromise in other areas.

Cheating lowers our self-concept. Whether or not we are fully aware of it, cheating sends us the message that we are not smart enough or responsible enough to make it on our own. We deny ourselves the celebration and satisfaction of authentic success.

An effective alternative to cheating is to become a master student. Ways to do this are described on every page of this book. ✗

> **Have some FUN!**

Contrary to popular belief, finals week does not have to be a drag.

In fact, if you have used techniques in this chapter, exam week can be fun. By planning ahead, you will have done most of your studying long before finals arrive. You can feel confident and relaxed.

When you are well prepared for tests, you can even use fun as a technique to enhance your performance. The day before a final, go for a run or play a game of basketball. Take in a movie or a concert. Watch TV. A relaxed brain is a more effective brain. If you have studied for a test, your mind will continue to prepare itself even while you're at the movies.

Get plenty of rest, too. There's no need to cram until 3 a.m. when you have used the techniques in this chapter.

On the first day of finals, you can wake up refreshed, have a good breakfast, and walk into the exam room with a smile on your face. You can also leave with a smile on your face, knowing that you are going to have a fun week. It's your reward for studying regularly throughout the term.

If this kind of exam week sounds inviting, you can begin preparing for it right now.

The test isn't over until . . .

Many students believe that a test is over as soon as they turn in the answer sheet. Consider another point of view: You're not done with a test until you know the answer to any question that you missed—and why you missed it.

This point of view offers major benefits. Tests in many courses are cumulative. In other words, the content included on the first test is assumed to be working knowledge for the second test, mid-term, or final exam. When you discover what questions you missed and understand the reasons for lost points, you learn something—and you greatly increase your odds of achieving better scores later in the course.

To get the most value from any test, take control of what you do at two critical points: the time immediately following the test, and the time when the test is returned to you.

Immediately following the test. After finishing a test, your first thought might be to nap, snack, rent a DVD, or go out with friends to celebrate. Restrain those impulses for a short while so that you can reflect on the test. The time you invest now carries the potential to raise your grades in the future.

To begin with, sit down in a quiet place and take a few minutes to write some Discovery Statements related to your experience of taking the test. Doing this while the test is still fresh in your mind increases the value of this technique. Describe how you felt about taking the test, how effective your review strategies were, and whether you accurately predicted the questions that appeared on the test.

Follow up with an Intention Statement or two. State what, if anything, you will do differently to prepare for the next test. The more specific you are, the better. If the test revealed any gaps in your knowledge, list follow-up questions to ask in class.

When the test is returned. When a returned test includes a teacher's comments, view this document as a treasure-trove of intellectual gold.

First, make sure that the point totals add up correctly and double-check for any other errors in grading. Even the best teachers make an occasional mistake.

Next, ask these questions:

- On what material did the teacher base test questions—readings, lectures, discussions, or other class activities?

- What types of questions appeared in the test—objective (such as matching items, true/false questions, or multiple choice), short-answer, or essay?

- What types of questions did you miss?

- Can you learn anything from the instructor's comments that will help you prepare for the next test?

Also see if you can correct any answers that lost points. To do this, carefully analyze the source of your errors and find a solution. Consult the following chart for help. ▧

Source of test error	Possible solutions
Study errors–studying material that was not included on the test, or spending too little time on material that *did* appear on the test	• Ask your teacher about specific topics that will be included on a test. • Practice predicting test questions. • Form a study group with class members to create mock tests.
Careless errors, such as skipping or misreading directions	• Read and follow directions more carefully–especially when tests are divided into several sections with different directions. • Set aside time during the next test to proofread your answers.
Concept errors–mistakes made when you do not understand the underlying principles needed to answer a question or solve a problem	• Look for patterns in the questions you missed. • Make sure that you complete all assigned readings, attend all lectures, and show up for laboratory sessions. • Ask your teacher for help with specific questions.
Application errors–mistakes made when you understand underlying principles but fail to apply them correctly	• Rewrite your answers correctly. • When studying, spend more time on solving sample problems. • Predict application questions that will appear in future tests and practice answering them.
Test mechanics errors–missing more questions in certain parts of the test than others, changing correct answers to incorrect ones at the last minute, leaving items blank, miscopying answers from scratch paper to the answer sheet	• Set time limits for taking each section of a test and stick to them. • Proofread your test answers carefully. • Look for patterns in the kind of answers you change at the last minute. • Change answers only if you can state a clear and compelling reason to do so.

Let go of test anxiety

If you freeze during tests and flub questions when you know the answers, you might be suffering from test anxiety.

A little tension before a test is good. That tingly, butterflies-in-the-stomach feeling you get from extra adrenaline can sharpen your awareness and keep you alert. You can enjoy the benefits of a little tension while you stay confident and relaxed. Sometimes, however, tension is persistent and extreme. It causes loss of sleep, appetite, and sometimes even hair. That kind of tension is damaging. It is a symptom of test anxiety, and it can prevent you from doing your best on exams.

Other symptoms include nervousness, fear, dread, irritability, and a sense of hopelessness. Boredom also can be a symptom of test anxiety. Frequent yawning immediately before a test is a common reaction. Though it suggests boredom, yawning is often a sign of tension. It means that oxygen is not getting to the brain because the body is tense. A yawn is one way the body increases its supply of oxygen.

You might experience headaches, an inability to concentrate, or a craving for food. For some people, test anxiety makes asthma or high blood pressure worse. During an exam, symptoms can include confusion, panic, mental blocks, fainting, sweaty palms, and nausea.

Symptoms after a test include the following:

Mock indifference: "I answered all the multiple choice questions as 'none of the above' because I was bored."
Guilt: "Why didn't I study more?"
Anger: "The teacher never wanted me to pass this stupid course anyway."
Blame: "If only the textbook weren't so dull."
Depression: "After that test, I don't see any point in staying in school."

Test anxiety can be serious—students have committed suicide over test scores. This anxiety can also be managed.

Test anxiety has two components: mental and physical. The mental component of stress includes all of your thoughts and worries about tests. The physical component includes bodily sensations and tension.

The following techniques can help you deal with the mental and physical components of stress in any situation, from test anxiety to stage fright.

Dealing with thoughts

Yell "Stop!" When you notice that your mind is consumed with worries and fears, that your thoughts are spinning out of control, mentally yell "Stop!" If you're in a situation that allows it, yell it out loud.

This action is likely to bring your focus back to the present moment and allow you to redirect your thoughts. Once you've broken the cycle of worry or panic, you can use any of the following techniques.

Daydream. When you fill your mind with pleasant thoughts, there is no room left for anxiety. If you notice yourself worrying about an upcoming test, replace visions of doom with images of something you like to do. Daydream about being with a special friend or walking alone in a favorite place.

Visualize success. Most of us live up—or down—to our own expectations. If we spend a lot of time mentally rehearsing what it will be like to fail a test, our chances of doing so increase. Instead, you can take time to rehearse what it will be like to succeed. Be specific. Create detailed pictures, actions, and even sounds as part of your visualization. If you are able to visit the room where you will take the test, mentally rehearse while you are actually in this room.

Focus. Focus your attention on a specific object. Examine details of a painting, study the branches on a tree, or observe the face of your watch (right down to the tiny scratches in the glass). During an exam, take a few seconds to listen to the sounds of concentration—the squeaking of chairs, the scratching of pencils, the muted coughs. Touch the surface of your desk and notice the texture.

Concentrate all of your attention on one point. Don't leave room in your mind for anxiety-related thoughts.

Praise yourself. Talk to yourself in a positive way. Many of us take the first opportunity to belittle ourselves: "Way to go, dummy! You don't even know the answer to the first question on the test." We wouldn't dream of treating a friend this way, yet we do it to ourselves.

An alternative is to give yourself some encouragement. Treat yourself as if you were your own best friend. Consider telling yourself, "I am very relaxed. I am doing a great job on this test."

Consider the worst. Rather than trying to put a stop to your worrying, consider the very worst thing that could happen. Take your fear to the limit of absurdity.

Imagine the catastrophic problems that might occur if you were to fail the test. You might say to yourself, "Well, if I fail this test, I might fail the course, lose my financial aid, and get kicked out of school. Then I won't be able to get a job, so the bank will repossess my car, and I'll start drinking." Keep going until you see the absurdity of your predictions.

After you stop chuckling, you can backtrack to discover a reasonable level of concern. Your worry about failing the entire course if you fail the test might be justified. At that point ask yourself, "Can I live with that?" Unless you are taking a test in parachute packing and the final question involves jumping out of a plane, the answer will almost always be yes. (If the answer is no, use another technique. In fact, use several other techniques.)

The cold facts are hardly ever as bad as our worst fears. Shine a light on your fears, and they become more manageable.

Zoom out. When you're in the middle of a test or another situation in which you feel distressed, zoom out. Think the way film directors do when they dolly a camera out and away from an action scene. In your mind, imagine that you're floating away and viewing the situation as a detached outside observer.

If you're extremely distressed, let your imagination take you even farther. See yourself rising above the scene so that your whole community, city, nation, or planet is within view.

From this larger viewpoint, ask yourself whether this situation is worth worrying about. A negative response is not a license to belittle or avoid problems; it is permission to gain some perspective.

Another option is to zoom out in time. Imagine yourself one week, one month, one year, one decade, or one century from today. Assess how much the current situation will matter when that time comes.

Dealing with the physical sensations of anxiety

Breathe. You can calm physical sensations within your body by focusing your attention on your breathing. Concentrate on the air going in and out of your lungs. Experience it as it passes through your nose and mouth.

Do this for two to five minutes. If you notice that you are taking short, shallow breaths, begin to take longer and deeper breaths. Imagine your lungs to be a pair of bagpipes. Expand your chest to bring in as much air as possible. Then listen to the plaintive chords as you slowly release the air.

Scan your body. Simple awareness is an effective technique to reduce the tension in your body.

Sit comfortably and close your eyes. Focus your attention on the muscles in your feet and notice if they are relaxed. Tell the muscles in your feet that they can relax.

Move up to your ankles and repeat the procedure. Next go to your calves and thighs and buttocks, telling each group of muscles to relax.

Do the same for your lower back, diaphragm, chest, upper back, neck, shoulders, jaw, face, upper arms, lower arms, fingers, and scalp.

Tense and relax. If you are aware of a particularly tense part of your body or if you discover tension when you're scanning your body, you can release this tension with the tense-relax method.

To do this, find a muscle that is tense and make it even more tense. If your shoulders are tense, pull them back, arch your back, and tense your shoulder muscles even more tightly. Then relax. The net result is that you can be aware of the relaxation and allow yourself to relax even more.

You can use the same procedure with your legs, arms, abdomen, chest, face, and neck. Clench your fists, tighten your jaw, straighten your legs, and tense your abdomen all at once. Then relax and pay close attention to the sensations of relaxation. By paying attention, you can learn to re-create these sensations whenever you choose.

Use guided imagery. Relax completely and take a quick fantasy trip. Close your eyes, free your body of tension, and imagine yourself in a beautiful, peaceful, natural setting. Create as much of the scene as you can. Be specific. Use all of your senses.

For example, you might imagine yourself at a beach. Hear the surf rolling in and the sea gulls calling to each other. Feel the sun on your face and the hot sand between your toes. Smell the sea breeze. Taste the salty mist from the surf. Notice the ships on the horizon and the rolling sand dunes. Use all of your senses to create a vivid imaginary trip.

Some people find that a mountain scene or a lush meadow scene works well. You can take yourself to a place you've never been or re-create an experience out of your past. Find a place that works for you and practice getting there. When you become proficient, you can return to it quickly for trips that might last only a few seconds.

With practice, you can use this technique even while you are taking a test.

Describe it. Focus your attention on your anxiety. If you are feeling nauseated or if you have a headache, concentrate on that feeling. Describe it to yourself. Tell yourself how large it is, where it is located in your body, what color it is, what shape it is, what texture it is, how much water it might hold if it had volume, and how heavy it is.

Be with it. As you describe your anxiety in detail, don't resist it. When you completely experience a physical sensation, it will often disappear. People suffering from severe and chronic pain have used this technique successfully.

Exercise aerobically. This is one technique that won't work in the classroom or while you're taking a test. Yet it is an excellent way to reduce body tension. Exercise regularly during the days that you review for a test. See what effect this has on your ability to focus and relax during the test.

Do some kind of exercise that will get your heart beating at twice your normal rate and keep it beating at that rate for 15 or 20 minutes. Aerobic exercises include rapid walking, jogging, swimming, bicycling, basketball, and anything else that elevates your heart rate and keeps it elevated.

Get help. When these techniques don't work, when anxiety is serious, get help. If you become withdrawn, have frequent thoughts about death or suicide, get depressed and stay depressed for more than a few days, or have prolonged feelings of hopelessness, see a counselor.

Depression and anxiety are common among students. Suicide is the second leading cause of death among young adults between the ages of 15 and 25. This is tragic and unnecessary. Many schools have counselors available. If not, the student health service or another office can refer you to community agencies that provide free or inexpensive counseling. You can also get emergency assistance over the phone. Most phone books contain listings for suicide prevention hot lines and other emergency services. ✖

TWENTY THINGS I LIKE TO DO

One way to relieve tension is to mentally yell, "Stop!" and substitute a pleasant daydream for the stressful thoughts and emotions you are experiencing.

In order to create a supply of pleasant images to recall during times of stress, conduct an eight-minute brainstorm about things you like to do. Your goal is to generate at least 20 ideas. Time yourself and write as fast as you can in the space below.

When you have completed your list, study it. Pick out two activities that seem especially pleasant and elaborate on them by creating a mind map. Write down all of the memories you have about that activity.

You can use these images to calm yourself in stressful situations.

journal entry 15

Discovery/Intention Statement

Do a timed, four-minute brainstorm of all the reasons, rationalizations, justifications, and excuses you have used to avoid studying. Be creative. List your thoughts in the space below by completing the following Discovery Statement.

I discovered that I . . .

_____

_____

_____

_____

_____

_____

_____

_____

_____

_____

_____

Next, review your list, pick the excuse that you use the most, and circle it. In the space below, write an Intention Statement about what you will do to begin eliminating your favorite excuse. Make this Intention Statement one that you can keep, with a timeline and a reward.

I intend to . . .

_____

_____

_____

_____

journal entry 16

Discovery Statement

Explore your feelings about tests. Complete the following sentences.

As exam time gets closer, one thing I notice that I do is . . .

_____

_____

When it comes to taking tests, I have trouble . . .

_____

_____

The night before a test, I usually feel . . .

_____

_____

The morning of a test, I usually feel . . .

_____

_____

During a test, I usually feel . . .

_____

_____

After a test, I usually feel . . .

_____

_____

When I get a test score, I usually feel . . .

_____

_____

_____

An online version of this exercise is available at

masterstudent.college.hmco.com

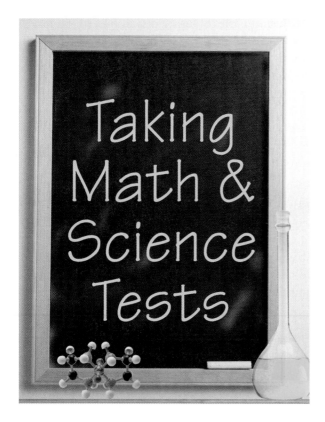

Taking Math & Science Tests

To approach math and science tests with confidence, back up to a bigger picture. For a moment, forget about tests. Start by learning ways to overcome any math or science anxiety that you feel. Next, choose courses with care. Also experiment with strategies for getting the most from class time and textbooks. Finally, review for tests by solving practice problems.

This article focuses on ideas for mastering math. Since math is crucial to many science courses, these suggestions can promote your success in both areas.

Overcome math and science anxiety

When they sit down to take a test in math or science, some capable students break out in a cold sweat. This is not a condition that you have to accept. Consider the following solutions.

Accept your current level of proficiency. To ensure that you have an adequate base of knowledge, tell the truth about your current level of knowledge and skill. Remember that it's OK to continue your study of math or science from your present level of ability—whatever that level might be.

Release irrational thoughts. When students fear math and science, they often say negative things to themselves about their abilities in these subjects. Many times this self-talk includes statements such as "I'll never be fast enough at solving math problems. . . . I'm one of those people who can't function in a science lab. . . . I'm good with words, so I can't be good with numbers."

Do some critical thinking about these statements. They can often be reduced to two simple ideas: "Everybody else is better at math and science than I am," and "Since I don't understand it right now, I'll never understand it." Both of these notions are illogical. If you lack confidence in your math and science skills, you are definitely not alone. To verify this, just ask other students. Also ask about what strategies they use to overcome confusion.

Then start some new self-talk. Use statements that affirm your ability to succeed in math and science: "When learning about math or science, I proceed with patience. . . . Any confusion I feel now will be resolved. . . . I learn math and science without comparing myself with others. . . . I ask whatever questions are needed to aid my understanding. . . . I am fundamentally OK as a person, even if I make errors in math and science."

Use systematic desensitization to diffuse anxiety. See anxiety as a learned response—one that you can "unlearn." You might be able to do this through a process that's sometimes used by people in psychotherapy. This process is called *systematic desensitization*:

- List some specific situations that trigger your math or science anxiety—for example, running out of time to answer all the questions on a test.

- Create a mental picture of yourself reacting in a new way to this trigger—such as budgeting your test time and finishing all the questions with time to spare.

- Next, set up a situation that *simulates* the situation you fear. For instance, create a mock test with the same number and kinds of questions that you anticipate will appear on your next test.

- Put yourself squarely in that simulated environment. For example, take your mock test in the actual exam room.

- Use relaxation techniques such as deep breathing at any time that you feel nervous.

- If your level of fear prevents you from functioning in your simulated situation, then back off a little and create a less demanding situation—such as a mock test with fewer or easier questions.

Your academic advisor or a counselor at your student health center may be able to help you use systematic desensitization. Ask for help—especially if your worries about math or science courses interfere with your daily life.

Choose courses with care

Success in math starts before you set foot in a classroom. Prior to enrolling in a math course, make sure that you have the background to understand it.

Assess your course readiness. Review your notes and textbook from your most recent math course. Also preview the assigned text for your next math course. If you have any doubts about your readiness for the course, meet with the teacher.

Math and science courses are often cumulative: the content of one course builds on the content of another. Talk to a math teacher or your advisor about what courses to take, and in what order.

Take math courses "back to back." You may find it tempting to take a break between required math courses. That's understandable, but this choice can make it harder for you to succeed.

Choose teachers with care. Ask around and discover which teachers have a gift for making math understandable. Look for math courses that tend to fill up early and find out who teaches them. Notice the office hours posted for math teachers; some may be more available to answer questions than others. Ask your academic advisor to recommend math teachers. Also ask friends to name their favorite math teachers—and to explain *why* they view these teachers as favorites.

Make the most of class time

Success in math and science depends on your active involvement. Attending class regularly, coming to class with homework finished, speaking up when you have a question, and seeking extra help when you need it are all crucial. In addition, experiment with the following strategies.

Review class work daily. If you want to succeed, make daily contact with math and science content. Warm up for each class session by reviewing the previous assignments, listing questions, and solving some extra problems.

Take useful notes. In your math notebook, leave several blank pages between each day's class notes. Fill these

pages with summaries of terms, definitions, equations, formulas, examples, and sample problems from your textbooks.

Also take complete notes. Success in math hinges on step-by-step learning. When your teacher works a problem in class on the board, copy each step exactly. Avoid skipping a step in your notes because it seems obvious. During a review session hours or days later, the gap in your notes could leave you scratching your head.

Get regular feedback and ask for help. Ask questions fearlessly—as soon as you're confused. The rapid pace and sequential nature of math courses make it essential for you to get help at the first sign of trouble. Help is available in many forms—your teacher, a math tutor, a study skills center, supplementary textbooks, computer-based tutorial programs, and more.

Use textbooks effectively

Math and science courses are often text-driven. That is, class activities follow the format of the book closely.

Read systematically. Read chapters and sections in order, as they're laid out in the text. Master one concept before going on to the next and to stay current with your reading.

Read actively. While reading your textbooks, stop at strategic points to reinforce your understanding of the material. At these points you can:

- Create a written list of key terms and translate each one into plain English.
- Copy diagrams, formulas, or equations.
- Work problems even if they're not assigned.
- List questions to ask in class.
- Close your book and mentally reconstruct the steps of an experiment or a mathematical proof.

Read slowly. It's ineffective to breeze through a math or science book as you would the newspaper. To get the most out of your text, be willing to read each sentence slowly and reread it as needed. A single paragraph may merit 15 or 20 minutes of sustained attention.

Practice solving problems

Since problem solving is so important to succeeding at math, develop a body of techniques that you can rely on. Start with the following suggestions and develop more techniques of your own.

Review problems you've solved before. Look over assigned problems and others. Make up your own variations on these problems. Work with a classmate and make up problems for each other to solve. The more problems you review, the more comfortable you're likely to feel solving new ones.

Divide problems by type. Make a list of the different kinds of problems and note the elements of each. By dividing problems into type or category, you can isolate the kinds of problems that are difficult for you. Practice those more and get help if you need it.

Read each problem several times. Read the problem at least twice before you begin. Read slowly. Be sure that you understand what is being asked. Let go of the expectation that you'll find the solution right away. You may make several attempts at solving the problem before you find a solution that works. Sometimes the sound of your voice will jar loose the solution to a problem. Talk yourself through the solution. Read equations out loud.

Translate problems into plain English. Putting problems into words aids your understanding. When you study equations and formulas, put those into words, too. The words help you see a variety of applications for each formula. For example, $5 + x$ can be translated as "a number added to 5." And, $x/2 = 10$ can be stated as "one-half of a number is 10."

List what you know and what you want to find out. Survey each problem for all of the givens. Look for what is to be proved or what is to be discovered. Consider using three columns labeled "What I already know," "What I want to find out," and "What relates the two." This last column is the place to record a formula that can help you solve the problem.

For clarity in problem solving, reduce the number of unknowns as much as you can. You may need to create a separate equation to solve each unknown.

The more problems you review, the more comfortable you're likely to feel solving new ones.

Draw an elaborate colored picture or a diagram if you are stuck. Sometimes viewing a visual representation will clear a blocked mind.

Choose a method to solve the problem. Before you start crunching numbers or punching a calculator, take a moment to plan your approach. Choose what arithmetic operations (addition, subtraction, multiplication, division) or formulas you will use.

Play with possible solutions. There's usually not one "right" way to solve a problem. Several approaches or formulas may work, though one may be more efficient than another. Be willing to think about the problem from several angles or to proceed by trial and error.

Check your work. One way to check your work is to estimate the answer before you compute it. Then ask yourself if the answer you actually got seems to be in the ballpark. In addition:

- *Use common sense.* Step back and ask if the solution seems reasonable at first glance. Reread the problem and re-mind yourself of the key question it asks. For example, if you're asked to calculate a discount for the price of an item, then that item should cost less in your solution.

- *Keep units of measurement clear.* Say that you're cal-culating the velocity of an object. If you're measur-ing distance in meters and time in seconds, then the final velocity should be in meters per second.

- *Put your answers to the test.* Plug your answer back into the original equation or problem and see if it works out correctly.

Savor solutions. Celebrate the times when you're getting correct answers. Relish the times when you feel relaxed and confident as you work or when you look over the last few pages and they seem easy. Then remember these times if you feel math or science anxiety.

PRACTICING CRITICAL THINKING

6

Create a short multiple choice test on a topic in a course you're taking right now. Ask several people from the class to take this exam.

Then, as a group, discuss the answer you chose for each question. Also talk about *why* and *how* you chose each answer. The purpose is to identify the strategies that different people use when answering a multiple choice question—especially when they are unsure of the correct answer.

You might discover some test-taking strategies that you would use in the future. List those strategies in the space below.

_____

_____

_____

_____

_____

_____

_____

_____

_____

_____

_____

_____

_____

_____

_____

_____

_____

Repeat this exercise by creating and discussing tests in other formats: short-answer, true/false, and essay.

Celebrate mistakes

Most of us are haunted by the fear of failure. We dread the thought of making mistakes or being held responsible for a major breakdown. We shudder at the missteps that could cost us grades, careers, money, or even relationships.

It's possible to take an entirely different attitude toward mistakes. Rather than fearing them, we could actually celebrate them. We could revel in our redundancies, frolic in our failures, and glory in our goof-ups. We could marvel at our mistakes and bark with loud laughter when we "blow it."

A creative environment is one in which failure is not fatal. Businesses, striving to be on the cutting edge of competition, desperately seek innovative changes. Smart managers know that innovation requires risk taking, despite the chance of failure.

Note: Nothing in this article amounts to an argument in favor of *making* mistakes in the first place. Rather, the intention is to encourage shining a light on mistakes so that we can examine them and fix them. Mistakes that are hidden cannot be corrected.

Following are some solid reasons to celebrate mistakes.

Celebration allows us to notice the mistake. Celebrating mistakes gets them out into the open. This is the opposite of covering up mistakes or blaming others for them. Hiding mistakes takes a lot of energy—energy that could be channeled into correcting errors.

Mistakes are valuable feedback. A manager of a major corporation once made a mistake that cost his company $100,000. He predicted that he would be fired when his boss found out. Instead, his boss responded, "Fire you? I can't afford to do that. I just spent $100,000 training you." Mistakes are part of the learning process. Not only are mistakes usually more interesting than most successes—they're also often more instructive.

Mistakes demonstrate that we're taking risks. People who play it safe make few mistakes. Making mistakes is evidence that we're stretching to the limit of our abilities—growing, risking, and learning. Fear of making mistakes can paralyze us into inaction. Celebrating mistakes helps us move into gear and get things done.

How to cram (even though you shouldn't)

Cramming is not the same as learning. When you rely on cramming, you cheat yourself out of a true education for one basic reason: You won't remember what you cram.

This point is especially important to recognize if you cram for mid-term exams. Some students think they are actually learning the material that they cram into their heads. They will be unpleasantly surprised during finals.

Cramming is also more work. It takes longer to learn material when you do it under pressure. You can't learn the same quantity of material in less time when you cram. You can learn some of the material, though with less comprehension and little or no long-term retention.

The purpose of cramming, therefore, is only to make the best of the situation. Cram to get by in a course so that you can do better next time. Cramming might help raise a grade if you have been reasonably attentive in class, have taken fair notes, and have read or skimmed most of the material for the course.

Make choices. Don't try to learn it all when you cram. You can't. Instead, pick out a few of the most important elements of the course and learn those backwards, forwards, and upside down.

Make a plan. Cramming is always done when time is short. It's easy to panic and jump right in. Taking a few minutes to create a plan first can actually save you time and allow you to work faster. After you've chosen what you want to study, determine how much time you have and set timelines for yourself.

Use mind map review sheets and flash cards. Condense the material you have chosen to learn onto mind maps. Choose several elements of the mind maps to put on 3x5 flash cards. Practice re-creating the mind maps, complete with illustrations. Drill yourself with the flash cards.

Recite and recite again. The key to cramming is repetitive recitation. Recitation can burn facts into your brain like no other study method. Go over your material again and again and again. One option is to tape-record yourself while you recite. Then play the tape as you fall asleep and as you get up in the morning.

Relax. Because you do not learn material well when you cram, you are more likely to freeze and forget it under the pressure of an exam. Relaxation techniques can be used to reduce test anxiety, both before and during the test.

Tell yourself it would have been more effective to study earlier and more often. Remind yourself that you will have an opportunity to do so next time and write an Intention Statement detailing how you plan to change your study habits.

Finally, lighten up. Our brains work better when we aren't criticizing ourselves. Give yourself permission to be the fallible human being you are.

Celebrating mistakes includes everyone. It reminds us that the exclusive club named the Perfect Performance Society has no members. All of us make mistakes.

Mistakes occur only when we aim at a clear goal. We can express concern about missing a target only if the target is there in the first place. If there's no target or purpose, there's no concern about missing it. Making a mistake affirms something of great value—that we have a plan.

Mistakes happen only when we're committed to making things work. Systems work when people are willing to be held accountable. Openly admitting mistakes promotes accountability. Imagine a school where there's no concern about quality and effectiveness. Teachers usually come to class late. Residence halls are never cleaned, and scholarship checks are always late.

The administration is in chronic debt, students seldom pay tuition on time, and no one cares. In this school, the word *mistake* would have little meaning. Mistakes become apparent only when people are committed to improving the quality of an institution. Mistakes go hand in hand with a commitment to quality.

Celebrating mistakes cuts the problem down to size. On top of the mistake itself, there is often a layer of regret, worry, and desperation about having made the mistake in the first place. Not only do people have a problem with the consequences of the mistake, but they also have a problem with themselves for making a mistake in the first place. When we celebrate mistakes, we eliminate that layer of concern. When our anxiety about making a mistake is behind us, we can get down to the business of correcting the mistake. ⊠

power process

Detach

This Power Process helps you release the powerful, natural student within you. It is especially useful whenever negative emotions are getting in the way of your education.

Attachments are addictions. When we are attached to something, we think we cannot live without it, just as a drug addict feels he cannot live without drugs. We believe our well-being depends on maintaining our attachments.

We can be attached to just about anything—expectations, ideas, objects, self-perceptions, people, results, rewards. The list is endless.

One person, for example, might be so attached to his car that he takes an accident as a personal attack. Pity the poor unfortunate who backs into this person's car. He might as well back into the owner himself.

Another person might be attached to his job. His identity and sense of well-being depend on it. He could become suicidally depressed if he gets fired.

We can be addicted to our emotions as well as to our thoughts. We can identify with our anger so strongly that we are unwilling to let it go. We can also be addicted to our pessimism and reluctant to give it up. Rather than perceive these emotions as liabilities, we can see them as indications that it's time to practice detachment.

Most of us are addicted, to some extent, to our identities: We are Americans, veterans, high achievers, bowlers, loyal friends, business owners, humanitarians, devoted parents, dancers, hockey fans, or birdwatchers. If we are attached to these roles, they can dictate who we think we are.

When these identities are threatened, we might fight for them as if we were defending our lives. The more addicted we are to an identity, the harder we fight to keep it.

Ways to recognize an attachment

When we are attached and things don't go our way, we might feel irritated, angry, jealous, confused, fatigued, bored, frightened, or resentful.

Suppose you are attached to getting an A on your physics test. You feel as though your success in life depends on getting an A. It's not just that you want an A. You *need* an A. During the exam, the thought "I must get an A" is in the back of your mind as you begin to work a problem. And the problem is difficult. The first time you read it, you have no idea how to solve it. The second time around, you aren't even sure what it's asking. The more you struggle to understand it, the more confused you get. To top it all off, this problem is worth 40 percent of your score.

As the clock ticks away, you work harder, getting more stuck, while that voice in your head gets louder: "I must get an A. I MUST get an A. I MUST GET AN A!"

At this point, your hands begin to sweat and shake. Your heart is pounding. You feel nauseated. You can't concentrate. You flail about for the answer as if you were drowning. You look up at the clock, sickened by the inexorable sweep of the second hand. You are doomed.

Now is a time to detach.

Ways to use this process

Detachment can be challenging. In times of stress, it might seem like the most difficult thing in the world to do. You can practice a variety of strategies to help you move toward detachment.

Practice observer consciousness. This is the quiet

state above and beyond your usual thoughts, the place where you can be aware of being aware. It's a tranquil spot, apart from your emotions. From here, you can observe yourself objectively as if you were someone else. Pay attention to your emotions and physical sensations. If you are confused and feeling stuck, tell yourself, "Here I am, confused and stuck." If your palms are sweaty and your stomach is one big knot, admit it.

Practice perspective. Put current circumstances into a broader perspective. View personal issues within the larger context of your community, your nation, or your planet. You will likely see them from a different point of view. Imagine the impact your present problems will have 20 or even 100 years from now.

Take a moment to consider the worst that could happen. During that physics exam, notice your attachment to getting an A. Realize that even flunking the test will not ruin your life. Seeing this helps you put the test in perspective.

Practice breathing. Calm your mind and body with breathing or relaxation techniques.

Note: It might be easier to practice these techniques when you're not feeling strong emotions. Notice your thoughts, behaviors, and feelings during neutral activities such as watching television or taking a walk.

Practice detaching. The key is to let go of automatic emotional reactions when you don't get what you want.

Rewrite the equation

To further understand this notion of detaching, we can borrow an idea from mathematics. An equation is a set of symbols joined by an equals sign (=) that forms a true statement. Examples are $2 + 2 = 4$ and $a + b = c$.

Equations also work with words. In fact, our self-image can be thought of as a collection of equations. For example, the thought "I am capable" can be written as the equation "I = capable." "My happiness depends on my car" can be written as "happiness = car." The statement "My well-being depends on my job" becomes "well-being = job." Each equation is a tip-off to an attachment. When we're upset, a closer look often reveals that one of our attachments is threatened. The person who believes that his happiness is equal to his current job will probably be devastated if his company downsizes and he's laid off.

Once we discover a hidden equation, we can rewrite it. In the process, we can watch our upsets disappear. The person who gets laid off can change his equation to "my happiness = my happiness." In other words, his happiness does not have to depend on any particular job.

People can rewrite equations under the most extreme circumstances. A man dying from lung cancer spent his last days celebrating his long life. One day his son asked him how he was feeling.

"Oh, I'm great," said the man with cancer. "Your mom and I have been having a wonderful time just rejoicing in the life that we have had together."

"Oh, I'm glad you're doing well," said the man's son. "The prednisone you have been taking must have kicked in again and helped your breathing."

"Well, not exactly. Actually, my body is in terrible shape, and my breathing has been a struggle these last few days. I guess what I'm saying is that my body is not working well at all, but I'm still great."

The dying man rewrote the equation "I = my body." He knew that he had a body and that he was more than his body. This man lived this Power Process and gave his son—the author of this book—an unforgettable lesson about detachment.

Some cautions

Giving up an addiction to being an A student does not mean giving up being an A student. And giving up an addiction to a job doesn't mean getting rid of the job. It means not investing your entire well-being in the grade or the job. Keep your desires and goals alive and healthy while detaching from the compulsion to reach them.

Notice also that detachment is different from denial. Denial implies running away from whatever you find unpleasant. In contrast, detachment includes accepting your emotions and knowing the details of them—down to every last thought and physical sensation involved. It's OK to be angry or sad. Once you accept and fully experience your emotions, you can more easily move beyond them.

Being detached is not the same as being apathetic. We can be 100 percent detached and 100 percent involved at the same time. In fact, our commitment toward achieving a particular result is usually enhanced by being detached from it.

Detach and succeed

When we are detached, we perform better. When we think everything is at stake, the results might suffer. Without anxiety and the need to get an A on the physics test, we are more likely to recognize the problem and remember the solution.

This Power Process is useful when you notice that attachments are keeping you from accomplishing your goals. Behind your attachments is a master student. By detaching, you release that master student. Detach. ◪

put it to work

You can apply many of the techniques discussed in this chapter directly to common situations in the workplace. For example, use the test-taking strategies when you take licensing exams, certification exams, and other tests in your career field. In addition, consider the following suggestions.

Seize opportunities to learn cooperatively. Forming study groups or committees helps you develop important workplace skills. Almost every job is accomplished by the combined efforts of many people. For example, manufacturing a single car calls for the contribution of designers, welders, painters, electricians, marketing executives, computer programmers, and many others.

Perhaps you prefer to complete your assignments by working independently. However, teamwork is often required in the workplace. Joining study groups now, while you are in school, can help you expand your learning styles and succeed in the workplace.

Apply your cooperative learning skills to working on project teams. To create a successful project team at work, combine the individual skills of team members in complementary ways. Major tasks in any project include:

- *Planning*—defining the desired outcomes, setting due dates for each task, and generating commitment to action.

- *Doing*—carrying out assigned tasks.

- *Reflecting*—meeting regularly to discuss what's working well and ways to improve the next phase of the project.

- *Interpreting*—discussing what the team has learned from the project and ways to apply that learning to the whole organization.

Many people are drawn to one of these tasks more than to others. Assign tasks to people based on their strengths and preferences.

One potential trap of working in teams is that one person ends up doing most of the work. This person might feel resentful and complain. If you find yourself in this situation, transform your complaint into a request. Instead of scolding team members for being lazy, request help. Ask team members to take over tasks that you've been doing. Delegate specific jobs.

Manage job stress. The same techniques that help you manage test anxiety can help you manage stress at work. Apply techniques for managing the mental and physical aspects of stress while interviewing for a job, making a presentation, doing a performance review, or carrying out any task that raises your anxiety level.

Celebrate mistakes. Recall a mistake you made at work and then write about it. In a Discovery Statement, describe what you did to create a result you didn't want ("I discovered that I tend to underestimate the number of hours projects take"). Then write an Intention Statement describing something you can do differently in the future ("I intend to keep track of my actual hours on each project so that I can give more accurate estimates").

Go for fun. Finally, see if you can adapt suggestions from "Have some FUN!" to cultivate enjoyment at work. One benefit of career planning (see Chapter Ten) is finding a job that allows you to follow your interests—in other words, to have fun. Successful people often eliminate the distinction between work and play in their lives. You're more likely to excel professionally when you're having a blast at your job. ◪

Name _____ Date _____/_____/_____

1. Preparing for tests can include creating review tools. Name at least two of these tools.

2. When answering multiple choice questions, it is better to read all of the possible answers before answering the question in your head. True or False? Explain your answer.

3. The presence of absolute qualifiers, such as *always* or *never*, generally indicates a false statement. True or False? Explain your answer.

4. When answering an essay question, which of the following techniques is least effective?
   (a) Make a quick outline before answering the question.
   (b) Save the best points for last.
   (c) Know standard essay question words.
   (d) Include part of the question in your answer.
   (e) Avoid filler sentences.

5. Grades are:
   (a) A measure of creativity.
   (b) An indication of your ability to contribute to society.
   (c) A measure of intelligence.
   (d) A measure of test performance.
   (e) C and D.

6. Describe how *detachment* differs from *denial*.

7. Success in a math course can start even before you set foot in the classroom. True or False? Explain your answer.

8. List at least three options for conducting a study group.

9. Describe at least three techniques for dealing with the thoughts connected to test anxiety.

10. Describe at least three techniques for dealing with the physical feelings connected to test anxiety.

learning styles application

The questions below will "cycle" you through four styles, or modes, of learning as explained in the article "Learning styles: Discovering how you learn" in Chapter One. Each question will help you explore a different mode. You can answer the questions in any order.

what if *Explain how a suggestion for managing test anxiety could help you manage stress in a situation that you face outside school.*

why *Name at least one benefit you could experience—in addition to better grades—by taking tests more effectively.*

how *Of the techniques that you gained from this chapter, choose one that you will use on your next test. Describe exactly how you intend to apply the technique.*

what *List three new techniques for reviewing course material or taking tests that you gained from reading this chapter.*

master student

profile

BARBARA JORDAN

(1936–1996) The first African American to become a state senator in Texas and the first African American to enter Congress since the Reconstruction.

So I was at Boston University in this new and strange and different world, and it occurred to me that if I was going to succeed at this strange new adventure, I would have to read longer and more thoroughly than my colleagues at law school had to read. I felt that in order to compensate for what I had missed in earlier years, I would have to work harder, and study longer, than anybody else. . . . I did my reading not in the law library, but in a library at my graduate dorm, upstairs where it was very quiet, because apparently nobody else studied there. So I would go there at night after dinner. I would load my books under my arm and go to the library, and I would read until the wee hours of the morning and then go to bed. . . .

I was always delighted when I would get called upon to recite in class. But the professors did not call on the "ladies" very much. There were certain favored people who always got called on, and then on some rare occasions a professor

would come in and would announce: "We're going to have Ladies Day today." And he would call on the ladies. We were just tolerated. We weren't considered really top drawer when it came to the study of law.

At some time in the spring, Bill Gibson, who was dating my new roommate, Norma Walker, organized a black study group, as we blacks had to form our own. This was because we were not invited into any of the other study groups. There were six or seven in our group—Bill, and Issie, and I think Maynard Jackson—and we would just gather and talk it out and hear ourselves do that. One thing I learned was that you had to talk out the issues, the facts, the cases, the decisions, the process. You couldn't just read the cases and study alone in your library as I had been doing; and you couldn't get it all in the classroom. But once you had talked it out in the study group, it flowed more easily and made a lot more sense. . . .

Finally I felt I was really learning things, really going to school. I felt that I was getting educated, whatever that was. I became familiar with the process of thinking. I learned to think things out and reach conclusions and defend what I had said.

In the past I had got along by spouting off. Whether you talked

about debates or oratory, you dealt with speechifying. But I could no longer orate and let that pass for reasoning because there was not any demand for an orator in Boston University Law School. You had to think and read and understand and reason. I had learned at twenty-one that you couldn't just say a thing is so because it might not be so, and somebody brighter, smarter, and more thoughtful would come out and tell you it wasn't so. Then, if you still thought it was, you had to prove it. Well, that was a new thing for me. I cannot, I really cannot describe what that did to my insides and to my head. I thought: I'm being educated finally. ✖

From *Barbara Jordan, a Self-Portrait* by Barbara Jordan and Shelby Hearon. Reprinted by permission of The Wendy Weil Agency, Inc. Copyright © 1978, 1979 by Barbara Jordan and Shelby Hearon.

For more biographical information about Barbara Jordan, visit the Master Student Hall of Fame on the *Becoming a Master Student* Web site at

masterstudent.college.hmco.com

7

Thinking

STUDENT VOICES

"*A Master Student practices critical thinking. . . . She does not always accept the first answer as the only answer, and constantly questions what is put before her. I am determined to get every ounce of information, to glean and hold onto it, use it, and mature my thinking.*"

—LYNN LINEBERGER

why
this chapter matters . . .

The ability to think creatively and critically helps you succeed in any course.

what
is included . . .

Critical thinking: A survival skill
Finding "aha!" and following through: Becoming a thorough thinker
Uncovering assumptions
Ways to fool yourself: Six common mistakes in logic
Overcome stereotypes with critical thinking
Gaining skill at decision making
Four ways to solve problems
"But I don't know what I want to do": Choosing a major
Asking questions
Power Process: "Find a bigger problem"
Master Student Profile: Paul Farmer

how
you can use this chapter . . .

Read, write, speak, and listen more effectively.
Learn strategies to enhance your success in problem solving. Apply thinking skills to practical decisions such as choosing a major.

As you read, ask yourself
what if . . .

I could solve problems more creatively and make decisions in every area of life with more confidence?

Critical thinking: A survival skill

Society depends on persuasion. Advertisers want us to spend money on their products. Political candidates want us to "buy" their stands on the issues. Teachers want us to agree that their classes are vital to our success. Parents want us to accept their values. Authors want us to read their books. Broadcasters want us to spend our time in front of the radio or television, consuming their programs and not those of the competition. The business of persuasion has an impact on all of us.

A typical American sees thousands of television commercials each year. And that's just one medium of communication. Add to that the writers and speakers who enter our lives through radio shows, magazines, books, billboards, brochures, Internet sites, and fundraising appeals—all with a product, service, cause, or opinion for us to embrace.

This leaves us with hundreds of choices about what to buy, where to go, and who to be. It's easy to lose our heads in the crosscurrent of competing ideas—unless we develop skills in critical thinking. When we think critically, we can make choices with open eyes.

Uses of critical thinking

Critical thinking underlies reading, writing, speaking, and listening. These are the basic elements of communication—a process that occupies most of our waking hours.

Critical thinking also plays an important part in social change. Consider that the institutions in any society—courts, governments, schools, businesses—are the products of a certain way of thinking. Any organization draws its life from certain assumptions about the way things should be done. Before the institution can change, those assumptions need to be loosened up or reinvented. In many ways, the real location of an institution is inside our heads.

Critical thinking also helps us uncover bias and prejudice. This is a first step toward communicating with people of other races, ethnic backgrounds, and cultures.

Crises occur when our thinking fails to keep pace with reality. An example is the world's ecological crisis, which arose when people polluted the earth, air, and water without considering the long-term consequences. Imagine how different our world would be if our leaders had thought like the first female chief of the Cherokees.

journal entry 17

Discovery/Intention Statement

Think back to a time when you felt unable to choose among several different solutions to a problem or several stands on a key issue in your life. In the space below, describe this experience.

I discovered that . . .

_____

_____

_____

Now scan this chapter to find useful suggestions for decision making, problem solving, and critical thinking. Note below at least four techniques that look especially promising to you.

Strategy   *Page number*

_____

_____

_____

_____

_____

_____

Finally, declare a time that you intend to explore these techniques in more detail, along with a situation coming up during this term in which you could apply them.

I intend to improve my thinking skills by . . .

_____

_____

_____

_____

_____

_____

_____

Asked about the best advice her elders had given her, she replied, "Look forward. Turn what has been done into a better path. If you are a leader, think about the impact of your decision on seven generations into the future."

Novelist Ernest Hemingway once said that anyone who wants to be a great writer must have a built-in, shockproof "crap" detector.[1] That inelegant comment points to a basic truth: As critical thinkers, we are constantly on the lookout for thinking that's inaccurate, sloppy, or misleading.

Critical thinking is a skill that will never go out of style. Throughout history, half-truths, faulty assumptions, and other nonsense have at one time been commonly accepted as true. Examples include:

- Illness results from an imbalance in the four vital fluids: blood, phlegm, water, and bile.

- Caucasians are inherently more intelligent than people of other races.

- Women are incapable of voting intelligently.

- We will never invent anything smaller than a transistor. (That was before the computer chip.)

- Computer technology will usher in the age of the paperless office.

The critical thinkers of history courageously challenged such ideas. These men and women pointed out that—metaphorically speaking—the emperor had no clothes.

Critical thinking is a path to freedom from half-truths and deception. You have the right to question what you see, hear, and read. Acquiring this ability is one of the major goals of a liberal arts education.

Critical thinking as thorough thinking

For some people, the term *critical thinking* has negative connotations. If you prefer, use *thorough thinking* instead. Both terms point to the same array of activities: sorting out conflicting claims, weighing the evidence, letting go of personal biases, and arriving at reasonable conclusions. This adds up to an ongoing conversation—a constant process, not a final product.

We live in a society that seems to value quick answers and certainty. This is often at odds with effective thinking. Thorough thinking is the ability to examine and re-examine ideas that might seem obvious. Such thinking takes time and the willingness to say three subversive words: "I don't know."

Thorough thinking is also the willingness to change our opinion as we continue to examine a problem. This calls for courage and detachment. Just ask anyone who has given up a cherished point of view in light of new evidence.

Skilled students are thorough thinkers. They distinguish between opinion and fact. They ask probing questions and make detailed observations. They uncover assumptions and define their terms. They make assertions carefully, basing them on sound logic and solid evidence. Almost everything that we call *knowledge* is a result of these activities. This means that critical thinking and learning are intimately linked.

It's been said that human beings are rational creatures. Yet no one is born a thorough thinker. This is a learned skill. Use the suggestions in this chapter to claim the thinking powers that are your birthright. The critical thinker is one aspect of the master student who lives inside you.

Accept your changing perspectives

Researcher William Perry found that students in higher education move through stages of intellectual development.[2] Students in earlier stages tend to think there is only one correct viewpoint on each issue, and they look to their instructors to reveal that truth. Later, students acknowledge a variety of opinions on issues and construct their own viewpoints.

Monitor changes in your thinking processes as you combine viewpoints. Distinguish between opinions that you accept from authorities and opinions that are based on your own use of logic and your search for evidence. Also look for opinions that result from objective procedures (such as using the *Why? What? How?* and *What if?* questions in this article) and personal sources (using intuition or "gut feelings").

Remember that the process of becoming a critical thinker will take you through a variety of stages. Give yourself time, and celebrate your growing mastery. ⬧

Finding "aha!" and following through:

Becoming a thorough thinker

Aha! is the burst of creative energy heralded by the arrival of a new idea. Aha! involves the sudden emergence of an unfamiliar pattern or an unusual combination of familiar elements.

This is an exhilarating experience. Nineteenth-century poet Emily Dickinson described *aha!* this way: "If I feel physically as if the top of my head were taken off, I know that is poetry."

Remember, however, that *aha!* does not always result in a timeless poem or a Nobel Prize. Also, it can be inspired by anything from playing a new riff on a guitar to figuring out why your car's fuel pump doesn't work.

The flip side of *aha!* is following through with critical thinking—taking the ideas you've created, testing them, and then taking further action. Many of us ignore this part of the thinking process. How many great moneymaking schemes have we had that we never pursued? How many good ideas have we had for articles that we never wrote? Genius resides in follow-through—the

application of perspiration to inspiration.

Stripped to its essence, critical thinking means asking and answering questions. The four basic questions in the Learning Styles Applications in this book—*Why? What? How?* and *What if?*—work well for this kind of thinking. For more details, see the last four suggestions in this article.

Creative thinking (*aha!*) and critical thinking (following through) are often presented as two separate skills. But for thorough thinkers, these are simply two milestones in a single, seamless process.

Choose when to think creatively

Creative thinking is useful in the early stages of planning and problem solving. Feel free to dwell in this domain for a while. When you face a problem, invent many possible solutions. If you narrow down your options too soon, you run the risk of missing an exciting solution or of neglecting a novel viewpoint.

Remember that creative thinking and critical thinking take place in a continuous cycle. After you've used critical thinking to narrow down your options, you can return to creative thinking at any time to generate new ones.

Conduct a brainstorm

The purpose of brainstorming is to generate as many solutions as possible. Sometimes the craziest, most outlandish ideas—although unworkable in themselves—can lead to new solutions.

First, define the issue or problem precisely. Write it down, stating it as a question—for example: "How can I add

Tangram

A tangram is an ancient Chinese puzzle game that stimulates the "play instinct" so critical to creative thinking. The cat figure above was created by rearranging seven sections of a square. Hundreds of images can be devised in this manner. Playing with tangrams allows us to see relationships we didn't notice before.

The rules of the game are simple: Use these seven pieces to create something that wasn't there before. Be sure to use all seven. You might start by mixing up the pieces and seeing whether you can put them back together to form a square.

Make your own tangram by cutting pieces like those above out of poster board. When you come up with a pattern you like, trace around the outside edges of it and see if a friend can discover how you did it.

money to my savings account each month even while I'm in school?"

Next, set a time limit for your brainstorming session. Use a clock to time it to the minute. Digital sports watches with built-in stopwatches work well. Experiment with various lengths of time.

Before you begin, sit quietly for a few seconds to collect your thoughts. Then start timing and write as fast as you can. Write down everything. Accept every idea. If it pops into your head, put it down on paper. Quantity, not quality, is the goal.

After the session, review and evaluate. Toss out any truly nutty ideas—after you give them a chance. For example, during your brainstorm on saving money, you might write: "Stop spending money on movies or other entertainment." Impossible? This idea could lead to a list of options for free fun—anything from playing a board game to giving or receiving a foot massage.

Cultivate creative serendipity

The word *serendipity* was coined by the English author Horace Walpole from the title of an ancient Persian fairy tale, "The Three Princes of Serendip." The princes had a knack for making lucky discoveries. Serendipity is that knack—the ability to see something unexpected and valuable.

History is full of serendipity. For instance, Scottish scientist Alexander Fleming was growing bacteria in a laboratory petri dish. A spore of *Penicillium notatum,* a kind of mold, blew in the window and landed in the dish, killing the bacteria. Fleming "accidentally" noticed this and isolated the active ingredient. Eventually it saved thousands of lives.

You can train yourself in the art of serendipity. Keep your eyes open. Multiply your contacts with the world. Meet new people. Join a book group. Go to plays, concerts, art shows, lectures, and movies. Then expect discoveries. Be prepared to recognize a useful idea, no matter where or when it appears.

Keep idea files

We all have ideas. "Creative" people are those who recognize ideas. record them, and follow up on them.

One way to record ideas is to jot them down on 3x5 cards. Collect quotations, random insights, notes on your reading, and useful ideas that you encounter in class. Collect jokes, too. File all of these away in a folder along with letters and articles clipped from magazines and newspapers. You can also create idea files on a computer.

Safeguard your ideas, even if you're pressed for time. Jotting down four or five words is enough to capture the essence of an idea. Then review your files regularly. Some amusing thought that came to you in November might be the perfect solution to a problem in March.

Play with ideas

It has been said that there are no new ideas—only new ways to combine old ideas. Creativity is the ability to discover those new combinations.

So look at the ideas that you collect from many angles. For example, put unrelated facts next to each other and see if you can invent a relationship between them—even if it seems absurd. Or take the obvious answers to a question—then toss them out. Ask yourself: "Well, I know *X* is true, but if *X* were *not* true, what would happen?" Also ask the reverse: "If that *were* true, what would follow next?" Or turn a problem upside down by picking a desired solution and brainstorming ways to achieve it. Ask other people for their ideas as well.

Create on your feet

A popular trend in executive offices is the "stand-up" desk—a raised working surface at which you stand rather than sit.

Standing has advantages over sitting for long periods. You can stay more alert and creative when you're on your feet. One theory is that our problem-solving ability improves when we stand, due to increased heart rate and blood flow to the brain.

Standing is great for easing lower-back pain, too. Sitting aggravates the spine and its supporting muscles.

This is a technique with tradition. If you search the Web for stand-up desks, you'll find models based on desks used by Thomas Jefferson, Winston Churchill, and writer Virginia Woolf. Consider setting your desk up on blocks or putting a box on top of your desk so that you can stand while writing, preparing speeches, or studying. Discover whether this approach works for you.

Term. A *term* is a key word or phrase—one that is often defined in a specific way. Imagine two people arguing about whether an employer should limit health care benefits to members of a family. To one person, the term *family* means a mother, father, and children; to the other person, the term *family* applies to any long-term, supportive relationship between people who live together. Chances are good that the debate will go nowhere until these people realize that they're defining the same term in different ways.

Conflicts of opinion can often be resolved—or at least clarified—when we define our key terms up front. This is especially true with abstract, emotion-laden terms such as *freedom, peace, progress,* and *justice.* Blood has been shed over the meaning of these words. Define them with care.

Assertion. An *assertion* is a complete sentence that contains one or more terms and directly answers a key question. For example, consider this sentence from the article "The Master Student" in Chapter One: "A master is a person who has attained a level of skill that goes beyond technique." This sentence is an assertion that answers an important question: How do we recognize a master?

Viewpoint. A *viewpoint* consists of several assertions that are logically related and supported by evidence. Viewpoints may also be called *opinions* or *arguments.*

Divergent thinking. The process of opening up alternatives and considering many different viewpoints is called *divergent thinking.* It's based on the assumption that having one good idea starts with having *lots* of ideas. Then you can pick and choose from among them, combining and refining ideas as you see fit. *Divergent thinking* is another term for *creative thinking.*

Convergent thinking. Out of all the possible viewpoints on an issue or alternative solutions to a problem, you'll often choose one that is the most reasonable or that provides the most workable basis for action. This process of narrowing down is called *convergent thinking.* Before you choose among viewpoints, generate as many of them as possible through divergent thinking. *Convergent thinking* is another term for *critical thinking.*

In any case, living with a problem invites a solution. Write down key questions, facts, opinions, and possible solutions on 3x5 cards and carry them with you. Look at them before you go to bed at night and record your first thoughts the next morning. The idea is to focus on the problem periodically—and then let go of it. Don't try to force a solution. Take a break from the problem and let it simmer in your subconscious mind for a while. Trust the creative process and let insights emerge in their own time.

Ask: *Why* am I considering this issue?

Critical thinking and personal passion go together. Begin critical thinking with a question that matters to you. Seek a rationale for your learning. Understand why it is important for you to think about a specific topic. You might want to arrive at a new conclusion, make a prediction, or solve a problem. By finding a personal connection with an issue, your interest in acquiring and retaining new information increases.

Ask: *What* are various points of view on this issue?

Dozens of viewpoints exist on every important issue—reducing crime, ending world hunger, preventing war, educating our children, and countless other concerns. Few problems allow for any single, permanent solution.

Imagine Karl Marx, Cesar Chavez, and Donald Trump assembled in one room to determine the most desirable economic system. Picture Mahatma Gandhi, Winnie Mandela, and General George Patton lecturing at a United Nations conference on conflict resolution. Visualize Fidel Castro, George W. Bush, and Mother Teresa in a discussion about distributing the world's resources equitably. When seeking out alternative points of view, let such events unfold in your mind.

You can take advantage of this diversity by seeking out alternative views with an open mind. When talking to another person, be willing to walk away with a new point of view—even if it's the one you brought to the table, now supported with new evidence.

When asking questions, let go of the temptation to settle for just a single answer. Once you have come up with an answer, say to yourself, "Yes, that is one answer. Now what's another?" Using this approach can sustain honest inquiry, fuel creativity, and lead to conceptual breakthroughs. But be prepared: The world is complicated, and critical thinking is a complex business. Some of your answers might contradict others. Resist the temptation to have all of your ideas in a neat, orderly bundle.

Ask: *How* well is each point of view supported?

Uncritical thinkers shield themselves from new information and ideas. As an alternative, you can follow the example of scientists, who constantly search for evidence that contradicts their theories. The following suggestions can help.

Look for logic and evidence. The aim of using logic is to make statements that are clear, consistent, and coherent. As you examine a speaker's or writer's assertions, you might find errors in logic—assertions that contradict each other or assumptions that are unfounded.

Also assess the evidence used to support points of view. Evidence comes in several forms, including facts, expert testimony, and examples. To think critically about evidence, ask questions such as:

- Are all or most of the relevant facts presented?

- Are the facts consistent with each other?

- Are the facts presented accurately—or in a misleading way?

- Are enough examples included to make a solid case for the viewpoint?

- Do the examples truly support the viewpoint?

- Are the examples typical? That is, could the author or speaker support the assertion with other examples that are similar?

- Is the expert credible—truly knowledgeable about the topic?

Consider the source. Look again at that article on the problems of manufacturing cars powered by natural gas. It might have been written by an executive from an oil company. Check out the expert who disputes the connection between smoking and lung cancer. That "expert" might be the president of a tobacco company.

This is not to say that we should dismiss the ideas of people who have a vested interest in stating their opinions. Rather, we can take their self-interest into account as we consider their ideas.

Understand before criticizing. Polished debaters can sum up their opponents' viewpoints—often better than the people who support those viewpoints themselves. Likewise, critical thinkers take the time to understand a statement of opinion before agreeing or disagreeing with it.

Effective understanding calls for listening without judgment. Enter another person's world by expressing her viewpoint in your own words. If you're conversing with that person, keep revising your summary until she agrees that you've stated her position accurately. If you're reading an article, write a short summary of it. Then scan the article again, checking to see if your synopsis is on target.

Watch for hot spots. Many people have mental "hot spots"—topics that provoke strong opinions and feelings. Examples are abortion, homosexuality, gun control, and the death penalty.

To become more skilled at examining various points of view, notice your own particular hot spots. Make a clear intention to accept your feelings about these topics and to continue using critical thinking techniques to explore them.

One way to cool down our hot spots is to remember that we can change or even give up our current opinions without giving up ourselves. That's a key message behind the articles "Ideas are tools" and "Detach." These Power Processes remind us that human beings are much more than the sum of their current opinions.

Ask: *What if* I could combine various points of view—or create a new one?

Each viewpoint can be seen as one approach among many possible alternatives. If you don't think that any one viewpoint is complete, then combine several of them. In the process, you might come up with something new.

For maximum clarity, put your new viewpoint in writing. Thoughts can move at blinding speed. Writing slows down that process. Gaps in logic that slip by us in thought or speech are often exposed when we commit the same ideas to paper. Writing down our thoughts allows us to compare, contrast, and combine points of view more clearly—and therefore to think more thoroughly. ☒

Consider the following argument:

Orca whales mate for life.
Orca whales travel in family groups.
Science has revealed that Orca whales are intelligent.
Therefore, Orca whales should be saved from
    extinction.

One idea underlies this line of thought:

Any animal that displays significant human
    characteristics deserves special protection.

Whether or not you agree with this argument, consider for a moment the process of making assumptions. Assumptions are assertions that guide our thinking and behavior. Often these assertions are unconscious. People can remain unaware of their most basic and far-reaching assumptions—the very ideas that shape their lives.

Spotting assumptions can be tricky since they are usually unstated and offered without evidence. And scores of assumptions can be held at the same time. Those assumptions might even contradict each other, resulting in muddled thinking and confused behavior. This makes uncovering assumptions a feat worthy of the greatest detective.

Letting assumptions remain in our subconscious can erect barriers to our success. Take the person who says, "I don't worry about saving money for the future. I think life is meant to be enjoyed today—not later." This statement rests on at least two assumptions: *saving money is not enjoyable*, and *we can enjoy ourselves only when we're spending money.*

It would be no surprise to find out that this person runs out of money near the end of each month and depends on cash advances from high-interest credit cards. She is shielding herself from some ideas that could erase her debt: Saving money can be a source of satisfaction, and many enjoyable activities cost nothing.

The stakes in uncovering assumptions are high. Prejudice thrives on the beliefs that certain people are inferior or dangerous due to their skin color, ethnic background, or sexual orientation. Those beliefs have led to flawed assumptions such as *mixing the blood of the races will lead to genetically inferior offspring* and *racial integration of the armed forces will lead to the destruction of morale.*

When we remain ignorant of our assumptions, we also make it easier for people with hidden agendas to do our thinking for us. Demagogues and unethical advertisers know that unchallenged assumptions are potent tools for influencing our attitudes and behavior.

Take this claim from an advertisement: "Successful students have large vocabularies, so sign up today for our

Uncovering assumptions

seminar on word power!" Embedded in this sentence are several assumptions. One is that a cause-and-effect relationship exists between a large vocabulary and success in school. Another is that a large vocabulary is the single or most important factor in that success. This claim also assumes that the advertiser's seminar is the best way to develop your vocabulary. In reality, none of these assumptions is necessarily true.

Assertions and opinions flow from our assumptions. Heated conflict and hard feelings often result when people argue on the level of opinions—forgetting that the real conflict lies at the level of their assumptions.

An example is the question about whether the government should fund public works programs that create jobs during a recession. People who advocate such programs might assume that creating such jobs is an appropriate task for the federal government. On the other hand, people who argue against such programs might assume that the government has no business interfering with the free workings of the economy. There's little hope of resolving this conflict of opinion unless we deal with something more basic: our assumptions about the proper role of government.

You can follow a three-step method for testing the validity of any viewpoint. First, look for the assumptions—the assertions implied by that viewpoint. Second, write down these assumptions. Third, see if you can find any exceptions to them. This technique helps detect many errors in logic. ◪

Ways to fool yourself

Six common mistakes in logic

Logic is a branch of philosophy that seeks to distinguish between effective and ineffective reasoning.

Students of logic look for valid steps in an argument, or a series of assertions. The opening assertions of the argument are the premises, and the final assertion is the conclusion.

Over the last 2,500 years, specialists in logic have listed some classic land mines in the field of logic—common mistakes that are called *fallacies*. These fallacies are included in just about every logic textbook. Following are six examples. Knowing about them before you string together a bunch of assertions can help you avoid getting fooled.

1 Jump to conclusions. Jumping to conclusions is the only exercise that some lazy thinkers get. This fallacy involves drawing conclusions without sufficient evidence. Take the bank officer who hears about a student failing to pay back an education loan. After that, the officer turns down all loan applications from students. This person has formed a rigid opinion on the basis of hearsay. Jumping to conclusions—also called *hasty generalization*—is at work here.

2 Attack the person. This mistake in logic is common at election time. An example is the candidate who

claims that her opponent has failed to attend church regularly during the campaign. People who indulge in personal attacks are attempting an intellectual sleight of hand to divert our attention from the truly relevant issues.

3 Appeal to authority. A professional athlete endorses a brand of breakfast cereal. A famous musician features a soft drink company's product in a rock video. The promotional brochure for an advertising agency lists all of the large companies that have used its services.

In each case, the people involved are trying to win your confidence—and your dollars—by citing authorities. The underlying assumption is usually this: *Famous people and organizations buy our product. Therefore, you should buy it too.* Or: *You should accept this idea merely because someone who's well known says it's true.*

Appealing to authority is usually a substitute for producing real evidence. It invites sloppy thinking. When our only evidence for a viewpoint is an appeal to authority, it's time to think more thoroughly.

4 Point to a false cause. The fact that one event follows another does not necessarily mean that the two events have a cause-and-effect relationship. All we can actually say is that the events might be correlated. For example, as children's vocabularies improve, they can get more cavities. This does not mean that cavities are the result of an improved vocabulary. Instead, the increase in cavities is due to other factors, such as physical maturation and changes in diet or personal care.

5 Think in all-or-nothing terms. Consider these statements: *Doctors are greedy. . . . You can't trust politicians. . . . Students these days are in school just to get high-paying jobs; they lack idealism. . . . Homeless people don't want to work.*

These opinions imply the word *all.* They gloss over individual differences, claiming that all members of a group are exactly alike. They also ignore key facts—for instance, that some doctors volunteer their time at free medical clinics and that many homeless people are children who are too young to work. All-or-nothing thinking is one of the most common errors in logic.

6 Base arguments on emotion. The politician who ends every campaign speech with flag waving and slides of her mother eating apple pie is staking her future on appeals to emotion. So is the candidate who paints a grim scenario of the disaster and ruination that will transpire unless she is elected. Get past the fluff and histrionics to see if you can uncover any worthwhile ideas. ⊠

Overcome stereotypes with critical thinking

Consider assertions such as "College students like to drink heavily," "People who speak English as a second language are hard to understand," and "Americans who criticize the President are unpatriotic."

These are examples of stereotyping—generalizing about a group of people based on the behavior of isolated group members. Stereotypes are a potent source of intellectual error. They are signals to shift our thinking skills into high gear—to demand evidence, examine logic, and insist on accurate information.

The word *stereotype* originally referred to a method used by printers to produce duplicate pages of text. This usage still rings true. When we stereotype, we gloss over individual differences and assume that every member of a group is the same.

Stereotypes infiltrate every dimension of human individuality. People are stereotyped on the basis of their race, ethnic group, religion, political affiliation, geographic location, job, age, gender, IQ, height, or hobby. We stereotype people based on everything from the color of their hair to the year of their car.

Stereotypes have many possible sources: fear of the unknown, uncritical thinking, and negative encounters between individual members of different groups. Whatever their cause, stereotypes abound.

In themselves, generalizations are neither good nor bad. In fact, they are essential. Mentally sorting people, events, and objects into groups allows us to make sense of the world. But when we consciously or unconsciously make generalizations that rigidly divide the people of the world into "us" versus "them," we create stereotypes and put on the blinders of prejudice.

You can take several steps to free yourself from stereotypes.

Look for errors in thinking. Some of the most common errors are:

- *Selective perception.* Stereotypes can literally change the way we see the world. If we assume that homeless people are lazy, for instance, we tend to notice only the examples that support our opinion. Stories about homeless people who are too young or too ill to work will probably escape our attention.

- *Self-fulfilling prophecy.* When we interact with people based on stereotypes, we set them up in ways that confirm our thinking. For example, when people of color were denied access to higher education based on stereotypes about their intelligence, they were deprived of opportunities to demonstrate their intellectual gifts.

- *Self-justification.* Stereotypes can allow people to assume the role of a victim and to avoid taking responsibility for their own lives. An unemployed white male might believe that affirmative action programs are making it impossible for him to get a job—even as he overlooks his own lack of experience or qualifications.

Create categories in a more flexible way. Stereotyping has been described as a case of "hardening of the categories." Avoid this problem by making your categories broader. Instead of seeing people based on their skin color, you could look at them on the basis of their heredity. (People of all races share most of the same genes.) Or you could make your categories narrower. Instead of talking about "religious extremists," look for subgroups among the people who adopt a certain religion. Distinguish between groups that advocate violence and those that shun it.

Test your generalizations about people through action. You can do this by actually meeting people of other cultures. It's easy to believe almost anything about certain groups of people as long as we never deal directly with individuals. Inaccurate pictures tend to die when people from different cultures study together, work together, and live together. Consider joining a school or community organization that will put you in contact with people of other cultures. Your rewards will include a more global perspective and an ability to thrive in a multicultural world.

Be willing to see your own stereotypes. The Power Process: "Notice your pictures and let them go" can help. One belief about ourselves that many of us can shed is *I have no pictures about people from other cultures.* Even people with the best of intentions can harbor subtle biases. Admitting this possibility allows us to look inward even more deeply for stereotypes. Every time that we notice an inaccurate picture buried in our mind and let it go, we take a personal step toward embracing diversity.

Gaining skill at decision making

When people refuse to make decisions, they leave their lives to chance. Philosopher Walter Kaufman calls this *decidophobia*—the fear of making decisions. He defines the alternative—autonomy—as "making with open eyes the decisions that give shape to one's life."[3]

We make decisions all of the time, whether we realize it or not. Even avoiding decisions is a form of decision making. The student who puts off studying for a test until the last minute might really be saying, "I've decided this course is not important" or "I've decided not to give this course much time."

Decide right now to apply some of the following suggestions, and you can take your overall decision making to new heights of effectiveness.

Recognize decisions. Decisions are more than wishes or desires. There's a world of difference between "I wish I could be a better student" and "I will take more powerful notes, read with greater retention, and review my class notes daily." Decisions are specific and lead to focused action. When we decide, we narrow down. We give up actions that are inconsistent with our decision. Deciding to eat fruit for dessert instead of ice cream rules out the next trip to the ice cream store.

Establish priorities. Some decisions are trivial. No matter what the outcome, your life is not affected much. Other decisions can shape your circumstances for years. Devote more time and energy to the decisions with big outcomes. Base your decisions on a life plan. The value of having a long-term plan for our lives is that it provides a basis for many of our year-to-year and week-to-week decisions. Being certain about what we want to accomplish this year and this month makes today's choices more clear.

Clarify your values. When you know specifically what you want from life, making decisions becomes easier. This is especially true when you define your values precisely and put them in writing. Saying that you value education is fine. Now give that declaration some teeth. Note that you value continuous learning as a chance to upgrade your career skills, for instance. That can make registering for next term's classes much easier.

Choose an overall strategy. Every time you make a decision, you choose a strategy—even when you're not aware of it. Effective decision makers can articulate and choose from among several strategies.

- *Find all of the available options and choose one deliberately.* Save this strategy for times when you have a relatively small number of options, each of which leads to noticeably different results.

- *Find all of the available options and choose one randomly.* This strategy can be risky. Save it for times when your options are basically similar and fairness is the main issue.

- *Limit the options; then choose.* When deciding which search engine to use on the World Wide Web, visit many sites and then narrow the list down to two or three that you choose.

- *Choose the first acceptable option that you find.* This strategy can work well when you have many options, and when thoroughly researching each option will take too much time or create too little benefit. For instance, when you're writing a paper and are pressed for time, write down the first five facts you find that directly support your thesis. You could look for more facts, but the extra investment of time might not produce enough usable results.

- *Choose to act on someone else's decision.* You use this strategy, for example, when you buy a CD based on a friend's recommendation. A more sophisticated version of this strategy is arbitration—people who are in conflict agree to act on the decision made by a third party, such as a judge, who listens to each person's case.

Use time as an ally. Sometimes we face dilemmas—situations in which any course of action leads to undesirable consequences. In such cases, consider putting a decision on hold. Wait it out. Do nothing until the circumstances change, making one alternative clearly preferable to another.

Use intuition. Some decisions seem to make themselves. A solution pops into our mind and we gain newfound clarity. Using intuition is not the same as forgetting about the decision or refusing to make it. Intuitive decisions usually arrive after we've gathered the relevant facts and faced a problem for some time.

Act on your decision. There comes a time to move from the realm of discovery and intention to the arena of action. Action is a hallmark of a true decision.

Evaluate your decision. Hindsight can be a valuable source of insight. After you act on a decision, observe the consequences over time. Reflect on how well your decision worked and what you might have done differently.

Four ways to solve problems

There is a vast literature on problem-solving techniques. Much of it can be traced to American philosopher John Dewey, who devised these steps of effective problem solving:

- Perceive a "felt difficulty" and state it clearly and concisely.

- Invent possible solutions.

- Rationally test each solution by anticipating its possible consequences.

- Act on the preferred solution, evaluate the consequences, and determine whether a new solution is needed.[4]

Much of what you'll read about problem solving amounts to variations on Dewey's steps. Think of problem solving as a process with four P's: Define the *problem*, generate *possibilities*, create a *plan*, and *perform* your plan.

1 **Define the problem.** To define a problem effectively, understand what a problem is—a mismatch between what you want and what you have. Problem solving is all about reducing the gap between these two factors.

Start with what you have. Tell the truth about what's present in your life right now, without shame or blame. For example: "I often get sleepy while reading my physics assignments, and after closing the book I cannot remember what I just read."

Next, describe in detail what you want. Go for specifics: "I want to remain alert as I read about physics. I also want to accurately summarize each chapter I read."

Remember that when we define a problem in limiting ways, our solutions merely generate new problems. As Einstein said, "The world we have made is a result of the level of thinking we have done thus far. We cannot solve problems at the same level at which we created them."[5]

This idea has many applications for success in school. An example is the student who struggles with note taking. The problem, she thinks, is that her notes are too sketchy. The logical solution, she decides, is to take more notes, and her new goal is to write down almost everything her instructors say. No matter how fast and furiously she writes, she cannot capture all of the instructors' comments.

Consider what happens when this student defines the problem in a new way. After more thought, she decides that her dilemma is not the *quantity* of her notes but their *quality*. She adopts a new format for taking notes, dividing her note paper into two columns. In the right-hand column she writes down only the main points of each lecture. And in the left-hand column she notes two or three supporting details for each point.

Over time, this student makes the joyous discovery that there are usually just three or four core ideas to remember from each lecture. She originally thought the solution was to take more notes. What really worked was taking notes in a new way.

2 **Generate possibilities.** Now put on your creative thinking hat. Open up. Brainstorm as many possible solutions to the problem as you can. At this stage, quantity counts. As you generate possibilities, gather relevant facts. For example, when you're faced with a dilemma about what courses to take next term, get information on class times, locations, and instructors. If you haven't decided which summer job offer to accept, gather information on salary, benefits, and working conditions.

3 **Create a plan.** After rereading your problem definition and list of possible solutions, choose the solution that seems most workable. Think about specific actions that will reduce the gap between what you have and what you want. Visualize the steps you will take to make this solution a reality and arrange them in chronological order. To make your plan even more powerful, put it in writing.

4 **Perform your plan.** This step gets you off your chair and out into the world. Now you actually *do* what you have planned. Ultimately, your skill in solving problems lies in how well you perform your plan. Through the quality of your actions, you become the architect of your own success.

Note that the four P's of this problem-solving process closely parallel the four key questions from the Learning Style Inventory.

Define the **problem**	**What** is the problem?
Generate **possibilities**	**What if** there are several possible solutions?
Create a **plan**	**How** would this possible solution work?
Perform your plan	**Why** is one solution more workable than another?

When facing problems, experiment with these four P's, and remember that the order of steps is not absolute. Also remember that any solution has the potential to create new problems. If that happens, cycle through the four P's of problem solving again. ▨

"But I don't know what I want to do"

Choosing a major

One decision that troubles many students in higher education is the choice of an academic major. Here is an opportunity to apply your skills at critical thinking, decision making, and problem solving. The following suggestions can guide you through this process.

Link your major to your goals. Your choice of a major can fall into place once you determine what you want in life. Before you choose a major, back up to a bigger picture. List your core values, such as contributing to society, achieving financial security and professional recognition, enjoying good health, or making time for fun. Also write down specific goals that you want to accomplish in 5 years, 10 years, or even 50 years from today.

Many students find that the prospect of getting what they want in life justifies all of the time, money, and day-to-day effort invested in going to school. Having a major gives you a powerful incentive for attending classes, taking part in discussions, reading textbooks, writing papers, and completing other assignments. When you see a clear connection between finishing school and creating the life of your dreams, the daily tasks of higher education become charged with meaning.

Studies indicate that the biggest factor associated with completing a degree in higher education is commitment to personal goals.[6] Your choice of a major and a related career are examples of those goals. Selecting the appropriate courses to complete your major is a form of planning that directly promotes your success.

Just choose—now. Don't delay the benefits of choosing a major. Even if you're undecided right now, you probably have an idea about what your major will be.

To verify this, do a short experiment. Search your school's catalog for a list of available majors. Read through the list two or three times. Then pretend that you have to choose a major today. Write down the first three ideas that come to mind.

Hold on to this list, which reflects your intuition or "gut feelings," as you perform the more arduous task of researching various majors and careers in detail. Your research might lead to a new choice of major—or it might simply confirm one of the majors on your original list.

Test your trial choice. When you've made a trial choice of major, take on the role of a scientist. Treat your choice as a hypothesis and then design a series of experiments to test it. For example:

- Study your school's list of required courses for this major, looking for a fit with your interests and long-term goals.

- Visit with instructors who teach courses in the major, asking about required course work and career options in the field.

- Discuss your trial choice with an academic advisor or career counselor.

- Enroll in a course related to your possible major.

- Find a volunteer experience, internship, part-time job, or service learning experience related to the major.

- Meet informally with students who have declared the same major.

- Interview someone who works in a field related to the major.

If these experiences confirm your choice of major, celebrate that fact. If they result in choosing a new major, celebrate that outcome as well.

Ask other people. Key people in your life might have valuable suggestions about your choice of major or career goals. Ask for their ideas and listen with an open mind.

At the same time, distance yourself from any pressure to choose a major or career that fails to interest you. If you make a choice based solely on the expectations of other people, you could end up with a job you don't enjoy—and a major barrier to your life satisfaction.

Learn more about yourself. Choosing a major can be more effective when you begin from a basis of self-knowledge. As you learn about your passions and potentials, let your choice of a major reflect that ongoing discovery. The exercises and Journal Entries in this book are a starting place. After reviewing what you have written, do any of them again and look for insights that bear on your choice of major.

Another path to self-knowledge includes questionnaires or inventories that are designed to correlate your interests with specific career choices. Your academic advisor or someone at your school's career planning and job placement office can give you more details about these inventories. You might wish to take several of them and meet with an advisor to interpret the results.

Keep in mind that there is no questionnaire, inventory, test, or other tool that can tell you exactly which career to choose or what goals to set for the rest of your life. Likewise, there is no expert who can make these choices for you. Inventories can help you gain self-knowledge, and other people can offer valuable perspectives. However, what you do with that knowledge and advice is entirely up to you.

Invent a major. When choosing a major, you might not need to limit yourself to those listed in your course catalog. Many schools now have flexible programs that allow for independent study. Through such programs you might be able to combine two existing majors, or invent an entirely new one of your own.

Choose a complementary minor. You can add flexibility to your academic program by choosing a minor to complement or contrast with your major.

The student who wants to be a minister could opt for a minor in English; all of those courses in composition can help in writing sermons. Or the student with a major in psychology might choose a minor in business administration, with the idea of managing a counseling service some day. An effective choice of a minor can expand your skills and career options.

Choose again. Keep your choice of a major in perspective. There is probably no single "correct" choice. Rather, your unique collection of skills is likely to provide the basis for majoring in several fields.

Odds are that you'll change your major at least once—and that you'll change careers several times during your life. You might even pursue a career that's unrelated to your major.

Many of the majors offered in higher education can help you prepare for several different careers, or for further study in graduate school. One benefit of higher education is mobility—gaining transferable skills that can help you move into a new career field at any time.

Viewing a major as a one-time choice that determines your entire future can raise your stress levels. Instead, look at choosing a major as the start of a continuing path of discovery, intention, and action. ▨

exercise 16

MAKE A TRIAL CHOICE OF MAJOR

Scan the list of majors offered at your school. You can find this list in the school catalog, which may be available online. Make a copy of this list or print it out.

Next, take the list and cross out all of the majors that you already know are not right for you. You will probably eliminate well over half the list.

Now scan the remaining majors. Next to the ones that definitely interest you, write "yes." Next to majors that you're willing to consider and are still unsure about, write "maybe."

Focus on your "yes" choices. See if you can narrow them down to three majors. List those here.

_____

_____

_____

Finally, write an asterisk next to the major that interests you most right now. This is your trial choice of major.

Asking questions

Thinking is born of questions. Questions open up options that might otherwise remain unexplored. Questions promote curiosity, create new distinctions, and multiply possibilities. Besides, teachers love them. One of the best ways to develop your relationship with a teacher is to ask a question.

Asking questions is also a great way to improve relationships with friends and coworkers. When you ask a question, you offer a huge gift to people—an opportunity for them to speak their brilliance and for you to listen to their answers.

Students often say, "I don't know what to ask." If you have ever been at a loss for what to ask, here are some ways to construct powerful questions about any subject you study in school, or about any area of your life that you choose to examine.

Let your pen start moving. Sometimes you can access a deeper level of knowledge by taking out your pen, putting it on a piece of paper, and writing down questions—even before you know what to write. Don't think. Just watch the paper and notice what appears. The results might be surprising.

Ask about what's missing. Another way to invent useful questions is to notice what's missing from your life and then ask how to supply it. For example, if you want to take better notes, you can write, "What's missing is skill in note taking. How can I gain more skill in taking notes?" Or "What's missing is time. How do I create enough time in my day to actually do the things that I say I want to do?"

Pretend to be someone else. Another way to invent questions is first to think of someone you greatly respect. Then pretend you're that person and ask the questions you think she would ask.

Begin a general question; then brainstorm endings. By starting with a general question and then brainstorming a long list of endings, you can invent a question that you've never asked before. For example:

What can I do when . . . ? What can I do when an instructor calls on me in class and I have no idea what to say? What can I do when I feel overwhelmed with assignments?

How can I . . . ? How can I get just the kind of courses that I want? How can I expand my career options? How can I become much more effective as a student, starting today?

When do I . . . ? When do I decide on a major? When do I transfer to another school? When do I meet with an instructor to discuss an upcoming term paper?

Ask what else you want to know. Many times you can quickly generate questions by simply asking yourself, "What else do I want to know?" Ask this question immediately after you read a paragraph in a book or listen to someone speak.

Attitudes of a critical thinker

Attitude	Sample statement
Truth-seeking	"Let's follow this idea and see where it leads, even if we feel uncomfortable with what we find out."
Open-minded	"I have a point of view on this subject, and I'm anxious to hear yours as well."
Analytical	"Taking a stand on the issue commits me to take some new action."
Systematic	"The speaker made several interesting points, and I'd like to hear some more evidence to support each one."
Self-confident	"After reading the book for the first time, I was confused. I'll be able to understand it after studying the book some more."
Inquisitive	"When I first saw that painting, I wanted to know what was going on in the artist's life when she painted it."
Mature	"I'll wait until I gather some more facts before reaching a conclusion on this issue."

The American Philosophical Association invited a panel of 46 scholars from the United States and Canada to come up with answers to the following two questions: "What is college-level critical thinking?" and "What leads us to conclude that a person is an effective critical thinker?"[3] After two years of work, this panel concluded that critical thinkers share the attitudes summarized in the chart.

PRACTICING CRITICAL THINKING

7

Statement #2:

_____
_____
_____
_____
_____
_____

The art of asking questions is just as important to critical thinking as answering them. One eye-opening way to create questions is to write something you're sure of and simply put a question mark after it. (You might need to rephrase the question for grammatical sense.) The question you create can lead to others.

For example, someone might say, "I would never take a philosophy course." This person can write "I would never take a philosophy course?" That suggests other questions: "In what ways would taking a philosophy course serve my success in school?" "Could taking a philosophy course help me become a better writer?"

In the space below, write three statements that you accept with certainty. Then rephrase each statement as a question.

Question #2:

_____
_____
_____
_____
_____
_____

Statement #1:

_____
_____
_____
_____
_____

Statement #3:

_____
_____
_____
_____
_____

Question #1:

_____
_____
_____
_____
_____
_____

Question #3:

_____
_____
_____
_____
_____
_____

power process

Find a bigger problem

Most of the time we view problems as barriers. They are a source of inconvenience and annoyance. They get in our way and prevent us from having happy and productive lives. When we see problems in this way, our goal becomes to eliminate problems.

This point of view might be flawed. For one thing, it is impossible to live a life without problems. Besides, they serve a purpose. They are opportunities to participate in life. Problems stimulate us and pull us forward.

Seen from this perspective, the goal becomes not to eliminate problems but to find problems that are worthy of us. Worthy problems are those that draw on our talents, move us toward our purpose, and increase our skills. The challenge is to tackle those problems that provide the greatest benefits for others and ourselves. Viewed in this way, problems give meaning to our lives.

Problems fill the available space

Problems seem to follow the same law of physics that gases do: They expand to fill whatever space is available. If your only problem is to write a follow-up letter to a job interview, you can spend the entire day thinking about what you're going to say, writing the letter, finding a stamp, going to the post office—and then thinking about all of the things you forgot to say. If, on that same day, you also need to go food shopping, the problem of the letter shrinks to make room for a trip to the grocery store. If you want to buy a car, too, it's amazing how quickly and easily the letter and the grocery shopping tasks are finished. One way to handle little problems is to find bigger ones. Remember that the smaller problems still need to be solved. The goal is to do it with less time and energy.

Bigger problems are plentiful

Bigger problems are not in short supply. Consider world hunger. Every minute of every day, people die because they don't have enough to eat. Also consider nuclear war, which threatens to end life on the planet. Child abuse, environmental pollution, terrorism, human rights violations, drug abuse, street crime, energy shortages, poverty, and wars throughout the world await your attention and involvement. You can make a contribution.

Worthy problems are those that draw on our talents, move us toward our purpose, and increase our skills.

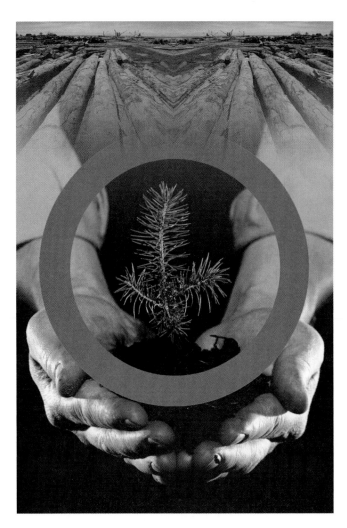

can experience efficiency and enthusiasm as natural parts of our daily routines. Energy and vitality can accompany most of our activities.

When we take on a bigger problem, we play full out. We do justice to our potentials. We then love what we do and do what we love. We're awake, alert, and engaged. Playing full out means living our lives as if our lives depended on it.

You can make a difference

Perhaps a little voice in your mind is saying, "That's crazy. I can't do anything about global problems" or "Everyone knows that hunger has always been around and always will be, and there is nothing anyone can do about it." These thoughts might prevent you from taking on bigger problems.

Realize that you *can* make a difference. Your thoughts and actions can change the quality of life on the planet.

This is your life. It's your school, your city, your country, and your world. Own it. Inhabit it. Treat it with the same care that you would a prized possession.

One way to find problems that are worthy of your talents and energies is to take on bigger ones. Take responsibility for problems that are bigger than you are sure you can handle. Then notice how your other problems dwindle in importance—or even vanish. ◪

Playing full out means living our lives as if our lives depended on it.

Play full out

Considering bigger problems does not have to be depressing. In fact, it can be energizing—a reason for getting up in the morning. Taking on a huge project can provide a means to channel your passion and purpose.

Some people spend vast amounts of time in activities they consider boring: their jobs, their hobbies, their relationships. They find themselves going through the motions, doing the same walk-on part day after day without passion or intensity. American author Henry David Thoreau described this kind of existence as "lives of quiet desperation."

Playing full out suggests another possibility: We can spend much of our time fully focused and involved. We

exercise 17

FIX-THE-WORLD BRAINSTORM

This exercise works well with four to six people. Pick a major world problem such as hunger, nuclear proliferation, poverty, terrorism, overpopulation, or pollution. Then conduct a 10-minute brainstorm about the steps an individual could take to contribute to solving the problem.

Use the brainstorming techniques explained earlier in this chapter. Remember not to evaluate or judge the solutions during the process. The purpose of a brainstorm is to generate a flow of ideas and record them all.

After the brainstorming session, discuss the process and the solutions that it generated. Did you feel any energy from the group? Was a long list of ideas generated? Are several of them worth pursuing?

put it to work

Strategies for creative and critical thinking can assist you in developing new products and services in the workplace. Some examples follow.

State the obvious and go for the opposite. One way to generate a burst of creativity followed by critical thinking is to take an idea that seems obvious and state its opposite. Then see if you can find evidence to support the opposite idea.

This principle has been used with great success in business. An example comes from Jan Carlzon, former president of the Scandinavian Airline SAS. Carlzon questioned an "obvious" truth—that upper management in any company should make most of the decisions. He went for the opposite idea and allowed rank-and-file employees to make daily decisions that directly affected customers. If a customer got bumped from a flight, an SAS counter clerk could decide on the spot whether to pay the customer's hotel bill for the night or find the customer an alternative flight on a competitor's airline. After implementing this policy, SAS's business grew dramatically.[7]

Find a smaller problem. After reading the Power Process: "Find a bigger problem," consider the merits of the opposite strategy. For example, you might feel overwhelmed with managing a complex, year-long project at work. One response is to give up—to quit. Another is to resign yourself to drudgery and dive into the project with a deep sigh.

"Find a smaller problem" offers an alternative: Just divide a huge project into many small jobs. Rather than worry about the project as a whole, turn your full attention to a small, specific task until it is complete. Do the same with the next small task, and the next. Just handle the details, one after another, until the project is finished.

The role of planning is critical. "Find a smaller problem" is not a suggestion to fill your days with busywork. When you plan effectively, the small jobs you do are critical to the success of the bigger project.

Experiment with the decreasing options technique. The decreasing options technique (DOT) is a decision-making strategy. It allows you to rank a large pool of ideas created by groups of people in meetings. Before you put DOT in action, go to an office supply store and get a package of several hundred adhesive dots—small stickers that can be attached to a sheet of paper. Then follow these steps:

- *Ask meeting participants to brainstorm solutions to a problem.* Permit all ideas to be expressed. Don't edit them yet. To save time, ask participants to submit ideas before the meeting takes place. That way you can summarize and post ideas ahead of time.

- *Summarize each idea in a single word or phrase on a large sheet of paper.* Write letters that are big enough to be seen across the meeting room. Place only one idea on each sheet of paper.

- *Post the sheets where all meeting participants can see them.*

- *Do an initial review of the ideas.* Ask participants if they can eliminate some ideas as obviously unworkable. Also group similar ideas together and eliminate duplications.

- *"Dot" ideas.* Give each participant a handful of sticker dots. Then ask participants to go around the room and place an adhesive dot next to the ideas that they consider most important.

- *Discuss the most important ideas.* Stand back and review the ideas. The high-priority concerns of the group will stand out clearly as the sheets with the most dots. Now you can bring these important ideas to the discussion table.

You can also use the DOT method online with bulletin boards or "virtual" meetings. Participants can use e-mail or networking software to post their ideas and manipulate computer graphics that look like sticker dots.

Name _____ Date _____/_____/_____

1. List four questions that can guide you on your path to becoming a critical thinker.

2. Explain what is meant in this chapter by *aha!*

3. Define *serendipity* and give an example.

4. Briefly discuss how to conduct a successful brainstorm.

5. List at least three ways to test your trial choice of major.

6. According to the text, *critical thinking* and *thorough thinking* are two distinct and different activities. True or False? Explain your answer.

7. Define *all-or-nothing thinking* and give an example.

8. Explain the suggestion "watch for hot spots" and describe its connection to critical thinking.

9. Name at least one fallacy involved in this statement: "Everyone who's ever visited this school has agreed that it's the best in the state."

10. List the four suggested steps for problem solving and give an example of each step.

learning styles application

The questions below will "cycle" you through four styles, or modes, of learning as explained in the article "Learning styles: Discovering how you learn" in Chapter One. Each question will help you explore a different mode. You can answer the questions in any order.

what if *Explain how you would modify a technique from this chapter to make it a more effective tool for decision making—or describe an original technique of your own.*

why *Think of a major decision you face right now and put it into the form of a question. Possible examples are "What major will I declare?" or "What is my top priority goal for this year?"*

how *Briefly describe how you will use a technique from this chapter to make a major decision.*

what *List a technique from this chapter that could help you make a major decision you face right now (such as the decision you list under* Why*).*

master student

PAUL FARMER

(1959–   ) A Harvard professor, renowned infectious-disease specialist, and the recipient of a MacArthur Foundation "genius" award. In medical school, found his life's calling—to diagnose and cure infectious diseases and to bring the lifesaving tools of modern medicine to those who need them most.

Dr. Farmer does not have anywhere near the name recognition of, say, Albert Schweitzer or Mother Teresa. But if any one person can be given credit for transforming the medical establishment's thinking about health care for the destitute, it is Paul Farmer.

Through the charity that Dr. Farmer helped found, Partners in Health, the health system, Zanmi Lasante (Creole for Partners in Health), not only cares for hundreds of thousands of peasants, but has also built schools and sanitation and water systems, vaccinated all the children, reduced the rate of H.I.V. transmission from mothers to babies, and successfully treated patients suffering from complicated drug-resistant strains of tuberculosis.

How has he done it? Dr. Farmer simply refuses to accept any excuse— no matter how reasonable—for not treating the poor. No doctors? We'll train them. High drug prices? We'll get the pharmaceutical companies to lower them. Misguided policies? We'll change them.

Working locally and globally simultaneously means pushing himself to extremes. He has a punishing schedule and rarely sees his Haitian-born wife, Didi, and daughter.

"The problem is, if I don't work this hard, someone will die who doesn't have to," he confesses in a rare moment of frustration. Dr. Farmer [was] pushed to branch out from Haiti after his colleague and kindred spirit, Jim Yong Kim, discover[ed] puzzling cases of lethal and drug-resistant strains of TB in the slums of Peru. Peru had an excellent TB control program. But in one of the horribly twisted ironies that tend to afflict the poor, the very medicine that was saving lives was also—through repeated treatments—breeding mutant strains resistant to conventional drugs.

Getting the medical establishment in Peru and at W.H.O. [World Health Organization], a United Nations agency, to change the prescribed regimen for TB drugs was formidable. Health experts dismissed the idea that complex diseases like drug-resistant TB or AIDS could even be treated in poor areas. In the end, Dr. Farmer and Dr. Kim prevailed, helping to lower the price of drugs and changing W.H.O.'s treatment guidelines. What's more, they had challenged the philosophy and the accuracy of cost-effectiveness analysis that ruled public health-care decisions at the highest level.

Near the end of [*Mountains Beyond Mountains*, author Tracy] Kidder details the wrenching efforts of some Partners in Health workers to help a 12-year-old Haitian boy suffering from a rare cancer. They hire a medevac helicopter for nearly $19,000 to bring the deathly ill boy to Boston for treatment. When he arrives the doctors learn the cancer has infiltrated his wasted body. He [died] three weeks later. To some it was an exercise in futility and excessive heroics. After all, how many other children could have been fed with that money?

But as Mr. Kidder explains, that kind of cost-benefit analysis is what Dr. Farmer has been fighting his whole life. If it were you, if it were your child and there was a chance to save him, would you think it was too much? Why, Dr. Farmer wants to know, don't people question why a young American doctor earns "five times what it cost to try to save a boy's life?"

For more biographical information on Paul Farmer, visit the Master Student Hall of Fame on the *Becoming a Master Student* Web site at

masterstudent.college.hmco.com

8

Communicating

why
this chapter matters . . .

Your communication abilities—
  including your skills at listening,
  speaking, and writing—are as
  important to your success as your
  technical skills.

what
is included . . .

Communicating creates our world
The communication loop: Receiving
  and sending
The fine art of conflict management
Choose your conversations and your
  community
Communicating across cultures
Dealing with sexism and sexual
  harassment
Writing on purpose
Giving credit where credit is due:
  Avoiding the high cost of plagiarism
Writing and delivering speeches
Power Process: "Employ your word"
Master Student Profile: Irshad Manji

how
you can use this chapter . . .

Listen, speak, and write more
  effectively.
Prevent and resolve conflict with other
  people.
Experience more satisfying
  relationships in all areas of your life.

As you read, ask yourself
What if . . .

I could use my capacity to make and
  keep agreements as a tool for
  creating my future?

Since English is not my native tongue, I have often felt intimidated com-municating with others. Master students are courageous, and even though I was fearful of speaking in class, I set a goal for myself to raise my hand at least once per day. My classmates respect my enthusiasm for learning and I've found it is easier to share now that I have practiced.

—SANTIAGO GONZALEZ

Communicating creates our world

Certain things are real for us because we can see them, touch them, hear them, smell them, or taste them. Books, pencils, tables, chairs, and food all are real in this sense. They enter our world in a straightforward, uncomplicated way.

Many other aspects of our lives, however, do not have this kind of reality. None of us can point to a *purpose*, for example. Nor would a purpose step up and introduce itself or buy us lunch. The same is true about other abstract concepts, such as *quality, intelligence, love, trust, human rights*, or *student success*.

Concepts such as these shape our experience of life. Yet they don't really exist until we talk about them. These concepts come alive for us only to the degree that we define and discuss them. Communicating brings our world into being.

According to communication theorist Lee Thayer, there are two basic life processes. One is acquiring and processing energy. The other is acquiring and processing information, also known as communication.[1] From this point of view, communicating is just as fundamental to life as eating.

Through communication, we take raw impressions and organize them into meaningful patterns. With our senses, we perceive sights, sounds, and other sensations. However, none of our sense organs is capable of perceiving *meaning*. We create meaning by finding patterns in our sensations and communicating them.

In our daily contact with other people and mass media, we are exposed to hundreds of messages. Yet the obstacles to receiving those messages accurately are numerous. For one thing, only a small percentage of communication is verbal. We also send messages with our bodies and with the tone of our voice. Throw in a few other factors, such as a hot room or background noise, and it's a wonder we communicate at all.

Another problem is that the message sent is often not the message received. Even the simplest message can get muddled. For some, the word *chair* conjures up the image of an overstuffed rocking recliner. Others visualize a metal folding chair. And some people think of the person who "chairs" a meeting. If things like this can be misunderstood, it's easy to see how complex ideas can wreak havoc.

Written communication adds a whole other set of variables. When you speak, you supplement the meaning of your words with the power of body language and voice inflection. When you write, those nonverbal elements are absent. Instead, you depend on your skills at word choice, sentence construction, and punctuation to get your message across. The choices that you make in these areas can serve as an aid—or a hindrance—to communication. ◪

journal entry 18

Discovery/Intention Statement

Think of a time when you experienced an emotionally charged conflict with another person. Were you able to resolve this dispute effectively? If so, list below the strategies you used. If not, describe what you could have done differently.

I discovered that I . . .

_____

_____

Now scan this chapter for ideas that can help you get your feelings across more skillfully in similar situations. List at least four ideas here, along with the page numbers where you can read more about them.

Strategy   *Page number*

_____

_____

_____

_____

Describe an upcoming situation in which you intend to apply these techniques. If possible, choose a situation that will occur within the next week.

I intend to . . .

_____

_____

_____

_____

_____

THE COMMUNICATION LOOP:
Receiving and sending

Communication is often garbled when we try to send and receive messages at the same time.

One effective way to improve your ability to communicate is to be aware of when you are the receiver and when you are the sender. If you are receiving (listening), just receive. Avoid switching into the sending (talking) mode. When you are sending, stick with it until you are finished.

Communication works best when each of us has plenty of time to receive what others send—that is, to *listen*—and the opportunity to send a complete message when it's our turn.

Choosing to receive

Listening well promotes success in school: more powerful notes, more productive study groups, and better relationships with students and instructors. A skilled listener is appreciated by friends, family, and business associates. The best salespeople and managers are the best listeners. People love a good listener.

To be a good listener, choose to listen. Once you've made this choice, you can use the following techniques to be a more effective listener. These ideas are especially useful in times of high emotional tension.

Be quiet. Silence is more than staying quiet while someone is speaking. Allow several seconds to pass before you begin to talk. This gives the speaker time to catch his breath and gather his thoughts. He might want to continue. Someone who talks nonstop might fear he will lose the floor if he pauses.

If the message being sent is complete, this short break gives you time to form your response and helps you avoid the biggest barrier to listening—listening with your answer running. If you make up a response before the person is finished, you might miss the end of the message—which is often the main point.

In some circumstances, pausing for several seconds might be inappropriate. Ignore this suggestion completely when someone asks in a panic where to find the nearest phone to call the fire department.

Maintain eye contact. Look at the other person while he speaks. Doing so demonstrates your attentiveness and helps keep your mind from wandering. Your eyes also let you "listen" to body language and behavior. When some of us avoid eye contact, not only do we fail to see—we also fail to listen.

This idea is not an absolute. While maintaining eye contact is important in some cultures, people from other cultures are uncomfortable with sustained eye contact. Some individuals learn primarily by hearing; they can listen more effectively by turning off the visual input once in a while. Keep in mind the differences among people.

Display openness. You can communicate openness by means of your facial expression and body position. Uncross your arms and legs. Sit up straight. Face the other person and remove any physical barriers between you, such as a pile of books.

Listen without response. This doesn't mean that you should never respond. It means waiting for an appropriate moment to respond. Avoid interrupting the sender.

Watch your nonverbal responses, too. A look of "Good grief!" from you can deter the other person from finishing his message.

Send acknowledgments. It is important to let the speaker know periodically that you are still there. Words and nonverbal gestures of acknowledgment convey to the speaker that you are interested and that you are receiving his message. These include "Umhum," "OK," "Yes," and head nods.

These acknowledgments do not imply your agreement. They just indicate that you are listening.

Feed back meaning. See if you can *briefly* state the essence of a person's message: "Let me see if I understood what you said . . ." or "What I'm hearing you say is . . . "

Listen beyond words. Be aware of nonverbal messages and behavior. You might point out that the speaker's body language seems to be the exact opposite of his words. For example: "I noticed you said you are excited, but you look bored."

Keep in mind that the same nonverbal behavior can have different meanings, depending on the listener's cultural background. Someone who looks bored might simply be listening in a different way.

Take care of yourself. People seek good listeners, and there are times when you don't want to listen. You might be distracted with your own concerns. Be honest. Don't pretend to listen. You can say, "What you're telling me is important, and I'm pressed for time right now. Can we set aside another time to talk about this?"

Listen for requests and intentions. An effective way to listen to complaints is to look for the request hidden in them.

"This class is a waste of my time" can be heard as "Please tell me what I'll gain if I participate actively in class." "The instructor talks too fast" might be asking "What strategies can I use to take notes when the instructor covers material rapidly?"

Viewing complaints as requests gives us more choices. Rather than responding with defensiveness or indifference, we can decide whether to grant the request.

Sending your messages

There are times when it's tough to send a message. Often, these times are emotionally charged. Described below are four techniques for delivering a message through tears, laughter, fist pounding, or hugging.

Replace "You" messages with "I" messages. It can be difficult to disagree with someone without his becoming angry or your becoming upset. When conflict occurs, we often make statements about the other person, or "You" messages:

"You are rude."
"You make me mad."
"You must be crazy."
"You don't love me anymore."

This kind of communication results in defensiveness. The responses might be:

"I am not rude."
"I don't care."
"No, *you* are crazy."
"No, *you* don't love *me!*"

"You" messages are hard to receive. They label, judge, blame, and assume things that might or might not be true. They demand rebuttal.

When communication is emotionally charged, psychologist Thomas Gordon suggests that you consider limiting your statements to descriptions about yourself.[2] Replace "You" messages with "I" messages.

"You are rude" might become "I feel upset."
"You make me mad" could be "I feel angry."
"You must be crazy" can be "I don't understand."
"You don't love me anymore" could become "I'm afraid we're drifting apart."

Suppose a friend asks you to pick him up at the airport. You drive 20 miles and wait for the plane. No friend. You decide your friend missed his plane, so you wait three hours for the next flight. No friend. Perplexed and worried, you drive home. The next day, you see your friend downtown.

"What happened?" you ask.

"Oh, I caught an earlier flight."

"You are a rude person," you reply.

Look for the facts, the observable behavior. Everyone will agree that your friend asked you to pick him up, that he did take an earlier flight, and that you did not receive a call from him. But the idea that he is rude is not a fact—it's a judgment.

He might go on to say, "I called your home and no one answered. My mom had a stroke and was rushed to Valley View. I caught the earliest flight I could get." Your judgment no longer fits.

When you saw your friend, you might have said, "I waited and waited at the airport. I was worried about you. I didn't get a call. I feel angry and hurt. I don't want to waste my time. Next time, you can call me when your flight arrives, and I'll be happy to pick you up."

"I" messages don't judge, blame, criticize, or insult. They don't invite the other person to counterattack with more of the same. "I" messages are also more accurate. They report our own thoughts and feelings.

At first, "I" messages might feel uncomfortable or seem forced. That's OK.

Just continue to practice this form of sending. The long-term rewards are worth it. As you practice, remember that an "I" message can include any or all of the following five elements:

- *Observations*. Describe the facts—the indisputable, observable realities. Talk about what you—or anyone else—can see, hear, smell, taste, or touch. Avoid judgments, interpretations, or opinions. Instead of saying, "You're a slob," say, "Last night's lasagna pan was still on the stove this morning."

- *Feelings*. Describe your own feelings. It is easier to listen to "I feel frustrated" than to "You never help me." Stating how you feel about another's actions can be valuable feedback for that person.

- *Wants*. You are far more likely to get what you want if you *say* what you want. If someone doesn't know what you want, he doesn't have a chance to help you get it. Ask clearly and avoid demands. Instead of saying, "Do the dishes when it's your turn—or else!" say, "I want to divide the housework fairly."

- *Thoughts*. Communicate your thoughts, and use caution. Beginning your statement with the word *I* doesn't make it an "I" message. "I think you are a slob" is a "You" judgment in disguise. Instead, say, "I'd have more time to study if I didn't have to clean up so often."

- *Intentions*. The last part of an "I" message is a statement about what you intend to do. Have a plan that doesn't depend on the other person. For example, instead of saying, "From now on we're going to split the dishwashing evenly," you could say, "I intend to do my share of the housework and leave the rest."

Be careful when expressing the last two suggestions in the previous list since they can contain hidden judgments or threats.

> *Most nonverbal behavior is unconscious. We can learn to be aware of it and choose our nonverbal messages.*

Remember that questions are not always questions. We use questions that aren't questions to sneak our opinions and requests into conversations. "Doesn't it upset you?" often means "It upsets me." "Shouldn't we hang the picture over here?" means "I want to hang the picture over here."

Communication improves when we say, "I'm upset" and "Let's hang the picture over here."

Choose nonverbal messages. How you say something can be more important than what you say. Your tone of voice and gestures add up to a silent message that you send. This message can support, modify, or contradict your words. Your posture, the way you dress, how often you shower, and even the poster hanging on your wall can negate your words before you say them. Most nonverbal behavior is unconscious. We can learn to be aware of it and choose our nonverbal messages.

Notice barriers to sending messages. Sometimes fear stops us from sending messages. We are afraid of other people's reactions, sometimes justifiably. Being truthful doesn't mean being insensitive to the impact that our messages have on others. Tact is a virtue; letting fear prevent communication is not.

Assumptions can also be used as excuses for not sending messages. "He already knows this," we tell ourselves. Predictions of failure can be barriers to sending, too. "He won't listen," we assure ourselves. However, that statement might be inaccurate.

Or we might predict, "He'll never do anything about it, even if I tell him." Again, making assumptions can defeat your message before you send it.

It's easy to make excuses for not communicating. If you have fear or some other concern about sending a message, be aware of it. Realize that you can communicate even with your concerns. You can choose to make them a part of the message: "I am going to tell you how I feel, and I'm afraid that you will think it's stupid."

Overcoming barriers to communication could be a matter of educational survival. A short talk with an advisor, a teacher, a friend, or a family member might solve a problem that could jeopardize your education. ⊠

journal entry 19

Discovery/Intention Statement

Think about one of your relationships for a few minutes. It can involve a parent, sibling, spouse, child, friend, hairdresser, or anyone else. In the space below, write down some things that are not working in the relationship. What bugs you? What do you find irritating or unsatisfying?

I discovered that . . .

_____

_____

_____

_____

_____

Now think for a moment about what you want from this relationship. More attention? Less nagging? More openness, trust, financial security, or freedom? Choose a suggestion from this chapter and describe how you could use it to make the relationship work.

I intend to . . .

_____

_____

_____

_____

_____

_____

exercise 18

WRITE AN "I" MESSAGE

First, pick something about school that irritates you. Then pretend that you are talking to the person who is associated with this irritation. In the space below, write down what you would say to this person as a "You" message.

_____

_____

_____

Now write the same complaint as an "I" message. Include at least the first three elements suggested in "The communication loop: Receiving and sending."

_____

_____

_____

_____

The fine art of conflict management

Conflict management is one of the most practical skills you'll ever learn. Think of ways to apply the following suggestions to a current conflict in your life.

State the problem openly. Using "I" messages, state the problem. Allow the other person in a particular conflict to do the same. You might have different perceptions. Knowing this, you can define the conflict clearly. It's hard to fix something unless everyone agrees on what's broken.

Focus on solutions. Define the conflict as a problem to be solved, not as a contest to be won. Let go of being "right" and aim for being effective instead. After stating the problem in terms that everyone accepts, dream up as many solutions as you can.

Choose one solution that is most acceptable to everyone involved and implement it. Agree on who is going to do what by when. Then keep your agreements.

Speak your mind. When we're locked in combat with someone, it's tempting to hold back—to say only a fraction of what we're thinking or feeling. This can be one more way to keep the conflict alive. An alternative is to "empty our buckets"—to let the words and the feelings flow spontaneously. Don't worry about making a perfect "I" statement. Just say the first things that come to mind. This is one way to get all of our cards on the table.

Commit to the relationship. Begin by affirming your commitment to the other person: "I care about you, and I want this relationship to last. So I'm willing to do whatever it takes to resolve this problem." Also ask the other person for a similar commitment.

Back up to common ground. List all of the points on which you are *not* in conflict: "I know that we disagree about how much to spend on a new car, but we do agree that the old one needs to be replaced." Often, such comments put the problem in perspective and pave the way for a solution.

Slow down the communication. In times of great conflict, people often talk all at once. Words fly like speeding bullets and no one is really listening.

When this happens, choose either to listen or to talk—not both at the same time. Usually, this slows down the pace, clears the smoke, and allows everyone to become more levelheaded.

Allow for cultural differences. People respond to conflict in different ways, depending on their cultural background. Some stand close, speak loudly, and make direct eye contact. Other people avert their eyes, mute their voices, and increase physical distance.

When it seems to you that other people are sidestepping or escalating a conflict, consider whether your reaction is based on cultural bias.

Permit the emotion. Crying is OK. Being upset is all right. Feeling angry is often appropriate. Allow the full range of your feelings. Often what's on the far side of anger is love.

Agree to disagree. Honest disagreement is a fact of life. We can peacefully coexist with other people—and respect them—even though we don't agree on fundamental issues. Conflict can be accepted even when it is not resolved.

Do nothing. Sometimes we worsen a conflict by insisting that it be solved immediately. An alternative is to sit tight and wait things out. Some conflicts resolve themselves with the passage of time.

See the conflict within you. When we're angry or upset, we can take a minute to look inside. Perhaps we were ready to take offense, waiting to pounce on something the other person said. Perhaps, without realizing it, we did something to create the conflict. Or maybe the other person is simply saying what we don't want to admit is true.

When these things happen, we can shine a light on our own thinking. A simple spot check might help the conflict disappear—right before our eyes. ▨

Choose your conversations and your community

Conversations can exist in many forms. One involves people talking out loud to each other. At other times, the conversation takes place inside our own heads, and we call it *thinking*. We are even having a conversation when we read a magazine or a book, watch television or a movie, or write a letter or a report. These observations have three implications that wind their way through every aspect of our lives.

Conversations shape our lives

One is that conversations exercise incredible power over what we think, feel, and do. We become our conversations. They shape our attitudes, our decisions, our opinions, our emotions, and our actions. Each of these is primarily the result of what we say over and over again, to ourselves and to others. If you want clues as to what a person will be like tomorrow, listen to what she's talking about today.

Conversation is constant

This leads to a second discovery. Given that conversations are so powerful, it's amazing that few people act on this fact. Most of us swim in a constant sea of conversations, almost none of which we carefully and thoughtfully choose.

Consider how this works. It begins when we pick up the morning paper. The articles on the front page invite us to a conversation about current events. Often the headlines speak of war, famine, unemployment figures, and other species of disaster. The advertisements start up a conversation about fantastic products for us to buy. They talk about hundreds of ways for us to part with our money.

That's not all. If we flip on the radio or television, or if we surf the Web, millions of other conversations await us.

Something happens when we tune in to conversation in any of its forms. We give someone else permission to dramatically influence our thoughts—the conversation in our heads. When we watch a movie, scenes from that movie become the images in our minds. When we read a book, passages from that book become the voice in our heads. It's possible to let this happen dozens of times each day without realizing it.

You have a choice

The real power of this process lies in a third discovery: We can choose our conversations. Certain conversations create real value for us. They give us fuel for reaching our goals. However, others distract us from what we want. They might even create lasting unhappiness and frustration.

We can choose more of the conversations that exhilarate and sustain us. Sometimes we can't control the outward circumstances of our lives. Yet no matter what happens, we can retain the right to choose our conversations.

Suppose that you meet with a political science instructor to ask about guidelines for writing a term paper. She instead begins discussing your poor writing skills and lack of preparation for higher education. This presents you with several options. One is to become angry and think about what a jerk the instructor is and to give up on the idea of learning to write well. Another option is to refocus the conversation by asking what you can do to improve your writing skills. The instructor might suggest working with a writing tutor or taking a basic composition class. These two sets of conversations will have vastly different consequences for your success in school.

The conversations you have are dramatically influenced by the people with whom you associate. If you want to change your attitudes about almost anything—prejudice, politics, religion, humor—choose your conversations by choosing your community. Spend time with people who speak about and live consistently with the attitudes that you value.

Sometimes this means choosing *not* to participate in certain conversations. Sometimes we find ourselves in conversations that are not empowering—gripe sessions, gossip, and the like. That's a time for us to switch the conversation channel. It can be as simple as changing the topic, politely offering a new point of view, or excusing ourselves and walking away.

When we choose our conversations, we discover a tool of unsurpassed power. This tool has the capacity to remake our thoughts—and thus change our lives. ⬚

Communicating across cultures

Communicating with people of other cultures is a learned skill—a habit. According to Stephen R. Covey, author of _The Seven Habits of Highly Effective People_, a habit is the point at which desire, knowledge, and skill meet.³ Desire is about wanting to do something. Knowledge is understanding what to do. And skill is the ability to do it.

Communicating across cultures starts from the first of those factors. When our actions are grounded in a sincere desire to understand others, we can be much more effective. When you truly value cultural diversity, you can use the following suggestions to develop knowledge and skills for a culturally diverse world.

Assume differences in meaning. Each day we can make an intention to act and speak with the awareness that cultures differ. One option is to look for several possible meanings of our words and actions.

Assume that differences in meaning exist, even if you don't know what they are. After first speaking to someone from another culture, don't assume that you've been understood or that you fully understand the other person. The same action can have different meanings at different times, even for members of the same culture. Check it out. Verify what you think you have heard. Listen to see if what you spoke is what the other person received.

Look for common ground. Some goals cross culture lines. Most people want health, physical safety, economic security, and education.

Likewise, most students want to succeed in school and prepare for a career. They often share the same teachers. They have access to many of the same resources at school. They meet in the classroom, on the athletic field, and at cultural events. The key is to honor the differences among people while remembering what we have in common.

Actively build relationships. Cultivate friends from other cultures. Do this through volunteering, serving on committees, or joining study groups—any activity in which people from other cultures are also involved. Then your understanding of other people can unfold in a natural, spontaneous way.

Aim for clear communication. If you're speaking to someone who doesn't understand English well, keep the following ideas in mind:

- Speak slowly and distinctly.
- To clarify your statement, don't repeat individual words over and over again. Restate your entire message in simple, direct language. Avoid slang.
- Use gestures to accompany your words.
- Since English courses for non-native speakers often emphasize written English, write down what you're saying. Print your message in capitalized block letters.
- Stay calm and avoid sending nonverbal messages that you're frustrated.

Ask for help. If you're unsure about how well you're communicating, ask questions: "I don't know how to make this idea clear for you. How might I communicate better?" "When you look away from me during our conversation, I feel uneasy. Is there something else we need to talk about?" "When you don't ask questions, I wonder if I am being clear. Do you want any more explanation?" Questions such as these can get cultural differences out in the open in a constructive way.

Look for individuals, not group representatives. Sometimes the way we speak glosses over differences among individuals and reinforces stereotypes. For example, a student worried about her grade in math expresses concern over "all those Asian students who are skewing the class curve." Or a Caucasian music major assumes that her African American classmate knows a lot about jazz. We can avoid such errors by seeing people as individuals—not spokespersons for an entire group.

Get inside another culture. You might find yourself fascinated by one particular culture. Consider learning as much about it as possible. Immerse yourself in that culture. Read novels, see plays, go to concerts, listen to music, look at art, take courses, or learn the language. Find opportunities to speak with members of that culture. Your quest for knowledge will be an opening to new conversations.

Celebrate your own culture. Learning about other cultures does not mean abandoning your own. You could gain new appreciation for it. You might even find out that members of your ethnic group have suffered discrimination. In the process of celebrating your own culture, you can gain valuable insights into the experiences of other people.

Find a translator, mediator, or model. People who move with ease in two or more cultures can help us greatly. Diane de Anda, a professor at the University of California—Los Angeles, speaks of three kinds of people who can communicate across cultures. She calls them *translators, mediators,* and *models.*[4]

A *translator* is someone who is truly bicultural—a person who relates skillfully to people in a mainstream culture and people from a contrasting culture. This person can share her own experiences in overcoming discrimination, learning another language or dialect, and coping with stress. She can point out differences in meaning between cultures and help resolve conflict.

Mediators are people who belong to the dominant or mainstream culture. Unlike translators, they might not be bicultural. However, mediators value diversity and are committed to cultural understanding. Often they are teachers, counselors, tutors, mentors, or social workers.

Models are members of a culture who are positive examples. Models include students from any racial or cultural group who participate in class and demonstrate effective study habits. Models can also include entertainers, athletes, and community leaders.

Your school might have people who serve these functions, even if they're not labeled *translators, mediators,* or *models.* Some schools have mentor or "bridge" programs that pair new students with teachers of the same race or culture. Students in these programs get coaching in study skills and life skills; they also develop friendships with possible role models. Ask your student counseling service about such programs.

Remember diversity when managing conflict. While in school or on the job, you might come into conflict with a person from another culture. Conflict is challenging enough to manage when it occurs between members of the same culture. When conflict gets enmeshed with cultural differences, the situation can become even more difficult. The following techniques can help:

■ *Keep your temper in check.* People from other cultures might shrink from displays of sudden, negative emotion—for example, shouting or pointing.

■ *Deliver your criticisms in private.* People in many Asian and Middle Eastern cultures place value on "saving face" in public.

■ *Give the other person space.* Standing too close can be seen as a gesture of intimidation.

■ *Address people as equals.* For example, don't offer the other person a chair so that she can sit while you stand and talk.

■ *Stick to the point.* When feeling angry or afraid, you might talk more than usual. A person from another culture—especially one who's learning your language—might find it hard to take in everything you're saying. Pause from time to time so that others can ask clarifying questions.

■ *Focus on actions, not personalities.* People are less likely to feel personally attacked when you request specific changes in behavior. "Please show up for work right at 9 a.m." is often more effective than "You're irresponsible."

■ *Be patient.* This guideline applies especially when you're a manager or supervisor. People from other cultures might find it difficult to speak candidly with someone they view as an authority figure. Encourage others to speak. Allowing periods of silence might help.

■ *Take time to comment when others do well.* However, avoid excessive compliments. People from other cultures might be uncomfortable with public praise and even question your sincerity.

Change the institution. We live in systems that can be racist. As a student, you might see people of color ignored in class. You might see people of a certain ethnic group passed over in job hiring or underrepresented in school organizations. And you might see gay and lesbian students ridiculed or even threatened with violence. One way to stop these actions is to point them out.

Federal civil rights laws, as well as the written policies of most schools, ban racial and ethnic discrimination. If your school receives federal aid, it must set up procedures that protect students against such discrimination. Find out what those procedures are and use them, if necessary.

Throughout recent history, much social change has been fueled by students. When it comes to ending discrimination, you are in an environment where you can make a difference. Run for student government. Write for school publications. Speak at rallies. Express your viewpoint. This is training for citizenship in a multicultural world. ▨

Discovery/Intention Statement

Briefly describe an incident in which you were discriminated against because you differed in some way from the other people involved. This could be any kind of difference, such as hair length, style of clothing, political affiliation, religion, skin color, sexual orientation, age, gender, economic status, or accent.

I discovered that I . . .

_____

_____

_____

Now, scan this chapter for ideas that could help you respond more effectively to discrimination, whether it occurs to you or someone else. List some ideas below that you intend to explore in more detail, along with their associated page numbers.

Strategy   *Page number*

_____

_____

_____

_____

_____

Students with disabilities

Equal opportunity for people with disabilities is the law. In the United States, both the Civil Rights Act of 1964 and the Rehabilitation Act of 1973 offer legal protection. The Americans with Disabilities Act of 1990 extends earlier legislation.

Ask for what you want. However, even the most well-intentioned instructors can forget about promoting learning for people with disabilities. To protect your rights, speak up while keeping the following ideas in mind.

Use available resources. A wealth of resources already exists to support your success in school. Check into services offered by your state. Departments of rehabilitation often provide funds for education or can help you find that money. State commissions on disabilities can guide you to services. In addition, the Job Accommodation Network (1-800-526-7234) offers help in placing employees with learning or physical disabilities.

Also find out about services at your school. Libraries might furnish books in Braille or on audiotapes for the visually impaired. Many counseling and student health centers target certain services to people with disabilities, including learning disabilities. Some schools offer disability resource centers. Other services to ask about include:

- Permits that allow you to park a car closer to classrooms.
- Note-taking services.
- Lecture transcriptions.
- Textbook-reading services and audio recordings.

- Sign language interpreters.
- Help in selecting courses and registering for classes.
- Assistants for laboratory courses in science.
- Shuttle buses for transportation between classes.
- Closed captioning for instructional television programs.
- TTY/TDD devices for students with hearing impairments.
- Assistance with taking tests.

Plan ahead. Meet with your counselor or advisor to design an educational plan—one that takes your disability into account. A key part of this plan is choosing instructors. Ask for recommendations before registering for classes. Interview prospective instructors and sit in on their classes. Express an interest in the class, ask to see a course outline, and discuss any adjustments that could help you complete the course. Some of the services you request might take extra time to deliver. Allow for possible delays as you plan your schedule.

Use empowering words. Changing just a few words can make the difference between asking for what you want and apologizing for it. When people refer to disabilities, you might hear words such as *special treatment* and *accommodation*. Experiment with using *adjustment* and *alternative* instead. The difference between these terms is equality. Asking for an adjustment in an assignment is asking for the right to produce equal work—not for special treatment that "waters down" the assignment.

Dealing with sexism and sexual harassment

Sexism and sexual harassment are real. These are events that occur throughout the year at schools and workplaces. Nearly all of these incidents are illegal or violate organizational policies.

Though men can be subjects of sexism and sexual harassment, women are more likely to experience this form of discrimination. Even the most well-intentioned people might behave in ways that hurt or discount women. Sexism is a factor when:

- Career counselors hint that careers in mathematics and science are not appropriate for women.

- Students pay more attention to feedback from a male teacher than from a female teacher.

- Women are not called on in class, their comments are ignored, or they are overly praised for answering the simplest questions.

- Examples given in a textbook or lecture assign women only to traditionally "female" roles, such as wife, mother, day care provider, elementary school teacher, or nurse.

- People assume that middle-aged women who return to school have too many family commitments to study adequately or do well in their classes.

Many kinds of behavior—both verbal and physical—can be categorized as sexual harassment. This kind of discrimination involves unwelcome sexual conduct. Examples of such conduct in a school setting are:

- Sexual touching or advances.
- Any other unwanted touch.
- Unwanted verbal intimacy.
- Sexual graffiti.
- Displaying or distributing sexually explicit materials.
- Sexual gestures or jokes.
- Pressure for sexual favors.
- Talking about personal sexual activity.
- Spreading rumors about someone's sexual activity or rating someone's sexual performance.

Point out sexist language and behavior. When you see examples of sexism, point them out. Your message can be more effective if you use "I" messages. Indicate the specific statements and behaviors that you consider sexist.

Observe your own language and behavior. Looking for sexist behavior in others is effective. Detecting it in yourself can be just as powerful. Write a Discovery Statement about specific comments that could be interpreted as sexist. Then notice if you say any of these things. Also ask people you know to point out occasions when you use similar statements. Follow up with an Intention Statement that describes how you plan to change your speaking or behavior.

You can also write Discovery Statements about the current level of intimacy (physical and verbal) in any of your relationships at home, work, or school. Be sure that any increase in the level of intimacy is mutually agreed upon.

Encourage support for women. Through networks, women can work to overcome the effects of sexism. Strategies include study groups for women, women's job networks, and professional organizations such as Women in Communications. Other examples are counseling services and health centers for women, family planning agencies, and rape prevention centers. Check your school catalog and library to see if any of these services are available at your school.

Set limits. Recognize your right to an education without the distraction of inappropriate and invasive behavior. Trust your judgment about when your privacy or your rights are being violated. Decide now what kind of sexual comments and actions you're uncomfortable with—and refuse to put up with them.

If you believe that you've been sexually harassed, report the incident to a school official. This person can be a teacher, administrator, or campus security officer. Check to see if your school has someone specially designated to handle your complaint, such as an affirmative action officer.

You can also file a complaint with the Office for Civil Rights (OCR), a federal agency that makes sure schools and workplaces comply with federal law. You can contact the OCR at 1-800-421-3481 or go to the agency's Web site. Your community might also offer resources to protect against sexual discrimination. Examples are public interest law firms, legal aid societies, and unions that employ lawyers to represent students.

Writing on purpose

Effective writing flows from a purpose. Discuss the purpose of your writing assignment with your instructor. Think about how you'd like your reader to respond after considering your ideas. Do you want him to think differently, to feel differently, or to take a certain action?

Your writing strategy will be greatly affected by how you answer these questions. If you want someone to think differently, make your writing clear and logical. Support your assertions with evidence. If you want someone to feel differently, consider crafting a story. Write about a character your reader can empathize with and tell how the person resolves a problem that the reader can relate to. And if your purpose is to move the reader into action, explain exactly what steps she should take and offer solid benefits for her doing so.

To clarify your purpose, state it in one sentence. For example, "The purpose of this paper is to define the term *success* in such a clear and convincing way that I win a scholarship from Houghton Mifflin."

Getting ready to write

Schedule and list writing tasks. Divide the ultimate goal—a finished paper—into smaller steps that you can tackle right away. Estimate how long it will take to complete each step. Start with the date your paper is due and work backward to the present. Say that the due date is December 1 and you have about three months to write the paper. Schedule November 20 as your targeted completion date, plan what you want to get done by November 1, then list what you want to get done by October 1.

Schedule time for rewrites before you begin. Allow at least one day in between revisions so that you can let the material sit. One guideline is to allow 50 percent of writing time for planning, research, and composing the first draft. Then give the remaining 50 percent to revising.

Generate ideas for a topic.
Brainstorm with a group. There's no need to create in isolation. Forget the myth of the lonely, frustrated artist hashing out his ideas alone in a dimly lit Paris café. You can harness the energy and the natural creative power of a group to assist you.

To get ideas flowing, start talking. Admit your confusion or lack of a clear idea. Then just speak. By putting your thoughts into words, you'll start thinking more clearly.

As soon as you get guidelines for the paper or speech, write down a list of topics that interest you. Write as many of these as you can think of in two minutes. Then choose one to begin. Remember that you can choose again later.

The most common pitfall is selecting a topic that's too broad. "Harriet Tubman" is not a useful topic for your American history paper. Instead, consider "Harriet Tubman's activities as a Union spy during the Civil War." Your topic statement can function as a working title.

Write a thesis statement. Clarify what you want to say about your topic by summarizing it in one concise sentence. This sentence is called a *thesis statement.*

You might write a thesis statement such as "Harriet Tubman's activities with the Underground Railroad led to a relationship with the Union army during the Civil

War." A statement that's clear and to the point can make your paper easier to write. You can always rewrite your thesis statement as you learn more about your topic.

A thesis statement is different from a topic statement. Like newspaper headlines, a thesis statement makes an assertion or describes an action. It is expressed in a complete sentence, including a verb. "Diversity" is a topic. "Cultural diversity is valuable" is a thesis statement.

Research. First, gain an overview of the subject. Discover the structure of your topic—its major divisions and branches. Follow this with more in-depth research guided by your outline. For suggestions, see Chapter Four: Reading and Chapter Five: Notes.

Outline. An outline is a kind of map. When you follow a map, you avoid getting lost. Likewise, an outline keeps you from wandering off the topic.

To create an outline, brainstorm a list of phrases that clarify and expand on your thesis statement. Turn each phrase into a complete sentence. Then arrange the sentences in a logical order. These can become topic sentences for key paragraphs in your paper.

Test your outline, revising it several times. Make sure that each word relates directly to your statement of purpose.

Writing a first draft

If you've planned your writing project and completed your research, you've already done much of the hard work. Now you can relax into writing your first draft.

To create your draft, expand each sentence in your outline into a full paragraph. Refer to your notes as you do this and add ideas of your own.

Remember that your first draft is not for keeps. Save quality for later, when you revise. Your goal at this point is simply to generate lots of material.

Don't worry about grammar, punctuation, or spelling for now. Write informally, as if you were explaining the subject to a friend.

Set your first draft down quickly. Pause occasionally to glance at your notes and outline. Avoid stopping to edit your work.

Free writing, a technique championed by writing teacher Peter Elbow, can also send a depth probe into your creative mind.[5] There's only one rule in free writing: Write without stopping. Set a time limit—say, 10 minutes—and keep your pencil in motion or your fingers dancing across the keyboard the whole time.

Give yourself permission to keep writing. Ignore the urge to stop and rewrite, even if you think what you've written isn't very good. It's OK if you stray from the initial subject. Just keep writing and let the ideas flow. Experiment with free-writing a draft as soon as your instructor assigns a paper.

Revising your draft

An effective way to revise your paper is to read it out loud. The eyes tend to fill in the blanks in our own writing. The combination of voice and ears forces us to pay attention to the details.

To begin revising, cut the passages that don't contribute to your purpose.

Approach your rough draft as if it were a chunk of granite from which you will chisel the final product. In the end, much of your first draft will be lying on the floor. What is left will be the clean, clear, polished product. Sometimes the revisions are painful. Sooner or later, every writer invents a phrase that is truly clever but makes no contribution to the purpose of the paper. Grit your teeth and let it go.

For maximum efficiency, make the larger cuts first—sections, chapters, pages. Then go for the smaller cuts—paragraphs, sentences, phrases, words.

In deleting passages, you've probably removed some of the original transitions and connecting ideas from your draft. The next task is to rearrange what's left of your paper or speech so that it flows logically. Look for consistency within paragraphs and for transitions from paragraph to paragraph and section to section.

When you're satisfied with flow, look at individual words and phrases.

In general, rely on nouns and verbs. Using too many adjectives and adverbs weakens your message and adds unnecessary bulk to your writing. Include details and be specific.

Also, use the active rather than the passive voice. For example, you can take *A project was initiated* and rewrite it as *The research team began a project.*

Format your paper following accepted standards for margin widths, endnotes, title pages, and other details. Ask your instructor for guidelines.

Finally, look over your paper with an eye for spelling and grammar mistakes.

When you're through proofreading, take a minute to savor the result. You've just witnessed something of a miracle—the mind attaining clarity and resolution. That's the aha! in writing. ⊠

Giving credit where credit is due

Avoiding the high cost of PLAGIARISM

There's a branch of law known as *intellectual property*. This field is based on the idea that original works—such as speeches, publications, and works of art—are not free for the taking. Anyone who borrows from these works is obligated to acknowledge the work's creator. This is the purpose behind copyrights, patents, and trademarks.

Using another person's words or pictures without giving proper credit is called *plagiarism*. This is a real concern for anyone who writes, including students. Plagiarism amounts to stealing someone else's work and claiming it as your own—the equivalent of cheating on a test.

Higher education consists of a community of scholars who trust each other to speak and write with integrity. Plagiarism undermines this trust. The consequences can range from a failing grade to expulsion from school.

There are several ways to avoid plagiarism when writing.

If your writing includes a passage, identifiable phrase, sequence of ideas, or visual image created by another person, be sure to acknowledge this fact.

Also be careful as you take notes. Clearly distinguish your own ideas from the ideas of others. If you use a direct quotation from another writer or speaker, put that person's words in quotation marks. Also note details about the source of the quotation: author, publication title, publisher, date, and page number. Many instructors will require you to add endnotes to your paper with this information, so include it with each quotation in your notes. Ask your instructor for examples of the format to use for endnotes.

If you do research online, you might find yourself copying sentences or paragraphs from a Web page and pasting them directly into your notes. This is the same as taking direct quotations from your source. To avoid plagiarism, identify such passages in an obvious way. Besides enclosing them in quotation marks, you could format them in a different font or color. Also capture relevant information about the Web page where the passages originally appeared: author, title, sponsoring organization, URL, publication date, revision date, and date that you accessed that page. For more information on crediting Internet sources, go online to the Modern Language Association's Web site at **http://www.mla.org/publications/style/style_faq/ style_faq4.**

Instead of using a direct quotation, you might choose to paraphrase an author's words. *Paraphrasing* means restating the original passage in different words, usually making it shorter and simpler. Paraphrase with care. Students who copy a passage word for word and then just rearrange or delete a few phrases are running a serious risk of plagiarism. Consider this paragraph:

Higher education also offers you the chance to learn how to learn. In fact, that's the subject of this book. Employers value the person who is a "quick study" when it comes to learning a new job. That makes your ability to learn a marketable skill.

Following is an improper paraphrase of that passage:

With higher education comes the chance to learn how to learn. Employers value the person who is a "quick study" when it comes to learning a new job. Your ability to learn is a marketable skill.

A better paraphrase of the same passage would be:

The author notes that when we learn how to learn, we gain a skill that is valued by employers.

Be sure to credit paraphrases in the same way that you credit direct quotations.

When you use the same sequence of ideas as one of your sources—even if you haven't summarized, para-phrased, or quoted—cite that source.

Finally, submit only your own original work, not materials that have been written or revised by someone else.

Out of a concern for avoiding plagiarism, some students go overboard in crediting their sources. You do not need to credit wording that's wholly your own. Nor do you need to credit general ideas. For example, the suggestion that people use a to-do list to plan their time is a general idea. When you use your own words to describe to-do lists, there's no need to credit a source. But if you borrow someone else's words or images to explain this idea, do give credit. ◪

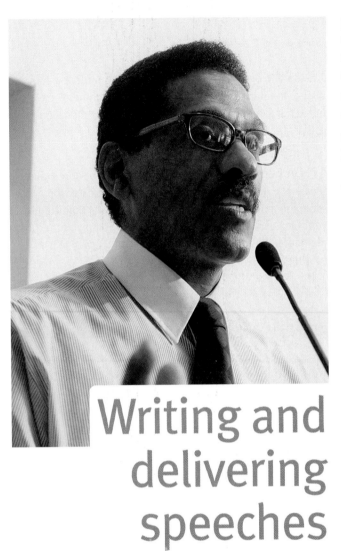

Writing and delivering speeches

The way you plan and present your speech can determine the number of audience members who will stay with you until the end. Polishing your speaking and presentation skills can also help you think on your feet and communicate clearly. These are skills that you can use in any course and in any career you choose.

Organize your presentation

Writing a speech is similar to writing a paper. Speeches are usually organized in three main parts: the introduction, the main body, and the conclusion.

To make an effective speech, be precise about your purpose and main point, or thesis. Speeches can inform, persuade, motivate, or entertain. Choose what you want to do, let your audience know what your intention is, and state your thesis early on.

Consider the length of your presentation. Plan on delivering about 100 words per minute. This is only a general guideline, however, so time yourself as you practice your presentation. Aim for a lean presentation—enough words to make your point but not so many as to make your audience restless. Be brief, be seated, and leave your listeners wanting more.

Write the introduction. In your introduction reveal the thesis and exactly what's coming. Whenever possible, talk about things that hold your interest. Include your personal experiences and start with a bang!

Consider this introduction to a speech on the subject of world hunger:

I'm very honored to be here with you today. I intend to talk about malnutrition and starvation. First, I want to outline the extent of these problems, then I will discuss some basic assumptions concerning world hunger, and finally I will propose some solutions.

You can almost hear the snores from the audience. Following is a rewrite:

More people have died from hunger in the past five years than have been killed in all of the wars, revolutions, and murders in the past 150 years. Yet there is enough food to go around. I'm honored to be here with you today to discuss solutions to this problem.

Most people pay attention for at least the first few seconds, so highlight your main points in the beginning sentences of your speech.

Write the main body. The main body of your speech is the content—70 to 90 percent of your presentation. In the main body, you develop your ideas in much the same way that you develop a written paper.

In speeches, transitions are especially important. Give your audience a signal when you change points, using meaningful pauses and verbal emphasis as well as transitional phrases: "On the other hand, until the public realizes what is happening to children in these countries . . ." or "The second reason hunger persists is . . ."

In long speeches, recap from time to time and preview what's to come. Use facts, descriptions, expert opinions, and statistics to hold your audience's attention.

Write the conclusion. At the end of the speech, summarize your points and draw your conclusion. You started with a bang; now finish with drama. Make it clear to your audience when you've reached the end. Avoid endings such as "This is the end of my speech." A simple standby is "So in conclusion, I want to reiterate three points: First, . . ." When you are finished, stop talking.

Create speaking notes. Some professional speakers recommend writing out your speech in full, then putting key words or main points on a few 3x5 cards. Number the cards so that if you drop them, you can quickly put them in order again. As you finish the information on

Get organized. As soon as you get the assignment, select a group leader and exchange contact information. Schedule specific times and places for planning, researching, writing, and practicing your presentation.

At your first meeting, write a to-do list including all of the tasks involved in completing the assignment. Distribute tasks fairly, paying attention to the strengths of individuals in your group. For example, some people excel at brainstorming while others prefer researching.

Get coordinated. Coordinate your presentation so that you have transitions between individual speakers. Practice making those transitions smooth.

Also practice using visuals such as flipboards, posters, DVDs, videotapes, or slides. To give visuals their full impact, make them appropriate for the room where you will present. Make sure that text is large enough to be seen from the back of the room.

Get cooperation. Presentations that get top scores take teamwork and planning—not egos. Communicate with group members in an open and sensitive way. Contribute your ideas and be responsive to the viewpoints of other members. When you do, your group is on the way to scoring well.

each card, move it to the back of the pile. Write information clearly and in letters large enough to be seen from a distance.

Some speakers prefer to use standard outlined notes. Another option is mind mapping. Even an hour-long speech can be mapped on one sheet of paper. You can also use memory techniques to memorize the outline of your speech.

Practice your presentation

Use your "speaker's voice." When you practice, do so in a loud voice. Your voice sounds different when you talk loudly, and this can be unnerving. Get used to it early on.

Practice in the room in which you will deliver your speech. Hear what your voice sounds like over a sound system. If you can't practice your speech in the actual room, at least visit the site ahead of time. Also make sure that the materials you will need for your speech, such as a computer or overhead projector and screen, will be available when you want them.

Make a recording. Many schools have recording equipment available for student use. Use it while you practice; then view the finished recording to evaluate your presentation.

Listen for repeated phrases. Examples include *you know, kind of, really*, plus any little *uh*'s, *umm*'s, and *ah*'s. When they pop up in your speech, remind yourself that you don't use those words anymore.

Keep practicing. Avoid speaking word for word, as if you were reading a script. When you know your material well, you can deliver it in a natural way. Practice your presentation until you could deliver it in your sleep; then run through it a few more times.

Deliver your presentation

Before you begin, get the audience's attention. If people are still filing into the room or adjusting their seats, they're not ready to listen. When all eyes are on you, then begin.

Deal with stage fright by noticing it. Tell yourself, "Yes, my hands are clammy. I notice that my stomach is slightly upset. My face feels numb." Allow these symptoms to exist. Experience them fully. When you do, they often become less persistent. Notice all of your thoughts and feelings; then gently release them.

Project your voice. When you speak, talk loudly enough to be heard. Avoid leaning over your notes or the podium.

Maintain eye contact. Find a few friendly faces around the room and imagine that you are talking to each person individually.

Notice your nonverbal communication. Only a fraction of our communication is verbal. Be aware of what your body is telling your audience. Contrived or staged gestures will look dishonest. Be natural. If you don't know what to do with your hands, notice that. Then don't do anything with them.

Pause when appropriate. Beginners sometimes feel that they have to fill every moment with the sound of their voice. Release that expectation. Give your listeners a chance to make notes and absorb what you say.

Have fun. One way to feel at ease while speaking is to look at your audience and imagine everyone dressed as clowns. Chances are that if you lighten up and enjoy your presentation, so will they. ◪

PRACTICING CRITICAL THINKING

8

Discuss a controversial issue of your choosing with a small group of classmates. At several points in your discussion, stop to evaluate your group's critical thinking. Answer the following questions in writing.

Are we staying open to opposing ideas, even if we initially disagree with them?

_____

_____

_____

_____

_____

Are we asking for evidence for each key assertion?

_____

_____

_____

_____

_____

Are we adequately summarizing one another's point of view before analyzing it?

_____

_____

_____

_____

_____

Are we foreseeing the possible consequences of taking a particular stand on any issue?

_____

_____

_____

_____

_____

Are we considering more than one solution to problems?

_____

_____

_____

_____

Are we willing to change our stands on issues or suspend judgment when appropriate?

_____

_____

_____

_____

Are we being systematic as we consider the issues?

_____

_____

_____

_____

power process

Employ your word

When you speak and give your word, you are creating—literally. Your speaking brings life to your values. In large part, others know who you are by the words you speak and the agreements you make. You can learn who you are by observing which commitments you choose to make and which ones you choose to avoid.

Your word makes things happen. Circumstances, events, and attitudes fall into place. The resources needed to accomplish whatever was promised become available. When you give your word, all this comes about.

The person you are right now is, for the most part, a result of the choices and agreements you've made in your life up to this point. Your future is determined largely by the choices and agreements you will make from this point on. By making and keeping agreements, you employ your word to create your future.

The world works by agreement

There are over six billion people on planet Earth. We live on different continents and in different nations, and communicate in different languages. We have diverse political ideologies and subscribe to various social and moral codes.

This complex planetary network is held together by people keeping their word. Agreements minimize confusion, prevent social turmoil, and keep order. Projects are finished, goods are exchanged, and treaties are made. People, organizations, and nations know what to expect when agreements are kept. When people keep their word, the world works. Agreements are the foundation of many things that we often take for granted. Language, our basic tool of communication, works only because we agree about the meanings of words. A pencil is a pencil only because everyone agrees to call a thin, wood-covered column of graphite a *pencil*. We could just as easily call them *ziddles*. Then you might hear someone say, "Do you have an extra ziddle? I forgot mine."

Money exists only by agreement. If we leave a $100 Monopoly bill (play money) on a park bench next to a real $100 bill (backed by the United States Treasury), one is more likely to disappear than the other. The only important difference between the two pieces of paper is that everyone agrees that one can be exchanged for goods and services and the other cannot. Shopkeepers will sell merchandise for the "real" $100 bill because they trust a continuing agreement.

Relationships work by agreement

Relationships are built on agreements. They begin with our most intimate personal contacts and move through all levels of families, organizations, communities, and nations.

When we break a promise to be faithful to a spouse, to help a friend move to a new apartment, or to pay a bill on time, relationships are strained and the consequences can be painful. When we keep our word, relationships are more likely to be satisfying and harmonious. Expectations of trust and accountability develop. Others are more likely to keep their promises to us.

Perhaps our most important relationship is the one we have with ourselves. Trusting ourselves to keep our word is enlivening. As we experience success, our self-confidence increases.

When we commit to complete a class assignment and then keep our word, our understanding of the subject improves. So does our grade. We experience satisfaction and success. If we break our word, we create a gap in our learning, a lower grade, and possibly negative feelings.

Ways to make and keep agreements

Being cautious about making agreements can improve the quality of our lives. Making only those promises that we fully intend to keep improves the likelihood of reaching our goals. We can ask ourselves what level of commitment we have to a particular promise.

At the same time, if we are willing to take risks, we can open new doors and increase our possibilities for success. The only way to ensure that we keep all of our agreements is either to make none or to make only those that are absolutely guaranteed. In either case, we are probably cheating ourselves. Some of the most powerful promises we can make are those that we have no idea how to keep. We can stretch ourselves and set goals that are both high and realistic.

If we break an agreement, we can choose to be gentle with ourselves. We can be courageous, quickly admit our mistake to the people involved, and consider ways to deal with the consequences.

Examining our agreements can improve our effectiveness. Perhaps we took on too much—or too little. Perhaps we did not use all the resources that were available to us—or we used too many. Perhaps we did not fully understand what we were promising. When we learn from both our mistakes and our successes, we can become more effective at employing our word.

Move up the ladder of powerful speaking

The words used to talk about whether or not something will happen fall into several different levels. We can think of each level as one rung on a ladder—the ladder of powerful speaking. As we move up the ladder, our speaking becomes more effective.

Obligation. The lowest rung on the ladder is *obligation*. Words used at this level include *I should, he ought to,*

someone better, they need to, I must, and *I had to.* Speaking this way implies that people and circumstances other than ourselves are in control of our lives. When we live at the level of obligation, we often feel passive and helpless to change anything.

Note: When we move to the next rung, we leave behind obligation and advance to self-responsibility. All of the rungs work together to reinforce this characteristic.

Possibility. The next rung up is *possibility*. At this level, we examine new options. We play with new ideas, possible solutions, and alternative courses of action. As we do, we learn that we can make choices that dramatically affect the quality of our lives. We are not the victims of circumstance. Phrases that signal this level include *I might, I could, I'll consider, I hope to,* and *maybe.*

Preference. From possibility we can move up to *preference*. Here we begin the process of choice. The words *I prefer* signal that we're moving toward one set of possibilities over another, perhaps setting the stage for eventual action.

Passion. Above preference is a rung called *passion*. Again, certain words signal this level: *I want to, I'm really excited to do that, I can't wait.* Possibility and passion are both exciting places to be. Even at these levels, though, we're still far from action. Many of us want to achieve lots of things and have no specific plan for doing so.

Planning. Action comes with the next rung—*planning*. When people use phrases such as *I intend to, my goal is to, I plan to,* and *I'll try like mad to,* they're at the level of planning. The Intention Statements you write in this book are examples of planning.

Promising. The highest rung on the ladder is *promising*. This is where the power of your word really comes into play. At this level, it's common to use phrases such as these: *I will, I promise to, I am committed, you can count on it.* This is where we bridge from possibility and planning to action. Promising brings with it all of the rewards of employing your word. ⬧

By making and keeping agreements, you employ your word to create your future.

put it to work

According to the National Association of Colleges and Employers, verbal and written communication tops the list of skills that companies look for in college graduates.[6] The techniques described in this chapter have many direct applications in the workplace.

Reread specific articles with the workplace in mind.

Simply by remembering to separate the processes of sending and receiving, you can immediately improve your relationships with both supervisors and employees.

Use ideas from "Writing and delivering speeches" to craft presentations that persuade your supervisor to increase your department budget—or give you a raise.

If you get into a personal conflict with a coworker, reread the article "The fine art of conflict management" and choose a suggestion to apply. As you read, visualize the suggestion working for you.

Use ideas from "Communicating across cultures" to develop specific skills. With the desire to communicate and gain knowledge of other cultures, you can become aware of your own biases, form alliances with people of other races and cultures, and point out the discrimination and racism that you observe in organizations. You can be an advocate for change.

Make effective presentations with visuals.

Presentations often include visuals such as overhead transparencies, flip charts, or "slides" created with presentation software. These can reinforce your main points and help your audience understand how your presentation is organized. In addition, visuals can serve as your speaking notes.

Use visuals to *complement* rather than *replace* your speaking. If you use too many visuals—or visuals that are too complex—your audience might focus on them and forget about you. To avoid this fate:

- Limit the amount of text on each visual. Stick to key words presented in short sentences and bulleted or numbered lists. Use a consistent set of plain fonts that are large enough for all audience members to see.

- Stick with a simple, coherent color scheme. Use light-colored text on a dark background, or dark text on a light background.

- Use consistent terminology in your speaking, your handouts, and your visuals. Inconsistency can lead people to feel lost or to question your credibility.

- Proofread your visuals for spelling and other mechanical errors.

Write for workplace audiences.

Good writing is a marketable skill. To verify this, flip through the help wanted section in a large Sunday newspaper. Note how many job descriptions call for good writing skills. Writing techniques can assist you in preparing memos, reports, e-mail messages, and Web sites.

Jakob Nielsen, author of *Designing Web Usability: The Practice of Simplicity*, suggests that effectively written Web pages are:

- *Concise*—free of needless words and organized so that the main point of each section and paragraph comes at the beginning.

- *Scannable*—prepared with subheadings and visuals that allow readers to skim and quickly find what they need.

- *Objective*—packed with credible facts and free of "hype," that is, vague claims presented without evidence.[7]

These three guidelines can assist you in *all* forms of business writing.

Work effectively in teams.

In their book *When Teams Work Best*, Frank LaFasto and Carl Larson summarize the lessons learned from studying 600 teams in both public and private organizations. These ranged from the Mount Everest climbing team to the workers who produced the Boeing 747 airplane.

According to these authors, the most common barrier to effective teamwork is an atmosphere of defensiveness. Team members can solve this problem by creating an environment in which all opinions are valued; resolving personal conflicts actively rather than ignoring them; staying focused on relevant problems rather than side issues; choosing leaders who allow all opinions to be expressed and keep the team focused; using a simple and clear process for decision making, allowing people to take immediate action without excess paperwork or time-wasting procedures; and defining the team's outcome clearly and how individual team members can contribute directly to that outcome.[8] ✖

Name _____ Date _____/_____/_____

1. List some examples of ways to display openness when someone is speaking to you.

2. Explain the meaning of the suggestion to "listen beyond words."

3. Define the word *conversation* as it is used in this chapter.

4. Reword the following complaint as a request: "You always interrupt when I talk!"

5. List at least three elements of an "I" message.

6. Define the terms *translator, mediator,* and *model* as explained in this chapter.

7. Which of the following should not be a concern when writing a first draft?
   (A) Refining your thesis statement.
   (B) Citations from outside resources.
   (C) Using an outline or map of your plan.
   (D) Freewriting to address all of the key points.

8. Define *plagiarism* and explain ways to avoid it.

9. Describe at least three techniques for practicing and delivering a speech.

10. What characteristic distinguishes the top five rungs of the ladder of powerful speaking from the bottom rung?

learning styles application

The questions below will "cycle" you through four styles, or modes, of learning as explained in the article "Learning styles: Discovering how you learn" in Chapter One. Each question will help you explore a different mode. You can answer the questions in any order.

what if *After reading this chapter, will you generally approach conflict management in a different way? Briefly explain your answer.*

why *Think of a conflict you are experiencing right now with an important person in your life. (If you cannot think of one, recall a conflict you've experienced in the past.) Do you think that any of the suggestions in this chapter could help you resolve this conflict? Briefly explain your answer.*

how *Describe when and where you plan to use a suggestion from this chapter to resolve a conflict with another person.*

what *Choose a specific suggestion from this chapter that could help you resolve a conflict you are experiencing right now with another person.*

master student profile

IRSHAD MANJI

(1969–   ) Controversial journalist, broadcaster, and author of The Trouble with Islam, *where she uses her "Muslim voice of reform, to concerned citizens worldwide" in an effort to explore faith and community, and the diversity of ideas.*

I t's to be expected that an author with a book on the verge of publication will lose her cool over a last-minute detail or two. Some might get nervous that their facts won't hold up and run a paranoid, final check. Others might worry about what to wear to their book party. When Irshad Manji's book was about to hit the stands, her concern was a bit different. She feared for her life.

Certain her incendiary book *The Trouble with Islam* would set off outrage in the Muslim community, she called the police, told them she was working on a book that was highly critical of Islam, and asked if they could advise her on safety precautions. They came to visit her Toronto apartment building several times and suggested she install a state-of-the-art security system, bulletproof windows, and hire a counterterrorism expert to act as her personal bodyguard.

In her short, plucky book she comes down hard on modern-day Islam, charging that the religion's mainstream has come to be synonymous with literalism. Since the 13th century, she said, the faith hasn't encouraged— or tolerated—independent thinking (or as its known in the faith, *ijtihad*).

The book, which is written like a letter, is both thoughtful and confrontational. In person, Ms. Manji embodied the same conflicting spirit. She was affable and wore a broad smile. Her upbeat, nervous energy rose to the task of filling in every potentially awkward pause. (One of her favorite factoids: "Prophet Mohammed was quite a feminist.")

Her journey scrutinizing Islam started when she was an 8-year-old and taking weekly religious classes at a *madrasa* (religious school) in suburban Vancouver. Her anti-Semitic teacher Mr. Khaki never took her questions seriously; he merely told her to accept everything because it was in the Koran. She wanted to know why she had to study it in Arabic, which she didn't understand, and was told the answers were "in the Koran."

Her questioning ended up getting her kicked out of school at 14, and she embarked on a 20-year-long private study of the religion. While she finds the treatment poured on women and foreigners in Islamic nations indefensible, she said that she continues to be a believer because the religion provides her with her values. "And I'm so glad I did because it was then I came to realize that there was this really progressive side of my religion and it was this tradition of critical thinking called *ijtihad*. This is what allows me to stay within the faith."

She calls herself a "Muslim refusenik" because she remains committed to the religion, and yet she doesn't accept what's expected of Muslim women. As terrorist acts and suicide bombings refuse to subside, she said it's high time for serious reform within the Islamic faith.

She said many young Muslim supporters are still afraid to come out about their support of her. "Even before 9/11 it was the young Muslims who were emerging out of these audiences and gathering at the side of the stage. They'd walk over and say, 'Irshad, we need voices such as yours to help us open up this religion of ours because if it doesn't open up, we're leaving the mosques.'"

She wants Muslims to start thinking critically about their religion and to start asking more questions. "Most Muslims have never been introduced to the possibility, let alone the virtue, of asking questions about our holy book," she said. "We have never been taught the virtue of interpreting the Koran in different ways." ⧄

From Lauren Mechling, "The Trouble with Writing About Islam," as appeared in *New York Sun*, November 26, 2004. Copyright © 2004. Reprinted by permission of *New York Sun*.

For more biographical information on Irshad Manji, visit the Master Student Hall of Fame on the *Becoming a Master Student* Web site at

masterstudent.college.hmco.com

9

Technology

why

this chapter matters . . .

Your skill with information technology may be as critical to your success as the ability to read, write, listen, and speak well.

what

is included . . .

Technology, satisfaction, and success
Connect to cyberspace
Finding what you want on the Internet
Write e-mail that gets results
Becoming an online learner
Thinking critically about information on the Internet
Joining online communities
Library—the buried treasure
Power Process: "Risk being a fool"
Master Student Profile: Mike Lazaridis

how

you can use this chapter . . .

Become an effective learner when you go online.
Find useful, accurate information on the Internet—and filter out irrelevant content.
Take part in online communities that promote your success.

As you read, ask yourself

what if . . .

I could stay up-to-date with information technology and use it with confidence to achieve my goals?

STUDENT VOICES

"*The most useful resource at my college is the student-run HelpDesk and Information Technology workshops. As an adult student coming from the workplace where computers were not a part of my primary responsibilities, I was intimidated by my classmates who seemed to know how to proficiently search the Web and use different applications. I relied on the IT workshops for assistance and it helped me to connect to other returning students who were in the same position as me.*"

—LI-CHENG LU

Technology, satisfaction, and success

Information technology pervades our lives. Computers are not only found on our desktops, in our libraries, and on our laps. They are also embedded in cars, appliances, automatic teller machines, grocery checkout lanes, and sometimes—given the latest advances in medical technology—the human body.

Several years ago, the Massachusetts Institute of Technology made headlines by making the content for all of its courses available on the Internet. At the time, this event seemed exotic. Today it is not far from the norm on many campuses.

Courses in higher education are no longer divided into separate categories—distance learning (delivered exclusively over the Internet) versus traditional courses (delivered by human beings standing in front of a classroom). A new model has emerged: the hybrid course that combines online instruction with class meetings and textbooks. Course management software such as WebCT and Blackboard creates virtual classrooms—sites on the World Wide Web where a teacher can post a syllabus, readings, announcements, tests, grades, and a digital "drop box" for student assignments. Digital discussions and debates can also take place via computer bulletin boards, chat rooms, and two-way audio and visual connections. In this chapter, the term *online learning* refers to all of these tools. You can use information technology to succeed in school, advance in your career, and achieve many other goals. Besides helping you complete your course work, computer applications can assist you in creating calendars, setting goals, and managing to-do lists. You can crunch numbers, maintain mailing lists, send and receive faxes, manage your finances, stay abreast of the news, and connect with people and organizations across the world. In addition, you can edit photos, create videos, produce audio files, and launch a personal Web site that introduces you to the worldwide online community.

There's more to technology savvy than just showing up on campus with your own computer or locating your school's computer labs. Knowing which hardware to use is an essential starting point. Mastering software applications such as word processing, databases, and spreadsheets will also help you succeed with technology in the classroom and in the workplace.

At the same time, succeeding with technology is not about becoming a "hacker" or an expert on the latest digital gadgets. Even students who major in computer science can fumble when it comes to online learning.

The bigger picture is that higher education offers you the chance to integrate technology with your own method of processing information. ▧

journal entry 21

Discovery/Intention Statement

Recall an incident when you felt frustrated during an attempt to use computer-based technology to complete a course assignment. Briefly describe what happened.

I discovered that I . . .

_____

_____

_____

Now skim this chapter for at least five ideas that you intend to explore in more detail—suggestions that could help you become a powerful online learner. Summarize each suggestion in a short phrase and list the page where you found it.

Strategy   *Page number*

_____

_____

_____

_____

Finally, describe a situation coming up this term—preferably within the next week—in which you could apply several of the suggestions you just listed.

I intend to . . .

_____

_____

_____

_____

Connect to cyberspace

You can take two paths to accessing information technology in higher education. One is through the resources offered by your school. The other is through your own technology resources, including a personal computer.

Many campuses have computer labs with equipment that's available for students for free. These labs can get crowded, especially during finals week or when other major assignments are due in large courses. To maintain your access to computers, find several sources of public computers on campus and check their availability.

With some creative thinking, you might find even more possibilities. A library on campus or in your community might offer public access. Some students get permission to use computers at their workplace after hours. Perhaps a friend or family member would be willing to loan you a computer or offer you computer time at his home. If you choose one of these options, be realistic about the number of hours that the computer will be available to you.

Your personal resources. You might find that it's more convenient to buy your own computer and peripheral equipment. Find out whether your campus bookstore or another outlet on campus sells computer hardware at a student discount. Also ask about getting an extended warranty with technical support. Other options include leasing a computer or buying a used one.

To make an informed purchase, take your time. Start by contacting an admissions counselor or academic advisor at your school and asking the following questions.

Should I get a laptop computer or a desktop computer? Laptop computers have the obvious advantage of portability. They also take up less space—a key consideration if you live in a dorm room. Yet laptops tend to be more fragile and more expensive than desktop computers.

Also, the portability of laptop computers makes them easy targets for thieves. If you get one, keep it in a secure place or always carry it with you in public. Don't leave your computer unattended, even for a few seconds. Treat your laptop the same way that you treat your wallet or purse. Your computer dealer can give you information about security devices for laptops. These include locks

and software that identifies the Internet addresses of stolen computers when thieves use them to go online.

What platform will work better for me—Windows or Macintosh? The majority of personal computers used in higher education and business settings are Windows-based. However, most campuses accommodate Macintoshes. You might also find that students with certain majors—such as art, music, or video production—favor Macintoshes. Ask your academic advisor for guidance in this area. If you use a Macintosh, look for software that freely exchanges files with Windows.

What hardware specifications should my computer meet? To find a personal computer that supports your academic success, think about technical specifications. These are the requirements that computers must meet in order to connect to the campus network and run software applications commonly used by students. In particular ask about recommendations for your computer's operating system, processor, memory, software, and Ethernet card or other device needed to connect to computer networks on campus.

Make sure that your system includes a way to make backup copies of all your computer files. One option is an optical drive, a piece of equipment built into newer computers, though you can buy it separately. An optical drive allows you to read and write data to compact discs (CDs), digital video discs (DVDs), or both.

What software do I need to successfully complete coursework? Many students find that a package—including a word processor as well as spreadsheet, database, and presentation software—meets their needs. Check with your campus bookstore to see if student discounts are offered on software packages. Also ask whether your school provides software to access the Internet (e-mail and Web browsers) and to protect your computer from viruses. ⊠

Finding what you want on the Internet

Go to:

:-) forward >

search

keyword

.com

< back

WWW .http:/

:-)

Imagine a library with millions of books—a place where anyone can bring in materials and place them on any shelf or even toss them randomly on the floor. That's something like the way information accumulates on the Internet. Finding your way through this maze can be a challenge. But it's worth it.

Experiment with different search sites. *Directories* offer extensive lists of Web pages, all grouped by topic. Think of directories as a table of contents for the Web.

Search engines find Web pages that relate to a specific topic. These programs scan millions of Web pages in the same way that a human indexer reviews hundreds of book pages.

Meta search engines draw on the capabilities of several search engines at once—similar to scanning several book indexes at the same time.

Each search site has different features. Some combine aspects of directories and search engines. Look for links on each search site that explain how to use advanced search capabilities. Find a few search sites you like and use them consistently. That way you get to know each one well and capitalize on its strengths.

Treat searches as dialogues with your computer. When doing research, start with a question you want to answer, such as "What mutual funds invest in bonds issued by the U.S. Treasury?" Write the question out as precisely as you can.

Next, identify the key words in this question—for example, *mutual funds, bonds,* and *U.S. Treasury.* Type these words into the search site.

Check three to five of these pages to see if they include answers to your original question. If not, rephrase your question and search again with different key words.

Use Boolean operators. Boolean operators include the words *AND, OR,* and *NOT.* For example, if you type *portfolios AND résumés,* you'll get a list of Web sites that refer to both portfolios and résumés. *Portfolios OR résumés* will give you sites that refer to either topic. *Portfolios NOT résumés* will give you sites that relate only to portfolios. With some search tools, a plus sign (+) func-

tions like the term *AND.* A minus sign (–) functions in the same way as the term *NOT.* ▨

exercise 19

EVALUATE SEARCH SITES

Use a computer to access several popular search sites on the Web. Possibilities include:

Alta Vista	www.altavista.com
Ask Jeeves	www.ask.com
Dogpile	www.dogpile.com
Excite	www.excite.com
Google	www.google.com
HotBot	www.hotbot.com
Yahoo!	www.yahoo.com

Choose a specific topic that you'd like to research—preferably one related to a paper or other assignment that you will complete this term. Identify key words for this topic and enter them in several search sites. (Open up a different window in your browser for each site.) Be sure to use the same key words each time that you search.

Next, evaluate the search sites by comparing the results that you got and the following factors:

- Simplicity of the site's design and use.
- Number of results you got.
- Presence of duplicate results.
- Quality of results—that is, their relevance to your topic.
- Number of sponsored results (links to the search site's advertisers or paid sponsors) and how clearly these results are identified.
- Number of results that are "dead" links (leading you to inactive Web sites).
- Options for doing advanced searches and the ease of using those options.

Write e-mail that gets results

Target your audience

Be conscious of the amount of e-mail that busy people receive. Send e-mail messages only to the people who need them, and only when necessary.

Write an informative subject line

Along with your name, the subject line is what a recipient sees when your message shows up in his e-mail box. Rather than writing a generic description, include a capsule summary of your message. "Biology 100 Report due next Tuesday" packs more information than "Report."

Think short

Keep your subject line short, your paragraphs short, and your message as a whole short. Most people don't want to read long documents on a computer screen.

Put the point first

People who use the Internet tend to skim rather than read in detail. To make sure your point gets across, put it at the top of the first paragraph. If your message will take up more than one screen's worth of text, break it up into short sections and add a heading for each section.

Consider how long your message might be stored

Your message could dwell in a recipient's in-basket for weeks or months. Think carefully about the impact of your message, both in the short term and the long term. When composing e-mail, be courteous. Edit sentences written in the heat of a strong emotion—sentences that you might regret later.

Review your message

Every message you send—even the shortest, most informal message—says something about your attention to detail. Put your best electronic foot forward. If you plan to send a long message, draft it in a word processing program first so that you can take advantage of spelling checkers and other editing devices. Then copy the text and paste it into the body of an e-mail message. Before you hit the "Send" button, ask someone else to review the message for clarity.

Test attachments

If you plan to send an attachment, do a dry run first. You might find that it takes a couple of tries to send attachments in a format that your recipient can read. For instructions on how to prepare files as attachments, see the "Help" feature in your e-mail program.

Note: Attachments sometimes come with computer viruses that can damage your hard disk. Open attachments only from people you know, and use antivirus software.

Reply promptly and consciously

Provide context. If you're responding to a question from a previous e-mail, include that question in your response.

Be aware of everyone who will receive your reply. If you hit the "Reply to all" button, your response will go to all of the people who received the original message—including those on the "cc" (carbon copy) line. Instead, you might want to reply to just one or two of these people.

Forward messages selectively

Think twice before forwarding generic messages from other sources—cartoons, joke files, political diatribes, and "inspirational" readings. Your recipients might already have an in-basket overflowing with e-mail. Such forwarded messages might be viewed as irritating clutter.

Protect your privacy

Any competent hacker can intercept a private message. Treat all online communication as public communication. Include only content that you're willing to circulate widely, and share personal data with caution. Before sending, ask yourself: "What would be the costs if this information were made public?"

Stay on top of your in-box

Read and respond to new messages promptly. Identify messages that you might refer to again. Sort these by date received, subject, or sender—whatever will help you retrieve them later. Consider printing out essential messages, such as schedules and lists of assignments. Most e-mail programs provide an option to save messages into folders for future reference. Use this option to organize messages that you send and receive. However, if there's little chance that you will refer to a message in the future, delete it now. Tame the e-mail tiger. ⊠

Becoming an online learner

Set yourself up for successful online learning by using specific strategies before courses begin. Also consider ways to stay on top of your online assignments after the course begins.

Before courses begin

Take a First Step about technology. Before you begin your next experience with online learning, practice telling the truth about your current skills in this area. Taking a First Step can uncover hidden strengths and help you make concrete plans to develop new technology skills. The *Becoming a Master Student* Web site has a special tool for this purpose. Go online to **masterstudent. college.hmco.com** and select the link to the E-Learning Readiness Self-Assessment.

Check out the technology requirements for your courses. You can begin to prepare for online learning even before you register for a course. Contact the instructor to see if you can get a course syllabus. Ask about the specifications your computer will need to meet and the applications you'll be expected to use. Your instructor might also assume that students have a certain amount of experience with online learning, so ask about that as well.

If you're planning to use a computer lab on campus, find one with hardware and software that meets course requirements.

Keep in mind that on-campus computer labs may not allow you to install software you own or software that comes loaded on a CD included with a textbook.

Do a trial run with course technology. Most online courses have been created using course-management software like WebCT or Blackboard. You do not need to install this software to access the online course, but you will need to know the procedure, access code, and password to get into the online course site. Get the details and then verify your access to course Web sites, including online tutorials, presentations, readings, quizzes, tests, assignments, and links to other sites. Also see if you can log on to course-based bulletin boards and chat rooms. Work

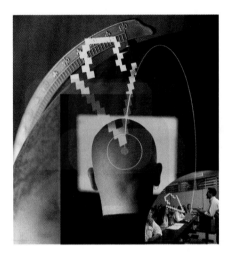

out any bugs well before the first assignment is due.

Locate support services. If you feel intimidated by technology, remember that there are living, breathing human beings who can help. Possibilities include instructors, people who staff computer labs, librarians, and on-campus technical support services. Computer dealers or manufacturers might offer similar resources, including online help and toll-free numbers for customer service. Locate helpful people and services *before* courses begin. Post their phone numbers next to your computer or in another place you can easily find them when hardware or software breaks down.

Develop a contingency plan. Murphy's Law of Computer Crashes states that technology tends to break down at the moment of greatest inconvenience. You might not find this piece of folklore to be true, but it's still wise to prepare for it in advance:

- Identify several on-campus computer labs with the technology you need.
- Find a technology buddy in each of your classes—someone who can update you on assignments and contact the instructor if you lose Internet access.
- Set up a backup e-mail account in case your Internet service provider goes offline. Many Web sites offer this service for free.
- Get complete contact information—address and office phone and fax numbers—for your instructors.
- Keep extra printer supplies—paper and toner or ink cartridges—always on hand. Don't run out of either on the day that a paper is due.

Set up files. Before classes meet, create a separate folder for each class on your computer's hard disk. Give each folder a meaningful name, such as *biology-spring2007*. Place all files related to a course in the appropriate folder. Doing this can save you from one of the main technology-related time-wasters—searching for lost files.

Also name individual files with care. Avoid changing extensions that identify different types of files, such as

.ppt for PowerPoint presentations or .pdf for files in the Adobe Reader portable document format. If you change extensions, you could have problems finding files later or sharing them with other users.

During your online courses

Take responsibility. All learning, especially online learning, depends on your initiative. Don't rely on an instructor to motivate you, particularly in courses that depend heavily on technology. Instead, manufacture your own motivation. Be clear about what you'll gain by doing well in the course. Relate course content to your personal goals. Don't wait to be contacted by your classmates and instructor. Initiate that contact on your own—right at the beginning of the course.

Manage your time. The temptation to procrastinate can be strongest with courses that take place mostly or totally online. Such courses can become invisible in your weekly academic schedule, creating the possibility of late-semester all-nighters for completing last-minute work.

Early in the term, create a detailed timeline with a due date for each assignment. Break big assignments into smaller steps and schedule a due date for each step. If possible, submit online assignments early. Staying ahead of the game will help you avoid an all-nighter at the computer during finals week.

The earlier you clarify expectations for online course work, the greater your opportunities to succeed. When you receive an online assignment, e-mail questions immediately. If you want to meet with an instructor in person, request an appointment several days in advance. In addition, download or print out online course materials as soon as they're posted on the class Web site. These materials might not be available later in the term.

Consider scheduling times in your daily or weekly calendar to complete online course work. Give these sched-uled sessions the same priority as regular classroom meetings. At these times, check for announcements relating to assignments, tests, and other course events.

Focus your attention. Some students are used to visiting Web sites while watching television, listening to loud music, or using instant messaging software. When applied to online learning, these habits can reduce your learning and imperil your grades. To succeed with technology, turn off the television, quit online chat sessions, and turn down the music. Stay in charge of your attention whenever you learn online.

Ask for feedback. To get the most from online learning, request feedback from your instructor via e-mail. When appropriate, ask for conferences by phone or in person. Be sure to check with your instructor to see how he wants e-mail messages from online course students to be addressed. Many teachers use a standard subject area format so that e-mails from online students can be quickly and easily recognized.

One powerful feature of technology is ease of file sharing. This feature makes it possible to share ideas and collaborate on projects with people who are located across campus—or around the world. Find out how to attach word processing files and other types of documents to your e-mail messages. Software such as Microsoft Word has a "tracking" feature that allows other people to insert comments into your files and even make suggested revisions. These alterations are highlighted on the screen, on a printout, or both. Use such tools to get feedback from both instructors and peers on your online assignments.

Contact other students. Make personal contact with at least one other student in each of your classes—especially those that involve lots of online course work. Meet with this person to share notes, quiz each other, critique papers, and do other cooperative learning tasks. This source of support can help you keep current with online work and promote your success. ⊠

> *If you feel intimidated by technology, remember that there are living, breathing human beings who can help.*

Thinking critically about information on the Internet

Sources of information on the Internet range from the reputable (such as the Library of Congress) to the flamboyant (such as the *National Enquirer*). This fact underscores the need for thinking critically about everything you see online.

Long before the Internet, critical thinking created value in every form of communication. Typos, mistakes, rumors, and downright lies can easily creep into print publications and television programs. Newspaper, magazine, and book publishers often employ fact checkers, editors, and lawyers to screen out errors and scrutinize questionable material before publication.

However, authors of Web pages and other Internet sources might not have these resources or choose to use them. People are free to post anything on the Internet, and this can include outdated facts as well as intentional misinformation. Do not assume that Internet content is more accurate or current than what you find in print.

Taking a few simple precautions when you surf the Internet can keep you from crashing onto the rocky shore of misinformation.

Distinguish between ideas and information. To think more powerfully about what you find on the Internet, remember the difference between information and ideas. For example, consider the following sentence: *Nelson Mandela became president of South Africa in 1994.* That statement provides information about South Africa. In contrast, the following sentence states an idea: *Nelson Mandela's presidency means that apartheid has no future in South Africa.*

Information refers to facts that can be verified by independent observers. *Ideas* are interpretations or opinions based on facts. These include statements of opinion and value judgments. Several people with the same information might adopt different ideas based on that information.

People who speak of the Internet as the "information superhighway" often forget to make the distinction between information and ideas. Don't assume that an idea is more current, reasonable, or accurate just because you find it on the Internet. Apply your critical thinking skills to all published material—print and online.

Look for overall quality. To begin thinking critically about a Web site, step back and examine the features of that site in general. Notice the effectiveness of the text and visuals as a whole. Also note how well the site is organized and whether you can navigate the site's features with ease. Look for the date that crucial information was posted, and determine how often the site is updated.

Next, take a more detailed look at the site's content. Link between several of the site's pages and look for consistency of facts, quality of information, and competency with grammar and spelling.

Also evaluate the site's links to related Web pages. Look for links to pages of reputable organizations. Click on a few of those links. If they lead you to dead ends, this might indicate a site that's not updated often—one that's not a reliable source for late-breaking information.

Look at the source. Think about the credibility of the person or organization that posts a Web site. Look for a list of author credentials and publications.

Notice evidence of bias or special interest. Perhaps the site's sponsoring organization wants you to buy a service, a product, or a point of view. If so, determine whether this fact colors the ideas and information posted on the Web site.

The domain in the Uniform Resource Locator (URL) for a Web site can give you clues about sources of information and possible bias. For example, distinguish between information from a for-profit commercial enterprise (URL ending in .com); a nonprofit organization (.org); a government agency (.gov); and a school, college, or university (.edu). In addition, reputable sites usually include a way for you to contact the author or sponsoring organization outside the Internet, including a mailing address and phone number.

Look for documentation. When you encounter an assertion on a Web page or some other Internet resource, note the types and quality of the evidence offered. Look for credible examples, quotations from authorities in the field, documented statistics, or summaries of scientific studies. Also look for source notes, bibliographies, or another way to find the original sources of information on your own.

Set an example. In the midst of the Internet's chaotic growth, you can light a path of rationality. Whether you're sending a short e-mail message or building a massive Web site, bring your own critical thinking skills into play. Every word and image that you send down the wires to the Web can display the hallmarks of critical thinking—sound logic, credible evidence, and respect for your audience. ▨

Joining online communities

Online communities come in many varieties. You can find them in three basic formats: e-mail lists, newsgroups, and chat rooms.

Listservs

Listservs consist of e-mail addresses for groups of people who want to automatically receive messages on a certain topic. To get the messages, you have to subscribe to the list.

Your instructors might use listservs to communicate with members of a class, especially when large numbers of students are involved.

When you subscribe to a listserv, you can send a message to a posting address at any time. Everyone who subscribes to the list will receive your message. Likewise, you will receive e-mails that other subscribers send to the posting address. Some lists are highly active, generating dozens of messages daily.

Newsgroups

Newsgroups—also called *Usenet groups, Web forums, bulletin boards*, and *discussion boards*—allow members to post and read e-mail messages. Usually, there is some type of subscribing process, which is often free. Once you subscribe to a group, you can choose whether you want to receive new e-mail messages as they appear, daily summaries of messages, or no e-mail messages at all. In the last case, you just view messages at the group's Web site at your convenience.

Newsgroups usually focus on a particular topic—anything from astronomy to Zen Buddhism. Some groups are moderated by a person or group that screens messages. Other groups are a free-for-all, open to any message from any person. Again, instructors might set up newsgroups for members of a class.

To access a newsgroup, you'll need special software. Today that software is often bundled into a Web browser such as Internet Explorer or an e-mail program.

Chat rooms

Chat rooms—sometimes called MUDs (multi-user domains) or MOOs (multi-user domains, object oriented)—allow you to send and receive messages live, in real time. This is as close to a live conversation as most computer users get while they're online. To join in, you'll need to download instant messaging software or use a similar application bundled with your Web browser.

Some chat rooms are set up for specific audiences and special purposes. Rooms might be ongoing or planned to last only for a limited time. For example, newspapers and magazines might create chat rooms that allow readers to discuss feature articles. Your teachers might also set up chat rooms where you and your classmates can take part in digital exchanges for the duration of a course. You might even do group exercises and role playing via chat rooms.

Consider the following suggestions for mastering online communities.

Learn the ground rules. Online communities have written policies about what kinds of messages are permitted. Often you'll receive these rules when you join. Look for a frequently asked questions (FAQ) file that explains the policies.

Stick to the topic. To make an effective contribution to the discussion, write courteous messages that are brief, informative, and relevant to the topic.

Review before you post. By observing what people write and what they don't, you'll learn the unwritten rules for that group. If you include statistics or quote material from someone else, cite the source. Avoid slang, jargon, and sarcasm, especially in class-related discussions. ✉

For more information on mastering online communities, visit

masterstudent.college.hmco.com

Library
the buried treasure

Knowing ways to unearth a library's treasures can enhance your writing, boost your presentation skills, help you plan your career, and enable you to continue learning for the rest of your life. In the early days of the Internet, researchers used to distinguish between sources published in print and sources published online. Today that distinction no longer holds so tightly. There are still benefits to actually going to a library to start your research. In addition to housing print and audiovisual materials, many libraries give you access to online sources—including special databases that are not available on the Web. Also remember that much published material is available only in print, not on the Internet. Books—a form of information technology that's been with us for centuries—still have something to offer.

Remember the best library resource. Libraries give you access to one resource that goes beyond the pages of a book or a site on the Web. That resource is a living person called a *librarian.*

Librarians have different specialties. Start with a reference librarian, who can usually tell you whether the library has the material that you want or direct you to another source, such as a business, community agency, or government office.

Librarians are trained explorers who can guide you on your expedition into the information jungle. Asking them for help can save you hours.

Take a tour. Libraries—from the smallest one in your hometown to the Smithsonian in Washington, D.C.—consist of just three basic elements:

- *Catalogs*—Online databases that list all of the library's accessible sources.
- *Collections*—Materials, such as periodicals (magazines and newspapers), books, audiovisual materials, and materials available from other collections via interlibrary loans.
- *Computer resources*—Internet access; connections to campus-wide computer networks; and databases stored on CD-ROMs, CDs, DVDs, or online. Through your library, you might have access to databases that are available only by subscription. Ask a librarian for a list of these and about how to access them.

Before you start your next research project, take some time to investigate all three elements of your campus or community library. Start with a library orientation session or tour. Step into each room and ask about what's available there. Find out whether the library houses any special collections or provides access to primary sources that are related to your major.

Search the catalog. A library's catalog lists the materials available in its collections. These listings used to be kept on index cards. Today, libraries catalog their materials on computers; some even include listings for several libraries. To find materials in a library's collections, do a keyword search—much like using a search engine on the Internet. The catalog is an alphabetical listing that is cross-referenced by subject, author, and title. Each listing carries the author's name, the title, the publisher, the date of publication, the number of pages and illustrations, the Library of Congress or Dewey decimal system number (for locating materials), and sometimes a brief description of the material. Some catalogs let you see if a book or periodical is on the shelf or checked out—and even allow you to put a hold on the materials you want.

Inspect the collection. When inspecting a library's collections, look for materials such as the following:

- *Encyclopedias*—Use leading print encyclopedias like *Encyclopaedia Britannica.* Specialized encyclopedias cover many fields and include, for example, *Encyclopedia of Psychology, Encyclopedia of the Biological Sciences, Encyclopedia of Asian History,* and *McGraw-Hill Encyclopedia of Science and Technology.*
- *Biographies*—Read accounts of people's lives in biographical works such as *Who's Who, Dictionary of American Biography,* and *Biography Index: A Cumulative Index to Biographical Material in Books and Magazines.*
- *Critical works*—Read what scholars have to say about works of art and literature in *Oxford Companion* volumes (such as *Oxford Companion to Art* and *Oxford Companion to African American Literature).*
- *Statistics and government documents*—Among many useful sources are *Statistical Abstract of the United*

States, Handbook of Labor Statistics, Occupational Outlook Handbook, and U.S. Census publications.

- *Almanacs, atlases, and gazetteers*—For population statistics and boundary changes, see *The World Almanac, Countries of the World,* or *Information Please.*

- *Dictionaries*—Consult *American Heritage Dictionary of the English Language, Oxford English Dictionary,* and other specialized dictionaries such as *Dictionary of Literary Terms and Literary Theory* and *Dictionary of the Social Sciences.*

- *Indexes and databases*—Databases contain publication information and an abstract, or sometimes the full text, of an article, available for downloading or printing from your computer. Your library houses print and CD-ROM databases and subscribes to some online databases; others are accessible through online library catalogs or Web links.

- *Reference works in specific subject areas*—These cover a vast range. Examples include the *Oxford Companion to Art, Encyclopedia of the Biological Sciences,* and *Concise Oxford Companion to Classical Literature.* Ask a librarian for more.

- *Periodical articles*—Find articles in periodicals (works issued periodically, such as scholarly journals, magazines, and newspapers) by using a periodical index. Use electronic indexes for recent works, print indexes for earlier works—especially for works written before 1980. Check to see which services your library subscribes to and the dates the indexes cover. Indexes might provide abstracts; some, such as Lexis-Nexis Academic Universe, Infotrac, OCLC FirstSearch, and *New York Times* Ondisc, provide the full text of articles. You might be able to access such indexes from a computer in your dorm room or apartment.

Access computer resources. Many libraries offer computers with Internet access. These computers are often available on a first-come, first-served basis, for free or for a nominal cost. Also remember that the Web gives you access to the online resources of many libraries. Some useful sites are Library of Congress (**http://lcweb.loc. gov**), Smithsonian Institution Libraries (**http://www. sil.si.edu/**), New York Public Library (**http://www.nypl. org/**), Internet Public Library (**http://www.ipl.org**), and WWW Virtual Library (**http://www.vlib.org**).[1]

Gain information literacy. *Information literacy* is the ability to locate, evaluate, use, and document sources of ideas and facts. Considering the variety of materials available at modern, fully equipped libraries, improving your ability to access information efficiently will help promote your success in school.

Start with the distinction between primary and secondary sources. *Primary sources* are often the researcher's dream. These are firsthand materials such as personal journals, letters, speeches, reports of scientific research, scholarly articles, field observations, archeological digs, and original works of art.

Secondary sources explain and comment on primary sources. Examples are nationally circulated newspapers such as the *Washington Post, New York Times,* and *Los Angeles Times.* Magazines with wide circulation but substantial treatment of current issues—such as the *Atlantic Monthly* and *Scientific American*—are secondary sources. So are general reference works such as the *Encyclopaedia Britannica.*

Secondary sources are useful places to start your research by getting an overview of your topic. They might even be all you need for informal research. Other research projects in higher education—major papers, presentations, theses, or manuscripts you want to publish—will call on you to find primary sources.

Once you find the sources you want, inspect each one. With print sources, look at the preface, publication data, table of contents, bibliography, glossary, endnotes, and index. (Nonprint materials, including online documents, often include similar types of information.) Also scan any headings, subheadings, and summaries. If you have time, read a chapter or section. Then evaluate sources according to their:

- *Relevance*—Look for sources that deal directly with your research questions. If you're in doubt about the relevance of a particular source, ask yourself: "Will this material help me achieve the purpose of my research and support my thesis?"

- *Currentness*—Notice the published date of your source material (usually found in the front matter on the copyright page). If your topic is time-sensitive, set some guidelines about how current you want your sources to be.

- *Credibility*—Scan the source for biographical information about the author. Look for education, training, and work experience that qualifies this person to publish on the topic. Also notice any possible sources of bias, such as political affiliations or funding sources that might color the author's point of view.

Keen researchers see facts and relationships. They focus their attention on the details, then discover unifying patterns. Far from being a mere academic exercise, library research can evolve into a path of continual discovery. ◪

Read the following two passages. Each makes a prediction about how computer technology could change our society over the next two decades.

Passage #1

Today's technology could evolve into a source of increasing tranquility. Software will search Web sites specifically for news and other information that interests you, screening out hordes of irrelevant data. Cell phones will give way to portable personal communicators that are completely voice-activated and small enough to wear on a necklace or wristband. Desktop and laptop computers will disappear from most homes as separate pieces of technology. Instead, computer chips will be embedded into most home appliances. Large, flat-panel screens—also voice-activated—will serve as a combination television, movie screen, and monitor for viewing Internet content. Rather than commuting to offices or schools, most people will work and educate themselves at home, leading to a slower, more relaxed pace of life.

Passage #2

We are on the verge of social disruption caused by technology. Advances in robotics will lead to machines that replace factory workers. White-collar workers of every variety will experience the same fate. Sophisticated automatic teller machines (ATMs) will completely replace human bank tellers. Most of the services now offered by travel agents, lawyers, accountants, tax preparers, investment advisors, and teachers will be automated in similar ways. Currently, people in these jobs stake their careers on access to special bodies of knowledge. In the future, thanks to easy-to-use software and vast digital libraries, this knowledge will be freely available to almost anyone. Many jobs will simply disappear, and it's not certain what will replace them. Massive unemployment could result in higher crime rates and urban decay along with record levels of suicide, alcoholism, and other drug addiction.

Assess the claims and evidence presented in the above passages. Then, in the space below, write a one-paragraph response—a prediction of your own about the future impact of technology. Be sure to include evidence to back up your prediction.

_____

_____

_____

_____

_____

_____

_____

_____

_____

_____

_____

_____

_____

_____

_____

_____

_____

Share your responses to this exercise on the Web and see what other students predict. Go online to

masterstudent.college.hmco.com

power process

Risk being a fool

A powerful person has the courage to take risks. And taking risks means being willing to fail sometimes—even to be a fool. This idea can work for you because you already are a fool.

Don't be upset. All of us are fools at one time or another. There are no exceptions. If you doubt it, think back to that stupid thing you did just a few days ago. You know the one. Yes . . . *that* one. It was embarrassing and you tried to hide it. You pretended you weren't a fool. This happens to everyone.

People who insist that they have never been fools are perhaps the biggest fools of all. We are all fallible human beings. Most of us, however, spend too much time and energy trying to hide our fool-hood. No one is really tricked by this—not even ourselves. And whenever we pretend to be something we're not, we miss part of life.

For example, many of us never dance because we don't want to risk looking ridiculous. We're not wrong. We probably would look ridiculous. That's the secret of risking being a fool.

It's OK to look ridiculous while dancing. It's all right to sound silly when singing to your kids. Sometimes it's OK to be absurd. It comes with taking risks.

The possibility of succeeding at any venture increases when we're comfortable with making mistakes— that is, with the risk of being a fool.

Taking risks is not being foolhardy

Sometimes it's not OK to be absurd. This Power Process comes with a warning label: Taking risks does *not* mean escaping responsibility for our actions. "Risk being a fool" is not a suggestion to get drunk at a party and make a fool of yourself. It is not a suggestion to act the fool by disrupting class. It is not a suggestion to be foolhardy or to "fool around."

"Risk being a fool" means recognizing that foolishness—along with dignity, courage, cowardice, grace, clumsiness, and other qualities—is a human characteristic. We all share it. You might as well risk being a fool because you already are one, and nothing in the world can change that. Why not enjoy it once in a while? Consider the case of the person who won't dance because he's afraid he'll look foolish. This same person will spend an afternoon tripping over his feet on a basketball court. If you say that his jump shot from the top of the key looks like a circus accident, he might even agree.

"So what?" he might say. "I'm no Michael Jordan." He's right. On the basketball court, he is willing to risk looking like a fool in order to enjoy the game.

He is no Fred Astaire, either. For some reason, that bothers him. The result is that he misses the fun of danc-

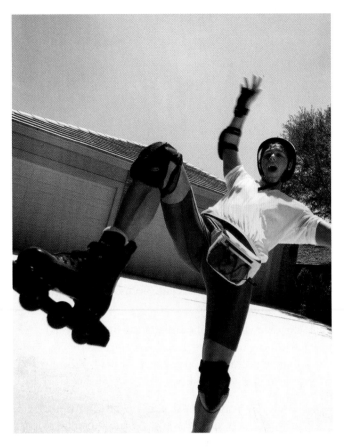

Consider these revised clichés: Anything worth doing is worth doing badly at first. Practice makes improvement. If at first you don't fail, try again.

Most artists and athletes have learned the secret of being foolish. Comedians are especially well versed in this art. All of us know how it feels to tell a joke and get complete silence. We truly look and feel like fools. Professional comedians risk feeling that way for a living. Being funny is not enough for success in the comedy business. A comedian must have the courage to face failure.

Courage is an old-fashioned word for an old-fashioned virtue. Traditionally, people have reserved that word for illustrious acts of exceptional people—the campaigns of generals and the missions of heroes.

This concept of courage is fine. At the same time, it can be limiting and can prevent us from seeing courage in everyday actions. Courage is the kindergartner who, with heart pounding, waves good-bye to his parents and boards the bus for his first day of school. Courage is the 40-year-old who registers for college courses after being away from the classroom for 20 years.

For a student, the willingness to take risks means the willingness to experiment with new skills, to achieve personal growth, and sometimes to fail. The rewards of risk taking include expanded creativity, more satisfying self-expression, and more joy.

ing. (Dancing badly is as much fun as shooting baskets badly—and maybe a lot more fun.)

There's one sure-fire way to avoid any risk of being a fool, and that's to avoid life. The writer who never finishes a book will never have to worry about getting negative reviews. The center fielder who sits out every game is safe from making any errors. And the comedian who never performs in front of an audience is certain to avoid telling jokes that fall flat. The possibility of succeeding at any venture increases when we're comfortable with making mistakes—that is, with the risk of being a fool.

Look at courage in a new way

Again, remember the warning label. This Power Process does not suggest that the way to be happy in life is to do things badly. Courage involves the willingness to face danger and risk failure. Mediocrity is not the goal. The point is that mastery in most activities calls for the willingness to do something new, to fail, to make corrections, to fail again, and so on. On the way to becoming a good writer, be willing to be a bad writer.

An experiment for you

Here's an experiment you can conduct to experience the joys of risk taking. The next time you take a risk and end up doing something silly or stupid, allow yourself to be totally aware of your reaction. Don't deny it. Don't cover it up. Notice everything about the feeling, including the physical sensations and thoughts that come with it. Acknowledge the foolishness. Be exactly who you are. Explore all of the emotions, images, and sensations surrounding your experience.

Also remember that we can act independently of our feelings. Courage is not the absence of fear but the willingness to take risks even when we feel fear. We can be keenly homesick and still register for classes. We can tremble at the thought of speaking in public yet still walk up to the microphone.

When we fully experience it, the fear of taking risks loses its power. Then we have the freedom to expand and grow. ▨

put it to work

Having a working knowledge of information technology will be an asset as you enter the workplace or change jobs.

The phrase *working knowledge* can have many different definitions over time, depending on the current state of technology and your personal goals.

You can use the cycle of discovery, intention, and action explained in this book to integrate technology continuously with your interests and career path. The idea is to continuously keep your technology skills updated for the workplace.

Step 1: Discover what you know about technology. Consider the following levels of knowledge and skill related to personal computers:

Discussing technology. People with this level of knowledge can walk into a computer store and describe what kind of hardware and software they want for home or professional use.

Performing basic functions. Examples are turning the computer off and on, opening and closing windows on a computer desktop, managing files and folders, installing software, and making backup copies of working files.

Finding information. This cluster of skills enables you to search the Internet or a library catalog to locate sources that can help you answer a specific question.

Creating and editing documents and presentations. With these types of skills, you can:

- Use a word processor to write a memo, letter, report, or research paper.

- Use a database program to organize bodies of data such as a mailing list.

- Use a spreadsheet to manage your household finances, track business expenses for your job, or run your own business.

- Use presentation software to create supporting visuals for a speech or a class you plan to teach.

Functioning in online communities. Included at this stage is the ability to use e-mail with attachments, listservs, newsgroups, chat rooms, and instant messaging software.

After reviewing the above list, write in a personal journal about your current skill with technology. Describe your strengths, along with any significant gaps in your knowledge or ability.

Step 2: Clarify your intentions for learning about technology. Next, describe what you'd like to be able to do with computer technology that you can't do now. Consider the skills you'll want to gain in order to meet your current career goals. Talk to people working in your chosen field and ask them how they use technology in their day-to-day work. Follow up by writing specifically about what you intend to learn.

Step 3: Act on your intentions. Find sources of information, ideas, and personal support as you act on your intentions to learn about technology. Options include:

- Books, periodicals, and Web sites about technology. These are available for people at all levels of technological savvy—from first-time computer users to management information specialists.

- Help screens and tutorials included with personal computer software.

- Courses offered through your school, workplace, library, or another community organization.

- A technology mentor—someone who can clearly answer your technology questions, demonstrate the skills you want to gain, and coach you as you sit at the keyboard.

Note: Plan to cycle through the above three suggestions many times in your career. Consider doing them every year to review your knowledge and update your technology skills for the workplace. ◩

Name _____ Date _____/_____/_____

quiz

1. List three strategies that you can use before courses begin to promote your success as an online learner.

2. List at least three criteria for evaluating search sites on the Web.

3. In general, you can assume that information you find on the Internet is more current and accurate than information you find in print materials. True or False? Explain your answer.

4. The Power Process in this chapter distinguishes between "being a fool" and "being foolhardy." Explain this distinction by giving an example.

5. Define the term *information literacy*.

6. List four strategies for writing effective e-mail messages.

7. Explain the difference between primary and secondary sources.

8. State the distinction between *ideas* and *information* given in this chapter and explain how it relates to thinking critically about Internet content.

9. Newsgroups are online communities that are also referred to as:
   (a) Usenet groups
   (b) Web forums
   (c) bulletin boards
   (d) discussion boards
   (e) all of the above

10. List three elements of a technology contingency plan.

learning styles application

The questions below will "cycle" you through four styles, or modes, of learning as explained in the article "Learning styles: Discovering how you learn" in Chapter One. Each question will help you explore a different mode. You can answer the questions in any order.

what if
Explain how a technique from this chapter could help you succeed as a user of technology in the workplace.

why
Name at least one benefit you could experience in school by gaining more skills with information technology. Examples of these skills include conducting Internet searches, studying online course material, accessing library materials, and joining online communities.

how
Of the techniques you gained from this chapter, choose one that you will use. Describe exactly how you intend to apply the technique.

what
List three techniques from this chapter that could significantly improve your skills as an online learner.

master student profile

MIKE LAZARIDIS

(1961–) CEO of Research in Motion and father of the Blackberry.

If we someday drive floating cars without wheels, or sprint to neighboring solar systems, it may be because physicists have learned to manipulate gravity, or reconciled the contradictions between Einstein's relativity and quantum theory, and linked the atom to the black hole.

Mr. Lazaridis says it may take a half-century to produce a major breakthrough. By then, he will be 91. He's prepared to be patient.

His company, though hardly immune to the technology-sector meltdown, is a rare creation—a tech firm that invented something people can actually name. His brainchild, the result of a white paper he wrote in three hours on his basement computer in 1997, has changed the way users talk and work and move their thumbs.

The Blackberry caught on first with stockbrokers; [today] its name is becoming as ubiquitous as Kleenex.

Slightly larger than a credit card, with a keyboard that requires thumb type, the Blackberry has spawned new slang: "Berry me," addicts say, even on Parliament Hill. Back at the Research in Motion headquarters in

Waterloo, however, everybody—including the boss they call Mike—still uses the more traditional, "Send me an e-mail."

"His curiosity is beyond bounds," says Ray Laflamme, an associate physicist at the Perimeter. "He wants to know the little details of how things work and the big pictures of where things are going. And he wants to connect the dots in between."

In high school, he juggled shop classes with the academic courses required for college. He spent hours tinkering with the equipment that a wealthy benefactor had donated to the school—an example he follows with local schools today—and it was there that he and Mr. Fregin met John Micsinszki, the electronics shop teacher. Mr. Micsinszki let the boys use the lab during the summer, and would take Mr. Lazaridis to ham-radio swap meets, where he could buy parts on the cheap.

Mr. Lazaridis is generous in his credit for all his teachers, but it was Mr. Micsinszki who once said to him: "Don't get too hooked on computers. Someday the person who puts wireless and computers together is really going to make something."

Mr. Lazaridis sat in his basement at midnight and e-mailed to his office the white paper titled "Success Lies in Paradox." When, he asked, is a tiny keyboard more efficient than a large one? When you use your thumbs.

That became the blueprint for the Blackberry, and the engineers in "the pit" went to work finding ways to keep the power demands small and the capacity big on a device then the size of a hamburger. "Have you saved a milliwatt today?" became the company's unofficial in-house slogan.

Indeed, pushing Canadians to understand the value of investing in education and basic research has become Mr. Lazaridis's self-appointed mission. He believes most of us take them for granted. Canada is too small to be good at everything, he argues, but could be world-class at many things, including raising the most educated population on earth.

A wooden model of the Avro Arrow sits on his desk at RIM—a reminder, he says, of the country's "great engineering capabilities" and the danger of missed opportunities. "We need to focus," he says. "You can't solve problems without knowledge. It's logic. If we're expecting to make the right decision, we need to be properly educated."

Reprinted with permission of *The Globe and Mail.*

For more biographical information on Mike Lazaridis, visit the Master Student Hall of Fame on the *Becoming a Master Student* Web site at

masterstudent.college.hmco.com

10

What's Next?

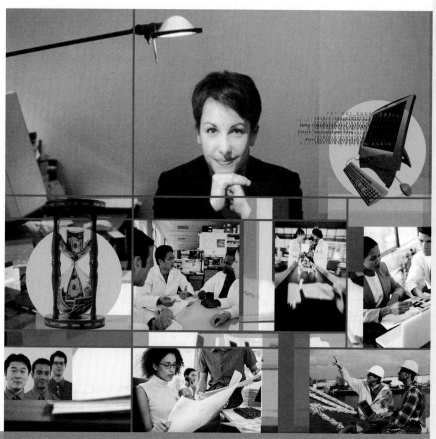

" *I believe the concept of a master student is more about a journey than a destination. It's not about straight A's or graduating at the top of the class, even though those are worthwhile goals. It doesn't end with getting a degree, either. It's more a philosophy of life, and a true master student never stops learning and growing. My journey to become a master student is just beginning.*"

—CATHY FREDERICK

why
this chapter matters . . .

You can use the techniques introduced in this book to set and achieve goals for the rest of your life.

what
is included . . .

Now that you're done—begin
". . . use the following suggestions to continue . . ."
Jumpstart your career plan
Use résumés and interviews to "hire" an employer
Cruising for jobs on the Internet
Creating and using portfolios
Service learning: The art of learning by contributing
The Discovery Wheel— Coming Full Circle
Power Process: "Be it"
Master Student Profile: Mia Hamm

how
you can use this chapter . . .

Choose the next steps in your education and career.
Document your continuing success with a portfolio.
Experience the joys of contributing.
Use a Power Process that enhances every technique in this book.

As you read, ask yourself
what if . . .

I could begin creating the life of my dreams—starting today?

Now that you're done—begin

If you used this book fully—if you actively participated in reading the contents, writing the journals, doing the exercises, practicing critical thinking, completing the learning styles applications, and applying the suggestions—you have had quite a journey.

Recall some high points of that journey. The first part of this book is about the nuts and bolts of education—the business of acquiring knowledge. It helps prepare you for making the transition to higher education and suggests that you take a First Step by telling the truth about your skills and setting goals to expand them. Also included are guidelines for planning your time, making your memory more effective, improving your reading skills, taking useful notes, and succeeding at tests. All of this activity prepares you for another aim of education—generating new knowledge and creating a unique place for yourself in the world. Meeting this aim leads you to the topics in the second part of this book: thinking for yourself, enhancing your communication skills, and mastering technology. All are steps on the path of becoming a master student. Now what? What's the next step?

As you ponder this question, consider the possibility that you can create the life of your dreams. Your responses to the ideas, exercises, and Journal Entries in this book can lead you to think new thoughts, say new things, and do what you never believed you could do. If you're willing to master new ways to learn, the possibilities are endless. This message is more fundamental than any individual tool or technique you'll ever read about.

There are people who scoff at the suggestion that they can create the life of their dreams. These people have a perspective that is widely shared. Please release it.

You are on the edge of a universe so miraculous and full of wonder that your imagination at its most creative moment cannot encompass it. Paths are open to lead you to worlds beyond your wildest dreams.

If this sounds like a pitch for the latest recreational drug, it might be. That drug is adrenaline, and it is automatically generated by your body when you are learning, growing, taking risks, and discovering new worlds inside and outside your skin. The world is packed with possibilities for master students. If you excel in adventure, exploration, discovery, and creativity, you will never lack for opportunities.

One of the first articles in this book is about transitions. You are about to make another transition—not just to another chapter of this book but to the next chapter of your life. Remember the process of discovery, intention, and action. This tool can help you master any change and achieve any goal. In the following pages, look for ways to reinforce this process. Use it to choose what's next for you. ▨

journal entry 22

Discovery/Intention Statement

Complete the following sentences with the first thoughts that come to mind.

From my life, I have discovered that I want . . .

_____

_____

_____

_____

_____

_____

_____

_____

To get what I want from my life, I intend to . . .

_____

_____

_____

_____

_____

_____

_____

_____

_____

"...use the following suggestions to continue ..."

Keep a journal. Psychotherapist Ira Progoff based his Intensive Journal System on the idea that regular journaling can be a path to life-changing insights.[1] To begin journaling, consider buying a bound notebook in which to record your private reflections and dreams for the future. Get one that will be worthy of your personal discoveries and intentions. Write in this journal daily. Record what you are learning about yourself and the world.

Take a workshop. Schooling doesn't have to stop at graduation, and it doesn't have to take place on a campus. In most cities, there are a variety of organizations that sponsor ongoing workshops, covering topics from cosmetology to cosmology. Use workshops to learn skills, understand the world, and discover yourself. You can be trained in cardiopulmonary resuscitation (CPR), attend a lecture on developing nations, or take a course on assertiveness training.

Read. Publications related to the topic of becoming a master student are recommended at the end of this book. Also ask friends and instructors what they are reading.

Take an unrelated class. Sign up for a class that is totally unrelated to your major. You can discover a lot about yourself and your intended future when you step out of old patterns.

Travel. See the world. Visit new neighborhoods. Travel to other countries. Explore. Find out what it looks like inside buildings that you normally have no reason to enter, museums that you never found interesting before, cities that are out of the way, forests and mountains that lie beyond your old boundaries, and far-off places that require planning and saving to reach.

Get counseling. Solving emotional problems is not the only reason to visit a counselor, therapist, or psychologist. These people are excellent resources for personal growth. You can use counseling to look at and talk about yourself in ways that might be uncomfortable for anyone except a trained professional.

Form a support group. Just as a well-organized study group can promote your success in school, an organized support group can help you reach goals in other areas of your life.

Find a mentor—or become one. Seek the counsel of experienced people you respect and admire. Use them as role models. If they are willing, ask them to be sounding boards for your plans and ideas. Many people are flattered to be asked.

You can also become a mentor for someone else.

Redo this book. Start by redoing one chapter or maybe just one exercise. If you didn't get everything you wanted from this book, it's not too late.

Another way to redo this book is to retake your student success course. People who do this often say that the second time is much different from the first. They pick up ideas and techniques that they missed the first time around and gain deeper insight into things they already know. ▧

exercise 20

DO SOMETHING YOU CAN'T

Few significant accomplishments result when people stick to the familiar. You can accomplish much more than you think you can.

Select something that you have never done before, that you don't know how to do, that you are fearful of doing, or that you think you probably can't do.

Be smart. Don't pick something that will hurt you physically, such as flying from a third-floor window. In your personal journal, write an Intention Statement describing exactly what you will do.

Next, do it. Put your intention into action. Of course, this is easier to say than to do. This exercise is not about easy. It is about discovering capabilities that stretch your self-image.

Finally, follow up by writing a Discovery Statement. Describe any changes in your perceived abilities as a result of doing this exercise.

Jumpstart
your career plan

A satisfying and lucrative career is often the goal of getting an education. It pays to define clearly both your career goal and your strategy for reaching that goal. Then you can plan your education effectively.

Career planning is an adventure that involves continuous exploration. There are dozens of effective paths to planning your career. Remembering the following ideas can help you begin this adventure now.

Acknowledge what you already know

When people learn study skills and life skills, they usually start with finding out things they don't know. That means discovering new strategies for taking notes, reading, writing, managing time, and the other subjects covered in this book.

Career planning is different. You can begin by realizing how much you know right now. You've already made many decisions about your career. This is true for young people who say, "I don't have any idea what I want to be when I grow up." It's also true for midlife career changers.

Consider the student who can't decide if she wants to be a cost accountant or a tax accountant and then jumps to the conclusion that she is totally lost when it comes to career planning. Another student feels equally lost because he doesn't know if he wants to be a veterinary assistant or a nurse.

These people are forgetting that they already know a lot about their career choices. The person who is debating the careers of tax accounting and cost accounting already knows that she doesn't want to be a doctor, playwright, or taxicab driver. She *does* know that she likes working with numbers and balancing books. And the person who can't decide between veterinary assistance and nursing has already ruled out becoming a lawyer, computer programmer, or teacher. He just doesn't know yet whether his bedside manner is more suitable for horses or for people.

Both of these people have already narrowed their list of career choices to a number of jobs in the same field—jobs that draw on the same core skills. In general, they already know what they want to be when they grow up.

This is probably true for you as well. To find out, do a simple exercise. First, find a long list of occupations. (One source is available online at the Occupational Informa-tion Network.) Using a stack of 3x5 cards, write down about 50 randomly selected job titles, one title per card.

Next, sort through the cards and divide them into two piles. Label one pile "Careers I've Definitely Ruled Out for Now." Label the other pile "Possibilities I'm Willing to Consider."

When you've finished sorting, notice which pile is larger. If you find that most of your cards end up in the "Definitely Ruled Out" pile, this indicates that you already have a career in mind.

See your career as your creation

Some people believe that they'll wake up one morning, see the heavens part, and receive a revelation about which career to choose. Many of them are still waiting for that magical day to dawn.

You can approach career planning in a different way. Instead of seeing a career as something you discover, view it as something that you choose. Rather than waiting to discover a single career that's exactly right for you, begin to *create* your career by choosing from several possibilities.

There's a big difference between these two approaches. Believing that the one "true" career for you will suddenly be revealed to you can lead to a lot of anxiety: "Did I discover the right one?" "What if I make a mistake?" "When will I know which career is right for me?"

In contrast, viewing your career as your own creation helps you to relax. Suppose that you've narrowed your list of possible careers to five, and you still find it hard to choose. Then just pick one. Any one. Many people will have five careers in a lifetime anyway. You might be able to do all of your careers eventually, and you may be able to begin with any career on your list. The important thing is to choose now.

One caution is in order: Choosing your career is not something to do in an information vacuum. Rather, choose after you've done a lot of research. This includes research into yourself—your skills and interests—along with a thorough knowledge of what careers are available in the workplace.

Discover your skills

Skills are the core content—the "skeleton"—of any job. A career consists of the skills that you use across several jobs in a related field. Learning the language of skills provides a key to planning your career, which can also help you choose your major.

Some students say, "I've just been taking general education and liberal arts courses. I haven't got any marketable skills." Think again. If you carefully define the word *skill*, you'll probably discover the you already have many skills to succeed in the workplace.

Some skills—such as the ability to repair fiber optic cables or perform brain surgery—are acquired through formal schooling, on-the-job training, or both. These abilities are called *content skills*. They reflect how much you know about a specific subject or how well you can perform a particular procedure. The ability to speak Spanish is a content skill. So are the abilities to program a computer, repair a car transmission, fix a broken television, or play the piano in a jazz band. All these activities call for specialized knowledge and activity.

However, there is another category of skills that we develop through experiences both inside and outside the classroom. We may never receive formal training to develop these abilities, yet they are key to success in the workplace. These are *transferable skills*.

Perhaps you've heard someone described in this way: "She knows what she's doing, but she's got lousy people skills." People skills—such as *listening* and *negotiating*—are transferable skills. Others include:

Analyzing
Attending to detail
Budgeting
Calculating
Coaching
Consulting
Counseling
Decision making
Drawing
Editing
Estimating costs
Evaluating
Interviewing
Learning
Managing time
Organizing
Planning
Problem solving
Reading
Researching
Selling
Serving customers
Speaking
Supervising
Thinking critically
Training
Working on teams
Writing

This is only a partial list. You can learn to recognize many more transferable skills. In fact, each chapter in this book covers a set of transferable skills—managing time, remembering information, reading, taking notes, and more.

Transferable skills apply across many different content areas. For example, if you do well at writing term papers in history, you can probably write well about English literature, computers, or just about anything else. Likewise, transferable skills help people thrive in any job—no matter what content skills they have. For example, you could transfer your skill at writing papers to a possible career in journalism, technical writing, or advertising copywriting. Just take your cue from the word *transferable*. Skills that you use to succeed in one situation can often *transfer* to success in another situation.

Recognizing all of your skills—content and transferable—can multiply your career options like magic. Say that you work part-time as an administrative assistant at a computer business that sells a variety of hardware and software. You take phone calls from potential customers, help current customers solve problems using their computers, and attend meetings at which your coworkers plan ways to market new products. You are developing skills at *selling, serving customers,* and *working on teams*. The same skills could help you land a job as a sales representative for a computer manufacturer or software developer.

The concept of transferable skills creates a powerful link between higher education and the work world. Many of the skills you're developing right now in school can be applied to your career.

The U.S. Department of Labor issued a series of reports created by the Secretary's Commission on Achieving Necessary Skills (SCANS). This influential series of documents lists essential skills for workers in the twenty-first century. You might find this list helpful in assessing your current skills and planning to develop new ones. Access it online by keying the title of the report into a search engine.

Plan by naming names

One step to a powerful career plan is to put it in writing. As you do, include names. Be specific. For example:

- *Name your job.* Take the skills you enjoy using and find out which jobs call for those skills. What are those jobs named? List them. Note that the same job might have different names.

- *Name your company—the agency or organization you want to work for.* If you want to be self-employed or start your own business, name the product or service you'd sell. Also list some possible names for your business. If you plan to work for others, name the organizations or agencies that are high on your list.

- *Name your contacts.* Take the list of organizations you just compiled. What people in these organizations are responsible for hiring? List those people and contact them directly. If you choose self-employment, list the names of possible customers or clients. All of these people are job contacts.

Expand your list of contacts by brainstorming with your family and friends. Come up with a list of names—anyone who can help you with career planning and job hunting. These people are your "contacts." Write each of these names on a 3x5 card or Rolodex card. You can also use a spiral-bound notebook or a computer to keep track of your contacts.

Next, call your contacts. After you speak with them, make brief notes about what you discussed. Also jot down any actions you agreed to take, such as making a follow-up call.

Consider everyone you meet to be a potential contact, and be prepared to talk about your career plan. Develop a "pitch"—a short statement of your career goal that you can easily share with your contacts. For example: "My major is architecture. I'm looking for an internship in an architecture firm for next summer. Do you know of any firms that hire interns?"

Remember your purpose

While digging deep into the details of career planning, take some time to back up to the big picture. Listing skills, researching jobs, and writing résumés are necessary and useful things to do. At the same time, attending only to these tasks can obscure our broadest goals. To get perspective, go back to the basics—a life purpose.

Your deepest desire might be to see that hungry children are fed, to make sure that beautiful music keeps getting heard, or to help alcoholics become sober. When such a large purpose is clear, smaller decisions about what to do are often easier.

A life purpose cuts through the stacks of job data and employment figures. Your life purpose is like the guidance system for a rocket. It keeps the plan on target while revealing a path for soaring to the heights.

Test your career choice—and be willing to change it

Once you have a possible career choice in mind, run some informal tests to see if it will work for you. For example:

- Contact people who are actually doing the job you're researching and ask them what it's like (an *information interview*).

- Choose an internship or volunteer position in a field that interests you.

- Get a part-time or summer job in your career field.

Skills that you use to succeed in one situation can often transfer to success in another situation.

The people you meet through these experiences are possible sources of recommendations, referrals, and future employment.

As you test your trial choice of career, keep opening up other options. Read books about careers and search for career-planning Web sites. Ask career counselors about skills assessments that can help you discover more about your skills and identify jobs that call for those skills. Take career-planning courses and workshops sponsored by your school. Become a regular visitor at the career-planning and job placement offices on campus.

Career planning is not a once-and-for-all proposition. Rather, career plans are made to be changed and refined as you gain new information about yourself and the world. If your present career no longer feels right, you can choose again—no matter what stage of life you're in. The process is the same whether you're choosing your first career or your fifth. ◪

RECOGNIZE YOUR SKILLS

This exercise about discovering your skills includes three steps. Before you begin, gather at least 100 3x5 cards and a pen or pencil. Allow about one hour to complete the exercise.

Step 1

Recall your activities during the past week or month. To refresh your memory, review your responses to the Time Monitor/Time Plan in Chapter Two. (You might even benefit from doing that exercise again.)

Write down as many activities as you can, listing each one on a separate 3x5 card. Include work-related activities, school activities, and hobbies. Some of your cards might read "washed dishes," "tuned up my car," or "tutored a French class."

In addition to daily activities, recall any rewards you've received or recognition of your achievements during the past year. Examples include scholarship awards, athletic awards, or recognitions for volunteer work. Again, list the activities that were involved.

Spend 20 minutes on this step, listing all of the activities you can recall.

Step 2

Next, look over your activity cards. Then take another 20 minutes to list any specialized knowledge or procedures needed to complete those activities. These are your *content skills*. For example, tutoring a French class requires a working knowledge of that language. Tuning a car requires knowing how to adjust a car's timing and replace spark plugs. You could list several content skills for any one activity. Write each skill on a separate card and label it "Content."

Step 3

Go over your activity cards one more time. Look for examples of *transferable skills*. For instance, giving a speech or working as a salesperson in a computer store requires the ability to persuade people. That's a transferable skill. Tuning a car means that you can attend to details and troubleshoot. Tutoring in French requires teaching, listening, and speaking skills.

Write each of your transferable skills on a separate card.

Congratulations—you now have a detailed picture of your skills. Keep your lists of content and transferable skills on hand when writing your résumé, preparing for job interviews, and other career-planning tasks. As you think of new skills, add them to the lists.

Use résumés and interviews to "hire" an employer

The logical outcome of your career plan is a focused job hunt. Mention the phrase *job hunting,* and many people envision someone poring through the help wanted sections in newspapers or on Web sites, sending out hundreds of résumés, or enlisting the services of employment agencies to find job openings and set up interviews.

Richard Bolles—author of *What Color Is Your Parachute?*—points out a fatal shortcoming of these job-hunting strategies: Most job openings are never advertised. Many employers turn to help wanted listings, résumés, and employment agencies only as a last resort. When jobs open up, they prefer instead to hire people they know—friends and colleagues—or people who walk through the door and prove that they're excellent candidates for available jobs.[2] Your best source of information about new jobs is people—friends, relatives, coworkers, and fellow students. Ask around. Tell everyone you want a job. In particular, tell people who might be able to create a job for you. Some jobs are created on the spot when a person with potential simply shows up and asks.

Use résumés to get interviews

A résumé is a piece of persuasive writing, not a dry recitation of facts or a laundry list of previous jobs. It has a basic purpose—to get you to the next step in the hiring process, usually an interview.

Begin your résumé with your name, address, phone number, and e-mail address. Then name your desired job, often called an "objective" or "goal." Follow with the body of your résumé—your skills, work experience, and education. In fact, you can use those last three topics as major headings printed in bold in a larger font. Also leave reasonable margins and space between paragraphs.

Write your résumé so that the facts leap off the page. Describe your work experiences in short phrases that start with active verbs: "*Supervised* three people." "*Wrote* two annual reports." "*Set up* sales calls." Whenever you can, give evidence that you used those skills to get measurable results. For example: "Our program reduced the average training time for newly hired people by 25 percent."

Use interviews to screen employers

You might think of job interviews as a time when a potential employer sizes you up and possibly screens you out. Consider another viewpoint—that interviews offer you a chance to size up potential employers and possibly screen *them* out.

To get the most from your interviews, learn everything you can about each organization that interests you. Get a feel for its strong points and know about its successes in the marketplace. Also find out what challenges the organization faces. As in a résumé, use interviews to present your skills as unique solutions for those challenges.

Job interviewers have many standard questions. Most of them boil down to a few major concerns:

- How did you find out about us?
- Would we be comfortable working with you?
- How can you help us?
- Will you learn this job quickly?
- What makes you different from other applicants?

Before your interview, prepare some answers to these questions.

If you get turned down for the job after your interview, don't take it personally. Every interview is a source of feedback about what works—and what doesn't work—in contacting employers. Use that feedback to interview more effectively next time.[3]

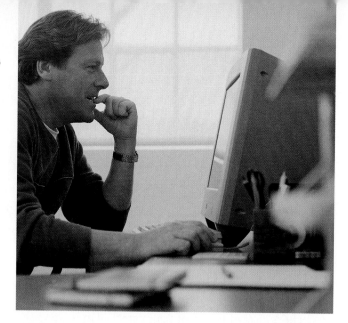

odern technology is creating new ways for you to plan your career and find jobs in the future. On the World Wide Web, you can research companies you'd like to work for, read lists of job openings, and post your résumé and a digital recording of yourself. Through faxes, overnight deliveries, mobile phones, and e-mail, you can stay in continual contact with potential employers. Widespread availability of high-speed Internet access has increased the number of long-distance job interviews being conducted via video conference or in a real time chat room, and has increased the possibility of sending an electronic portfolio attachment with a résumé.

According to one estimate, about two million people go online every month to hunt for jobs. That's a testament to the potential power of the digital medium and to some of its pitfalls as well. When you're looking for a job, the strength of the Internet—the sheer density of data—can also lead to frustration:

- The haphazard organization of the Internet makes it hard for potential employers to find your résumé when you post it online. The organizations you most want to work for might avoid using the Internet to find job applicants.

- Job openings listed on the Internet can be heavily skewed to certain fields, such as jobs for computer professionals or people in other technical fields.

- Across all fields, the majority of job openings are not listed on the Internet (or in newspaper want ads, for that matter).

This is not meant to disparage the Internet as a tool for job hunters and career planners. The point is that posting a résumé on a Web site will not automatically lead to an e-mail in-basket that's bursting to its digital seams with job offers. For an effective job search, view the Internet as just one resource.

With this caveat in mind, you might choose to post your résumé online and scan Internet job ads. If you do, begin with sites such as that for JobBank USA (**http://www.jobbankusa.com**), which links to over 20 search engines for finding job openings. Also check CareerBuilder.com (**http://www.CareerBuilder.com**) for want ads, updated weekly, from major U.S. newspapers. When responding to ads and posting résumés online, avoid some common mistakes. One is to use word processing software to create lots of fancy formatting for your résumé and then attach it to an e-mail message. Many Web sites are not powerful enough to handle such formatting and will garble your attachments. Instead, skip the word processing and paste your résumé right

Cruising for jobs on the Internet

into an e-mail message. Proofread it one more time before you hit the "Send" button.

Some people create personal Web pages to highlight their accomplishments and entice employers. If you go this route, keep your page simple and easy to download. Some Web hosts will want to run banner ads on your page. These ads are widely seen as tacky. Avoid them.

Even if you don't choose to post a digital résumé or Web page, you can access career-planning resources on the Internet. Begin with "gateway" sites that offer organized links to many career-related pages on the World Wide Web. For instance, the Riley Guide (**http://www.rileyguide.com**) gives an overview of job hunting on the Internet.

Also check JobHuntersBible.com (**http://www.jobhuntersbible.com**), a site maintained by Richard Bolles, author of *What Color Is Your Parachute?* This site focuses on effective ways to use the Internet. And for some revealing figures, visit sites such as Salary.com to find out the current pay scales of typical jobs in your field. One way in which the Internet can really help you is in researching organizations before you contact them. Chances are good that the company you're interested in has a Web site. Go to the site to gather information, discover the names of key players, and view financial data. Doing so will show potential employers that you've done your homework. That can make a favorable impression and even land you a job. ◻

Intention Statement

Even if you are not sure of your career preference, write a career plan right now. Include three elements: a career goal, a list of steps you can take to prepare for that career, and a timeline for reaching that career goal.

Your plan might be incomplete or tentative. No problem. You can change this plan later—or even throw it out and start all over. Career planning is a continual cycle of discovery, intention, and feedback.

The point is to dive into the process and make career planning a lifelong habit. This habit can radically affect the quality of your life.

You can plan now, with no further research. Go ahead. There's nothing to lose and lots of space to write in. Make an outline, do a mind map—use any format you like. Discover what you already know.

Mind map, outline, or write down your career plan now. Begin using the following space and continue as needed on a sheet of separate paper. You can also use a computer for this purpose.

Creating and using portfolios

In medieval times, artisans who wished to join a guild presented samples of their work. Furniture makers showed cabinets and chairs to their potential mentors. Painters presented samples of their sketches and portraits. Centuries later, people still value a purposeful collection of work samples. It is called a portfolio.

The word *portfolio* derives from two Latin terms: *port,* which means "to move," and *folio,* which means "papers" or "artifacts."[4] True to these ancient meanings, portfolios are movable collections of papers and artifacts.

Portfolios differ from résumés. A résumé lists facts, including your interests, skills, work history, and accomplishments. Although a portfolio might include these facts, it also includes tangible objects to verify the facts— anything from transcripts of your grades to a videotape that you produced. Résumés offer facts; portfolios provide artifacts.

Photographers, contractors, and designers regularly show portfolios filled with samples of their work. Today, employers and educators increasingly see the portfolio as a tool that's useful for everyone. Some schools require students to create them, and some employers expect to see a portfolio before they'll hire a job applicant.

Enjoy the benefits—academic, professional, and personal

A well-done portfolio benefits its intended audience. To an instructor, your portfolio gives a rich, detailed picture of what you did to create value from a class. To a potential employer, your portfolio gives observable evidence of your skills and achievements. In both cases, a portfolio also documents something more intangible—your levels of energy, passion, and creativity.

Portfolios benefit you in specific ways. When you create a portfolio to document what you learned during a class, you review the content of the entire course. When you're creating a portfolio related to your career, you think about the skills you want to develop and ways to showcase those skills. And when you're applying for work, creating a portfolio prepares you for job interviews. Your portfolio can stand out from stacks of letters and résumés and distinguish you from other applicants.

Creating a portfolio helps you reflect on your life as a whole. When selecting artifacts to include in your portfolio, you celebrate your accomplishments. You discover key themes in your experience. You clarify what's important to you and create goals for the future. Portfolios promote the cycle of discovery, intention, and action presented in Journal Entries and exercises throughout this text. To create a portfolio, experiment with a four-step process:

1. Collect and catalog artifacts.

2. Plan your portfolio.

3. Assemble your portfolio.

4. Present your portfolio.

Collect and catalog artifacts. An artifact is any object that's important to you and that reveals something about yourself. Examples include photographs, awards, recommendation letters, job descriptions for positions you've held, newspaper articles about projects you've done, lists of grants or scholarships you've received, programs from performances you've given, transcripts of your grades, or models you've constructed.

Taken together, your artifacts form a large and visible "database" that gives a picture of you—what you value, what you've done, and what skills you have. You can add to this database during every year of your life. From this constantly evolving collection of artifacts, you can create many portfolios for different purposes and different audiences.

Start collecting now. Write down the kinds of artifacts you'd like to save. Think about what will be most useful to you in creating portfolios for your courses and your job search. In some cases, collecting artifacts requires follow-up. You might call former instructors or employers to request letters of recommendation. Or you might track down newspaper articles about a service-learning project you did.

To save hours when you create your next portfolio, start documenting your artifacts. On a 3x5 card, record the "five W's" about each artifact: *who* was involved with it, *what* you did with it, *when* it was created, *where* it was created, and *why* the artifact is important to you. File these cards and update them as you collect new artifacts. Another option is to manage this information with a computer, using word processing or database software.

Plan your portfolio. When you're ready to create a portfolio for a specific audience, allow some time for planning. Begin with your purpose for creating the portfolio—for example, to demonstrate your learning or to document your work experience as you prepare for a job interview.

Also list some specifics about your audience. Write a description of anyone who will see your portfolio. List what each person already knows about you and predict what else these people will want to know. Answer their questions in your portfolio.

Being aware of your purpose and audience will serve you at every step of creating a portfolio. Screen artifacts with these two factors in mind. If a beautiful artifact fails to meet your purpose or fit your audience, leave it out for now. Save the artifact for a future portfolio.

Assemble your portfolio. With a collection of artifacts and a written plan, you're ready to assemble your portfolio. Arrange artifacts according to your design. Also include elements to orient your audience members and guide them through your portfolio. Such elements can include:

■ A table of contents.

■ An overview or summary of the portfolio.

■ Titles and captions for each artifact.

■ An index to your artifacts.

Although many portfolios take their final form as a collection of papers, remember that this is just one possibility. You can also create a bulletin board, a display, or a case that contains your artifacts. You could even create an audio or video recording or a digital portfolio in the form of a personal audio or video Web site.

Present your portfolio. Present your portfolio to friends and people in your career field, and request their feedback. That feedback will give you plenty of ideas about ways to revise your portfolio. A portfolio is a living document. Update it as you acquire new perspectives and skills. ⊠

Service learning
The art of learning by contributing

As part of a service-learning project for a sociology course, students volunteer at a community center for older adults. For another service-learning project, history students interview people in veterans' hospitals about their war experiences. These students plan to share their interview results with a psychiatrist on the hospital staff.

Meanwhile, business students provide free tax-preparation help at a center for low-income people. Students in graphic arts classes create free promotional materials for charities. Other students staff a food cooperative and community credit union.

These examples of actual projects from the National Service-Learning Clearinghouse demonstrate the working premise of service learning—that volunteer work and other forms of contributing can become a vehicle for higher education.

Service starts with selfishness. To get the most from service learning, consider an unusual idea: Giving to others follows from giving to yourself. In fact, this book urges you to be selfish—to get whatever *you* want out of your education and the rest of your life.

One result of successful selfishness is the capacity to contribute to others. Contributing is what's left to do when your own needs have been fulfilled. People who are satisfied with life can share that satisfaction with others. It is not easy to contribute to another person's joy until you experience joy yourself.

Also remember that our lives depend on mutual contribution. Every time that we ride in a car or board a plane, for example, we depend on others for our lives. Each day, we depend upon the sensibilities of countless people—from cab drivers to world leaders—for our safety. Service learning is a natural extension of this idea. This form of learning reminds us that human beings depend on each other in order to survive.

One caution: Contributing is not the same as knowing what is best for other people. We can't know. True contributing occurs only after you find out what other people want or need and then determine that you can lovingly support their having it.

Plan for service learning. When you design a service-learning project, remember to:

- Work with a community agency that has experience with students. Make sure that the agency has liability insurance to cover volunteers.

- Handle logistics. Integrating service learning into your schedule can call for detailed planning. If your volunteer work takes place off campus, arrange for transportation and allow for travel time. Also arrange to get academic credit for your participation.

- Reflect on your service-learning project. Write Discovery Statements about what you want to gain from service learning and how you feel about what you're doing. Follow up with Intention Statements about what you'll do differently for another project.

- Include ways to evaluate your project. From your Intention Statements, create action goals and outcome goals. *Action goals* state what you plan to do and how many people you intend to serve—for instance, "We plan to provide 100 hours of literacy tutoring to 10 people in the community." *Outcome goals* describe the actual impact that your project will have: "At the end of our project, 60 percent of the people we tutor will be able to write a résumé and fill out a job application." Build numbers into your goals whenever possible. That makes it easier to evaluate the success of your project.

- Create a way to build long-term impact into your project. Find other students or community members who are willing to step in and take over for you when the term ends.

- Celebrate mistakes. If your project fails to meet its goals, have a party. State—in writing—the obstacles you encountered and ways to overcome them. The solutions you offer will be worth gold to the people who follow in your footsteps. Sharing the lessons learned from your mistakes is an act of service in itself. ✉

PRACTICING CRITICAL THINKING

10

Critical thinking includes the habit of persistence. Skilled thinkers know that some ideas call for continual testing. These people recognize insights that have implications for action over many weeks, months, or years.

Becoming a Master Student is designed to promote this kind of insight and action. The book presents far more success strategies than you can apply during a single term. Some of its suggestions might not apply to your life right now. However, those same suggestions could become useful next month, next term, or next year.

With this thought in mind, plan to keep *Becoming a Master Student* and use it again. Imagine that your book has a mouth. (Visualize the mouth.) Also imagine that it has arms and legs. (Visualize them.) Picture your book sitting on a shelf or table that you see every day. Imagine a time when you might be having trouble in school and struggling to be successful as a student. Visualize your book jumping up and down, shouting, "Use me! Read me! I might have the solution to your problem, and I know I can help you solve it."

Other ways to continue the process you started with *Becoming a Master Student* are these:

* Keep it on the coffee table, in the kitchen, or in the bathroom.

* Keep it near your bedroom nightstand.

* Loan the book to someone else; then talk about it with that person.

* Teach your favorite suggestions from this book to your friends and family members.

* Tear out specific articles and share them with family members or friends.

* In your calendar or appointment book, schedule periodic times to review *Becoming a Master Student*.

In addition, take a few minutes to review your responses to the exercises and journal entries throughout this book. In the space below, list five major discoveries that you made during this course—insights to take with you for the future.

_____

_____

_____

_____

_____

_____

_____

_____

_____

Now revisit the intentions you created while using this book. These may include goals that go well beyond the end of this course. List five such goals below. If possible, include goals that relate to your choice of major and your career plan.

_____

_____

_____

_____

_____

_____

_____

_____

_____

_____

_____

_____

THE DISCOVERY WHEEL—COMING FULL CIRCLE

Do this exercise online at `masterstudent.college.hmco.com`

This book doesn't work. It is worthless. Only you can work. Only you can make a difference and use this book to become a more effective student.

The purpose of this book is to give you the opportunity to change your behavior.

The fact that some-thing seems like a good idea doesn't necessarily mean that you will put it into practice. This exercise gives you a chance to see what behaviors you have changed on your journey toward becoming a master student.

Answer each question quickly and honestly. Record your results on the Discovery Wheel on this page and

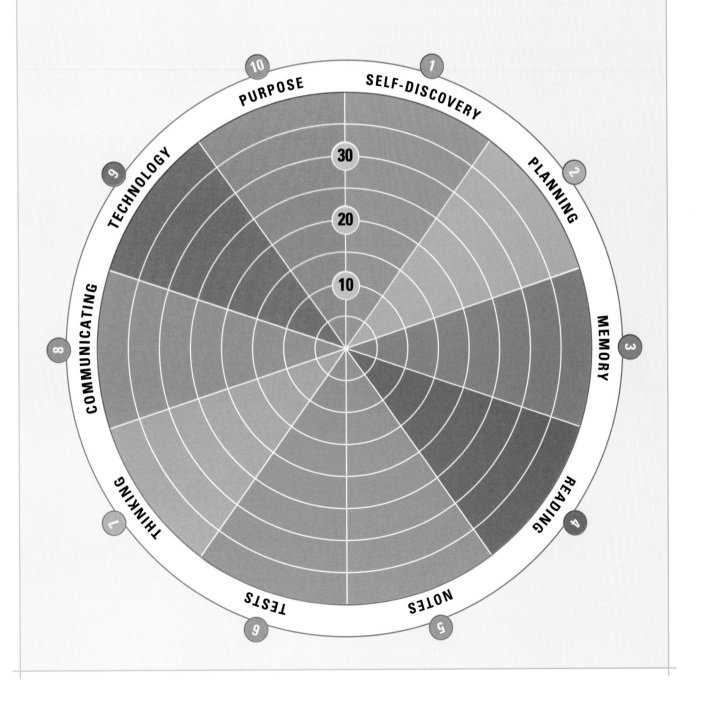

then compare it with the one you completed in Chapter One.

The scores on this Discovery Wheel indicate your current strengths and weaknesses on your path toward becoming a master student. The last Journal Entry in this chapter provides an opportunity to write about how you intend to change. As you complete this self-evaluation, keep in mind that your commitment to change allows you to become a master student. *Your scores might be lower here than on your earlier Discovery Wheel.* That's OK. Lower scores might result from increased self-awareness and honesty, and other valuable assets.

Note: The online version of this exercise does not include number ratings, so the results will be formatted differently than those described here. If you did your previous Discovery Wheel online, do it online again. This will help you compare your two sets of responses more accurately.

5 points
This statement is always or almost always true of me.

4 points
This statement is often true of me.

3 points
This statement is true of me about half the time.

2 points
This statement is seldom true of me.

1 point
This statement is never or almost never true of me.

1. _____ I enjoy learning.
2. _____ I understand and apply the concept of multiple intelligences.
3. _____ I connect my courses to my purpose for being in school.
4. _____ I make a habit of assessing my personal strengths and areas for improvement.
5. _____ I am satisfied with how I am progressing toward achieving my goals.
6. _____ I use my knowledge of learning styles to support my success in school.
7. _____ I am willing to consider any idea that can help me succeed in school—even if I initially disagree with that idea.
8. _____ I regularly remind myself of the benefits I intend to get from my education.

_____ Total score (1) *Motivation*

1. _____ I set long-term goals and periodically review them.
2. _____ I set short-term goals to support my long-term goals.
3. _____ I write a plan for each day and each week.
4. _____ I assign priorities to what I choose to do each day.
5. _____ I plan regular recreation time.
6. _____ I adjust my study time to meet the demands of individual courses.
7. _____ I have adequate time each day to accomplish what I plan.
8. _____ I am confident that I will find the resources to finance my education.

_____ Total score (2) *Planning*

1. _____ I am confident of my ability to remember.
2. _____ I can remember people's names.
3. _____ At the end of a lecture, I can summarize what was presented.
4. _____ I apply techniques that enhance my memory skills.
5. _____ I can recall information when I'm under pressure.

6. _____ I remember important information clearly and easily.

7. _____ I can jog my memory when I have difficulty recalling.

8. _____ I can relate new information to what I've already learned.

_____ Total score (3) *Memory*

1. _____ I preview and review reading assignments.

2. _____ When reading, I ask myself questions about the material.

3. _____ I underline or highlight important passages when reading.

4. _____ When I read textbooks, I am alert and awake.

5. _____ I relate what I read to my life.

6. _____ I select a reading strategy to fit the type of material I'm reading.

7. _____ I take effective notes when I read.

8. _____ When I don't understand what I'm reading, I note my questions and find answers.

_____ Total score (4) *Reading*

1. _____ When I am in class, I focus my attention.

2. _____ I take notes in class.

3. _____ I am aware of various methods for taking notes and choose those that work best for me.

4. _____ I distinguish important material and note key phrases in a lecture.

5. _____ I copy down material that the instructor writes on the chalkboard or overhead projector.

6. _____ I can put important concepts into my own words.

7. _____ My notes are valuable for review.

8. _____ I review class notes within 24 hours.

_____ Total score (5) *Notes*

1. _____ I feel confident and calm during an exam.

2. _____ I manage my time during exams and am able to complete them.

3. _____ I am able to predict test questions.

4. _____ I adapt my test-taking strategy to the kind of test I'm taking.

5. _____ I understand what essay questions ask and can answer them completely and accurately.

6. _____ I start reviewing for tests at the beginning of the term.

7. _____ I continue reviewing for tests throughout the term.

8. _____ My sense of personal worth is independent of my test scores.

_____ Total score (6) *Tests*

1. _____ I have flashes of insight and often think of solutions to problems at unusual times.

2. _____ I use brainstorming to generate solutions to a variety of problems.

3. _____ When I get stuck on a creative project, I use specific methods to get unstuck.

4. _____ I see problems and tough decisions as opportunities for learning and personal growth.

5. _____ I am willing to consider different points of view and alternative solutions.

6. _____ I can detect common errors in logic.

7. _____ I construct viewpoints by drawing on information and ideas from many sources.

8. _____ As I share my viewpoints with others, I am open to their feedback.

_____ Total score (7) *Thinking*

1. _____ I am candid with others about who I am, what I feel, and what I want.

2. _____ Other people tell me that I am a good listener.

3. _____ I can communicate my upset and anger without blaming others.

4. _____ I can make friends and create valuable relationships in a new setting.

5. _____ I can effectively resolve conflict.

6. _____ I can persuade others to accept my ideas by writing a research paper or speaking in public.

7. _____ I am aware of my biases and am open to understanding people from other cultures, races, and ethnic groups.

8. _____ I can point out examples of discrimination and sexual harassment and effectively respond to them.

_____ Total score (8) *Communicating*

1. _____ I learn effectively from course materials and activities that are posted online.

2. _____ I can efficiently find information on the Internet.

3. _____ I think critically about information and ideas that I access online.

4. _____ I write clear and concise e-mail messages that generate the results I want.

5. _____ My online communication is fair and respectful to other people.

6. _____ I monitor new technology that can support my success in school.

7. _____ I monitor new technology that can support my success in my career.

8. _____ I effectively use libraries to find the resources and information I want.

_____ Total score (9) *Technology*

1. _____ I see learning as a lifelong process.

2. _____ I relate school to what I plan to do for the rest of my life.

3. _____ I learn by contributing to others.

4. _____ I revise my plans as I learn, change, and grow.

5. _____ I am clear about my purpose in life.

6. _____ I know that I am responsible for my own education.

7. _____ I take responsibility for the quality of my life.

8. _____ I am willing to accept challenges even when I'm not sure how to meet them.

_____ Total score (10) *Purpose*

Filling in your Discovery Wheel

Using the total score from each category, shade in each section of the Discovery Wheel on page 237. Use different colors, if you want. For example, you could use green to denote areas you want to work on. When you have finished, complete the following Journal Entry.

journal entry 24

Discovery/Intention Statement

The purpose of this Journal Entry is to (1) review both of the Discovery Wheels you completed in this book, (2) summarize your insights from doing them, and (3) declare how you will use these insights to promote your continued success in school.

Again, a lower score on the second Discovery Wheel does not necessarily indicate decreased personal effectiveness. Instead, the lower score could result from increased honesty and greater self-awareness.

	Chapter 1	Chapter 10
Motivation		
Time		
Memory		
Reading		
Notes		
Tests		
Thinking		
Communicating		
Technology		
Purpose		

Comparing the Discovery Wheel in this chapter with the Discovery Wheel in Chapter One, I discovered that I . . .

_____

_____

_____

_____

_____

_____

_____

In the next six months, I intend to review the following articles from this book for additional suggestions I could use:

_____

_____

_____

_____

_____

_____

_____

→ Transferring to another school

Transferring to a different school involves making a decision that will have a major impact on your education. This is true at many points in higher education—when you're transferring from a two-year to a four-year school, or when you're choosing a graduate school.

Selecting a school for the next step in your higher education is like choosing a career. First, you define the profile of an ideal prospective school, much as you would that of an ideal job. Next, you create a profile of yourself—your skills, background, experience, learning style, and other preferences. Then you seek a reasonable fit between yourself and your ideal job.

Start by digging up facts about each school you're considering. Identify the number of students, the class sizes, the student to faculty ratio, the admissions criteria, the availability of degrees, the costs, and the location. Remember, there is no one "right" school for you, and you could probably thrive at many schools (perhaps even your current one).

power process

Be it

All of the techniques in this book are enhanced by this Power Process.

To tap into its full benefits, consider that most of our choices in life fall into three categories. We can:

- Increase our material wealth (what we have).
- Improve our skills (what we do).
- Develop our "being" (who we are).

Many people devote their entire lifetime to the first two categories. They act as if they are "human havings" instead of human beings. For them, the quality of life hinges on what they have. They devote most of their waking hours to getting more—more clothes, more cars, more relationships, more degrees, more trophies. "Human havings" define themselves by looking at the circumstances in their lives—what they have.

Some people escape this materialist trap by adding another dimension to their identities. In addition to living as "human havings," they also live as "human doings." They thrive on working hard and doing everything well. They define themselves by how efficiently they do their jobs, how effectively they raise their children, and how actively they participate in clubs and organizations. Their thoughts are constantly about methods, techniques, and skills.

Look beyond doing and having

In addition to focusing on what we have and what we do, we can also focus on our being. While it is impossible to live our lives without having things and doing things, this Power Process suggests that we balance our experience by giving lots of attention to who we are—an aspect of our lives that goes beyond having and doing. Call it *soul, passion, purpose,* or *values*. Call it *being*. This word describes how we see ourselves—our deepest commitments, the ground from which our actions spring.

The realm of being is profound and subtle. It is also difficult to capture in words, though philosophers have tried for centuries. Christian theologian Paul Tillich described this realm when he defined *faith* as "ultimate commitment" and the "ground of being." In the New Testament, Jesus talked about being when he asked his followers to love God with all of their heart, soul, and mind. An ancient Hindu text also touches on being: "You are what your deep, driving desire is."

If all this seems far removed from taking notes or answering test questions, read on. Consider an example of how "Be it" can assist in career choices. In a letter to his father, a young man wrote:

We just went to see the Dance Theatre of Harlem. It was great! After the last number, I decided that I want to dance more than anything. I have a great passion to do it, more than anything else I can think or dream of. Dancing is what will make me happy and feel like I can leave this earth when my time comes. It is what I must do. I think that if I never fulfill this passion, I will never feel complete or satisfied with what I have done with my life.

In his heart, this man *is* a dancer now, even before his formal training is complete. From his passion, desire, commitment, and self-image (his *being*) comes his willingness to take classes and rehearse (*doing*). And from his doing he might eventually *have* a job with a professional dance company.

Picture the result as you begin

The example of the dancer illustrates that once you have a clear picture of what you want to *be,* the things you *do* and *have* fall more naturally into place.

The idea is this: Getting where you want to be by what you do or by what you have is like swimming against the current. Have → do → be is a tough journey. It's much easier to go in the other direction: be → do → have.

Usually, we work against nature by trying to have something or do something before being it. That's hard. All of your deeds (what you do) might not get you where you want to be. Getting all of the right things (what you have) might not get you there either.

Take the person who values athletics and wants to master tennis. He buys an expensive racket and a stylish tennis wardrobe. Yet he still can't return a serve. Merely having the right things doesn't deliver what he values.

Suppose that this person takes a year's worth of tennis lessons. Week after week, he practices doing everything "right." Still, his game doesn't quite make it.

What goes wrong is hard to detect. "He lost the match even though he played a good game," people say. "Something seemed to be wrong. His technique was fine, but each swing was just a little off." Perhaps the source of his problem is that he cannot see himself as ever mastering the game. What he has and what he does are at war with his mental picture of himself.

You can see this happen in other areas of life. Two people tell the same joke in what seems to be the same way. Yet one person brings a smile, while the other person has you laughing so hard your muscles hurt. The difference in how they do the joke is imperceptible. When the successful comedian tells a joke, he does it from his experience of already being funny.

Change the way you see yourself, and watch your actions and results shift as if by magic.

To have and do what you want, be it. Picture the result as you begin. If you can first visualize where you want to be, if you can go there in your imagination, if you can be it today, you set yourself up to succeed.

Be a master student now

Now relate this Power Process to succeeding in school. All of the techniques in this book can be worthless if you operate with the idea that you are an ineffective student. You might do almost everything this book suggests and still never achieve the success in school that you desire.

For example, if you believe that you are stupid in math, you are likely to fail at math. If you believe that you are not skilled at remembering, all of the memory techniques in the world might not improve your recall. Generally, we don't outperform our self-concept.

If you value success in school, picture yourself as a master student right now. Through higher education you are gaining knowledge and skills that reflect and reinforce this view of yourself.

This principle also works in other areas of life. For example, if you value a fulfilling career, picture yourself as already being on a path to a job you love. Use affirmations and visualizations to plant this idea firmly in your mind. Change the way you see yourself, and watch your actions and results shift as if by magic.

While you're at it, remember that "Be it" is not positive thinking or mental cheerleading. This Power Process works well when you take a First Step—when you tell the truth about your current abilities. The very act of accepting who you are and what you can do right now unleashes a powerful force for personal change.

Flow with the natural current of be → do → have. Then watch your circumstances change.

If you want it, be it. ◩

put it to work

Master students can transition to master employees using skills practiced in college.

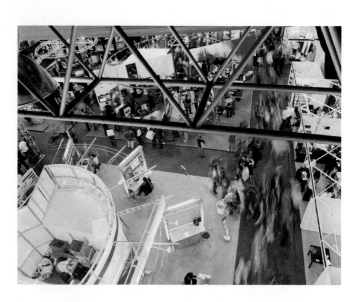

Plan for change. Even the most brilliant people can fall flat when predicting trends in business and the workplace. Case in point: Thomas Watson, founder of IBM, said, "I think there's a world market for about five computers."[5]

Still, you can benefit from making predictions about changes in the workplace that affect your own employment opportunities. Keep up-to-date with breaking changes as you decide what's next in your career. This is easier to do than ever before, thanks to resources mentioned throughout this book:

- *The Internet.* Use your skills in searching the Internet to find Web sites devoted to your field. Start by keying your job title into a search engine such as Google or Yahoo! Also search for career-related listservs—programs that distribute e-mail messages to groups of people with similar interests.

- *Periodicals.* Read the business sections of the *New York Times* and the *Wall Street Journal*, for example. Most newspapers also have online editions, as do general-interest magazines such as *Time* and *Business Week.*

- *Professional associations.* People in similar jobs like to band together and give each other a heads up on emerging trends—one reason for professional associations. These range from the American Medical Association to the Society of Actuaries. There's bound to be one for people in your field. Ask colleagues and search the Internet. **Note:** Many associations post Web sites and publish newsletters or trade magazines.

- *Conferences and conventions.* Many professional associations sponsor annual meetings. Here's where you can meet people face-to-face and use your networking skills. Print and online publications are powerful sources of news, but sometimes nothing beats plain old schmoozing.

Consider coaching. Consider receiving life coaching as a way to continue the cycle of discovery, intention, and action you started in this book. A life coach is someone with training in counseling or a related field who meets with clients several times per month in person or over the phone. Life coaches can help you define your personal values, align your daily life with those values, write goals and action plans, and create projects that allow you to contribute to others. With the support of a life coach, you can start now to envision the jobs you want to have in 5 years, 10 years, and 20 or more years into the future. You can set comprehensive, long-term goals in every other area of your life as well. Like other professionals, life coaches charge for their services. Fees vary widely. Consider life coaching even if you can afford only a few hours of this service a year.

You can also meet with friends to offer each other free coaching. Start by redoing the exercises and Journal Entries in this book, sharing the results, and inventing new exercises of your own. The results can be dramatic.

Continue the conversation about success. As you begin your life beyond this student success course, continue to engage in a conversation about what you want from your life and how you intend to get it. You can experience success as you define it and live the life of your dreams. ⊠

Name _____ Date _____/_____/_____

1. Briefly discuss the meaning of "Now that you're done—begin."

2. Explain how *content skills* and *transferable skills* differ. Give one example of each kind of skill.

3. Explain how career planning can be a process of choosing instead of a process of discovery.

4. According to the text, service to others and selfishness are unrelated. True or False? Explain your answer.

5. Describe the three main types of life choices explained in the Power Process: "Be it."

6. Using the Power Process: "Be it" eliminates the need to take action. True or False? Explain your answer.

7. If your scores are lower on the Discovery Wheel the second time you complete it, that means your study skills have not improved. True or False? Explain your answer.

8. List at least three typical questions that employers tend to ask during job interviews.

9. Describe a flaw associated with the typical job-hunting strategy of looking through help wanted advertisements. Suggest an alternative approach to job hunting.

10. List at least three ways that you can continue on your path of becoming a master student after completing this book.

learning styles application

The questions below will "cycle" you through four styles, or modes, of learning as explained in the article "Learning styles: Discovering how you learn" in Chapter One. Each question will help you explore a different mode. You can answer the questions in any order.

what if Consider this statement from the first article in this chapter: "You are on the edge of a universe so miraculous and full of wonder that your imagination at its most creative moment cannot encompass it. Paths are open to lead you to worlds beyond your wildest dreams." If you adopted this statement as a working principle, what would you do differently on a daily basis?

why Consider your experience with this book and your student success class. Which of your attitudes or actions changed as a result of this experience?

how List one suggestion from this book that you would like to apply but have not yet acted upon. Describe exactly how you will implement this suggestion.

what List five suggestions from this book that you've already applied. Rate each suggestion for its effectiveness on a scale of 1 to 5 (1 is most effective, 5 is least effective).

master student
profile

MIA HAMM

(1972–   ) Three-time U.S. Soccer Athlete of the Year and core member of the gold medal–winning women's soccer team in the 1996 and 2004 Olympics, she is also the founder of the Mia Hamm Foundation.

Learning how to deal with obstacles on the soccer field will no doubt help you off the field as well. Life, like soccer, isn't always fair. There are tackles from behind, your friends will sometimes let you down, referees miss calls, and sometimes your parents will blame you for things you didn't do. It is how you deal with these hurdles that to a large extent can determine how successful a person you are.

One of the most difficult situations I've ever had to deal with was the death of my brother Garrett. The painful emotional toll it took on my family and me was incredible. I missed the first two games of our Olympic Victory Tour in April 1997 to be with my family, but I knew that even though the game I love paled in importance compared to losing Garrett, I needed to get back on the field. The athletic field is where Garrett and I had so many great moments together, and I knew he would have wanted me out there. I knew also one of the best ways to deal with my grief was to play and to be with my teammates, so I joined

the team in Milwaukee for our third game of the tour.

To focus mentally after that ordeal was one of the biggest challenges I've faced, and I must admit I really struggled to cope with my emotions and concentrate on soccer, but my teammates were remarkable in their caring for me and my family. There's no way I could have come back without their support and love, and I will always be grateful.

My first game back was against South Korea, and Milwaukee was deluged by rain. The field was covered in water, and you couldn't kick a ball further than five feet without it stopping dead in a huge puddle. Still, the fans came out. These were the same fans who had helped me organize a charity indoor soccer game the year before in Milwaukee to raise money for bone-marrow research. They packed the stadium despite conditions that might have canceled any other sporting event, and they cheered loudly when we took the field—or the lake, as it were.

The game started, and something amazing happened that I'll remember forever. Just thirty seconds into the match, the ball popped loose in front of the goal and I whacked it into the net. All the emotion from the fans and my teammates and from my ordeal rushed in at once. It was a truly

overwhelming experience. I ran toward the stands and slid in the puddles before I was buried underneath a pile of soggy teammates.

It took a good dose of mental toughness combined with the support of my team to get me back on the field. It also showed me that you can overcome even the most tragic events if you put your mind to it and accept help from others. Mental toughness requires great patience and sacrifice. You must be willing to battle through the difficulties even if it's a long, arduous process, like recovering from a serious knee injury. The way I have been taught to regain the mental edge when having troubles is to make life or the game as simple as possible. If you have all these insecurities or frustrations when you step on the field, you are giving yourself a hundred different reasons to fail. Those are pretty tough odds. Focus on what you know you can do.

Source: Pages 38–40 from *Go for the Gold: A Champions Guide to Winning in Soccer and Life* by Mia Hamm and Aaron Heifetz Copyright ©1999 by Mia Hamm. Reprinted by permission of HarperCollins Publishers, Inc.

For more biographical information about Mia Hamm, visit the Master Student Hall of Fame on the *Becoming a Master Student* Web site at

masterstudent.college.hmco.com

photo credits

endnotes

Introduction

1. U.S. Department of Labor, Bureau of Labor Statistics, "Education pays . . . ," August 7, 2003, http://www.bls.gov/emp/emptab7.htm (accessed May 3, 2004). National Center for Education Statistics, "Annual Earnings of Young Adults," http://www.nces.ed.gov/ programs/coe/2002/section2/indicator16.asp, 2002 (accessed January 13, 2004).
2. H. Wechsler, J. E. Lee, M. Kuo, M. Seibring, T. F. Nelson, and H. P. Lee, "Trends in College Binge Drinking during a Period of Increased Prevention Efforts: Findings from Four Harvard School of Public Health Study Surveys, 1993–2001," *Journal of American College Health* 50, no. 5 (2002): 203–217.
3. B. F. Skinner, *Science and Human Behavior* (Boston: Free Press, 1965).

Chapter 1

1. Carl Rogers, *Freedom to Learn* (Columbus, OH: Merrill, 1969).
2. Howard Gardner, *Frames of Mind: The Theory of Multiple Intelligences* (New York: Basic Books, 1993).
3. David A. Kolb, *Experiential Learning: Experience as the Source of Learning and Development* (Englewood Cliffs, NJ: Prentice-Hall, 1984).
4. William James, *Pragmatism and Other Essays* (New York: Washington Square, 1963).

Chapter 2

1. Alan Lakein, *How to Get Control of Your Time and Your Life* (New York: New American Library, 1973; reissue 1996).
2. Dorothy Lee, *Freedom and Culture* (Englewood Cliffs, NJ: Prentice-Hall, 1959).
3. Jane B. Burka and Lenora R. Yuen, *Procrastination: Why You Do It, What to Do About It* (Reading, MA: Addison-Wesley, 1983).
4. M. A. Just, P. A. Carpenter, T. A. Keller et al., "Interdependece of Nonoverlapping Cortical Systems in Dual Cognitive Tasks," *NeuroImage* 14, no. 2 (2001): 417-426.

Chapter 3

1. Donald Hebb, quoted in D. J. Siegel, "Memory: An Overview," *Journal of the American Academy of Child and Adolescent Psychiatry* 40, no. 9 (2001): 997-1011.
2. Holger Hyden, "Biochemical Aspects of Learning and Memory," in *On the Biology of Learning*, ed. Karl H. Pribram (New York: Harcourt, Brace & World, 1969).

3. CNN.com, "Ethical Debate over Potential 'Viagra for the Mind,'" March 11, 1999, http://www.cnn.com/SPECIALS/views/y/1999/ 03/utley.memory.mar11/#1 (accessed April 15, 2002).

Chapter 4

1. G. S. Gates, "Recitation as a Factor in Memorizing," *Archives of Psychology* 40 (1917).
2. R. Rosnow and E. Robinson, eds., *Experiments in Persuasion* (New York: Academic Press, 1967).
3. William Glasser, *Take Effective Control of Your Life* (New York: Harper & Row, 1984).
4. School of Information Management and Systems, University of California, Berkeley, "How Much Information? 2003," October 27, 2003, http://www.sims.berkeley.edu/research/projects/how-much-info-2003/execsum.htm (accessed February 20, 2004).
5. John Morkes and Jakob Nielsen, "Concise, Scannable and Objective: How to Write for the Web," 1997, http://www.useit.com/ papers/webwriting/writing.html (accessed February 20, 2004).

Chapter 5

1. Walter Pauk and Ross J. Q. Owens, *How to Study in College*, Eighth Edition (Boston: Houghton Mifflin, 2005).
2. Tony Buzan, *Use Both Sides of Your Brain* (New York: Dutton, 1991).
3. Gabrielle Rico, *Writing the Natural Way* (Los Angeles: J. P. Tarcher, 1983).
4. Joseph Novak and D. Bob Gowin, *Learning How to Learn* (New York: Cambridge University Press, 1984).
5. David P. Ausubel, *Educational Psychology: A Cognitive View* (New York: Holt, Rinehart and Winston, 1968).
6. William Glasser, *Take Effective Control of Your Life* (New York: Harper & Row, 1984).
7. Viktor Frankl, *Man's Search for Meaning* (New York: Simon & Schuster, 1970).
8. W. E. B. Du Bois, *The Souls of Black Folk* (New York: Bantam, 1989).

Chapter 6

1. Adapted from Linda Wong, *Essential Study Skills*, Fourth Editiion. Copyright © 2002 by Houghton Mifflin Company. Reprinted with permision.

Chapter 7

1. Quoted in Theodore A. Rees Cheney, *Getting the Words Right: How to Rewrite, Edit and Revise*, repr. ed. (Cincinnati, OH: Writer's Digest Books, 1990).
2. William G. Perry, Jr., *Forms of Intellectual and Ethical Development in the College Years: A Scheme* (New York: Holt, Rinehart, and Winston, 1970).
3. Walter Arnold Kaufman, *Without Guilt and Justice: From Decidophobia to Autonomy* (New York: Delta, 1975).
4. John Dewey, *How We Think* (Boston, D.C. Heath, 1910).
5. Quoted in Alice Calaprice, ed., *The Expanded Quotable Einstein* (Princeton, NJ: Princeton University Press, 2000).
6. Joe Cuseo, "Academic-Support Strategies for Promoting Student Retention and Achievement during the First Year of College," University of Ulster Office of Student Transition and Retention, http://www.ulst.ac.uk/star/data/cuseoretention.htm#peestud (accessed September 4, 2003).
7. Jan Carlzon, *Moments of Truth* (New York.: HarperCollins, 1989).

Chapter 8

1. Lee Thayer, "Communication—Sine Qua Non of the Behavioral Sciences," in *Vistas in Science,* ed. David L. Arm (Albuquerque: University of New Mexico, 1968).
2. Thomas Gordon, *Parent Effectiveness Training: The Tested New Way to Raise Responsible Children* (New York: New American Library, 1975).
3. Stephen R. Covey, *The Seven Habits of Highly Effective People: Restoring the Character Ethic* (New York: Simon & Schuster, 1989).
4. Diane de Anda, *Bicultural Socialization: Factors Affecting the Minority Experience* (Washington, DC: National Association of Social Workers, 1984).

5. Peter Elbow, *Writing with Power: Techniques for Mastering the Writing Process* (New York: Oxford University Press, 1981).
6. National Association of Colleges and Employers, "Recreate Yourself: From Student to the Perfect Job Candidate," http://www.jobweb.com/joboutlook/2004outlook/outlook5.htm (accessed December 15, 2003).
7. Jakob Nielsen, *Designing Web Usability: The Practice of Simplicity* (Indianapolis: New Riders, 1999).
8. LaFasto and Larson refer to their book *When Teams Work Best* in their online article: Center for Association Leadership, "The Zen of Brilliant Teams," http://www.centeronline.org/knowledge/article.cfm?ID=1884&, July 2002 (accessed January 5, 2004).

Chapter 9

1. From Ann Raimes, *Universal Keys for Writers.* Copyright 2005 by Houghton Mifflin Company. Reprinted with permission.

Chapter 10

1. Ira Progoff, *At a Journal Workshop* (New York: Dialogue House, 1975).
2. Richard Nelson Bolles, *What Color Is Your Parachute?* (Berkeley: Ten Speed Press, updated annually).
3. This article includes material from *Career Planning*, Third Edition, by Dave Ellis, Stan Lankowitz, Ed Stupka, and Doug Toft. Copyright © 2003 by Houghton Mifflin Company. Reprinted with permission.
4. Martin Kimeldorf, *Peterson's Portfolio Power: The New Way to Showcase All Your Job Skills and Experiences* (Lawrenceville, NJ: Peterson's Guides, 1997).
5. Charles Hard Townes in Martin Moskovits, ed., *Science and Society, the John C. Polanyi Nobel Laureates Lectures* (Concord, Ontario: Anansi Press, 1995), 8.

additional reading

Adler, Mortimer, and Charles Van Doren. *How to Read a Book*. New York: Touchstone, 1972.

Anthony, Jason, and Karl Cluck. *Debt-Free by 30*. New York: Plume, 2001.

Bandler, Richard, and John Grinder. *Frogs into Princes: Neuro-Linguistic Programming*. Moab, UT: Real People, 1979.

Beckham, Barry, ed. *The Black Student's Guide to Colleges*. New York: Madison Books UPA, 1996.

Birkerts, Sven. *The Gutenberg Elegies: The Fate of Reading in an Electronic Age*. New York: Ballantine, 1994.

Boston Women's Health Book Collective. *The New Our Bodies, Ourselves*. New York: Simon & Schuster, 1996.

Brown, Alan C. *Maximizing Memory Power*. New York: Wiley, 1986.

Buzan, Tony. *Make the Most of Your Mind*. New York: Simon & Schuster, 1977.

Chaffee, John. *Thinking Critically*. Boston: Houghton Mifflin, 2003.

Corey, Gerald. *I Never Knew I Had a Choice*. Monterey, CA: Brooks-Cole, 1982.

Covey, Stephen R. *First Things First*. New York: Simon & Schuster, 1994.

Deida, David. *The Way of the Superior Man*. Austin, TX: Plexus, 1997.

Dumond, Val. *The Elements of Nonsexist Usage*. New York: Prentice-Hall, 1990.

Elgin, Duane. *Voluntary Simplicity*. New York: Morrow, 1993.

Ellis, Dave. *Creating Your Future: Five Steps to the Life of Your Dreams*. Boston: Houghton Mifflin, 1998.

Ellis, Dave, and Stan Lankowitz. *Human Being: A Manual for Happiness, Health, Love and Wealth*. Rapid City, SD: Breakthrough Enterprises, 1995.

Ellis, Dave, Stan Lankowitz, Ed Stupka, and Doug Toft. *Career Planning*. Boston: Houghton Mifflin, 2003.

Facione, Peter. *Critical Thinking: What It Is and Why It Counts*. Millbrae, CA: California Academic Press, 1996.

Fletcher, Anne. *Sober for Good*. Boston: Houghton Mifflin, 2001.

Gawain, Shakti. *Creative Visualization*. New York: New World Library, 1998.

Gibaldi, Joseph. *MLA Handbook for Writers of Research Papers*. New York: Modern Language Association, 1999.

Glasser, William. *Schools Without Failure*. New York: Harper & Row, 1968.

Golas, Thaddeus. *The Lazy Man's Guide to Enlightenment*. New York: Bantam, 1993.

Greene, Susan D., and Melanie C. L. Martel. *The Ultimate Job Hunter's Guidebook*. Boston: Houghton Mifflin, 2004.

Higbee, Kenneth L. *Your Memory: How It Works and How to Improve It*. Englewood Cliffs, NJ: Prentice-Hall, 1996.

Hill, Napolean. *Think and Grow Rich*. New York: Fawcett, 1996.

Hurtado, Sylvia, et al. *Enacting Diverse Learning Environments: Improving the Climate for Racial/Ethnic Diversity in Higher Education*. Ashe-Eric Higher Education Reports, 1999.

James, William. *Talks to Teachers on Psychology and to Students on Some of Life's Ideals*. New York: Norton, 1983.

Keyes, Ken, Jr. *Handbook to Higher Consciousness*. Berkeley, CA: Living Love, 1974.

Keyes, Ralph. *Timelock: How Life Got So Hectic and What You Can Do About It*. New York: HarperCollins, 1991.

Kolb, David A. *Experiential Learning: Experience as the Source of Learning and Development*. Englewood Cliffs, NJ: Prentice-Hall, 1984

Lathrop, Richard. *Who's Hiring Who?* Berkeley, CA: Ten Speed Press, 1989.

LeBoeuf, Michael. *Imagineering: How to Profit from Your Creative Powers*. New York: Berkley, 1990.

Light, Richard J. *Making the Most of College: Students Speak Their Minds*. Cambridge, MA: Harvard University Press, 2001.

Lucas, Jerry, and Harry Lorayne. *The Memory Book*. New York: Ballantine Books, 1975.

Mallow, Jeffry V. *Science Anxiety: Fear of Science and How to Overcome It*. New York: Thomond, 1986.

Manning, Robert. *Credit Card Nation: The Consequences of America's Addiction to Credit*. New York: Basic Books, 2000.

McCarthy, Michael J. *Mastering the Information Age*. Los Angeles: J. P. Tarcher, 1991.

McCutcheon, Randall. *Can You Find It? Twenty-Five Library Scavenger Hunts to Sharpen Your Research Skills*. Minneapolis, MN: Free Spirit, 1991.

Nolting, Paul D. *Math Study Skills Workbook*. 2nd ed. Boston: Houghton Mifflin, 2005.

Orman, Suze. *The Road to Wealth*. New York: Riverhead, 2001.

Pauk, Walter and Ross J. Q. Owens. *How to Study in College*. 8th ed. Boston: Houghton Mifflin, 2005.

Pennebaker, James W. *Opening Up: The Healing Power of Confiding in Others*. New York: Morrow, 1990.

Pirsig, Robert. *Zen and the Art of Motorcycle Maintenance*. New York: Perennial Classics, 2000.

Raimes, Anne. *Universal Keys for Writers*. Boston: Houghton Mifflin, 2005.

Rajneesh, Bhagwan S. *Journey Toward the Heart*. New York: Harper and Row, 1980.

Rial, Arlyne. *Speed Reading Made Easy*. Garden City, NY: Doubleday, 1985.

Robbins, John. *Diet for a New America: How Your Food Choices Affect Your Health, Happiness and the Future of Life on Earth*. New York: HJ Kramer, 1998.

Ruggiero, Vincent Ryan. *Becoming a Critical Thinker*. 4th ed. Boston: Houghton Mifflin, 2002.

Schacter, Daniel L. *Searching for Memory: The Brain, the Mind, and the Past*. New York: HarperCollins, 1997.

Scharf-Hunt, Diana, and Pam Hait. *Studying Smart: Time Management for College Students*. New York: HarperPerennial, 1990.

Schlosser, Eric. *Fast Food Nation*. Boston: Houghton Mifflin, 2001.

Strunk, William, Jr., and E. B. White. *The Elements of Style*. New York: Macmillan, 1979.

The American Heritage Dictionary, 4th Ed.

Thiederman, Sondra. *Profiting in America's Multicultural Marketplace: How to Do Business Across Cultural Lines*. New York: Lexington Books, 1992.

Tobias, Sheila. *Succeed with Math: Every Student's Guide to Conquering Math Anxiety*. New York: College Board, 1995.

Ueland, Brenda. *If You Want to Write: A Book About Art, Independence and Spirit*. St. Paul, MN: Graywolf, 1987.

U.S. Department of Education. *The Student Guide*. Published yearly. (Federal Student Aid Information Center, P.O. Box 84, Washington, DC 20044-0084, 1-800-4-FED-AID)

Watkins, Ryan, and Michael Corry. *E-learning Companion: A Student's Guide to Online Success*. Boston: Houghton Mifflin, 2005.

Weil, Andrew. *Health and Healing*. Boston: Houghton Mifflin, 1995.

Weil, Andrew. *Natural Health, Natural Medicine*. Boston: Houghton Mifflin, 1998. Welch, David. *Decisions, Decisions: The Art of Effective Decision Making*. Amherst, NY: Prometheus, 2002.

Winston, Stephanie. *Getting Organized*. New York: Warner, 1978.

Wurman, Richard Saul. *Information Anxiety*. New York: Doubleday, 1989.

Wurman, Saul Richard. *Information Anxiety 2*. Indianapolis: QUE, 2001.

251

index

as memory technique, 74, 86
of presentations, 197–198
of workspace, 86
Outcome goals, 53
Outlines
format for, 120
prereading, 93
prewriting, 195
Overlearning, 75

Paradox, 29
Paragraphs, 116–117
Paraphrasing, 196
Participation, 28
Part-time jobs, 229
Passive voice, 195
Pasteur, Louis, 78
Pauk, Walter, 118
Peers, 3, 212. *See also* Cooperative learning
Peg system, 82
Perception, 183
Periodical articles, 216, 244
Perry, William, 162
Physical exercise, 9, 147
Pictures. *See also* Visuals
as memory technique, 74, 79
in notes, 116
use of mental, 106–107
Plagiarism, 196
Planning. *See also* Time management
explanation of, 14, 50
financial, 62–63
long-term, 59–60, 66
motivation and, 50
for problem solving, 171
to-do lists for, 56
Portfolios, 233–234
Power Process
Be here now, 64–65
Be it, 242–243
Detach, 154–155
Discover what you want, 15–16
Employ your word, 200–201
Find a bigger problem, 176–177
I create it all, 128–129
Ideas are tools, 40–41
Love your problems, 84–85
Notice your pictures, 106–107
Risk being a fool, 218–219
Praise, 146
Preferred learning mode, 37
Prefixes, 100
Presentations
delivery of, 198
geared to learning styles, 42
group, 198
organization of, 197–198
practicing delivery of, 198
visuals in, 202
Preview, prereading, 93
Primacy-recency effect, 97
Primary sources, 216

Problems
as barriers, 84–85
control of, 85
determining worthy, 176–177
Problem solving
math and science, 150–151
methods for, 171
while standing, 164
Process preferences, 42
Procrastination, 57, 61, 66, 212
Professional associations, 244
Progoff, Ira, 226
Projects, 42
Put it to work. *See* Workplace applications
Question Card (Q-Card), 77
Questions
critical thinking and, 174
essay, 141–142
following lectures, 125
multiple-choice, 140
predicting test, 138
as reading technique, 93–94
that aren't questions, 186
true/false, 140–141

Reading. *See also* Textbooks
active, 150
activities after, 96–97
activities during, 94–95
activities prior to, 93–94
aloud, 98, 104
with children underfoot, 103–104
difficult material, 98–99
improving speed in, 101–102
mastery through, 226
muscle, 91, 92, 108
taking notes while, 126
using dictionary during, 100
visual images in, 106–107
workplace applications for, 108
Reciting
as memory technique, 75
as reading technique, 95–97
when cramming, 153
your notes, 119
Recognize your skills (Exercise), 230
Recordings, 118
Reference works, 216
Reflection, 94
Reflective observation, 35, 36
Rehabilitation Act of 1973, 192
Relationships, 200–201
Relaxation
to maintain health, 9
as memory technique, 74
to promote concentration, 101
to reduce test anxiety, 140, 146, 153, 155
Relax (Exercise), 102
Religious institutions, 10
Remembering your car keys—or anything
else (Exercise), 78
Research

library, 215–216
plagiarism and, 196
on writing topics, 195
Research notes, 126
Resignation, 128
Responsibility, 28, 128–129
Rest, 9, 58
Résumés, 231
Review
after reading, 97
of notes, 114, 121
before tests, 136–137
Review notes, 126
Revised drafts, 195
Rewards, 6, 57
Rhymes, 81
Right-brained people, 119
Riley Guide, 232
Risk being a fool (Power Process),
218–219
Risks
challenges associated with, 218–219
mistakes from taking, 152
willingness to take, 28
Rogers, Carl, 29
Roommates, 59
Routines, 104

Saccades, 101
SCANS reports, 228
Schedules, 60, 136. *See also* Time
management
Scholarships, 63
School catalogs, 10
Schools. *See also* Higher education
cost of, 1, 62–63
transferring to other, 241
School security agencies, 10
Schumann-Heink, Madame, 78
Science classes
anxiety over, 149–150
making choices for, 150
problem solving for, 150–151
using class time in, 150
using textbooks for, 150
Search engines, 209
Seating, 114
Secondary sources, 216
Secretary's Commission on Achieving
Necessary Skills (SCANS), 228
Self-awareness, 28
Self-concept, 143
Self-direction, 29
Self-discipline, 14
Self-fulfilling prophecy, 76
Self-help groups, 9
Self-judgment, 13
Self-justification, 169
Self-knowledge, 173
Self-management skills, 39
Serendipity, 164
Service learning, 235

MONDAY	TUESDAY	WEDNESDAY	THURSDAY	FRIDAY	SATURDAY	SUNDAY

Name _____

Month _____

MONDAY	TUESDAY	WEDNESDAY	THURSDAY	FRIDAY	SATURDAY	SUNDAY

Name _____

Month _____